"Oh, how I wish I had this book through the decades I have volunteered for self-help and non-profit mental health groups and in my neighborhood!!! So much valuable information. A real roadmap. And it's such a fun read. Thank you, Maurine and Jeanne, for putting this down so we know where we are going without having to learn from all our mistakes."

Celinda Jungheim, *Board Chair Emeritus, Recovery International*

"There is definitely a need for this book. Our society today has a crucial need for activism to address the problems we are facing. People all over the world are organizing to address social problems; it is important for them to know a practical approach to accomplishing social change."

Dona J. Reese, *Professor at the School of Social Work, Southern Illinois University*

"Within minutes of starting to read this book, I started connecting the ideas to current projects I'm involved with. The authors balance rationale and purpose with practical ideas and specific examples that ring true. There is something for everyone to learn and apply. I want the book! [It is] urgently needed to compensate for manipulative change agents who are taking advantage of societal divisions to benefit the already-too-powerful."

Sarah Heyer, *Assistant Coordinator, Carbondale Conversations for Community Action*

"Successfully used some practices listed in this book to plan a warming center for local homeless. Waiting for the full book to come to print so I can acquire it."

Scott Martin, *Carbondale Interfaith Council, President*

"This is an essential guide to community-building. I can see local governments, libraries, churches, grassroots action groups, employers, and employees building consensus, overcoming obstacles, and achieving their goals with the help of this book."

Diana Brawley Sussman, *Carbondale Public Library Director and Co-chair of Nonviolent Carbondale*

"*Making Change: Facilitating Community Action* is as clear and straightforward as its title, offering step-by-step methods, real-life examples and helpful graphics. I wish I'd had this resource when I was a new minister in town, and I look forward to applying its lessons to act more effectively."

Rev. Sarah C. Richards, *Carbondale Unitarian Fellowship, Carbondale, IL*

MAKING CHANGE

Every community has issues or opportunities that need to be addressed. The expert knowledge of community members could be the key to creating lasting change. By making community members into facilitators, *Making Change: Facilitating Community Action* suggests they can guide community members through the process of making change and to help them determine their goals and methods.

The aim of this book is to enable facilitators to identify concerns and address, enable and foster change at the local level through effective facilitation. This book follows a six-stage model for creating change. Beginning with issue awareness, it continues through getting to know the team they are working with, seeking information on the issue and community, through facilitating the planning and community development through evaluation. This book focuses on the human side of the change process while also teaching the practical skills necessary for individuals to reach their goal.

Making Change is for people interested in making change to improve their community, including students, community activists, local government and educational leaders.

Jeanne L. Hites Anderson is a professor emerita of St Cloud State University, St Cloud, Minnesota. She began facilitating while working in the business world in training and performance improvement. She found through her volunteer work that there were many overlapping practices between change initiatives in business and the community.

Maurine Pyle is a Quaker facilitator with over 40 years of social change experience in a wide variety of professional and volunteer settings. She is committed to a form of leadership known as servant leadership. She holds master's degrees in Organizational Development and Linguistics.

MAKING CHANGE

Facilitating Community Action

JEANNE L. HITES ANDERSON AND
MAURINE PYLE WITH ILLUSTRATIONS
BY NICK PYLE

NEW YORK AND LONDON

First published 2021
by Routledge
52 Vanderbilt Avenue, New York, NY 10017

and by Routledge
2 Park Square, Milton Park, Abingdon, Oxon, OX14 4RN

Routledge is an imprint of the Taylor & Francis Group, an informa business

© 2021 Taylor & Francis

The right of Jeanne Anderson and Maurine Pyle to be identified as authors of this work has been asserted by them in accordance with sections 77 and 78 of the Copyright, Designs and Patents Act 1988.

All rights reserved. No part of this book may be reprinted or reproduced or utilised in any form or by any electronic, mechanical, or other means, now known or hereafter invented, including photocopying and recording, or in any information storage or retrieval system, without permission in writing from the publishers.

Trademark notice: Product or corporate names may be trademarks or registered trademarks, and are used only for identification and explanation without intent to infringe.

Library of Congress Cataloging-in-Publication Data
Names: Anderson, Jeanne (Author of Making change), author. | Pyle, Maurine (Author of Making change), author.
Title: Making change : facilitating community action / Jeanne Anderson and Maurine Pyle.
Description: New York, NY : Routledge Books, 2020. | Includes bibliographical references and index.
Identifiers: LCCN 2020004573 (print) | LCCN 2020004574 (ebook) | ISBN 9780367444778 (hardback) | ISBN 9780367444761 (paperback) | ISBN 9781003009962 (ebk)
Subjects: LCSH: Social change. | Group facilitation. | Political participation.
Classification: LCC HM831 .A54 2020 (print) | LCC HM831 (ebook) | DDC 303.4—dc23
LC record available at https://lccn.loc.gov/2020004573
LC ebook record available at https://lccn.loc.gov/2020004574

ISBN: 978-0-367-44477-8 (hbk)
ISBN: 978-0-367-44476-1 (pbk)
ISBN: 978-1-003-00996-2 (ebk)

Typeset in Sabon
by Apex CoVantage, LLC

Visit the eResources: www.routledge.com/9780367444761

In recognition of his significant contributions to the fields of community development and prevention, we dedicate our book to William Lofquist, our friend and mentor.

We also dedicate this book to all community activists working toward the well-being of our communities, our environment, and our world.

BRIEF CONTENTS

List of Tables and Figures   xxix
Acknowledgments   xxxii
Preface   xxxiii

STAGE 1
Issue Awareness   1

  1 The Beginning   3

  2 Reflect, Observe and Wonder Abstract   10

  3 Detours   15

STAGE 2
Getting to Know You   19

  4 Reflective Facilitation   21

  5 Calling the First and Subsequent Meetings   29

  6 Recruit and Retain Volunteers   36

  7 Clearing Mental Space for Facilitation   46

  8 Building Rapport and Unity   50

STAGE 3
Information Seeking   57

  9 Mental Models and Frameworks   59

  10 Spectrum of Attitudes   67

11	What's Happening Now?	72
12	Visioning	80
13	Change Resistance and Readiness	91
14	Wondering and Hypothesis Testing	105
15	Planning Perspectives	117
16	Force Field Analysis: Upsetting the Equilibrium	124
17	Identifying the Play and the Players in a Community	130
18	Getting Grounded: Collecting Data Together	138

STAGE 4
Facilitation of Planning — 151

19	Getting Started on Planning for Change	153
20	Where Are We Going and How Will We Get There? Strategies and Tactics	164
21	Effective Learning Objectives	172
22	No Tin Cups: Fundraising and Stewardship	177
23	Building Alliances and Collaboration	194
24	Choreography of Conversation	203
25	Setting the Stage for Productive Meetings	214
26	Listening Deeply	222
27	Observing the Action	229
28	Asking Good Questions	235
29	Trouble on the Team	246

STAGE 5
Community Development   257

30   Choosing and Developing a Solution   259

31   Communication   271

32   Programs   283

33   Policy Change   295

34   Physical Environment   303

35   Support   309

36   Monitoring and Managing Change   317

STAGE 6
Evaluation and Conclusion   327

37   Leadership, Sustainability and Renewal   329

38   Evaluation   339

39   Disengagement: It's Been Nice, but I Really Must Be Going   348

Index   354

CONTENTS

List of Tables and Figures xxix
Acknowledgments xxxii
Preface xxxiii

STAGE 1
Issue Awareness   1

1   **The Beginning**   3
     What's in This Chapter?   3
        Objectives   4
     A Story About Beginning a Change   4
     What These Concepts Are About   4
     Participation   6
     Responsibility   7
     Changing Conditions   7
     Spectrum of Attitudes   7
     The Facilitation of Change Model   8
     Try It!   9
     Summary   9
     Citations   9

2   **Reflect, Observe and Wonder Abstract**   10
     What's in This Chapter?   10
        Objectives   11
     A Story About Reflecting, Observing and Wondering   11
     What This Technique Is About   12
     The Importance of Reflection   12
     Making Observations   12
     Wondering   13
     How to Carry Out Observing and Noticing Techniques   13
     Try It! Observing Your Community   14
     Summary   14
     Citations   14

3   **Detours**   15
     What's in This Chapter?   15
           Objectives   15
     A Story About Activity Traps and Finding Your Way Through the Maze   16
     What This Technique Is About   17
     How to Carry Out This Technique   17
     Try It!   18
     Summary   18
     Citations   18

STAGE 2
Getting to Know You   19
     What's in This Section   19
     What This Section Is About   20

4   **Reflective Facilitation**   21
     What's in This Chapter?   21
           Objectives   22
     A Story About Reflection: Race Unity Conversation   22
     What This Technique Is About   23
     How to Carry Out This Technique   24
     Journaling Buttons and Biases   24
           Social Biases Can Be Either Implicit or Explicit   25
                 Before the Meeting: Clear a Mental Space   26
                 During the Meeting: Provide Neutral Guidance   26
     After the Meeting: Debriefing   27
     Try It   27
     Summary   27
     Citations   28

5   **Calling the First and Subsequent Meetings**   29
     What's in This Chapter?   29
           Objectives   30
     A Story About Calling a First Meeting   30
     What This Technique Is About   31
     How to Carry Out This Technique   32
           First Steps for a Facilitator   32
           How to Call the First Meeting   33
     Calling Subsequent Meetings   34
     Try It!   34
     Summary   35
     Citations   35

6   **Recruit and Retain Volunteers**   36
     What's in This Chapter?   36
           Objectives   37
     A Story About Recruiting Volunteers   37
     What This Technique Is About   38

Volunteer Service   38
Characteristics of Volunteers   39
   Life Stages   39
   Gender, Marital, Parental and Educational Status   40
   Motivations   40
Recruiting Volunteers   40
Recruiting Strategies   40
Retaining Volunteers   41
Making Doers Out of the Supporters   43
How to Carry Out This Technique   43
Social Media   43
Personal Invitation   44
Retention   44
Try It!   44
Summary   45
Resources   45
Citations   45

7 Clearing Mental Space for Facilitation   46
What's in This Chapter?   46
   Objectives   47
A Story About Preparing to Facilitate   47
What This Technique Is About   48
Mindfulness for Facilitators   48
How to Carry Out This Technique   48
Try It!   49
Summary   49
Citations   49

8 Building Rapport and Unity   50
What's in This Chapter?   50
   Objectives   50
A Story About Creating Your Own Dream Team   51
What This Technique Is About   53
What "Ice" Isolates People From Each Other?   53
I-to-We   54
How to Carry Out This Technique   54
Try It!   55
Summary   55
Citations   55

STAGE 3
Information Seeking   57

9 Mental Models and Frameworks   59
What's in This Chapter?   59

　　　　Objectives　59
　　　A Story About Mental Models　60
　　　What This Technique Is About　61
　　　　Identify Your Group's Mental Models　63
　　　How to Carry Out This Technique　65
　　　Try It!　65
　　　Summary　66
　　　Citations　66

10　Spectrum of Attitudes　　　　　　　　　　　　　　　　　　　　　　　　67
　　　What's in This Chapter?　68
　　　　Objectives　68
　　　A Story About Attitudes Toward Beneficiaries of Change　68
　　　Viewing People as Resources　69
　　　What This Technique Is About　69
　　　How to Carry Out This Technique　70
　　　Examine the Spectrum of Attitudes with Your Group　70
　　　　Set Up Your Protocol　70
　　　Try It!　70
　　　Summary　71
　　　Citations　71

11　What's Happening Now?　　　　　　　　　　　　　　　　　　　　　　　72
　　　What's in This Chapter?　72
　　　　Objectives　73
　　　A Story About What's Happening Now and Desired Outcomes　73
　　　What This Technique Is About　73
　　　　Brainstorm "What's Happening Now"　73
　　　Root Causes　74
　　　　SWOT Analysis: Strengths and Weaknesses, Opportunities and Threats　76
　　　Choose High-Priority, High-Yield Issues　76
　　　Locating and Establishing Indicators　77
　　　How to Carry Out This Technique　78
　　　　"What's Happening Now" Method 1 for Small Groups　78
　　　　"What's Happening Now" Method 2 for Large Groups　78
　　　Try It!　78
　　　Summary　79
　　　Citations　79

12　Visioning　　　　　　　　　　　　　　　　　　　　　　　　　　　　　　80
　　　What's in This Chapter?　81
　　　　Objectives　81
　　　A Story: Situational Blindness　81
　　　What This Technique Is About　83
　　　Small-Scale Visioning　84
　　　Large-Scale Visioning　85

      A Hunger-Free St. Michael Parish   86
    How to Carry Out This Technique   86
      Brainstorming: Gathering the Wisdom of the Group   86
        Brainstorming Methods   87
    Recharging a Group That Is Stuck   88
      OK, Now What?   89
    Try It!   89
    Summary   89
    Citations   90

13 Change Resistance and Readiness   91
    What's in This Chapter?   91
      Objectives   92
    A Story About Change Readiness: Open Housing in Winston-Salem,
        North Carolina, 1968   92
    What This Technique Is About   93
    Types of Change   93
    Individuals and Change   95
    Resistance   96
    Resilience   97
    Opposition   98
    Community Readiness   98
    The Change Timeline   99
    Readiness Levels   100
    Making Plans   100
    How to Carry Out This Technique   101
    Collecting Readiness Data   102
    Analyzing Qualitative Data From Interviews or Surveys   102
    Try It!   102
    Summary   103
    Citations   103

14 Wondering and Hypothesis Testing   105
    What's in This Chapter   105
      Objectives   106
    A Story About Reading in Prison   106
    What This Technique Is About   106
    Clarifying the Problem   107
    Hypothesis   107
    Contributing Factors   109
    The Fishbone Diagram   109
    Indicators   111
    Searching for Data on Indicators   113
    Hypothesis Testing   113
    Action Steps   114
    How to Carry Out This Technique   114

Try It! 114
Summary 115
Citations 115

15 Planning Perspectives — 117
What's in This Chapter? 117
    Objectives 117
A Story About Planning Perspectives 118
What This Technique Is About 119
Grids and Units of Change 119
Focus on Outcomes and Conditions 120
Purpose 121
The Four Action Quadrants 121
How to Carry Out This Technique 122
An Example 122
Try It! 122
Summary 123
Citations 123

16 Force Field Analysis: Upsetting the Equilibrium — 124
What's in This Chapter? 125
    Objectives 125
A Story About Analysis: A Skateboarder's Solution 125
What This Technique Is About 125
How to Carry Out This Technique 126
An Example 126
Try It! 128
    Exercise #1 128
    Exercise #2 128
Summary 129
Citations 129

17 Identifying the Play and the Players in a Community — 130
What's in This Chapter? 130
    Objectives 131
A Story: Maurine Plays a *Columbo* Role in a New Project 131
What This Technique Is About 132
Identifying the Community, Their Cultures and Values 132
Who Needs to Be Aware of the Plan? 134
Key Members 135
Who Has Influence in the Community? 135
Who Is "Outside" the Community? 135
How to Gather the Information 135
Identifying the Play 136
The Community Description 136

How to Carry Out This Technique   137
Try It!   137
Summary   137
Citations   137

18 Getting Grounded: Collecting Data Together — 138
What's in This Chapter?   138
  Objectives   139
A Story About Data Collection   139
Local Data Collection   140
Conclusion   141
What This Technique Is About   141
Why Collaborate?   141
Principles of Collecting Data Together   142
Acquiring Research Partners   143
Sustaining Partnerships   144
Conducting Participatory Data Gathering and Evaluation   145
Data Collection   145
Sharing Findings and Decisions With the Team   146
Sharing the Findings With the Community   148
How to Carry Out This Technique   148
Try It!   148
Summary   149
Resources   149
Citations   149

STAGE 4
Facilitation of Planning — 151

19 Getting Started on Planning for Change — 153
What's in This Chapter?   153
  Objectives   153
A Story: Conversation for Race Unity   154
  Step 1: Seeking Allies for Awareness-Building and Information-Sharing   155
  Step 2: Networking for Organizational and Community Resources   155
  Step 3: Cooperative Creation of New Resources   155
What These Techniques Are About   156
Review Your Research   157
SWOT Analysis   157
Perspectives, Paradigms and Sources of Design   159
Planning Change Strategies and Tactics   160
How to Carry Out These Techniques   160
Try It!   161
Summary   162
Citations   163

20 Where Are We Going and How Will We Get There? Strategies and Tactics   164
What's in This Chapter?   165
    Objectives   165
A Story: How the Quakers Changed Direction on Their
    Vision of a Retreat Center   165
What This Technique Is About   166
    Examples of Community Development Strategies   167
Tactics   167
    How to Develop Strategies and Tactics   167
Project Timeline   168
How to Carry Out This Technique   169
Try It!   170
Summary   171
Resources   171
Citations   171

21 Effective Learning Objectives   172
What's in This Chapter?   172
    Objectives   172
A Story: If You Don't Know Where You Are Going, Any Path Will Do   173
What This Technique Is About   174
Example: Hunger-Free St. Michael Parish   174
How to Carry Out This Technique   175
SMART Objectives   176
Try It!   176
Summary   176
Citations   176

22 No Tin Cups: Fundraising and Stewardship   177
What's in This Chapter?   177
    Objectives   178
A Story About Funding Homes for Veterans   178
What This Technique Is About   179
Creating a Fundraising Plan   179
Methods of Fundraising   179
    Sponsorships   179
    Individual Giving   180
    Build a Fundraising Network   181
    Fundraising Events   182
    In-Kind Donations   182
    Fee-For-Service   183
    Grants   183
Accountability and Stewardship   183
How to Carry Out These Techniques   184
    Create a Fundraising Plan   184

Fundraising Strategies 185
    Conduct Meetings Seeking Donations 185
    Build a Fundraising Network 186
    Events 186
    In-Kind Donations 187
    Fee-For-Service 187
    Grants 187
    Demonstrating Accountability and Stewardship 189
    Communications 191
    Software to Assist With Fundraising 191
Try It! 191
Summary 192
Resources 192
    Donation Forms and Web Pages 192
    Free Software for Fundraising 192
    Sources for Grant Searches 192
    Websites for More Information 192
Citations 193

23 Building Alliances and Collaboration   194
What's in This Chapter? 194
    Objectives 195
A Story About Opening Dialogue 195
What This Technique Is About 196
Alliances With Outside Organizations 196
Bridge Cultural, Social and Community Values 198
Build the Community and Methods of Collaborating 199
Alliances With Outside People 200
How to Carry Out This Technique 200
Try It! 201
Summary 201
Resources 201
Citations 202

24 Choreography of Conversation   203
What's in This Chapter? 203
    Objectives 204
A Story About Communication: Mr. Mayor Attends a
    Race Unity Group Meeting 204
What This Technique Is About 205
    Step 1: Which Dance Step Is Appropriate? 205
    Step 2: Who Leads? Who Follows? 205
    Step 3: Cutting In 205
The Arts of Observation and Reflection 206
Keeping in Step (Taking Cues From the Dance-Master) 207

Communication Styles   208
How to Break Up Tensions in the Group—Introducing New Steps   209
How to Carry Out This Technique   210
Try It!   211
   Exercise #1: Describe How You Would Facilitate   211
   Exercise #2: Practice Observing a Meeting   213
Summary   213
Citations   213

25 Setting the Stage for Productive Meetings   214
What's in This Chapter?   215
   Objectives   215
A Story About Productive and UNproductive Meetings:
   Gun Violence in Our Town   215
What This Technique Is About   216
Plan to Accommodate Attendees   216
Plan to Socialize   216
Plan a Team Culture Discussion   216
Plan the Agenda   217
Plan to Record Key Information   217
Plan for Interactive Activities   217
Room Set-Up   217
Prepare Yourself   217
Opening the Meeting   218
During the Meeting   218
   Observing   218
Stay on Task   218
Conclude the Meeting: Agreements,
   Actions and Decisions   219
How to Carry Out This Technique   219
   Planning   219
   Open the Meeting   220
   During the Meeting   220
   Meeting Conclusion   220
Try It!   220
Summary   220
Citations   221

26 Listening Deeply   222
What's in This Chapter?   222
   Objectives   223
A Story About Listening   223
What This Technique Is About   224
   Removing the Barriers to Listening   224
   Talking and Not Understanding   224
   Biases   224

Distractions and Interruptions   224
Expectations   224
Presence   224
Eye Contact   225
Nonverbal Feedback   226
Ask Questions   226
Connection   227
How to Carry Out This Technique   227
Try It!   227
Summary   228
Citations   228

27 Observing the Action   229
What's in This Chapter?   229
Objectives   230
A Story About Observation of Participants   230
What This Technique Is About   230
Communication Across Cultures   231
How to Carry Out Observations of Participants   231
Practice Observing   232
Try It!   234
Exercise #1   234
Exercise #2   234
Summary   234
Citations   234

28 Asking Good Questions   235
What's in This Chapter?   235
A Story About Asking Questions   236
What This Technique Is About   237
Why Do People Ask Questions?   237
Questioning and Teamwork   238
Asking Questions   239
Types of Questions   239
Questions Through the Change Process   239
Delivering Questions   242
Use Silence   242
Encourage Participation   242
Responding to Answers   242
How to Carry Out This Technique   243
Questions and Teamwork   243
Questions Throughout the Planning Cycle   243
Try It!   243
Summary   243
Citations   244
Citations for Studies Cited in the Story   244

29 Trouble on the Team   246
    What's in This Chapter? 247
        Objectives 247
    A Story About an Elephant in the Living Room 247
    Let's Ask the Key Question Again—What's Happening Now? 248
    Back to Our Story 248
    What These Techniques Are About 249
        What Is the Role of Conflict in Community Development? 249
    How to Address the Problem of Conflict in a Healthy Way 249
    What Are Some Typical Issues That Can Cause Conflict? 250
    How to Carry Out These Techniques 251
    Resolutions 251
    Situational Blindness 252
    Poor Communication 254
    Try It! 254
        The Scenario 254
    What You Need to Do 255
    Summary 255
    Citations 255

STAGE 5
Community Development   257

30 Choosing and Developing a Solution   259
    What's in This Chapter? 260
        Objectives 260
    A Story: A New Librarian Comes to Town 260
    What This Technique Is About 261
    How to Carry Out This Technique 261
        Who Should Be Involved? 261
        Searching for Promising Practices or Interventions 261
        Attributes of Promising Practices or Interventions 262
    Team Decision Process 263
    Gain Consensus for Group Commitment 264
    Analyze Costs and Benefits 264
    Matching Solutions to Causes 265
    Design and Development 265
    Evaluation 268
    Try It! 268
    Summary 269
    Citations 269

31 Communication   271
    What's in This Chapter? 271
        Objectives 272
    A Story About Communication as a Strategy 272

What This Technique Is About   273
How to Carry Out These Techniques   273
    Guidelines for Emissary Work   273
Guidelines for Word-of-Mouth Promotion   274
Guidelines for Public Behaviors That Others Will Emulate   277
Guidelines for Sharing Ideas and Stories   277
Guidelines for Stories in the Local News Media   277
Guidelines for Communications in Print and Visuals   278
Guidelines for Communication in Social and Other Media   279
Guidelines for Reporting Results   279
Other Methods   280
Evaluating Communications   280
Try It!   280
Summary   281
Citations   282

32 Programs   283
What's in This Chapter?   283
    Objectives   284
A Story About Program Intervention: Renew   284
What This Technique Is About   286
    Creating Training   286
How to Carry Out This Technique   287
    About the Learners   287
    Analyzing the Content   287
The Lesson Plan for a Face-to-Face Training   289
Creating Job-Aids   291
Mentoring and Coaching   292
Try It!   293
Summary   294
Citations   294

33 Policy Change   295
What's in This Chapter?   295
    Objectives   296
A Story About the 3Rs Project—Reading Reduces Recidivism   296
What This Technique Is About   297
How to Carry Out This Technique   297
    Who Should Be Involved?   297
    What's Happening Now?   297
Desired Outcomes   298
Information Seeking   299
Planning   299
    Tell Your Story   299
    Timing   300
    Networking   300

Policy Enactment   301
Policy Evaluation   301
Try It!   301
Summary   302
Citations   302

34 Physical Environment   303
What's in This Chapter?   303
  Objectives   304
A Story About Creating a Mountain Biking Trail   304
What This Technique Is About   304
How to Carry Out This Technique   305
  Who Should Be Involved?   305
What's Happening Now?   305
Desired Outcomes   306
Information Seeking   306
Planning   306
Try It!   307
Summary   308
Citations   308

35 Support   309
What's in This Chapter?   309
  Objectives   310
A Story About Community Support   310
What This Technique Is About   311
How to Carry Out This Technique   312
  Who Should Be Involved?   312
What's Happening Now?   312
Desired Outcomes   313
Information Seeking   313
Planning the Support Group   313
  Facilitation of Support Groups   313
  Meetings   313
Getting the Word Out   314
Additional Support Materials   314
Implementing the Support Group   314
Evaluating the Support Group   315
Try It!   315
Summary   315
Citations   315

36 Monitoring and Managing Change   317
What's in This Chapter?   317
  Objectives   318
A Story About Managing Change   318

What This Technique Is About   319
Get People Ready for Change   320
Monitor Progress   320
    Implementation and Maintenance   321
    Change Management   321
    Risks   322
    Quality   322
    Report Results   322
How to Carry Out This Technique   323
    Monitor Progress   323
Remove Obstacles   323
Build on the Change   323
Manage Risks   323
Manage Quality   324
Report Results   324
Try It!   324
Summary   324
Citations   325

STAGE 6
Evaluation and Conclusion 327

37 Leadership, Sustainability and Renewal 329
    What's in This Chapter?   329
        Objectives   330
    A Story About Mentorship for Leadership Development   330
    What This Technique Is About   330
        Preventing Rollback   330
    Leadership for Organizational Renewal   331
    Leadership Development   334
    How to Carry Out This Technique   335
        Sustaining the Change   335
    Renewing the Organization   335
    Leadership Development   336
    Try It!   338
    Summary   338
    Citations   338

38 Evaluation 339
    What's in This Chapter?   339
        Objectives   340
    A Story About Evaluation   340
    What This Technique Is About   341
    How to Carry Out This Technique   341
    Who Should Be Involved?   342

Write the Questions 342
Select the Data Collection Method 342
    Surveys 342
    Interviews 343
    Observations 343
    Archival Records 345
Test the Survey, Interview or Observation Form 345
Prepare to Analyze the Data 346
Collect and Analyze Your Data 346
Report Results 346
Try It! 346
Summary 347
Citations 347

39 Disengagement: It's Been Nice, but I Really Must Be Going 348
What's in This Chapter? 349
    Objectives 349
A Story About Disengaging From the Action 349
What This Technique Is About 349
When to Step Aside 350
How to Carry Out This Technique 351
    How to Step Aside 351
When Objectives Are Complete 351
Formal Exit Meeting 351
The Agenda 352
Final Written Report 352
Reflection for Continued Professional Development 352
Try It! 352
Summary 353
Citations 353

Index 354

TABLES AND FIGURES

FIGURES

S1.0	Facilitation of Change Model Stage 1: Issue Awareness.	1
1.1	Lofquist's Spectrum of Attitudes.	8
1.2	Facilitation of Change Model.	8
S2.0	Facilitation of Change Model Stage 2: Getting to know you.	19
5.1	Changing conditions.	31
6.1	Life stages of volunteers.	39
6.2	Retaining volunteers.	41
6.3	Rock's SCARF model of human needs.	42
8.1	Plan openers that change perceptions from "I" to "We."	55
S3.0	Facilitation of Change Model Stage 3: Information seeking.	57
9.1	One participant's drawing of the change process.	60
9.2	A second participant's drawing of the change process.	61
9.3	A third participant's drawing of the change process.	61
9.4	Combined change process drawing.	62
9.5	A framework is like a tent structure.	63
9.6	Activity traps keep you so busy you forget your goal.	64
10.1	Lofquist's Spectrum of Attitudes (1989) adapted.	69
11.1	Easel paper headings for exploration of "What's happening now?".	73
11.2	Digging for root causes results in more effective solutions.	75
11.3	Elements of change.	75
11.4	Example of brainstormed lists focused on drug use.	76
11.5	Example SWOT analysis.	77
12.1	Creativity requires being willing to "color outside the lines."	84
12.2	Everyone may believe they have a good idea, but that is the wisdom of one person. Better ideas are often the result of a team effort.	87
12.3	Easel paper headings for exploration of vision of ideal outcomes.	87
13.1	Readiness critical quadrant: Transformational change.	94
13.2	Ideal individual change cycle.	95
13.3	Individual change cycle with resistance.	96
13.4	Change adoption timeline.	97
13.5	Change commitment timeline.	99
14.1	Testing hypotheses.	107
14.2	Prison library brainstorm.	109
14.3	Fishbone diagram.	110
14.4	Activist's fishbone diagram.	111
14.5	Gauging progress.	112

15.1	Planning perspectives.	118
15.2	Arenas of action.	120
15.3	Focus continuum showing possible units of change.	121
15.4	Purpose continuum.	121
16.1	Push and pull forces.	126
16.2	Force Field Analysis diagram.	127
16.3	Skateboard park analysis.	127
16.4	Retreat center Force Field Analysis.	128
17.1	Overlapping communities.	133
17.2	Steps in change adoption.	134
18.1	Six factors leading to effective collaborations.	142
18.2	Main data collection points in the change process.	147
18.3	Analysis and interpretation process.	148
S4.0	Facilitation of Change Model Stage 4: Facilitation of Planning.	151
19.1	Planning perspectives.	156
19.2	SWOT matrix.	157
19.3	SWOT analysis for conversation for race unity.	158
19.4	Design of change strategies.	159
19.5	Benefits of approaches to design of change strategies.	160
19.6	SWOT matrix.	162
20.1	Alignment of tactic, strategy and goal.	166
20.2	How to write a tactic.	168
20.3	PERT chart.	169
20.4	Gantt chart.	169
21.1	Components of learning objectives.	175
22.1	Donor cycle.	180
22.2	"Viral" fundraising model.	182
22.3	Grant process.	183
22.4	Accountability and use of financial data for decision-making.	184
22.5	Donor pyramid.	185
23.1	Levels of networking with other organizations.	196
23.2	Allies integration.	197
24.1	Communication styles.	209
25.1	Meeting room arrangements.	218
26.1	Components of deep listening.	225
28.1	Using questions to establish relationships.	238
28.2	The change cycle.	240
29.1	Conflict resolution methods.	252
29.2	Situational awareness.	253
S5.0	Facilitation of Change Model Stage 5: Community development.	257
30.1	Selecting solutions.	263
30.2	Design and development process.	267
31.1	Relative impact of word of mouth versus advertising.	274
31.2	Picture of Tina to be included in message example that appeals to emotion.	276
31.3	Brochure design.	278
32.1	Events of Learning.	287
32.2	Events of Instruction.	288
32.3	Analyzed content for processing jars in pressure canner.	289
32.4	Types of job-aids.	291
36.1	Gauging progress in community development.	319
36.2	The change process.	320

36.3 Monitor and manage implementation. 321
S6.0 Facilitation of Change Model Stage 6: Evaluation and conclusion. 327
37.1 Change commitment timeline. 331
37.2 Organization change phases. 332
37.3 Continuing planning. 333
37.4 Organizational renewal cycle. 336
38.1 Evaluation process. 341

TABLES

2.1   Observing the community: Things to look for. 13
4.1   Common cognitive biases and how to reduce their effect. 25
5.1   Special considerations for intercultural, older or disabled meeting participants. 33
8.1   Examples of icebreakers for a community development meeting. 54
14.1 Activists' indicators. 112
20.1 Differences between strategies and tactics. 167
20.2 Tactics aligned with strategy and goal. 168
20.3 Tactics aligned with strategy and goal for Hunger-free St. Michael. 170
21.1 Goals and objectives for St. Michael Parish Hunger-free Committee. 175
21.2 Goals and objectives for sustainability committee. 176
22.1 Donor communications. 190
22.2 Donor stewardship plan template. 191
24.1 Communication styles adapted from Merrill and Reid (1981). 209
24.2 Responding to people with different communication styles. 211
27.1 Facilitator responses to participant behaviors. 233
28.1 Possible questions and probes. 244
30.1 Match solutions to causes. 266
30.2 Causes and solutions example. 267
30.3 Intervention design document template. 268
30.4 Causes and solutions analysis template. 269
30.5 Intervention design template. 269
31.1 Communication planning template. 281
32.1 SWOT analysis for *ReNEW*. 285
32.2 Choosing between coaching and mentoring. 292
32.3 Lesson plan template. 293
33.1 Policy planning template. 302
34.1 Environment concept plan template. 307
38.1 Playground observation checklist. 344

ACKNOWLEDGMENTS

We wish to thank William Lofquist, who prompted us to write this book to give evidence of the value of his theories and practices which have influenced people worldwide to seek "the wellbeing of all" through community development, and for his first person story on open housing in Winston-Salem, North Carolina. On behalf of all those who have been touched by Bill's compassion, we express our gratitude to him. We also wish to thank Mary Lofquist. Behind every great man, there is a woman holding it together.

We wish to commend Nick Pyle for providing the illustrations at the head of each chapter.

We are indebted to David Lynn, who was instrumental in helping us to formulate the basis for our book over the course of a marathon weekend by sharing his expertise as a professional facilitator and collaborator with Bill in many community change projects.

We wish to thank P. Michael Hebert for his feedback on several chapters, and for his contribution of the appendix on negotiation, which is a derivation of part of an unpublished work by P. Michael Hebert and Amon Burton. We thank both of you.

We wish to thank Diana Brawley Sussman, Director of the Carbondale Public Library, for sharing the story of how Nonviolent Carbondale emerged from a small community and then spread nationwide. Her work with Sparrow Coalition and homeless individuals at the library is also inspirational.

We wish to commend Fern Chappell, who made the initial effort that led to the formation of Race Unity Group of Carbondale; and to Scott Martin, Carbondale Interfaith Council president, who has sustained the Conversation at the Newman Center every Tuesday night.

First person stories by Kara Dunkel and Margaret Katranides about how local institutions were founded and grew have added authenticity to our book. Recognition must be given also to Barbara Kessell, who confirmed the background information in the 3Rs story and for her commitment to proving that *Reading Reduces Recidivism*. We also appreciate having the account of the restoration of the Euyerma Hayes Center as recounted by Sumera Mahkdoom.

We wish to clarify that the organizations mentioned in our book, such as Touch of Nature, Annapolis Friends Meeting, Rotary Club of Carbondale–Breakfast, Avenue of the Righteous (Illinois), Sparrow Coalition, Good Samaritan, and Illinois Yearly Meeting are all real; however, some of our stories were slightly fictionalized accounts, or names of individuals have been changed by request of the participants. Our thanks to Nick Pyle for the winsome drawings at the start of each chapter.

We thank Todd Anderson for his patience, support and insightful feedback on each chapter, and all of the people involved in community change that have tried out our techniques and sent us their comments and suggestions.

PREFACE

The focus of this book is facilitation of community action. Why facilitation? Every community has issues or opportunities that need to be addressed, and community members are the experts on their hopes and dreams for the community. The role of a facilitator is to guide community members through the process of making change. Facilitators take a neutral stance on solutions selected and instead use their understanding of people, group dynamics and the change process to help community members determine where they want to go and how to get there. In that way, the community will create change that they understand and accept.

WHO CAN BENEFIT FROM THIS BOOK?

This book is for people interested in making change to improve their community. It is especially for those new to facilitation of change or community development. This might include college classes in social work, social responsibility, criminal justice, public health and public advocacy. It might also include volunteers, educational leaders, local human rights commissions, social workers, clergy, activists, school boards and local governmental agencies such as police departments. This book focuses on the human side of the change process while teaching the necessary skills to reach a common goal.

BOOK DESIGN

This book is structured around a six-stage process:

- Issue awareness.
- Getting to know the change team.
- Seeking information on the change.
- Facilitation of the planning process.
- Implementation of community development.
- Evaluation.

Each chapter is designed with objectives and exercises requiring creativity and critical thinking. The eResources for this book include appendices with supplemental information for learners, instructor resources with terms and concepts introduced in each chapter, annotated citations and example solutions for each chapter's exercise. To access eResources, go to eResources: www.routledge.com/9780367444761

The aim of this book is to enable community *facilitators* to identify concerns and address, enable and foster change at the local level through effective facilitation. The text covers visioning, effectively conducting meetings, data collection, building alliances, developing leadership skills, teamwork, facilitating the development process and implementing, evaluating and sustaining the change. It provides practical tools for collaboration on data collection, analysis, building alliances, developing change strategies, implementation and evaluation of the results.

STAGE 1

Issue Awareness

At the beginning of a problem-solving process, we become aware of an issue by noticing its symptoms, or someone points it out to us. Keeping in mind that everyone has different perspectives on an issue, we need to clarify the issue as a team and to listen to each of the perspectives. This part is key, because when we select problems to solve and solutions to use, the best solutions are those that meet everyone's needs.

This book follows a six-stage model for creating change. Beginning with issue awareness, it continues through getting to know the team you will be working with, seeking information about the issue and the community, facilitating the planning process and then continuing through community development, and evaluation.

Figure S1.0 Facilitation of Change Model Stage 1: Issue Awareness.

THE BEGINNING

Figure 1.0

WHAT'S IN THIS CHAPTER?

Community change initiatives often begin with a small group of people who are aware of an issue and come together to do something about it. However, to really get change moving requires a large number of people to become aware, take responsibility and participate in taking action, including the people most impacted. This chapter discusses the *spectrum of attitudes* that people bring to community development and defines three key principles for community development—*participation, responsibility and changing conditions*. Finally, it introduces the six-stage facilitation to change model.

Objectives

By the end of this chapter, you will be able to:

- Describe issues in your community that need attention.
- Reflect on your attitudes toward people most directly affected by these issues. Would you work on solving the issue *for* them or *with* them?
- Describe how you might use principles of participation, responsibility and changing conditions to address this issue.
- Describe the six stages in the facilitation of change model.

A STORY ABOUT BEGINNING A CHANGE

There was something about her face that was compelling us all to look in her direction. She was not only pretty in a conventional way, but attractive in the sense that she attracted people like a magnet. There was an internal glow, a light shining in her face that was causing all of us to turn in her direction. What was she saying? With an emotional and broken-voiced appeal, she asked us to notice the homeless people standing on the street corners in our town. Most of us had passed them by with barely a glance or, more likely, with feelings of shame that we were among the "haves", but they had nothing at all but a cardboard sign with a pleading message—"Will work for food." But she had noticed their pain and suffering and called our attention to the human "litter" at our door, which we were merely shifting aside. Pastor Christine had a heart for the homeless, and she single-handedly turned all of us around to look back at them to see what we could do. This was the genesis of the Homeless Coalition.

Within six months, Pastor Christine had gathered about 100 citizens who were concerned about the growing homeless population in their town. In small groups, they met with her over time to ask what they could do about this problem and how they could help solve it. Some were businesspeople who thought the town was beginning to look down-at-the-heels, and others were church people who felt a charitable impulse to help the down-and-outers. Among the initial founders of the Homeless Coalition were a wide spectrum of supporters ranging from academics, human service professionals, government officials and a variety of volunteers who all cared about their town and its future. Christine knew she needed to find a way to get them all on board, so she called a town meeting to hold a visioning session to bring them all together and find out what to do next.

WHAT THESE CONCEPTS ARE ABOUT

Getting on board is a metaphor often used by organizers who are appealing to people to change direction or join a new movement. The image of boarding a train can be helpful as a way to imagine ourselves in this scene. At the initial stage of any change process, people share the same excitement as train riders experiencing new vistas and new relationships, hopping on when they are ready and getting off when they are done. As new people join the process, there can be a surge of energy and a renewal of the community.

The first person we meet when boarding a train is the conductor, a skilled person who helps us to embark on a new journey. The facilitator can be viewed as a type of conductor, someone who has the experience, patience and ability to answer questions and solve problems along the way. Just like on a train journey, there will be unexpected detours, such as when an avalanche of snow covers the tracks, causing the train to be rerouted since the destination must be altered due to changing conditions. Sometimes you travel in the dark and can't see the unfolding landscape, and you have to trust that progress is being made. The role of the facilitator, like that of a conductor on a train, is to keep the process on track even when things break down or conditions change.

Train riders sometimes just want to get to their destination, but others have a communal attitude. You never know who you will meet on a train, but you can usually expect to meet people who are different from yourself. First-time riders bring fresh viewpoints and are guided by the more experienced travelers who know how things work. Both perspectives are useful as the journey continues. Patterns and habits must change repeatedly when new riders get on and cars are added. Riders come aboard with an expectation of arriving on schedule; however, there will be many stops and starts along the way to changing any social condition.

As the group moves along in its developmental perspective, flexibility is needed. An effective conductor/facilitator listens to participants and observes changes in conditions. The journey is unfolding gradually, and no one knows when it will end. The facilitator can offer confidence that the destination will be reached eventually, even if the timing for arrival at the destination is not certain. Along the way there will be frustrations and successes, and with the help of careful facilitation, new directions will emerge from the visioning process. By carefully pursuing collective decision-making with skill and tact, the facilitator can ensure that the desired results will be produced.

The first thing that must be done before taking a journey is to determine the destination. In other words, the traveler needs a clear goal. Pastor Christine could see that among her 100 supporters there were at least 10 different ideas of how to approach the problem of homelessness. The police and the mayor wanted to halt panhandling, the church folks were feeling distressed by trying to meet needs of people experiencing homelessness one by one and the social activists saw homeless people as a cause. Pastor Christine decided to use a visioning approach as a first step to clarify at least a few of the initial directions the Homeless Coalition could take. She invited two trained facilitators from a local agency to lead the town meeting. That was a smart move, because the facilitators were neutral and had the skills to help coalesce the myriad opinions into a proposed destination for the journey.

Homelessness is a complex issue that is deeply rooted in conditions of poverty and injustice. Soon after the town meeting, the members began to learn the truth of the old adage, "It takes a lot of track to turn a big train around." Although well-intentioned, they did not yet know that they were in for a very long ride. At this point, Maurine entered the scene, offering to become their volunteer facilitator to conduct them through the next phase, which is **action planning**.

At the end of the town meeting, excitement and enthusiasm were running high. Fifteen people had signed on to continue the conversation over a three-month period with a clear goal to address issues of homelessness in our town. Now it was time to think about choosing a framework for how the newly formed community of activists would proceed during the action planning phase. As their volunteer facilitator, Maurine recommended the framework of **community development** which she had practiced for many years as a social activist, knowing that it would provide a much-needed framework to contain the energy of the group and help them to look forward in the same direction.

Along the way in her training as a professional group facilitator, Maurine had encountered a wise and experienced teacher, William Lofquist, who had thought deeply about the concept of community development for many years. In his book, *The Technology of Development* (1996), he offers this definition:

> In recent years much emphasis has been placed on . . . technologies . . . We have put much less emphasis on a technology of development for creating better communities. In this framework, *development is defined as an active process of creating conditions* [circumstances that exist in a particular situation] *and fostering personal attributes* [characteristics of a person] *which promote the well-being of people.* Conditions and personal attributes are two realities which are closely intertwined. It is difficult to consider one without giving attention to the other.
>
> (p. 1; emphasis in original)

Clift, Wojciakowski, and Wojciakowski (2011) said that "Community development, in both concept and action, is dependent on a group of like-minded people working together to improve and further grow a local community" (p. 180). Lofquist has broadened this definition to include fostering personal and collective attributes that go beyond just solving problems. Simply stated, changed hearts can change the direction of society toward the common good.

When using a community development framework, the first question to ask is "**What is happening now?**" We need first to see the current conditions before we can create a new set of conditions. By asking questions, we are setting out on a journey of discovery and finding new and unexpected ways of responding to situations as they unfold. At the beginning, most activists tend to choose a problem-solving approach, and the solutions can seem simple. At the initial meeting of the Homeless Coalition, some of the ideas that were put forth were to provide free bedding or toothbrushes to homeless people seen around town. However, eventually we saw more complex sets of conditions unfolding and a more effective set of ideas emerged to respond to them, but it took some time for reorientation.

Maurine offered the group an introduction to community development as an alternative framework to "business as usual" and educated the team members on how this change process might evolve developmentally. Many were skeptical and wanted to fix old systems to make them run more smoothly. Community development is a **radical** method, meaning it begins at the roots, emerging from the bottom. Here is how she introduced the new process in a nutshell:

- Development arises spontaneously and directly from <u>awareness</u> and concerns of community members.
- Development follows needs organically, not complying with preset formulas within existing organizations.
- Development seeks to hear from those most directly affected by the concern being addressed.
- Development acknowledges and supports emerging leadership in the community.
- Development is an ongoing process that is designed to extend beyond the current generation's lifespan.

The first organizational step was to hold regular volunteer meetings and set up a team structure to address the five directions which were highlighted in the visioning exercise. At the very first meeting, Maurine could see that we would need to apply more of Lofquist's theory base to give the group a good start-up. He states that there are three undergirding principles for community development—participation, responsibility and changing conditions. Let's take them one by one to see how they were implemented in the project.

PARTICIPATION

The first principle is **participation**:

> When people have an opportunity to participate in decisions and shape strategies that vitally affect them, they will develop a sense of ownership in what they have determined and commitment to seeing that the decisions are sound, and the strategies are useful, effective and carried out. This theory is basic to a democratic society.
>
> (Lofquist, 1996, p. 4)

By inviting volunteers to self-select the team that was their personal focal point, there was an initial opportunity for each of them to participate in decision-making. This led to an immediate commitment to go forward in a research and development mode with many people taking leadership at the outset. It almost felt like a horse race as the teams tried to outdo each other in providing much-needed data on homelessness at the national and local level. A spirit of friendly competition was evident. People were fully engaged.

More important for a successful change initiative is for participants to include the people impacted, not just the volunteers. As Michael Wilkinson (2004) says, "You can achieve more effective results when the solutions are created, understood and accepted by the people impacted" (p. 2).

RESPONSIBILITY

The next principle is **responsibility**:

> How one takes responsibility for oneself in relation to other people helps determine the quality of the relationship. When people agree to work together toward mutually desirable goals that promote their mutual well-being, a sense of corporate or community responsibility emerges.
>
> (Lofquist, 1989, p. 13)

A spirit of cooperation became evident when people began to realize that each of them had a particular gift to offer to the group. Some members were highly skilled in their professional lives and could provide expertise in particular areas. Others had life experiences as volunteer leaders. The group began to feel like a community of like-minded people on a mission to solve a problem. But then the question arose: What exactly were the parameters of the problem of homelessness? Recalling the story of the three blind men trying to describe the elephant—"Was it like a wall, a hose, a snake?"—Maurine could see the group struggling to come to agreement. As they moved forward, it became apparent that there would be many disagreements over the definition of homelessness and how we could go about working together to solve it. In a sense each person had taken personal responsibility but had not yet come to understand that mutuality of purpose was essential.

CHANGING CONDITIONS

The third principle is **changing conditions**: Conditions were changing, and people were also changing their attitudes. Rather than focusing on who was right or who is the smartest, they needed to learn about the benefits of **focusing on conditions** rather than on the people. There is also a strong tendency to focus on symptoms of the problem rather than on the causes. How could we view the issue in its entirety? By asking a simple question over and over: **What is happening now?**

The teams needed more data from the people most affected by homelessness, the people living on the street. Then Maurine offered the group a radical suggestion—"Let's ask them to tell us how they see the problem." But the teams resisted mightily—"Why would we talk to them? We are the experts." The team members had fallen into the habit of treating the homeless as objects rather than as resources. But Maurine insisted on holding a session with some homeless people as our informants, as well as some school and agency personnel who were on the front lines helping them. This was an eye-opening experience for many of the team members. As they heard directly from the people experiencing homelessness, the conversation shifted to, "We need to listen to them more. We don't really know about homelessness." The teams had turned a corner when we realized that the people that we wanted to do things "for" or "to" could become our partners and resources in the change process.

The number one rule of **focusing on conditions** is:

> Persons who own the problem of concern (if the beginning point is a problem) can become resources, giving them access to positive roles, using their perspectives and encouraging them to use their energies in positive ways. This can result in enhanced self-esteem. Joint ownership of the problem conditions is made possible, when that is appropriate, as is joint participation in achieving a solution.
>
> (Lofquist, 1989, p. 27)

SPECTRUM OF ATTITUDES

It was clear that the members of the Homeless Coalition experienced a shift in perspective from viewing homeless people as objects to resources after they listened to them. The diagram shown in Figure 1.1

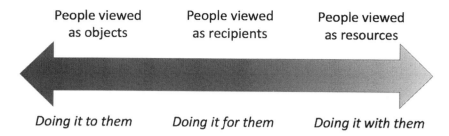

Figure 1.1 Lofquist's Spectrum of Attitudes.

Figure 1.2 Facilitation of Change Model.

became useful as they viewed other groups, like the police or the mayor, in a similar way. By shifting toward viewing them as resources, the project became more successful at utilizing all of the resources in the community. A healthy perspective toward the people experiencing homelessness was critical for any effective initiative. Additionally, people impacted by the project need to participate and take responsibility for the solutions if they are to be accepted. In Chapter 10, Spectrum of Attitudes will be explored in more detail.

THE FACILITATION OF CHANGE MODEL

The six-stage facilitation of change model, shown in Figure 1.2, will be used and explained step by step throughout the book. Each stage corresponds to a part of the book. In this stage (Chapters 1–3), we examine issue awareness. In Stage 2, we address getting to know the team members. Stage 3 focuses on how to seek and find information that will help your change initiative plan effectively. This leads to the facilitation of planning in Stage 4. Stage 5 is about the actual implementation of your community development plans, and Stage 6 is about how to sustain the change and your organization's leadership, evaluation of the change initiative and disengagement of the facilitator.

TRY IT!

Change begins with awareness and reflection. Discuss the following questions:

1. What issues in your community are begging for attention and action? Who is most affected by the issue? Are other community members also concerned and talking about it? Why do you suppose things are the way they are?
2. As you think about those people most affected by the issue, consider your own attitude toward them. If you were to work on the issue, how would you view them? As objects, recipients or resources? Would you work on solving the issue *for* them or *with* them? (More on this in Chapter 9.)
3. Effective change requires activists to use principles of participation, responsibility and changing conditions. Consider these questions:
    a. How can community members be invited to participate in making decisions and planning strategies affecting them?
    b. How can participants be encouraged to take personal responsibility, at the same time that they work together in mutuality of purpose?
    c. How can a group of community members work together to change conditions affecting their common well-being?

SUMMARY

Community change initiatives often begin with a small group of people who become aware of a problem or opportunity in the community or the environment, meet and commit to work together to do something about it to enhance the well-being of community members. This section begins with the small group beginning the process through observing, noticing and wondering why things are the way they are, and how they can be changed. This chapter also discussed the spectrum of attitudes toward others that participants bring to community development. Finally, it discusses principles for community development—participation, responsibility and changing conditions.

CITATIONS

Clift, F., Wojciakowski, C., & Wojciakowski, M. (2011). Community development. In K. A. Agard (Ed.), *Leadership in nonprofit organizations: A reference handbook* (Vol. 2, pp. 180–186). Thousand Oaks, CA: SAGE Publications, Inc. doi:10.4135/9781412979320.n21

Lofquist, W. A. (1989). *Technology of prevention workbook*. Tucson, AZ: AYD Publications.

Lofquist, W. A. (1996). *Technology of development*. Tucson, AZ: Development Publications.

Wilkinson, M. (2004). *The secrets of facilitation: The S.M.A.R.T. guide to getting results with groups*. San Francisco, CA: Jossey-Bass/Wiley.

2. REFLECT, OBSERVE AND WONDER ABSTRACT

Figure 2.0

WHAT'S IN THIS CHAPTER?

A community change gets started when community members notice opportunities or issues that need to be addressed. The goal of all community change is to ensure the well-being of members or the environment. The change process begins with observing and noticing that things are not as they should be. Look around your community and ask yourself: Do all families have access to the supports, services and opportunities they need? Are children thriving? Is the environment healthy and safe? How is the community dealing with these issues? Are they being swept under the rug, or is an effort made to change conditions to improve the community well-being?

Objectives

By the end of this chapter, you will be able to:

- Conduct a basic observation in the community on which to wonder and reflect.

When several people notice that there are issues to be addressed in a community, they may come together to discuss what can be done. They may refer the issue to an existing council or committee, or they might assemble a core group to address the issue, beginning by collecting data to better understand the community and its needs and articulate the issues. Next, they usually invite community members into conversations, especially those directly affected, to address the issues and improve the well-being of community members.

Let's begin with **observation**. Look around. What do you first notice? What is drawing your attention to the problem you seek to solve?

A STORY ABOUT REFLECTING, OBSERVING AND WONDERING

When the Interfaith Council (a council of different faith groups such as Muslims and Christians working together in the community) founded Good Samaritan in the 1970s, conditions were different from how they are now. The shelter service was designed to address temporary homelessness caused by a missed paycheck or unpaid electric bills. Now severe economic disparities and the closing of the Industrial Age is leaving many more people, including families, permanently homeless. Bill Lofquist has called the current human service system "yesterday's solution for today's problems" (Lofquist, personal communication, March 19, 2016). At the very heart of his community development theory is the concept that conditions are constantly changing. We needed to ask, "What's happening now?"

As a member of the Council, Maurine asked if she could lead a community **reflection** for clergy and congregations using the question, "What does it mean to be homeless in Carbondale?" She was hoping to awaken the community to these changing conditions and to shake people out of their stereotyping of people who had no place to live. A large group gathered at a church one night for this facilitated conversation. Maurine gave each person an index card and asked them to respond to several questions in writing before the group began any discussion.

- What kinds of people are homeless?
- How do they appear to us?
- What are the conditions of homeless people in our town?
- What skill sets do they have for survival?
- How do we often react as community members to the needs of homeless people?
- What are some changing economic conditions that could be affecting homelessness?

Then, one by one, she asked for the written comments to be read aloud and wrote them on big sheets of easel paper on the wall. She asked the group to make some **observations** on what they were hearing. This process kept the group from entering too quickly into discussion with its usual back and forth of ideas. People were hearing fresh insights without adding their own spin on what was said. The next step was to ask the question, "I **wonder** what we could do to address these changing conditions by community action." This is the step that Lofquist (1983) calls Community Development. The group was moving away from a problem-solving approach to imagining new solutions to address the changing conditions of homelessness. They heard that this is a nationwide economic problem and not merely a local human services issue. Homelessness is a "wicked problem" and will require a larger solution than simply offering a cot and three hot meals a day. New services are needed like more permanent housing, which would challenge the entire city—government, the merchants, the religious institutions and the university—to address the changing conditions of homelessness in the town. Where would this lead next when it becomes apparent that the shelter movement is inadequate?

WHAT THIS TECHNIQUE IS ABOUT

Pastor Christine had noticed people standing on street corners with signs asking for money. She viewed the homeless people coming to her church for aid as economic refugees, not panhandlers. When she listened deeply to their stories, she discovered that they were jobless veterans or former coal miners or factory workers. Instead of seeing them as guilty parties, she noticed their despair over losing everything familiar—home, family, job, dignity. It drew her heart toward them in compassion for their hopeless condition in life. This was the observation starting the Homeless Coalition.

THE IMPORTANCE OF REFLECTION

This technique is *not* the formal data collection that assesses community needs. Rather, it is simply about looking around to see what captures your attention in your community. Observing requires that we release our current perceptions and enter an open space in our minds with all our senses being alert. This takes reflection. What do you notice—see, hear, smell, touch or sense—in this present moment?

An advantage of observation is that you can see real people behaving naturally in real-life situations. You can learn what may be difficult or inappropriate to learn via surveys or interviews. A disadvantage of observation is that it is subjective: Our ingrained ways of thinking, or our *thought-habits*, can obscure new information and ignore the changing conditions. Often we walk around absentmindedly. Good observation depends on stepping outside of our usual ways of thinking, but this is done only reflectively. We usually view the world through a veil of assumptions, memory and habits. By consciously calming the mind and then looking around us as if for the first time, we can lift the veil. By noticing with fresh eyes, we can arrive at a new and deeply thoughtful understanding and thus free ourselves from preconceptions.

Cognitive science has revealed that human beings are *not* naturally reflective. We are mainly reactors. For example, as I walk down the street and see a disheveled person, I grab my purse tightly as a gesture of self-protection. Other physical symptoms are a tightened stomach, nervousness or quickening of my breath. My brain is reacting with fear. Is he a robber or a panhandler? Police are not the only people who are profiling strangers. We do it all the time. Our human brains are programmed to immediate stereotyping of the unfamiliar and secondary responses of fight or flight. But if we can see these reactions as just a place to start, they need not become hardened guidelines. Such physical and mental reactions are a substitute for perception; they can get in our way, or they can be lifesavers. Only by reflecting and testing our observations with others can we determine what is true and what is merely an adrenaline response of the body to a stimulus. This same reflectivity is necessary when making observations of the community, and of the facilitation and group processes in meetings (Bens, 2017).

MAKING OBSERVATIONS

Why observe and see as if for the first time? Most of what we see is filtered through a perceptual framework, or **mental model**. Ray Dalio notes that there is a tendency of people "to slowly get used to unacceptable things that would shock them if they saw them with fresh eyes" (Dalio, 2017, p. 476).

Like Pastor Christine, we need to see accurately what is in front of us. The things you observe in your community that can and should be changed to make it more livable—this is the starting place.

Table 2.1 Observing the community: Things to look for.

Category	Description
Physical Disorder	Litter on the street and in yards, graffiti, abandoned vehicles
Physical Order	Lack of graffiti, signs noting Neighborhood Watch, rules, clean playground facilities in good repair, street lighting
Decay	Abandoned homes and commercial buildings, broken windows, dark spaces
Other Physical	Other signs of decay such as neglected street or sidewalk damage
Social Disorder	Individuals that appear homeless, panhandling, individuals congregating with verbal conflict, physical conflict, potential drug activity, potential prostitution activity, loud music
Social Order	Individuals congregating with no conflict, neighbors on porches, individuals in neighborhoods, children playing outside
Other Social	Police patrol, police interacting

Source: Adapted from Harvey, DiLuca, Hefner, Frabutt, and Shelton (2013)

Community change is about community members observing, noticing, reflecting and getting excited and energized about something that needs to be done to create the community they desire.

Table 2.1 provides a list of *easily observable* indicators you might notice that can show that the community could benefit from this type of excitement and action. Other factors of community well-being are less easily observed. These factors might include arts, culture and leisure programming; children and youth opportunities; community engagement; economy; education; financial self-sufficiency; health; housing; and public safety (Kim, 2016). Many cities, counties and state agencies have statistical data available to the public on their websites. This information can be used to validate your observations. After observing, gather with others and share stories. What did other people notice? What are their hopes and dreams for the community? What did they identify as most important to address? If they noticed and identified the same things that you did, then you have verified your observations. This chapter addresses how this process begins.

Social situations such as the meeting discussed here can also be observed but are a bit more complicated. Formal data collection will be discussed in Chapter 18.

WONDERING

Once we have observed something, we may begin to wonder about the patterns we saw in our observations. That wondering, asking ourselves "Why?" is the first step on the path to making change. If we can determine why or how something happens, we can gather more information and test our ideas. For instance, Pastor Christine, observing the homeless people in her town, came to view the homeless as economic refugees, meaning that economic issues such as job loss and lack of social supports were a prominent cause for their homelessness. How could that educated guess be tested? Once we can identify causes, we can begin to identify solutions.

HOW TO CARRY OUT OBSERVING AND NOTICING TECHNIQUES

It is important to remember that at this point, your observation is not formal data collection. That step will come later. This observation is preliminary and subjective, and it is about identifying community issues that call your attention and beg to be addressed.

1. Choose neighborhoods, parks or shopping areas of your community.
2. Prepare to observe by imagining that you are a tourist or journalist seeing the area for the first time. How would you describe it? Look at the colors. What color is the sky today? The sidewalk. See the contrast between the pavement and street signs. What colors are people wearing?
3. Put thoughts of other things aside so you can effectively observe.
4. Take a camera to take pictures to help you remember later.
5. Walk or drive through the area, observing what is happening. Try to be unobtrusive. Don't gaze too long at anyone. Look away from time to time.
6. What do you notice? What is drawing your attention? What are people doing? Look for gestures and body language. Observe also who is talking to whom. Are people making eye contact? Do you note any physical tensions or emotions? Or do you notice that nobody is around? Do you hear noise or observe conflict?
7. Notice the context. Is the area clean and well kept, or is litter or graffiti visible?
8. Next, begin wondering. Imagine that you are a person you have been observing. What would you be thinking or feeling if you exhibited the particular behavior that you observed?
9. What did you notice that you would seek to solve?
10. Verify your observation with others that have been in the area. Are your observations similar?
11. Look for community data available on city, county and state websites for information on community well-being that may validate your observations.

TRY IT! OBSERVING YOUR COMMUNITY

You might want to print the list just presented or create your own list to remind you of things to look for. Pick a neighborhood or two, walk or drive through and observe the characteristics of physical and social order or decay. Use a camera or cell phone to snap pictures of the environment to help you remember. What caught your eye? Use empathy and wonder about the behaviors you observed. Talk to other people in the community. Do your observations compare to what they have noticed?

SUMMARY

The beginning of change can be as simple as noticing those things that suggest a barrier to children and families having the social supports and physical surroundings to thrive. Later in the process, you will use your observations to plan and carry out formal data collection to assess the community needs and priorities.

CITATIONS

Bens, I. (2017). *Facilitating with ease! Core skills for facilitators, team leaders and members, managers, consultants, and trainers* (4th ed.). Hoboken, NJ: John Wiley & Sons.

Dalio, R. (2017). *Principles: Life and work*. New York: Simon & Schuster.

Harvey, L. K., DiLuca, K. L., Hefner, K., Frabutt, J. M., & Shelton, T. L. (2013). Systematic observations of neighborhood order: Assessing the methodology in evaluating community-based initiative. *Journal of Applied Social Science, 7*(1), 42–60.

Kim, Y. (2016). *Community wellbeing indicators and the history of beyond GDP* (Research & Policy Brief, 73). Cornell University's Community & Regional Development Institute. Retrieved from https://cardi.cals.cornell.edu/sites/cardi.cals.cornell.edu/files/shared/PolicyBriefJune-16_draft5.pdf

Lofquist, W. A. (1983). *Discovering the meaning of prevention*. Tucson, AZ: Development Publications.

DETOURS

3

Figure 3.0

WHAT'S IN THIS CHAPTER?

In Chapter 1 we told a story about the founding of the Homeless Coalition as an example of how an action for change gets started in a local community. In this chapter we will take a look at how, with the help of a facilitator, a stalled project can begin moving again after taking a detour from its original starting point.

Objectives

- Describe how to re-energize a stalled project by identifying key logs (the logs which would free up a logjam if they are moved) that need to be cleared.
- Describe why you want to get the right people on the team.

- Describe why you want to select the right organizations with which to enter into an alliance.
- Describe activity traps and how they can derail your efforts.

A STORY ABOUT ACTIVITY TRAPS AND FINDING YOUR WAY THROUGH THE MAZE

When Pastor Christine founded the Homeless Coalition, the team she gathered at first believed that the problem of homeless people in their town would be simply alleviated, not realizing that they were entering a maze. Their efforts to alleviate *symptoms* of homelessness such as poor hygiene or worn and dirty clothing became **activity traps** (pursuits that keep people so busy that they lose sight of their goals), distracting them from their original goal. Years later, the solutions seemed farther away and more complex than they could have ever imagined at the beginning.

Homelessness has deep and tangled roots—poverty, lack of affordable housing, barriers to public systems, economic injustice, addiction and racism, just to name a few. These challenges being faced by the Homeless Coalition first led to intense research into the problem by several teams of very intelligent people. Finally, by inviting homeless people to advise them, they realized that they did not know as much about homelessness as the people they were attempting to help. By treating them as resources and not as objects, progress could be made.

Let's pick up our story two years later, to see where the use of a community development framework led to new directions. When you enter a maze, it is important to realize that there is a way out. To find the solution, you need to keep your focus.

The Homeless Coalition needed to consider the need to engage with community leaders to solve this problem. A crisis helped to accelerate the creation of new relationships. Frigid weather caused a crisis for the city government because there was no winter shelter available for the marginalized homeless people who could not be served by the Good Samaritan Shelter for various reasons. The city manager opened up City Hall to allow people to come in from the cold. The Homeless Coalition offered to supply cots and volunteers for the temporary shelter for a few nights. The result was chaos. A lack of showers, food and, mostly, supervision led to many headaches and complaints. No one was happy with the situation. Then the city manager asked members of the Homeless Coalition and the Interfaith Council to help him find a solution.

Two organizational meetings were held with leaders, with Maurine serving as the facilitator, including the mayor, city manager, chief of police and staff of the health department, social services and others to determine the scope of the problem with homelessness in the city and to design a temporary winter shelter. By reducing the problem to one aspect that could be solved immediately, there seemed to be a way out of the maze of hopelessness arising from feeling that nothing could be done. If homelessness can be viewed as a public health problem, this takes away blaming the homeless people for their condition. There was a way out of the maze.

Lessons Learned:

- When following a maze, keep your focus and recognize that you are not alone. Watch for indicators (something measurable that represents desired outcomes) as you process and follow the progress of others.
- Don't get stuck in activity traps that keep us so busy with the activities we are doing that we lose sight of the point of those activities (Odiorne, 1974).
- Patience and persistence pay off in the end.
- You can enter by one door and exit by another, but you must be near an open door while it is still open.
- The best solutions in problem-solving are on a spectrum. There are no one-size-fits-all solutions.

What can we do when the train track is blocked? Take the detour, of course.

The Homeless Coalition train had a full head of steam when it started out but ran into some problems when the initial strategy did not work. Let's go back and review how the volunteers found ways to detour around the barriers on the rails without the project becoming derailed.

WHAT THIS TECHNIQUE IS ABOUT

There are few people that have never experienced a project stalling for some reason. Many change projects in US organizations have experienced such problems (Mourier & Smith, 2001). You might have a good team, good goals and objectives, good strategies, and then BOOM! Reality hits. The project has hit a logjam. Why? It might have been stakeholders that had been left out, poor decisions, lack of budget or resources, lack of team buy-in and sense of urgency, or something completely outside your control. This technique is about getting started—and getting restarted when the process becomes stalled.

> *Logjam*: an impasse or deadlock in a process.
> *Key logs*: metaphorically, a key issue or problem, which if addressed, would make the current problem or logjam easy to solve.

Urgency is necessary to keeping projects moving (Meredith & Mantel, 2006). Sometimes things stall because someone failed to deliver, but you will do better to avoid discussing why something stalled out or who is to blame. Urgency grows only by looking forward, not backward. Most of the people on community development teams, unlike those in business, are volunteers. Blame is one way to lose volunteers, so it is wise not to go down that road. Sometimes volunteers do drop the ball for understandable reasons. If necessary, talk to the person or persons individually, outside the meeting. Avoid blame, and simply ask:

1. What has been completed?
2. What can you do next?
3. When can you have the next step done?

If they can't pick up the ball, find someone else to do it. Invite the person who dropped the ball to let you know when they are ready to pitch in again. Between meetings, touch base with those responsible for actions to find out how it's going, and if they need anything to get the job done.

Fuzzy goals and objectives, and unclear strategies, can all drain a project of its energy, but nothing seems to drain energy more than a distant deadline. Because many of the change projects addressed by communities are huge, universal human problems, like homelessness, success for our true goals may be decades, even centuries away. The only way to maintain energy for this kind of issue is to *break it into smaller achievable goals*, such as winter shelter, meals or help for people with mental health issues.

If your organization is stalled out because of a lack of resources, partnering with other nonprofit organizations can both help organizations to boost efficiency and effectiveness, and help push broader social and systems change that neither organization could achieve alone. The purpose for the collaboration needs to be clear even before the organizations determine how they will work together.

HOW TO CARRY OUT THIS TECHNIQUE

Determine if you are missing any stakeholders. Do some personal emissary work (personally speaking to stakeholders on behalf of the project to invite them to a meeting) to get all the stakeholders together.

Make alliances or relationships between organizations that could assist your project. Ask the other organizations to send a liaison (someone who will maintain communication for mutual understanding and cooperation between organizations) to a meeting with your project team. Take everything you've done to this point and present it to all stakeholders of your project. Describe the stalled project and its logjam while avoiding any blame. Speculate together on the *key logs* that may be stalling forward momentum. Ask the stakeholders:

- Are the right people on the team?
- Are the right organizations your allies?
- Are the goals and objectives clear and achievable? Can they be achieved within a year?
- Do you have a way to observe and measure your team's success? (See Chapters 10 and 17 for more on indicators and data collection.)
- Do you have local data on which to base your choice of strategies?
- Have you identified strategies that can be adapted to your local needs?
- Does your team have a sense of urgency?
- Which one key factor of those listed here would break the logjam if it were moved?

Describe what was happening when you started and your team's vision of what success looks like, including any measures or indicators. (More on initial assessments will be covered in Chapter 11 and visioning in Chapter 12). Determine which logjams to clear and how and why you will clear them. Rally people around the cause by showing them why this project matters.

TRY IT!

Imagine that you are a facilitator for a community committee to provide winter shelter to the homeless. It is already early November, and no decisions have been made on a temporary winter shelter for the homeless. Your organization has been offered a former church building, but your committee's decision making has been brought to a standstill because of concerns about the resources required and responsibility for a building. December will bring temperatures in the thirties (Fahrenheit) when it would be inhumane and dangerous to expect the homeless to sleep on sidewalks. It is already Saturday, and the next meeting is Thursday. As the facilitator, you need to get the project moving quickly. Using the actions described under "How to Carry Out This Technique," write an agenda that is likely to break the logjam. List other items that need to be done before the meeting.

SUMMARY

This chapter covered a step-by-step approach to re-energize a stalled project, including identifying key logs that need to be cleared to get things moving, as well as including the right people on the team and making allies with the right organizations.

CITATIONS

Meredith, J. R., & Mantel, S. J. (2006). *Project management: A managerial approach.* Hoboken, NJ: John Wiley & Sons.

Mourier, P., & Smith, M. (2001, October). Restarting a stalled project. *Security Management,* (10), 32–35.

Odiorne, G. S. (1974). *Management and the activity trap* (1st ed.). New York: Harper & Row.

STAGE 2
Getting to Know You

Figure S2.0 Facilitation of Change Model Stage 2: Getting to know you.

WHAT'S IN THIS SECTION

1. How you, the facilitator, "ground" yourself before beginning a facilitation so that you can see clearly, engage the participants, observe the process with fresh eyes and respond effectively throughout the facilitation process.
2. Several techniques for facilitating reflectively, include:
    - Clearing a mental space for facilitation.
    - Seeking unity: Moving groups from I to We.
    - Identifying participants' attitudes toward the focus of the change: *spectrum of attitudes*.

WHAT THIS SECTION IS ABOUT

Reflective facilitation, as an art form, involves careful planning before any change process ever begins. Speaking metaphorically, it can be compared to intentional gardening. First, there is the *gardener* (facilitator) and then the *garden* (the focus or concern), and finally, *gardening* (actions taken throughout the change process). Reflection generally involves slowing down and thinking ahead or looking back with a calm mind. Just as the gardener waits and observes the garden as it grows, the facilitator is observing the group process, listening to reactions of group members and continuously evaluating actions and outcomes. The facilitator, like a gardener, plays an attentive role in planning and implementing all phases of any group process. Just as one would create a garden design before beginning to plant, a time of reflection is essential before moving into a group process. One might say that shining some light on the garden will elicit new growth after the planting has begun. Essentially, this is the art of reflection.

The current climate of human culture and communication, all around the globe, is almost hyperactive. We live in fast-moving times, with scant attention being paid to listening or reflecting. The Media, both professional and social media, is the driving force by setting the pace with constant sound bites and fast takes. Although it has often been claimed that humans are the only species that can reflect, the reality is far from that. We are mostly being controlled by our thoughts rather than the other way around. Huston Smith, in his landmark study on Hinduism, offers another perspective on our capacity as humans to be reflective:

> The motion of the average mind, say the Hindus, are about as orderly as those of a crazed monkey cavorting about its cage. Nay, more like the prancings of a drunk crazed monkey. Even so, we have not conveyed its restlessness; the mind is like a drunken, crazed monkey that has St. Vitus' Dance. To do justice to our theme, however, we must go one final step. The mind is like a drunken crazed monkey with St. Vitus' Dance who has just been stung by a wasp.
>
> (Smith, 2009, p. 48)

Demanding that people pay attention is like an ineffective teacher commanding her fractious students to listen, while waving her hands frantically. On the other hand, what is the antidote for this all-too-human tendency of steering away from reflection? One method is the facilitator modeling reflective behavior through more listening and less talking in such a way that it alters a group's communication style. At the heart of the matter is that reflection allows for more emotions, feelings and associations to come forth. People who are being "listened to" in a deeper way are more likely to mirror this behavior.

For example, when was the last time you turned off all your electronic devices and just sat quietly with your own thoughts? A test might be taking one hour a day with nothing in your hands or in your ears. Being alone with your own thoughts will clear fertile ground for creativity and innovation. If your mind is always occupied with electronic devices, you are currently conditioned to respond immediately to electronic prompts from others. If you, as the facilitator, expect others to pay attention to you, first you need to learn how to pay attention to your own mind.

REFLECTIVE FACILITATION   4

Figure 4.0

WHAT'S IN THIS CHAPTER?

When we are planning to make significant changes to the social condition, there needs to be time set aside for deeply rooted reflection. When planning a strategy or action, what is the first step? Think it out! Returning to the gardening metaphor, the gardener would not simply toss some seeds onto untilled soil and expect to have them take root. The first thing a good gardener does is **clear the space**; you have some weeding and tilling to do before you take any action. In this case, begin by clearing your mind of any extraneous messages that could distract your thought process. Allow yourself some dreamtime where ideas simply float to the surface of your mind and are written down (or sketched in images) on a piece of paper. **What do you see?**

Objectives

By the end of this chapter, you will be able to:

- Reflect on your own buttons and biases so you can avoid those pitfalls and maintain your neutrality during facilitation.
- Use relaxation techniques to clear your mental space and calm yourself before a meeting.
- While providing neutral guidance, listen deeply and create a physical, emotional and intellectual space where people can come together, think, speak freely and make decisions together.

As an exercise in reflection, let's look at the Conversation for Race Unity, where we will see a mixed racial group coming together around a noble purpose: they had set a high bar for themselves of improving racial communication in a segregated city. Their stated purpose was:

> to build an interracial community based on listening respectfully to each other's life stories. As we listen to one another, we will be building a community that strengthens our understanding and compassion for one another. All ages are welcome to attend.

These are high-sounding words with good intentions behind them; and yet great difficulties can arise in actual practice because "after you build utopia, people will move in." By that quip I mean that real people have real communication habits that can clash even when trying to achieve a noble goal. Unique conversationalists entered this idealized setting with communication styles like grandstanding, overlapping speech, hesitancy, aggression and inaudibility. Here is the story of how the group members learned the art of deep listening by slowing down and listening to a story; and feeling it, holding it and accepting it as true.

A STORY ABOUT REFLECTION: RACE UNITY CONVERSATION

The weekly conversation is a walk-in group with an ever-changing landscape of participants that includes young and old, highly educated adults or those with limited formal education, and different cultures, religions and races. Quite a mix of people! Their chief reasons for attending are curiosity and a desire to make new friends across the racial barrier. Facilitation is led by a different person each week, so in the beginning there was a need to create some guidelines to assure that everyone had a fair chance at being heard. Initially, the group agreed to use a talking stick, a ritual object from Native American tradition, which allows only one person to speak, the holder of the stick, while all others agreed to listen without debating or interrupting when the stick-holder was speaking.

This model of communication provided some necessary training in how to listen because it restrained speech into sequences and assured that even the quietest person would have a turn. But after a while the group members became restive and pushed back, saying to Maurine, the facilitator, "We want to talk!" People quickly resumed their speech patterns of competing for floor time and rebutting the comments of another person who spoke before them; their recently acquired practice of reflection and deep listening soon flew out the window. They soon found this style of conversation problematic. As time went by, they returned to a modified listening model which respected each person's right to be heard. Through trial and error, they learned that cooperation was essential to achieving unity in speech and in relationships.

Lessons Learned:

- Both as individuals and as a group, they needed to learn how to be reflective, which is characterized by deep thinking.
- Ultimately, reflection depends on becoming a deeper listener. That means paying careful attention to the words and intentions of the speaker without blaming, judging or interrupting them.

> *Deep thinking*: using all of our thinking facilities including analytical and creative abilities and refocusing on the issue at hand each time we lose focus (which is often typically) until we have completed the thought. Note: deep thinking is more effective if a brief break is taken about every 40 minutes or so.
> *Deep listening*: Deep listening involves listening-to-learn, listening for understanding, rather than agreement, and asking good questions to explore the new learning. Deep listening can occur on the intrapersonal (listening to yourself), interpersonal and group levels. More on deep listening practice is found in Chapter 26.
> *Focused attention*: The brain's ability to attend to a target thought for a period of time. There are at least three kinds of focus: inner, other, and outer focus (Goleman, 2015) that are affected by our cognition and our perception.

WHAT THIS TECHNIQUE IS ABOUT

How can we prepare ourselves to be more reflective facilitators? Parker Palmer, Quaker educator and author, says that we need to develop what he calls "habits of the heart (which are) deeply ingrained ways of seeing, being, responding to life that involve our minds, our emotions, our self-images, our concepts of meaning and purpose" (Palmer, 2011, p. 253). These habits require in turn both modesty and audacity. He lists them as follows:

- An understanding that we are all interconnected.
- An awareness of the value of our differences.
- An ability to hold tension in ways that produce energy, creativity and insight.
- A sense of empowerment to speak and act to create positive change.
- A capacity to create a feeling of fellowship among group members that allows us to work toward change (Palmer, 2011).

Here are some examples to consider. William Lofquist anchors his theory of development in the concept that we need to *take seriously the well-being of others*. This is easier when we are aware that we are all in the community, with its attendant issues, *together*. At the same time, we also need to see and value the differences, or "otherness" among us. Studies have shown that diverse groups are more effective at solving problems (Hong & Page, 2004; Bang & Frith, 2017), but it is not enough to put diverse people together. The best groups must think and interact in effective ways.

When we include all people of whatever culture, language, skin color, gender identity, physical capability or age, we are embracing difference and creating vital communities. Or, as Horton the Elephant so succinctly put it, "A person's a person no matter how small" (Dr. Seuss, 1954).

In communities, the members of our group often come together out of concern for issues *within the community*. When this happens, their concern may give rise to passion and a need to speak out. Other concerned people may not have that same sense of voice or agency (sense of control of one's actions in the world) (Palmer, 2011) through which positive change can take place. In this case, they need the support of the facilitator and the group to speak their mind. This support comes from the community; the sense of fellowship that needs to be created among the group and lends courage to its members so that they can both speak and act.

HOW TO CARRY OUT THIS TECHNIQUE

Reflective facilitation is helping the team think together so they can plan and implement together. In order to do that, facilitators need to *know themselves well* so they can bring their strengths, avoid pitfalls and remain neutral. These begin with personal reflection and end with reflecting on the process; so that team members can see clearly what is happening during the discussion. Several methods can be used for personal reflection. We will discuss four methods that work well together: journaling, clearing mental space, providing neutral guidance and debriefing.

JOURNALING BUTTONS AND BIASES

A *hot button* is something that causes a person to stop listening consciously and deeply and start listening unconsciously or defensively. Hot buttons get under our skin and cause anger or frustration. Hot buttons are individual, so different things irritate different people. Jeanne's personal button as a facilitator is when someone dominates the conversation, not allowing others to say anything. Knowing what her buttons are helps her to diminish their effect. This is where a **journal** can help you reflect and become aware of your own buttons and biases. Facilitators who make regular efforts to consider their own thoughts and actions in light of different contexts and use ongoing reflection in the form of critique of their own biases will often be more successful at remaining neutral during facilitation.

Use an empty notebook to explore your thinking:

1. To find out what your buttons are, think back to meetings where someone really annoyed you. What was the issue? (If you have not had that experience in meetings, think about your reaction to people on television, news or social media.)
2. Write down what they said or did. How does this hot button affect your behavior? How did you feel? Did you begin to perspire or clench your jaw? Write that down. Next time a button is pushed, you can recognize the physical symptoms and slow the cascade of reactions.
3. Now, *reflect* for a moment about the possible cause of your reaction. Usually it is something beneath the surface that needs to be studied honestly, nonjudgmentally and compassionately. Perhaps it is an unresolved pain from years ago. Keep in mind that this reflection process is not easy and requires courage.
4. *Take a deep breath* or take a walk and *let go* of the pain. Next time the button is pushed, it will feel a little less intense, so you can *respond* more calmly.
5. Take this a step further and practice having a conversation about the issue with a trusted friend (Jana & Freeman, 2016).

As human beings we all have experiences, values and cultural contexts which are lenses for how we see the world. This results in *bias*—the tendency to favor one thing over another. Biases result from interactions of memory, attention, attribution (how people explain causes) and other mental processing. *Cognitive biases* are automatic and unconscious. They may arise from:

- Our brain's information-processing shortcuts or heuristics.
- Distortions caused during storage and retrieval from our memory.
- Our brain's limited capacity in processing information quickly.

Most biases are harmless, like the tendency to enjoy or dislike coffee, but under some circumstances can lead to highly negative outcomes. As a facilitator, you will need to identify and *set aside those biases* that interfere with sound thinking, relationships and wise facilitation, because if they are not avoided, they can lead to errors in judgments, decisions and relationships. Table 4.1 lists seven of approximately 100 common thinking biases that can influence our decisions and how to reduce their effect.

Table 4.1 Common cognitive biases and how to reduce their effect.

Bias	What it is	Strategy to reduce it
Feelings Heuristic	A heuristic is a fast, automatic mental shortcut (usually based on experiences) used in decision-making when emotion is a factor. If your feelings towards a strategy are positive, then you are more likely to judge risks as low and benefits as high. Conversely, if your feelings or gut reaction are negative, then you may judge the risks high and the benefits low.	Take some time to reflect on the decision. Imagine the possible consequences, both intended and unintended. Analyze it, think about it and discuss it.
Anchoring	The first information we receive influences how we judge all other information we receive after that (Hardman, 2009).	Don't rush to make a decision. Weigh the data and facts, and carefully interpret them before deciding. Ask for time to decide if necessary.
Confirmation bias	Our tendency to hear only information that agrees with our existing beliefs or ideas and ignore that which does not agree.	Question and challenge the facts and your judgments. Look at the pros and cons of an idea. Consider alternatives. Pay attention to what you like and what you fear.
Conservatism bias	This is a bias toward earlier evidence rather than newer evidence.	Remember that things are changing constantly, which means we continually get to learn new things.
Halo Effect	If we have this bias, we assume that if a person, organization or approach is successful in one area, it will be in another.	Resist first impressions by questioning and reflecting on them. Avoid generalizations.
Information bias	More information is not necessarily better. If we have an information bias, we continue to seek more information, even if it will not affect our decisions.	Focus on what needs to be known to make your decision and avoid clouding the decision with an overwhelming amount of data.
Status quo bias	This is a bias toward preferring things to remain the way they are.	You (or your community) don't have to stick to the status quo. You can change and maximize the potential of the community.

You might recognize one or more of these biases in your own thinking. Everyone has them, so it is difficult to be rational, objective thinkers. However, by recognizing them at work in our decision-making, we can reduce their effect.

When we think of biases, we often think of social biases. Social biases can include positive or negative perspectives and categorizing people with respect to race, gender, sexual orientation, tall/short, fat/thin, disability, ethnic origin or religion, to name a few. These biases can make it harder to look at things from someone else's perspective.

Social Biases Can Be Either Implicit or Explicit

In the case of explicit bias, individuals are aware of their biased attitudes (positive or negative) toward certain groups. Implicit biases, however, are *unconscious* feelings, perceptions, attitudes, and stereotypes that have developed as a result of prior experiences (Fridell, 2013). Jana and Freeman (2016) indicated that, by becoming more self-aware, we can move beyond our social biases. To move beyond those biases, talk to a trusted friend or family member. The U.S. Department of Justice noted that "implicit biases can be reduced through the very process of discussing them and recognizing them for what they are" (n.d., p. 2).

1. Use your journal to reflect on your social biases or overgeneralized beliefs about particular groups of people. How does the bias affect your life? Is it really possible that everyone in the group is the same?
2. Restate any generalizations you find yourself making. Restate the generalization so that they reflect your actual experience. (Instead of saying "all shoppers wearing hijabs are loud," restate it to say "some of the shoppers wearing hijabs that you have encountered were loud.")
3. When you recognize and write down a bias, stereotype or generalization, you can then *discuss it with a trusted friend*, which can reduce their effect on your relationships with others who are different from you.
4. Ask yourself why you think that way and work to change your perspective.

Before the Meeting: Clear a Mental Space

Clearing a mental space helps a facilitator to be mindful of what is going on during the meeting, including awareness of his or her own thinking processes (inner focus) and reading what other people are doing and saying (other focus) and what is going on in the larger context (outer focus). Adriansen and Krohn define it this way: "Mindfulness is to be present in the moment and to cultivate a state of non-judgmental openness in order to relinquish our control of the world, including our own cognitive processes" (2014, p. 26).

There are several ways for a facilitator to clear a mental space and allow for mindful, reflective facilitation before leading a meeting:

- Progressive muscle relaxation.
- Mindfulness meditation.
- Yoga, tai chi, and Qi Gong.
- Repetitive or centering prayer.
- Guided imagery.

Here we will describe the first method. Progressive muscle relaxation involves conscious attention to different body parts. Lie down or sit in a comfortable position and begin by relaxing the toes. Next, move to the arch and relax those muscles. Move then to the heel, then to the ankle and then allow the attention to gradually move through the entire body. This usually takes 30 to 45 minutes. Other methods may take less or more time, depending on the level of stress you are feeling. One quick and effective method is covered in Chapter 7.

During the Meeting: Provide Neutral Guidance

- Keep in mind your own cognitive and social biases so you can neutralize them during the meeting.
- Create a safe and creative space for decisions (covered in Chapter 23). Make sure everyone has had the opportunity to express their concerns. Promote the expression of diverse perspectives (Kaner, Lind, Toldi, Fisk, & Berger, 2014) and foster a sense of equal status, goals, cooperation and participation that can help reduce prejudice among the diverse members of your team (Allport, 1954).
- Listen deeply and reflect the process and group meanings back to the participants (covered in Chapter 24)
- Remember that what a facilitator thinks of the ideas or proposals expressed by members of the change team doesn't really matter. The goal is to make sure everyone feels heard respectfully (Neal & Neal, 2011) and to keep the meeting energy rolling.

- If you are a *member* of the community rather than an outside facilitator, and the team is asking your honest reaction to an idea, you can defer offering an opinion. If you are pressed, you might say, "OK, I am taking off my facilitator hat for a moment . . ." Then return to the neutral role of the facilitator after you offer your opinion. More important than your own opinions, however, is making sure everyone at the meeting is heard. Forming tolerant, respectful and open-minded relationships, listening deeply and inviting each person to comment can help make that happen.

AFTER THE MEETING: DEBRIEFING

- After the meeting, ask anyone who expressed concerns or resistance if they felt that the decisions made reflected their thinking or were acceptable. If the decisions did not, those concerns should be addressed at the next meeting. On a sheet of easel paper, write down the heading "Unresolved Concerns" and then make a list of the concerns. Post the concerns at the next meeting and discuss them.
- After the meeting, use your journal to take notes about what worked and what didn't during the meeting, including what worked to help you facilitate neutrally.

TRY IT

Imagine that you are facilitating a meeting of a committee addressing issues in your community of immigrants from an African country, and several have been invited to the meeting as stakeholders. Your goal is to plan and conduct a meeting reflectively.

1. Begin by reflecting on your buttons and biases related to the group of immigrants. Have you had unfortunate encounters in the grocery store? A parking lot? Note these in your journal.
2. Describe any overgeneralizations or biases you might have, and then rewrite them so they better describe your actual experiences.
3. Discuss the bias with a trusted friend.
4. Decide how you will clear the mental space.
5. Describe how you might create a safe and creative space for attendees.
6. Write a brief agenda.
7. Describe how you will respond if pressed to give your opinion.
8. Describe how you will debrief with participants that had expressed concerns or objections.
9. Describe how you will journal what worked and what didn't during the meeting.

SUMMARY

This chapter covered how to reflect on your own buttons and biases so you can avoid those pitfalls and maintain your neutrality during facilitation. We briefly touched on using mindfulness or relaxation techniques to clear your mental space and calm yourself before a meeting. Finally, we covered providing neutral guidance, listening deeply and creating a physical, emotional and intellectual space where people can come together, think, speak freely and make decisions together. This will be addressed in greater depth in future chapters.

Let's take a few steps forward to examine the situation more closely and design your action planning. Each step will be given full treatment in the next chapters of Stage 2.

- Calling a meeting.
- Clear your mental space.
- Getting to know you.

CITATIONS

Adriansen, H. K., & Krohn, S. (2014). Mindfulness for group facilitation: An example of Eastern philosophy in Western organizations. *Group Facilitation, 13*, 17–28. Retrieved from https://pure.au.dk/portal/files/79477067/Mindfulness_for_Group_Facilitation_Adriansen_Krohn.pdf

Allport, G. W. (1954). *The nature of prejudice.* Cambridge, MA: Perseus Books.

Bang, D., & Frith, C. D. (2017). Making better decisions in groups. *Royal Society Open Science, 4*(170193). doi:10.1098/rsos.170193

Department of Justice. (n.d.). *Police-community relations toolkit: Understanding bias: A resource guide.* Retrieved from www.justice.gov/crs/file/836431/download

Fridell, L. (2013, Fall). This is not your grandparents' prejudice: The implications of the modern science of bias for police training. *Translational Criminology*, 10–11. Retrieved from http://cebcp.org/wp-content/TCmagazine/TC5-Fall2013

Geisel, T. S. (Dr. Seuss) (2019). *Horton hears a who.* Crawfordsville, IN: Random House Books for Young Readers. (Original work published 1954.)

Goleman, D. (2015). *Focus: The hidden driver of excellence.* New York: Harper Paperbacks.

Hardman, D. (2009). *Judgment and decision making: Psychological perspectives.* New York: John Wiley & Sons.

Hong, L., & Page, S. E. (2004). Groups of diverse problem solvers can outperform groups of high-ability problem solvers. *Proceedings of the National Academy of Science USA, 101*, 16385–16389. doi:10.1073/pnas.0403723101

Jana, T., & Freeman, M. (2016). *Overcoming bias: Building authentic relationships across differences.* Oakland, CA: Berrett-Koehler.

Kaner, S., Lind, L., Toldi, C., Fisk, S., & Berger, D. (2014). *Facilitator's guide to participatory decision-making* (3rd ed.). San Francisco, CA: Jossey-Bass.

Lofquist, W. A. (1989). *Technology of prevention workbook.* Tucson, AZ: AYD Publications.

Neal, C., & Neal, P. (2011). *The art of convening: Authentic engagement in meetings, gatherings, and conversations.* San Francisco, CA: Berrett-Koehler Publishers.

Palmer, P. J. (2011). *Healing the heart of democracy: The courage to create a politics worthy of the human spirit.* San Francisco, CA: Jossey-Bass.

Smith, H. (2009). *The world's religions.* New York: Harper Collins.

CALLING THE FIRST AND SUBSEQUENT MEETINGS

5

Figure 5.0

WHAT'S IN THIS CHAPTER?

Change requires that a *core group* of people get excited about improving their community, organization or business and use that energy to move a change forward. How do you find and excite these people? Often a community change begins with a meeting, but many of us sit through too many meetings at work. You want to call a meeting only when collaboration and interaction are important, such as when you have opportunities or intractable problems to address, projects, plans or decisions to be made. Often, a small steering committee including gatekeepers meets to plan for larger group meetings. This is especially useful in communities where elders (and experienced leaders, young or old) are important gatekeepers to the larger community.

Objectives

By the end of this chapter, you will be able to:

- Call the first meeting of a *core* change team effectively.
- Call productive subsequent meetings.

A STORY ABOUT CALLING A FIRST MEETING

The group meeting to plan for the Homeless Coalition included some gatekeepers, influencers and people with needed skills such as facilitation skills. However, they realized that important people were missing. They agreed to reach out to the missing groups such as Hispanics in the community, local Black clergy, legislators, representatives of the mental health community, and persons with addictions, AA and those who serve these groups.

After a visioning meeting, the core group had a focus to use when inviting people to the meeting: "The Homeless Coalition is a community partnership addressing local issues of homelessness and poverty." The group planned to focus that meeting on the conditions causing poverty and homelessness and meeting participants' past experiences leading to effective planned change. The group then planned the agenda (which follows), time and place. Look at the agenda to find examples of engaging and collaborative methods planned.

Homeless Coalition—Community Meeting Agenda

1. Opening Reading from Emma Lazarus poem on the Statue of Liberty
   Give me your tired, your poor
   Your huddled masses yearning to breathe free
   The wretched refuse of your teeming shore
   Send these, the homeless, tempest-tossed to me
   I lift my lamp beside the golden door (1883)
2. Wisdom Circle formation—we are here to listen and to learn from one another. The talking stick is a symbol free and equal speech. Only one person speaks, the one who holds the stick. Talking stick symbols:
   - Music wood—the breath of God blows through it—empty yourself to become a hollow reed.
   - Rabbit fur—soften your words, do not speak in anger.
   - Crow feather—speak the truth.
   - Turkey feather—generosity.
   - Beads—green for spring, yellow for summer, red for fall, white for winter—changing seasons, life is ever changing.
   - Buffalo fur—strength and endurance.
   - Iridescent shells—conditions are constantly changing.
   - Crane breast feather—leadership—be farsighted.
   - Turquoise—the eye of God is always upon us.
3. About speaking and listening in this circle:
   - Speak using few words—simply and directly and with humility.
   - No single person holds the entire truth.
   - Speak from the heart as well as from the head.
   - Listen deeply to the person who holds the stick.

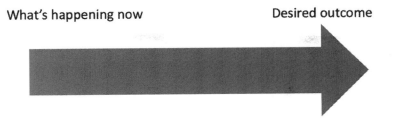

Figure 5.1 Changing conditions.

WHAT BRINGS YOU TO THIS CIRCLE?

Example: I am president of the Community Interfaith Council. I have been listening to the news of how many people in our community cannot find a place to live. I come here to learn with all of you how we can change this condition of homelessness.

4. Three principles undergirding community development:
    - **Participation**—when people have an opportunity to participate in decisions and shape strategies that vitally affect them, they will develop a sense of ownership in what they have determined and the commitment to carry it out.
    - **Responsibility**—no person can ever be responsible for another person. How one takes responsibility for oneself in relation to other people helps determine the quality of the relationship. When people agree to work together toward mutually desirable goals that promote mutual well-being, a sense of corporate or community responsibility emerges.
    - **Changing conditions**—when people work together to create conditions that promote their mutual well-being, not only is a clear sense of the common good strengthened and pursued, but the individuals involved are provided opportunities for personal growth and development as well.
5. Focusing on conditions:
    - Situations are created in which every person's perspective of those conditions can become important to understanding and changing them (see Figure 5.1). Work together in small groups to describe "what's happening now."
    - People become allies in working toward mutual goals, mutually arrived at.
    - People are treated as resources rather than as objects or recipients.
    - Successful experiences in planned change can be carried into other condition-improving activity. Share experiences with successful planned change.

WHAT THIS TECHNIQUE IS ABOUT

To call your first core community change meeting, you will need to think about what you hope to achieve with the meeting and write a summary of what the meeting is about. The summary can be helpful to

> *Change team*: the core group guiding change planning and implementation.
> *Gatekeepers*: people that control access to something, such as a group or resource in a community.
> *Influencers*: people who have built a reputation for their knowledge and expertise on a particular topic and can sway or influence the thinking or action of others. These are people who impact the community through participation in events and institutions such as fundraising events, school board, park board, city council, service clubs and church groups.

invite people because people usually want to know why they should give up their time to attend a meeting. Write a brief description of the community issue that explains the idea so that the reader can understand it within a short time, say no more than one minute.

Think about people who are concerned or interested in the topic for the meeting, beginning with influencers in the community. Community change is generally a grassroots change process. It should *not* be about authorities, specialists or "experts" telling community members what they should do. Interested people, gatekeepers and influencers will be the target audience invited for this meeting. You may already know some of these people based on the conversations you had when you verified your observations (discussed in Chapter 2). If not, you will need to generate a list of influencers.

Next, you will need to schedule a date and time that will be possible for participants to attend and determine how the meeting will be conducted. For instance, Jeanne was a co-facilitator of a global group working on how an organization could become more globally inclusive. Her challenge was to hold a meeting via web conference with influencers in every U.S. time zone and in Mumbai, India. They had to find a time and a technology that would work for everyone.

There are also special meeting considerations to keep in mind when you are including intercultural participants or elders. In the example just mentioned, time zones and technology were primary considerations, because the participants were all fluent in English and culturally competent. However, that was not the case in a local community group in which there were several new immigrants. Neither group of participants on the committee was familiar with the language or culture of the other group. We had to rely heavily on cultural liaisons and translators. However, there was strong motivation on both sides to resolve community issues, so we relied on some of the suggestions in Table 5.1 to help us do our work.

Elders, for the sake of this discussion, are those age 65 or older, some of whom may be developing hearing, vision or mobility issues. These people are often retired and concerned citizens, frequently doing volunteer work and likely to participate in community change efforts. With broad life experience, they can be invaluable participants, so you will want to make sure they can participate fully. Suggestions listed in Table 5.1 helped create a safe and creative space for all participants.

Finally, **create an agenda,** because you won't want to waste anyone's time. Most people will want answers to two questions early on: why am I here, and why should I care (Stewart & Tao, 2017)? This question is a good topic to start your agenda. Also, you need to plan the meeting activities so that everyone is comfortable contributing and working together toward the same goal. Finally, keep in mind that an agenda may need to be flexible, especially when people attend the meeting with their own items that they want to cover. Some things you may want to cover include answers to questions such as:

- What is the history of the condition or issue of concern?
- What information do we have about the situation?
- When reviewing data, what numbers, words or phrases stand out?
- What are the actual conditions we are trying to achieve?
- What resources do we have to achieve those conditions?

Now you will be ready to promote the meeting. Call each of the people you wish to invite and share the meeting summary to persuade them to attend. Send out the agenda to invited people and ask for input.

HOW TO CARRY OUT THIS TECHNIQUE

First Steps for a Facilitator

A facilitator sets the stage for his or her role early in the project. At the beginning of your engagement with any group, the facilitator needs to pose some questions to those inviting him or her to facilitate:

- What is your relationship to the group? Leader, facilitator or group member?
- Will you be a paid or volunteer facilitator?

Table 5.1 Special considerations for intercultural, older or disabled meeting participants.

Special Participant Considerations

Participant	Concerns	Suggestions
Intercultural participants	■ Facilitator or non-peers in the group may influence participants ■ When language fluency is not strong, directions and questions may be difficult to explain to participants ■ Information from diverse groups may be difficult to synthesize ■ Desire to save face may influence answers to questions ■ May need additional time for translation ■ Printed materials may be problematic for those with poor English literacy	■ Gain trust of those attending ■ Find out about the cultural norms (for instance, to determine if separate seating or even meetings must be available for men and women) ■ Practice reflection on presuppositions/assumptions ■ Detailed directions on language and culture may be helpful for co-facilitators ■ Compare to other people and sources to check validity of interpretations of participant comments, preferably a cultural liaison ■ Printed materials may be translated (verbally or in writing) for those with poor English literacy
Elders (age 65 and over) or those with disabilities	■ Older participants may have experienced a decline in visual or auditory perception ■ Older participants may tire more easily than young participants ■ Memory and information processing may be slower ■ Breadth of life experience may yield important insights ■ Accessibility of the meeting room can be problematic, especially in older buildings	■ Older facilitators are often sensitive to the needs of older participants ■ Place elders near front so they can hear or see better ■ Increase illumination and contrast to improve readability; try to avoid glare or poor lighting ■ Use 12- to 14-point type for printed materials ■ Keep meetings short (less than 1.5 hours) ■ Use a quiet room and reduce reverberations in the room caused by bare walls and floors ■ Speak clearly ■ Accessibility of the meeting room should be considered—are curb cuts, ramps and/or elevators available?

- What is your timeline for your term as facilitator? When will your work be complete and under what conditions (especially if you are a paid facilitator)?
- Will your departure impede the progress of the project or leave an opening for new leadership?
- Do you have a plan for mentoring a new facilitator and passing the baton? How will you prepare new leaders?
- Is there a role for you after your term as facilitator?

How to Call the First Meeting

Describe the focus or purpose of the meeting. Write down the objectives for the meeting. The objectives should align with the focus and should be specific and easy to measure. Use these two ideas and write a summary of the meeting and its purpose.

Brainstorm a list of interested people and those who may influence community opinions and perspectives. This task is better done in a group: ask interested people for suggestions of influencers.

Identify an appropriate time and place for the meeting. This means a time when people are available to come, and a place that is comfortable and familiar or at least neutral to participants. Also, if necessary, use technology such as web conferencing to include people who might otherwise be left out.

Create your agenda so that you will accomplish the intent, using engaging, collaborative and interactive strategies. According to Laborie and Stone (2016), you can tell when participants are engaged when they are:

- Focused and attentive.
- Active.
- Enthusiastic and eager.
- Spontaneous.
- Curious and inquisitive.
- Willing (p. 38).

Call each of the people you want at the meeting, share the meeting summary and persuade them to come. If the people you are inviting are geographically far away and tech savvy, you can try a video conference to invite them.

After the meeting, informally evaluate the results. Did the right group of people show up, including community leaders and influencers? Did those people indicate a willingness to continue with the project? If they do not show these characteristics, rethink steps 4 and 6, then try again. Use what you learned from the first meeting to create a more successful meeting.

CALLING SUBSEQUENT MEETINGS

Calling meetings of ongoing committees, councils and project teams is quite a different process. First, send out a request for items to the entire project team email list. This gets members' thinking juices flowing and gives them an equal opportunity to add to the discussion. Second, contact the key stakeholders to ask if they have any issues to add like Old Business/New Business. Third, send out a proposed agenda to give latecomers one more chance to add something. Fourth, arrange the agenda items to handle the more difficult or lengthy discussions up front followed by reports from committees. Finally, add a section called "Open Agenda" at the bottom to address current events and announcements. (See the following sample agenda.)

Proposed Agenda for Council Meeting on February 27 at Sufi Community Center

1. Good Samaritan report
2. Winter housing crisis for marginalized homeless
3. CAIRS
4. RAID
5. Communications Team formation
6. Southern Illinois Immigration Rights Project (SIIRP)
7. Treasurer's report
8. Open Agenda

TRY IT!

Think of a meeting you will facilitate soon. If you don't have a meeting to facilitate soon, think of one you will attend. Describe the meeting's purpose or focus and objectives. Write a summary of the meeting and brainstorm a list of people who should be there for the meeting to achieve the objectives. Identify a time and place that will be appropriate for all the possible participants. Finally, create an agenda that will accomplish the objectives using engaging collaborative strategies.

SUMMARY

Calling the first meeting can have challenges for community developers, including clearly defining the intent in a compelling way that can interest community leaders and influencers when they are invited. A second challenge is to invite those who will get excited about a community issue and be willing to work to address it. Create an agenda that will accomplish your purpose while engaging the participants. Finally, evaluate the meeting. Did you accomplish the purpose, or were the participants uninterested or even resistant? Learn from the first meeting and try again using a different approach, and perhaps invite people who are less resistant to the proposed project.

CITATIONS

Laborie, K., & Stone, T. (2016). Interact + engage. *TD: Talent Development*, 70(1), 36–40.

Stewart, M., & Tao, T. (2017). *Momentum: Creating effective, engaging and enjoyable meetings*. Austin, TX: Lioncrest Publishing.

6 RECRUIT AND RETAIN VOLUNTEERS

Figure 6.0

WHAT'S IN THIS CHAPTER?

The mainstay of many organizations working on community change is volunteers. Some fortunate groups find that interested people are attracted to the change team, but often they need to be recruited. How do you recruit them, and how do you keep them? The answer to this question has changed dramatically in the last 40 years. Knowing the characteristics of volunteers, their intrinsic motivations and what they want is a key place to start. Knowing what you need is also important.

Objectives

By the end of this chapter, you will be able to:

- Determine the skills, needs and intrinsic motivations of each potential volunteer.
- Determine your organization's needs to find the right person for the job.
- Invite and persuade them to volunteer.
- Prepare to engage and recognize volunteers.
- Retain volunteers.

A STORY ABOUT RECRUITING VOLUNTEERS

For three decades Maurine has been using Quaker methods as a blueprint for her work in community development. Whether she was engaged in prison reform, interfaith collaboration or prevention activities, she always found that Quaker social change methods really worked best; for example, engaging with people using consensus decision-making and conflict resolution, to name just two. Here is a story of how she employed these methods to create a successful project to address one of the most difficult issues in world history—the Holocaust.

In the 1990s Maurine became involved as a volunteer with an interfaith organization in the Chicago area called the Avenue of the Righteous. Their mission is to honor the Holocaust rescuers and bring their lessons to life today. At that time, she was employed at National-Louis University where she was a newly hired admissions director and part-time faculty member.

One afternoon she received a phone call at her office from Ruth Goldboss, one of the founders of the Avenue. Ruth is the kind of person who is always on fire with a new idea. Her ideas are usually very good, so Maurine listened carefully. Ruth said she had a vision of a drama which would teach children about altruism using one of the stories of the Righteous Gentiles who rescued Jews during the Holocaust. A few years prior Ruth had helped to create a memorial park in Evanston which honors the deeds of these unsung heroes. Ruth asked Maurine if she would help her reach someone in the college's drama department with this idea. Maurine agreed to carry the message forward. When she spoke to the theater arts director, he loved the idea and immediately asked the Dean of Arts and Sciences to support the project. The Dean loved the idea and persuaded the higher university officials to support it. They liked it too!

Using the principle of *intrinsic* motivation (self-motivated action) as a method for recruiting volunteer support, Maurine began to invite the Avenue of the Righteous volunteers to become partners with the university to produce the play. There was initial excitement over the project, but eventually there was an impasse over the budget. At one point the Dean asked Ruth to produce an advisory committee for the project that would be impressive enough to the president of the university so he would endorse releasing funds from the public relations budget. Ruth then reached out to a retired U.S. Supreme Court justice and secured him as a volunteer on the advisory committee. He was intrinsically motivated as a Jew to lend his name and credibility to the project. Having a star quality volunteer like him on the advisory committee gave the go-ahead to the project.

Within two years the Honor of Humanity Project emerged as a collaborative effort of the local interfaith community group and the university, and they produced an original play for children called *Angel in the Night* which won a national award and is currently being produced in schools across the country. At the end of the project, which had brought national press attention to the small university, Maurine received a letter of commendation from the Development Department director. He wrote, "I never saw you do it, and I never knew how you did it, but I know this would never have happened if you had not come here." What happened? How could one phone call produce so much? While no one was watching, Maurine was grounding this effort solidly with well-established and tested methods of community development. They do work effectively.

Lessons Learned:

- Every individual you want to recruit is unique and has their own intrinsic motivation.
- Before inviting them to volunteer, think about their skills, desires and motivations.
- Ask yourself (and the volunteer) if the role you are inviting them to take would be motivating for them.

WHAT THIS TECHNIQUE IS ABOUT

Back in the 1960s, Jeanne became a teenage Red Cross volunteer after she heard a Red Cross spokesperson during one of her high school assemblies. A few students had signed up, and every Wednesday after school they caught a bus to the VA hospital with a group of volunteers from other schools. They loyally filled the hospital's fixed schedule, in part because they had fun with their group of volunteer friends, new and old. Also, they had a passion and felt like they made a difference by visiting with disabled patients who were veterans from World War II, the Korean War and the Vietnam War. The youth volunteers chatted with the veterans, went with them to movies at the hospital, even held a talent show with them. They also took mobility-impaired patients for walks and fed those who were unable to feed themselves. That was then, this is now. Many youth volunteers still want to make a difference, but not necessarily on a fixed schedule.

VOLUNTEER SERVICE

The first steps in recruiting volunteers are to determine:

- What you need your volunteers to do. Write a description of the tasks, roles and responsibilities. Then describe the skills and passions needed by the volunteers. Use these to write a *job description*. A job description describes the nature of the work performed and whether the staff is paid or unpaid (volunteer). The purpose of a job and the key functions to be performed are described in the job description. A job description is used for hiring and placing staff, and for evaluation of their work.
- What time commitment you need? Can these jobs be done by short-term volunteers? Or do you need a longer-term commitment? Short-term commitments can lead to longer-term commitments (McKee & McKee, 2012).
- Where does the job need to be done? On site? Can any of the jobs be done virtually on a volunteer's own time schedule?
- Will the responsibilities challenge volunteers and help them develop new skills? Will they meet new people and broaden their network of acquaintances in the community? In organizations with direct client contact, particularly with vulnerable populations, policies and procedures are critical for all concerned, clients, staff and volunteers. *Vulnerable populations* are those requiring utmost care, including "children, minors, pregnant women, fetuses, human in vitro fertilization, prisoners, employees, military persons and students in hierarchical organizations, terminally ill, comatose, physically and intellectually challenged individuals, institutionalized, elderly individuals, visual or hearing impaired, ethnic minorities, refugees . . . economically and educationally disabled" (Shivayogi, 2013).

When the volunteer has direct client contact, make sure any necessary *policies* and *procedures* are in place and available to volunteers when they begin, just as you would for paid staff. Policies are written to help an organization to reach its goals and are available in a form that is widely accessible. Policies and procedures are designed to guide all decisions, actions and activities that take place within the organization. Procedures describe how things are done within the organization. You may

need to provide training on the specific methods used to carry out policies in the day-to-day operations of the organization.
- Determine the reporting structure for volunteers, and what their relationship will be to other staff.

CHARACTERISTICS OF VOLUNTEERS

There are some key characteristics of volunteers that you will need to address if you wish to recruit and retain volunteers: their life stages, their gender, their motivations and how they prefer to serve. It is important to be aware that there are cultural differences in motivations for volunteering and differences among racial and ethnic groups in rates of volunteering. Volunteers also tend to have higher levels of education.

Life Stages

People generally volunteer in greater numbers during their teen years, middle adulthood and late adulthood (Rosenthal & Baldwin, 2001) (shown in Figure 6.1).

- During *early adulthood*, energetic twentysomethings are trying to establish careers and romantic relationships. They may be pursuing further education in college or graduate school, starting their career and seeking romantic relationships. People ages 20–24 have a fairly low rate of volunteering compared to other life stages, but after age 25, volunteerism picks up (Bureau of Labor Statistics, 2016).
- People over 25 may choose to volunteer for career reasons, such as networking or internships, or because they have a passion for a cause and want to see a change in society or politics. They might also volunteer because a friend asked them. The current young adults are technology savvy and tend to be impatient (McKee & McKee, 2012). They also prefer short-term (sometimes called *episodic* or *micro-volunteering*), flexible (sometimes online), challenging and rewarding assignments that use their skills and experience. You might find that those short-term volunteer stints may lead to future volunteering on a longer-term basis.
- During *middle adulthood*, men often find their time taken up with work and family. They may accept short-term, flexible volunteer opportunities, but their volunteer work often revolves around

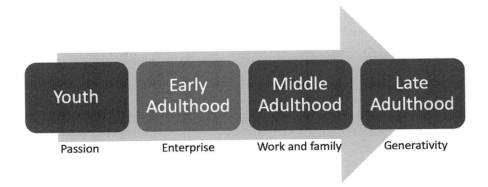

Figure 6.1 Life stages of volunteers.

their family. Opportunities for family volunteering may interest them. Women in that age group are more likely to volunteer than men, regardless of marital, work or parental status.
- In *late adulthood*, when the children have left home and people retire, they find time to volunteer again. They may be looking for a way to contribute meaningfully for the betterment of society (Armstrong, 2008) or out of concern for the next generation (generativity) (Yamashita, Keene, Lu, & Carr, 2019).

Gender, Marital, Parental and Educational Status

According to the Bureau of Labor Statistics (2016), women (27.8%) volunteered at higher rates than men (21.8%) regardless of educational level, age or life stage. Married people and those with children under 18 also volunteer at higher rates than those with other marital or parental status (often in schools) (Haski-Leventhal et al., 2016). Better-educated people tend to volunteer at higher rates than others.

Motivations

The best ways of motivating and retaining volunteers depend in part on their reasons for volunteering. In general, most volunteers are motivated by:

- Community service.
- Career advancement.
- A sense of well-being (Yamashita et al., 2019).

In addition, they are likely to want:

- Personal growth.
- Sense of purpose.
- High quality and friendly guidance, feedback and trust.
- Autonomy with regard to how they give their time.
- To overcome anxiety or fear. Some volunteers are motivated by a shared anxiety or fear that a pending change in their community will adversely impact people such as themselves and by their desire to direct the change towards a positive outcome.
- Opportunities to socialize and make new friends.
- Fun!

Generalities aside, it is important to remember that each person is unique and driven by their own intrinsic motivation. When a volunteer is intrinsically motivated, they are energized from within to do something out of will and interest for the task and need no outside rewards.

RECRUITING VOLUNTEERS

Using what you know about potential volunteers, you can plan how your volunteers might serve your organization and your recruitment strategies.

RECRUITING STRATEGIES

Generally, announcements and notes posted on community bulletin boards are not very effective at recruiting the right person for the job, with consideration for their talents and interests. There are already huge numbers of nonprofits competing for people's time.

- *Social media*: Some nonprofit organizations use a social media strategy effectively for recruiting. They use blogs and websites with chatbots to answer questions and apps such as LinkedIn and Facebook to tell stories that matter. The stories should describe how volunteering can allow people to provide community service and provide volunteers with a sense of well-being. Or they might communicate how they can learn skills or obtain networks of people that might lead to career advancement. Moreover, effective social media campaigns seem to be the most human, fun and original. They create community with their followers through interactivity, fresh stories, pictures and videos. They might ask for ideas or pertinent pictures. They also ask questions and share advice. When they find people are particularly engaged, they invite them to volunteer. If people inquire about volunteering, *respond immediately*! The more time that elapses from the point when a person contacts your organization, the more likely your potential volunteer will disappear.
- *Personal invitation*: Like the social media approach, probably the most effective method is to ask your team to help you brainstorm a list of people who are a good fit for the position, and then share the job of *personally* asking people to volunteer. Personalize your message for the potential volunteer: Every individual you want to recruit is unique and has their own intrinsic motivation. Before inviting them to volunteer, think about their skills, desires and motivations. Ask yourself if the role you are inviting them to take would be motivating to them. For instance, you know the person you are about to talk to has a passion for providing winter shelter for the homeless. If so, would the role be fulfilling for them? Discuss this when inviting them to volunteer, rather than using the same script for everyone you recruit.
- *What potential volunteers want to know*: Volunteers will want to know how they sign up to volunteer, what they will do and how much time they are asked to contribute (shorter is often better). In the past, the mainstay of nonprofits may have been be the regularly scheduled on-site volunteer, like my volunteer work at the VA hospital; but that's not for everyone. Many people have tight schedules with work and family. When they still want to contribute in some way, consider opportunities for episodic or "micro-volunteering" like marching in a parade for your organization. Another possibility is virtual volunteer work done online, like the United Nations' online volunteering where an individual might work on your web site or do writing, editing, research, teaching or training. Emphasize how their skills and interests can benefit the cause. Finally, give volunteers some autonomy on how and when they serve.

RETAINING VOLUNTEERS

Make it easy for volunteers to sign up and to get to the necessary location to get the job done (or allow them to serve online, if possible) at a time that works for everyone. Be prepared and welcome them when they arrive.

It is not enough to recruit volunteers: volunteers need to be retained (see Figure 6.2). Three keys to retaining volunteers are *guidance*, *trust* and *fun*. Many volunteers want to have a sense of purpose and challenging tasks where they learn new skills that they can apply in their careers. Give them mundane tasks like cleaning or setting out chairs for a meeting, and they may not come back a second time; but giving them challenging tasks requires that you also provide guidance.

Figure 6.2 Retaining volunteers.

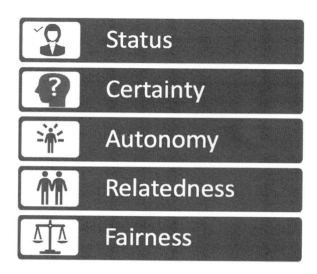

Figure 6.3 Rock's SCARF model of human needs.

- *Guidance* is the direction you use when working with your volunteers, including sharing your description of roles and responsibilities, policies and procedures as well as your expectations, and providing training, regular feedback and evaluation. Having access to such guidance can increase their sense of certainty about what they will be doing in their future volunteer work. Introduce them to their tasks gradually, while providing feedback. This guidance leads to volunteers' personal growth. Feedback is probably the number one thing you can do to motivate and retain volunteers. Knowledge of results means knowing how much of a difference they make to the clients you serve and in achieving the goal of your organization. David Rock's (2008) model described five human needs that can guide your collaborations and work with volunteers (see Figure 6.3).

  Most people are concerned about *status*—their relative importance to others. This implies that how we provide guidance can make a difference. Framing feedback in a positive way can improve a volunteer's sense of their relative importance to a project. Guidance along with fair and positive feedback can also lead to a sense of well-being. It can also convey fairness in the exchanges between the volunteers and the volunteer supervisor.

  It is important to *recognize volunteer efforts*, both immediately when the work is being done and over the long haul. Many organizations have annual celebrations of volunteers. Even if they have volunteered for a short time, they should be thanked, appreciated and celebrated.

- Just as important as guidance is *trust*. You want to convey to your volunteers the belief that you can depend on each of them, and they can depend on you, to achieve your common purpose. That includes sharing the confidence that the volunteer will get the job done. This increases the volunteer's feelings of autonomy, which may bring volunteers back a second and third time.

- Finally, make volunteering *fun*. Fun contributes to volunteers' sense of well-being and desire for relationships. Many people enjoy the opportunity for making new friends and working on a team. Providing food allows volunteers the chance to socialize. You might also make doing the work fun by creating volunteer team challenges or competitions. These social approaches can increase volunteer's sense of relatedness with other volunteers and staff.

MAKING DOERS OUT OF THE SUPPORTERS

Sometimes we have loyal supporters who don't volunteer. Why not? The simple answer to this is that perhaps *they have not been asked*. Perhaps they don't know you need the help. A personal invitation to do something for your organization that would give them satisfaction or stretch their skills might be what they are waiting for. Ask for help. It may not be comfortable, but research suggests that human beings are hardwired to say yes to requests for help from certain people (Grant, 2018; Pfaff, 2015). It can be as simple as how you frame the question. Make sure they understand that:

- You or the organization has a genuine need for their help.
- They have skills or knowledge that others don't have.
- It's not because others are lazy or haven't tried (Grant, 2018).

Jeanne was once on the board of a nonprofit organization with a board member named Jim. He attended each monthly board meeting but had not volunteered for any tasks for some time. He was a whiz at creating simple graphic instructions (job-aids) to help people do tasks, but when someone suggested that job-aids for the volunteer evaluators would be helpful for annual workshops coming up in three months, he didn't speak up. After the meeting, she asked him about it. He said he wanted to contribute but was under pressure with his consulting job. She asked how long he thought he would be tied up. He said he thought he would be busy for at least the next month. Just before the next board meeting, she caught him in the hall and asked how things were going. He said the consulting contract was winding down, and he would be pleased to create the job-aid, as long as he could work with someone who was knowledgeable about that the evaluators did.

Lessons Learned:

- Asking someone in person to do something using his particular skills made a big difference.
- "No" doesn't always mean no. Respectful repetition of a request, perhaps at a later time, will sometimes produce a different answer.
- Giving Jim autonomy over when and how he got the job done made it easier for him to say "yes."
- Working with someone who knew the evaluator's job gave Jim personal growth.

HOW TO CARRY OUT THIS TECHNIQUE

Determine what you need volunteers to do. List the tasks and skills needed, the expected time commitment and location for the volunteer service. Prepare relevant policies and procedures, particularly if they will be working directly with clients who are members of vulnerable populations. Finally, determine who will be responsible for volunteer supervision and what the relationship is of paid staff to the volunteers.

SOCIAL MEDIA

Use your choice of social media to share stories about the benefits provided by the nonprofit to the community and the satisfaction expressed by current volunteers. Think about the list of volunteer motivations and look for testimonials, pictures or videos that communicate the community service and how volunteering satisfies the volunteers. Create interactions to use such as friendly competitions, quizzes or questions. When you find a very engaged follower who fits your organization's needs, invite them to volunteer. Make it quick and easy for them by providing all the information they need to sign up, tasks, time commitment, location and why they would make a good volunteer.

PERSONAL INVITATION

Brainstorm with a group to engender a list of people that might be a good fit for the position. Create a persuasive message that describes how volunteering can allow people to provide community service and provide volunteers with a sense of satisfaction. Or it might communicate how the volunteer can learn skills or networks with people that might help with career advancement. Include the tasks, time commitment, location and why they would make a good volunteer. Personalize the message for the individuals you will invite to volunteer. Divide the list with others in the brainstorm group and share the task of personally contacting potential volunteers and inviting them to volunteer.

RETENTION

Welcome the new recruit. Make sure anyone who answers the phone or email is welcoming. Allow the volunteer some say over how they give their time. You want them to be happy to be there. Provide initial guidance in the form of training or mentorship, keeping in mind what kind of training they would value. Make it interesting and hands-on. Communicate the organization's purpose and how the volunteer will make a difference. Create trust. As your volunteers work, provide feedback so they know how they are doing. Make sure they feel the work is interesting, is meaningful and uses their skills. Bored volunteers often don't come back.

Consider creating opportunities to work on a team and try team challenges to keep groups of volunteers close while having fun. Track volunteer hours and scheduling using volunteer management tools. Provide food and opportunities to socialize with other volunteers. Use the information on volunteer hours (see Figure 6.3) to show appreciation and celebrate volunteers.

TRY IT!

Imagine that you are on the newly created homeless coalition board for your town. The founding group has decided that they are ready to recruit volunteers. The homeless coalition plans to serve warm meals to the homeless at the local community center beginning December 1 and will need to accomplish several tasks, so it will need volunteers who can do each of the tasks. They will need to:

1. Share this information with homeless people in the area.
2. Notify social services staff that work with the homeless.
3. Pick up food donations from local grocery stores.
4. Cook the meals.
5. Clean the community center after the meal.

What you need to do is:

- Describe tasks that need to be done and skills needed to do them.
- Describe the time commitments and location.
- Create a persuasive message for any one of the volunteer tasks (your choice).
- Describe how you will welcome volunteers.
- Describe the guidance, training and feedback that will be provided for any one of the volunteer tasks (your choice).
- Look at the Free Volunteer Management Tools listed at https://www.g2.com/categories/volunteer-management/free
    - Select one or more of these tools to schedule and track hours of volunteers. Describe why you selected the software.

- Describe how you will provide food and opportunities for volunteers to socialize with other volunteers.
- Describe how you will show appreciation and celebrate volunteers.

SUMMARY

The lifeblood of most nonprofit organizations working on community change is volunteers. This chapter covered:

- The characteristics of volunteers and what motivates them.
- Determining what you need to find the right person for the job.
- How to invite and persuade people to volunteer, and how to retain them.

RESOURCES

Free Volunteer Management Tools:
https://www.g2.com/categories/volunteer-management/free

CITATIONS

Armstrong, T. (2008). *The human odyssey: Navigating the twelve stages of life*. New York: Sterling.

Bureau of Labor Statistics. (2016). *Volunteering in the United States 2015*. Unites States Department of Labor. Retrieved from www.bls.gov/news.release/volun.toc.htm

Grant, H. (2018). *Reinforcements: How to get people to help you*. Brighton, MA: Harvard Business Review Press.

Haski-Leventhal, D., Metz, E., Hogg, E., Ibrahim, B., Smith, D. H., & Wang, L. (2016). Volunteering in three life stages. In *The Palgrave handbook of volunteering, civic participation, and nonprofit associations* (pp. 682–701). London: Palgrave Macmillan.

McKee, J., & McKee, T. (2012). *The new breed: Understanding and equipping the 21st century volunteer* (2nd ed.). Loveland, CO: Group Publishing.

Pfaff, D. W. (2015). *The altruistic brain: How we are naturally good*. Oxford, England: Oxford University Press.

Rock, D. (2008). SCARF: A brain-based model for collaborating with and influencing others. *NeuroLeadership Journal, 1*(1), 44.

Rosenthal, R. J., & Baldwin, G. (2001). *Volunteer engagement 2.0: Ideas and insights changing the world*. Hoboken, NJ: Jossey-Bass.

Shivayogi, P. (2013). Vulnerable population and methods for their safeguard. *Perspectives in Clinical Research, 4*(1), 53–57.

Yamashita, T., Keene, J. R., Lu, C.-J., & Carr, D. C. (2019). Underlying motivations of volunteering across life stages: A study of volunteers in nonprofit organizations in Nevada. *Journal of Applied Gerontology, 38*(2), 207–231.

7 CLEARING MENTAL SPACE FOR FACILITATION

Figure 7.0

WHAT'S IN THIS CHAPTER?

Facilitating well requires authenticity, trustworthiness, confidence. It requires that we bring our own unique presence into the meeting room (Ghais, 2005). Facilitation can be a stressful experience, particularly when the focus of the change draws strong emotions from participants. As Suzanne Ghais says, "Facilitation is not for wimps" (2007, p. 2). However, it can also be enormously satisfying and rewarding.

Preparing to facilitate a change process involves many things such as touching base with people involved and gathering information, but more importantly, it involves preparation to clear the mental space of the facilitator to become more mindful throughout the process. Approaching facilitation mindfully will result in greater adaptability (Hunter & McCormick, 2008), resilience and awareness (Adriansen & Krohn, 2016). Clearing space *before* a meeting can also help you to become less judgmental, resulting in enhanced awareness of your own emotions as well as the emotions and behavior patterns of participants *during* the meeting. This awareness allows you to maintain a calm, creative meeting, or to embrace and resolve conflicts that can arise.

Objectives

By the end of this chapter, you will be able to:

- Define "mindfulness" for facilitators.
- Prepare to facilitate mindfully by clearing the mind before a meeting.

A STORY ABOUT PREPARING TO FACILITATE

Usually Jeanne would take 10 to 30 minutes before facilitating meetings to clear her mental and emotional space. She would close her office door, close her eyes, breathe calmly and pay attention to the concerns that arose in her mind. Then she would determine a time in the near future when the concern would be addressed. At that point, she could generally put it out of mind for the time being and focus on the facilitation.

Shortly before she planned to sit down to clear space, a friend's twin sister came to her door with a troubled look on her face. She told the facilitator that her sister had passed away in a car accident during an early winter snowstorm. She shared the time and date of the memorial service. By the time her friend's sister left, there was no time left for customary meditation, so the facilitator gathered her things and went to the meeting as planned.

The facilitation on this day was with a group of participants that she had worked with before, so they were well acquainted. Although she was a bit agitated, the meeting started as usual. However, about 10 minutes into the meeting, one of the older participants raised her hand and in a kindly voice, said:

"You don't seem yourself today. Is everything OK?"

Jeanne paused a moment as she thought about how comfortable the group would be if she was honest. Then she admitted "No, actually it's not. Just moments ago, I learned that a good friend passed away in a car accident yesterday."

A sharp intake of breath was heard from several of the participants. "Why didn't you say something?" asked the older woman.

"We can reschedule," suggested another participant.

At a previous meeting, the group had considered leadership and sustainability for the group. After some discussion, the group decided to continue the meeting and elected one of the participants to lead the meeting with coaching from Jeanne. This decision allowed the group to begin preparing one of their own to lead in the future, while taking some of the facilitation load off Jeanne.

At the end of the meeting, the woman who earlier had inquired if anything was wrong approached the facilitator. "I'm so glad you trusted us enough to tell what was going on. In the end, it got us started on implementing our leadership plans. Thanks so much, for your flexibility and skillful facilitation."

Lessons Learned:

- Good facilitation requires focus and attention to listen deeply (Barrett & Kirk, 2000) and to be aware of the emotions and behavior patterns of participants.
- It is difficult to be aware of your own emotions when mental noise has not been dismissed and a mental space has not been cleared.

- To focus on the present—that is, the facilitation—you need to focus and refocus throughout the process.
- Clearing the mind is a type of meditation that improves mental focus (Pagnoni, 2012).
- It takes a clear knowledge of the participants and confidence to be authentic in difficult situations, but ultimately it can result in increased trust in your work as a facilitator.

WHAT THIS TECHNIQUE IS ABOUT

Justice and Jamieson (2006) define facilitation as "enabling groups to succeed." As the facilitator, you will be responsible for designing and managing the processes of the meeting and reducing difficulties that people sometimes have when collaborating to solve problems. You will be working toward helping the participants take responsibility and contribute to the project. As a result, while you prepare for facilitation, you may become preoccupied with details of preparing support materials, planning the agenda, the timing of exercises or breaks, carrying out what the meeting sponsors have asked of you, and a myriad of other thoughts and feelings.

MINDFULNESS FOR FACILITATORS

Clearing a space is a just-in-time mindfulness technique to fully engage in the present moment in a spirit of nonjudgmental openness, which is valuable when facilitating. It can produce a sense of calm and help you properly interpret the mood and energy level of the participants (Adriansen & Krohn, 2016). Accurate interpretation can also help you decide what you need to do next to keep the meeting productive.

There are many types of mindfulness techniques. This particular technique is about awareness and attention (Kabat-Zinn, 2016), including conscious attention to thoughts, feelings and body sensations, and the environment around you.

HOW TO CARRY OUT THIS TECHNIQUE

Clearing space can take as little as five minutes. You might want to set a timer for that amount of time. If you are often interrupted in your home or workspace, you might want to close your door and even turn off the lights.

1. Sit down in a comfortable position and close your eyes.
2. Breathe deeply. Pay attention to your breath going in and out. Feel the effects on your body.
3. Be in the moment, exactly as it is, without any judgment. Try not to think of anything past or present.
4. Thoughts, feelings or sensations will arise. Accept what comes to mind by acknowledging it, and then let it go. If the thought or feeling keeps returning and feels demanding, you may want to make a note of it for a future time when you will deal with the issue. Then you can let it go and move on.
5. Pay attention to sounds and perceptions of the space around you, both inside the room and outside. Sense the temperature and dimensions of the room you are in.
6. Finally, explore what you feel like after clearing space; do you feel any changes after sitting for five minutes?

This technique can also be used as a facilitator-led exercise during a meeting when energy or emotions are running too high.

TRY IT!

The next time you lead a meeting, instead of rushing headlong to begin facilitating, pause for a moment beforehand to clear a small mental space and see what happens. Does it change anything that happens during the meeting?

SUMMARY

The ability of a facilitator to stay focused on the present experience with nonjudgmental attentiveness can help to foster the calm, relaxed, creative environment needed for planning change. This is often called mindfulness—a mental state characterized by focused attention and awareness of the present moment, and nonjudgmental acknowledgment and acceptance of feelings, thoughts and bodily sensations. Mindfulness can result in increased awareness of emotional and behavior patterns among participants, and the ability to reduce or creatively use conflict to plan a more effective change. It can also lead to an increased sense of well-being and resilience for facilitators. Finally, clearing space is good practice for the observation you will do during the meeting.

CITATIONS

Adriansen, H. K., & Krohn, S. (2016). Mindfulness for group facilitation: An example of Eastern philosophy in Western organizations. *Group Facilitation: A Research & Applications Journal, 13*, 17–28. Retrieved from https://pure.au.dk/ws/files/79477067/Mindfulness_for_Group_Facilitation_Adriansen_Krohn.pdf

Barrett, J., & Kirk, S. (2000). Running focus groups with elderly and disabled elderly participants. *Applied Ergonomics, 31*(6), 621–629. doi:10.1016/S0003-6870(00)00031-4

Ghais, S. (2005). *Extreme facilitation: Guiding groups through controversy and complexity.* San Francisco, CA: Jossey-Bass/Wiley.

Hunter, J., & McCormick, D. W. (2008, August). *Mindfulness in the workplace: An exploratory study.* Paper presented at the 2008 Academy of Management Annual Meeting, Anaheim, CA. Retrieved from www.mindfulnet.org/MindfulnessintheWorkplace.pdf

Justice, T., & Jamieson, D. W. (2006). *The facilitator's fieldbook.* New York: AMACOM.

Kabat-Zinn, J. (2016). *Mindfulness for beginners: Reclaiming the present moment and your life.* Louisville, CO: Sounds True.

Pagnoni, G. (2012). Dynamical properties of BOLD activity from the ventral posteromedial cortex associated with meditation and attentional skills. *The Journal of Neuroscience: The Official Journal of the Society for Neuroscience, 32*(15), 5242–5249. doi:10.1523/JNEUROSCI.4135-11.2012

8 BUILDING RAPPORT AND UNITY

Figure 8.0

WHAT'S IN THIS CHAPTER?

People gather around a community concern with passionate interest and may not be aware that the first step before planning change is to build relationships within the team. Beneath the surface is a vital construction project that will determine how the team will work together.

Objectives

By the end of this chapter, you will be able to:

- Define the "ice" that may prevent people from being comfortable sharing, contributing and working together.
- Brainstorm methods to help melt the ice and help participants understand and jointly embrace the purpose of the change.
- Carry out socialization in which individuals become a team, leading to effective teamwork to create community change.

Beyond the simple greeting ("How do you do?") is the stage of socialization intended to build a bridge strong enough to carry the group forward. The facilitator must help create relationships that last using a variety of rituals at the outset. To be more explicit, ask yourself what is likely to be most effective. Name tags? Sign-in sheets? Icebreakers? You could pass a talking stick (feather, stone) and ask participants, "What is your name and affiliation?" "Why have you come to this meeting?" "Why are you passionate about this issue?"

If you were preparing to bake a cake, you would first assemble everything you need, making sure you have all the ingredients and tools before launching into the process of baking. The beginning of a change action follows much the same wisdom. Take time to build relationships before designing your action steps.

William Lofquist's theory of community development speaks about how this initial process works:

- People can collaborate on joint goals, increasing the possibility of unity within the group.
- People who are intended to benefit from a community change can lend their perspectives and their energies in positive ways to enhance the change efforts.
- People who take joint ownership of the conditions causing or influencing the problem can make a collaborative effort in accomplishing a solution. (1989, p. 27)

When members of a group have rapport, they get along well enough to communicate, discuss, even disagree. This makes the communication process easier and usually more effective. Rapport can come from having things in common, such as an initial experience. This is one of the first tasks of the facilitator—to create a positive climate and establish rapport. When participants don't know one another and need to interact comfortably with each other and with the facilitator, they will need a way to get acquainted. Often, this is carried out through icebreakers, although there are other first experiences that set the tone and provide a common experience. For instance, a reading from the Emma Lazarus poem on the Statue of Liberty was used by a group organizing to address poverty and homelessness. This experience can be followed by small group introductions and discussions of the poem's meanings to the individuals.

A STORY ABOUT CREATING YOUR OWN DREAM TEAM

In sports contexts we often hear about a "dream team" where you get to pick your favorite players for an imagined playoff. But in the real world of teambuilding, you rarely get a choice. Your partners might be members of your office, faith organization or service club. This will probably not result in a perfect fit, and at times you will wish that you had a choice of your team members. Plus, your team members are often your equals, so you cannot simply outvote them.

You can glean some principles from this recent story of a Quaker organization that was facing a big problem. Take note that Quakers do not vote and do not believe in hierarchy decision-making. They have developed a unique bottom-up style of governance that is now being copied in other settings, such as with teams in corporations. Here is a story of how consensus can be used as a methodology for team building.

Setting: Midwestern America on the prairie; at a rural setting two hours from the nearest large cities
Time frame: 2002–2006
Population: Urban and rural demographic (i.e. Quakers who are city residents and country residents)
Narrator of this story: Presiding officer (Maurine acting as facilitator)
Main Characters: Quaker facilitator, Building and Grounds Committee Chair, the Newcomer, the yearly meeting members, the resident rural Quaker Meeting.
A *bit of background*: In 1875 when Quakers on the prairie were envisioning their annual regional gathering place, called a Yearly Meeting, they imagined a meetinghouse that could seat 800 people. Quakers who inherited that old building have commented with wry amusement that people must have been much thinner in those early days. Even so, the historic building is impressive, like a huge old barn. At the time that this story happened in the 21st century, the yearly meeting population was about 1000, and the buildings on the property were too small and in bad repair. The resident Meeting (the last remaining rural Meeting) was serving as the steward of the old yearly meetinghouse and keeping it maintained. The Building and Grounds Committee worked with the resident trustees on work weekends to handle larger projects like painting or adding a small feature like a bathroom, but no big projects had been undertaken since a room replacement years ago.

The old meetinghouse was falling apart, and no one wanted to tackle a big restoration project. Then someone surprising showed up on the scene. A newcomer who had joined the resident Meeting could see that there was a problem with the building's foundation listing to one side, but the Building and Grounds clerk was resistant to her assessment. With a wry sense of humor, he countered by saying, "just tip your head to the side."

Just prior to the retreat: During a business meeting, the newcomer bounced up and down on a corner of the old meetinghouse floor that was spongy and asked, "I wonder how much longer before I fall through the floor to the basement?" She could see what the old-timers were missing because it was in their *blind spot*. The building was in immediate danger from neglect, and the elders were being conservative with their funds because they could not imagine how they would pay for the restoration. Her action challenged the group to face the fact that their historic building was crumbling, and they could not delay. Later she convinced the stewards of the property (the resident Meeting), to hire an engineer to assess the property. The report was shocking to everyone. There were dangers to health and safety as well as big structural problems with the old building.

There was no agreement or precedent for how to proceed with such a large project; however, a skilled facilitator and a Quaker (Maurine) stepped up and offered to help. At first when she suggested leading a vision retreat, her offer was not accepted. The presiding clerk sniffed at such a *newfangled notion* saying, "We have never done it that way." After a while, the clerk relented and a visioning retreat was planned inviting all-comers, and not just "the usual suspects."

Planning the retreat: Maurine considered how she could move factions from opposition to consensus. The retreat location that was selected was a community college between the urban and rural Quaker meetings for convenience and *neutrality*. A general invitation was sent out, and some different types of people came who previously were uninvolved in the Yearly Meeting. This added some spice to the proceedings since it was not just insiders making decisions. The facilitator herself was not holding any office at that time, so not many people knew about her or her facilitation skill set. This helped because she could play both an insider and outsider role in the process of leading the retreat. She was *not identified with any factions*. Finally, she chose an icebreaker and brainstorm methods that would separate ideas from people and move people towards working as a team.

The retreat: Maurine began the meeting by passing a talking stick and inviting each participant to identify their Quaker meeting name and what had motivated them to come. This served both as an icebreaker and a way to define the purpose of the retreat. The facilitator asked them, "Why have you come to this vision retreat?"—a useful question which elicited a variety of responses. An old farmer from the resident Meeting said, "I looked around and saw that all the old men have died, so I guessed it was my turn to become a trustee." He was willing to step into the traditional role of a Quaker elder. Others said they had come because they represented their local meetings. This was the beginning of consensus process among the 20 Quaker meetings.

The focus question for the visioning was, "How should we be using our historic property?" Using a card storm process, each person wrote down a brainstorm of 10 ideas in response to the question. Then they were asked to choose their top three ideas. In groups of three, they shared their best ideas with each other. Finally, they were directed to reach consensus on the three ideas as a group. The facilitator called up these ideas in waves and put the cards on the wall using tape. She then began to ask them, "Do you see any cards that belong together?" By grouping these cards and probing the conversation, six different collections of cards emerged. Then she invited the participants to name a commonly held description of each collection. Thus, a consensus was forming as we heard a loud and clear message that we wanted to restore our buildings and create a year-round retreat center!

The next step after the visioning retreat was to return to the business meeting with this new charge. Returning to our original metaphor of facilitation as a train, the track that had been blocked now had a detour.

Lessons Learned:

- A newcomer can offer a fresh perspective and shake up the thinking of those who are unable to see the situation clearly anymore.
- Asking for advice from professional consultants who *remain neutral* can help team members to rethink the original problem. This unfreezes old paradigms.
- Consensus building begins with thinking creatively and separating ideas from the person who offered it originally. This quickly moves the group from **I-to-We** thinking.
- It is unwise to begin with "we don't have the money" because it stops the creative process. The funding question should be considered last.

WHAT THIS TECHNIQUE IS ABOUT

With change projects, there is often a group of diverse people that come together. This may present difficulty in becoming an effective team when:

- People have never met.
- People attending include those who will benefit from the community change (such as the homeless) who are different from other participants.
- They come from different parts of the community with different backgrounds, cultures, values and perspectives.
- They may have different levels of authority, which may intimidate some team members, especially when they represent "Big Money."

WHAT "ICE" ISOLATES PEOPLE FROM EACH OTHER?

An important first job for the facilitator is to determine what "ice" might keep team members isolated. In our story, by asking key players, Maurine determined that a key difference in perspective was the rural perspective of farmers and others from the country and the urban perspective of people from the city and suburbs. Using the talking stick and the question "Why did you come?" Maurine was able to help melt the ice. An opening or icebreaker is an energizing and engaging activity that helps people warm up and get acquainted, and it relieves tensions or inhibitions. It may be a question, event, game or challenge that begins a conversation. Often an element of fun is involved. Varieties of icebreakers or openers include:

- Introductions
- Introduction to or segue into the meeting topic
- Activity based on the meeting topic

An example of each type of icebreaker is shown in Table 8.1.

While there are literally thousands of icebreakers in books and on the Internet, you can see from the examples that you can also develop openers or icebreakers of your own that reinforce the meeting topic. As you facilitate these activities, build a positive climate by showing participants right from the start that they matter:

- Your welcome as they come in the door.
- Consistent positive messages of empathy and encouragement begin to build a positive climate where participants can feel comfortable sharing their thoughts and working with others.
- When you share your thoughts, your appreciation of the comments of participants and even situational humor, you are modeling the type of positive environment that you want to build.

Table 8.1 Examples of icebreakers for a community development meeting.

Type of Opener or Icebreaker	Example
Introduction	Break the participants into groups of four. Ask them to give their names and then describe to the group their five favorite places in the community and say why.
Introduction to or segue into the meeting topic	Before the meeting, place on each table a sheet of easel paper and a marker. Break the participants into groups of four by counting off. Tell the new groups to think for a minute and then to describe to their group the *one* word that describes a healthy community. Record the words and share with the larger group.
Activity based on the meeting topic	Before the meeting, place on each table a sheet of easel paper and a marker. Break the participants into groups of four by counting off. Ask each group to brainstorm and record descriptions of "what's happening now" in the community. After 10 minutes, have the group tape the easel paper to the wall so everyone can read the descriptions.

I-TO-WE

It takes planning to lay foundations for good group decisions (Tropman & Mills, 2014). When participants walk into the meeting, they may know a few other people, but many people walk in as individuals who simply have an interest in the topic. A goal from the beginning of the meeting is to move the people from individual to team thinking (as shown in Figure 8.1). A cohesive team can work together and produce effective results. It might take more than one opening activity to build that cohesion (Miller, 2004).

The goals of these openers are to help participants:

- Understand and commit to the group's goals.
- Trust each other and be willing to risk expressing different ideas openly and respectfully (Mears & Voehl, 1994).
- Sense group belonging.
- Express different viewpoints to pave the way for creativity and innovation.
- Make good decisions together.
- Be willing to continuously assess their process and progress.

HOW TO CARRY OUT THIS TECHNIQUE

1. Define the ice: Are participants complete strangers to one another? What are their main differences? How will they *become comfortable working with the others*?
2. Consider the focus of the meeting and how you can *create a sense of common purpose* and team membership.
3. Use one of the ideas in Table 8.1, or browse books such as Miller's *Quick Meeting Openers* (2008) or some of the many web sites devoted to meeting openers or icebreakers for inspiration. Think of meeting openers you have experienced in the past.
4. Brainstorm meeting openers focused on helping participants become comfortable working with other participants with a common sense of purpose.
5. After the meeting, evaluate the effectiveness of the openers/icebreakers and revise if necessary.

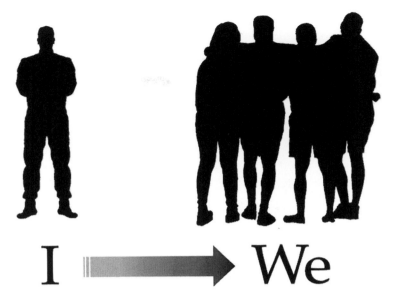

Figure 8.1 Plan openers that change perceptions from "I" to "We."

TRY IT!

Think of a meeting you will facilitate soon. If you don't have a meeting to facilitate soon, think of one you will attend. Describe any possible ice that might exist: do all attendees know one another? What are their differences? Make a plan for how you can help them become comfortable sharing, contributing and working together? Next, describe how can you help them understand and embrace the purpose of the change. Share your ideas with someone you trust that will also attend the meeting to get their feedback.

SUMMARY

Building relationships is a key first action for a meeting facilitator, especially when the group will be working together planning change. Often this process begins with the meeting opener or icebreaker. The goal for the opener is to introduce people to each other in a way that will help them become comfortable working together toward a common goal. To do so, the facilitator or steering committee will need to consider the nature of the "ice," and the purpose of the meeting, and then design the meeting opener.

CITATIONS

Lofquist, W. A. (1989). *Technology of prevention workbook*. Tucson, AZ: AYD Publications.
Mears, P., & Voehl, F. (1994). *Team building: A structured learning approach*. Delray Beach, FL: St. Lucie Press.
Miller, B. C. (2004). *Quick team-building activities for busy managers: 50 exercises hat get results in just 15 minutes*. New York: AMACOM.
Miller, B. C. (2008). *Quick meeting openers for busy managers*. New York: AMACOM.
Tropman, J. E., & Mills, B. (2014). *Effective meetings: Improving group decision-making* (3rd ed.). Beverly Hills, CA: Sage Publications.

STAGE 3
Information Seeking

After forming a team and getting to know others working on a change project, we get to the stage of **information seeking**. Imagine that you have just opened a 1000-piece picture puzzle and laid all the pieces out on the table. What is the first step? Find the framing straight-edge pieces, right? First, look at the picture on the puzzle box and reflect on it. What do you see? Is this an Escher puzzle with tricky changes of perception, or is it a simple photograph? The next steps will lead to the answer. That is what we need to do when beginning a change process: look at information such as who the players are, readiness for change and where we are now. This information forms the straight edges of the puzzle. Within the straight edges, our planning will then fill in the strategies for change.

Figure S3.0 Facilitation of Change Model Stage 3: Information seeking.

In this stage, we will cover **information seeking**.

In order to make the best choices of strategies to solve problems or take advantage of opportunities, we will need some information about our team, organization and our community. This information will help us to:

- Set the stage by exploring mental models or frameworks, exploring the spectrum of attitudes, what's happening now and visioning.
- Analyze the readiness for change, analyze planning perspectives, determine the play and the players, and locate or collect data and that information for wondering and hypothesis testing.

This process usually takes several meetings.

MENTAL MODELS AND FRAMEWORKS

9

Figure 9.0

WHAT'S IN THIS CHAPTER?

At this point, a working team needs to anchor their efforts by becoming aware of their own mental models and grounding their work in objective data (Wind, Crook, & Gunther, 2005). A **mental model** is a way of explaining how things work in the real world. There are various sorts of mental models, including images or diagrams, classifications or categories, concepts and causal stories.

Objectives

By the end of this chapter, you will be able to:

- Describe or draw your mental models for how change initiatives work in the real world.
- Explore and describe the strengths and limits of your model.
- Explore other models and new approaches.

- Analyze the relevance of the mental models against the actual, current environment to generate new models.
- Describe what you can do to overcome inhibitors to change.

A STORY ABOUT MENTAL MODELS

A workshop was held one Martin Luther King Jr. Day at the community's conference center to identify and prioritize community issues and possible solutions. The planning team invited the mayor, members of the city council, school board and other influencers as well as issuing an open invitation to community members. The turnout was huge because of community concerns, the convenient day and excellent promotion.

Key topics had been identified beforehand and included: Education, Health, Youth Opportunities, Racism and Housing. After the initial discussion covering ground rules and goals for the day, participants self-selected into groups according to their interests. Because of the large turnout, the icebreaker was held in the smaller groups. Each person in the group was given markers and paper, and they drew images representing their framework for the change process. In the Education group, one image looked like the one in Figure 9.1.

The person who drew this picture was a faculty member from the nearby college, who was familiar with Lewin's change process model. Another group member, a member of upper management from a local manufacturing company, drew an image like the one in Figure 9.2 showing a continuous improvement model of development, similar to the image used by Lynn and Lofquist (2007, p. 2).

A third participant drew a cyclical process showing the steps of the change process (Figure 9.3).

Other images were similar to these three. Each person shared their knowledge, and the discussion helped each person to articulate their mental models. The group was able to build a more comprehensive model to take back to the large group. In the process, they got to know each other, and what knowledge and talents each person brought to the group. There are several models for community development, and more than one can be used, but it is important that the group agrees to their approach. In our examples you will see that some groups are faith based and some are not. All of the examples show the use of participatory planning which is community-driven and taps the assets and talents of the community members to obtain sustainable results.

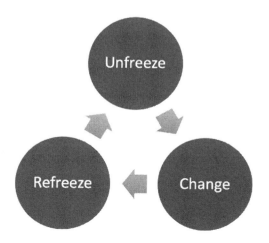

Figure 9.1 One participant's drawing of the change process.

Figure 9.2 A second participant's drawing of the change process.

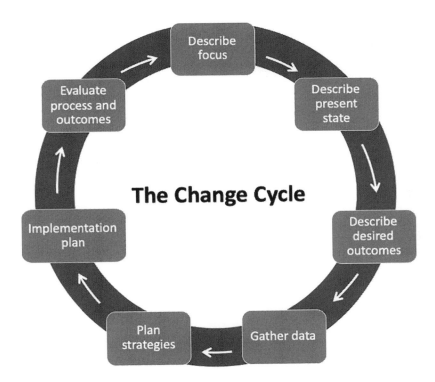

Figure 9.3 A third participant's drawing of the change process.

WHAT THIS TECHNIQUE IS ABOUT

William Lofquist emphasizes that "the most basic skill, and one without which little community development work is likely to happen, is the facilitation of the use of a framework with groups, mostly small and occasionally larger groupings" (Lynn & Lofquist, 2007, p. 36). What is a framework? We need to understand that concept at the very beginning of our process.

Figure 9.4 Combined change process drawing.

Framework: An essential supporting substructure like a skeleton—a basic structure underlying a system or concept.

Planning and decision-making require much hard work when done from the ground up. A framework represents "tried and true" guidelines for planning change. There is more than one way to do things, but a good framework is one of the available tools to help you plan and carry out your change process better and faster.

Imagine that you have been tasked with putting up a pup tent. What do you do first? Lay out the cloth, put up the tent poles, stretch out the guy lines and stake it down firmly. That sounds pretty simple, doesn't it? It is not! What if the site you originally chose has sandy gravel or is prone to flooding? Your first effort may be unworkable, so you will have to pull up stakes and move to another site. Similarly, your first exposure to a problem may prove to be entirely wrong and unworkable, so you will have to gather more information or look at the problem from a new perspective.

What do the guy lines do in a tent structure (Figure 9.5)? They provide the necessary tension to hold the whole operation together. In the same way, we need to arrive at similar perspectives with our colleagues and agree to certain guidelines and keep the project operations tight as we go along. Slippage can cause erosion to the foundation of our project, and it all could roll downhill in a rainstorm.

Securing the process by clearly identifying our frameworks and the process steps, like properly using the tent pole, guy lines and stakes, is essential for the longevity and effectiveness of any project. A **framework**

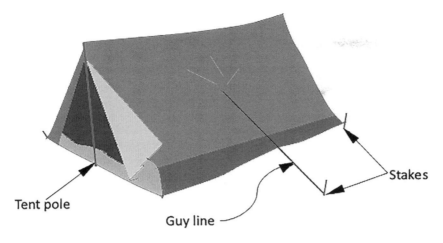

Figure 9.5 A framework is like a tent structure.

is the set of ideas used to plan and make decisions about our change project. The framework is based on our mental models of how the world works and how things fit together, which may or may not be accurate. All too often, people tend to oversimplify complex problems or adopt erroneous information. This is why Senge (2006) says that it is important to reflect on our mental models and to share our ideas of how things work with others in the group to make sure our mental models are accurate and usable. Otherwise, our ways of thinking may limit our creativity and strategies: "new insights fail to get put into practice because they conflict with deeply held internal images of how the world works" (p. 163). By articulating our mental models, we can identify and correct blind spots and come to agreement on a framework to nurture its use. Peter Senge noted:

> The discipline of working with mental models starts with turning the mirror inward; learning to unearth our internal pictures of the world, to bring them to the surface and hold them rigorously to scrutiny. It also includes the ability to carry on 'learningful' conversations that balance inquiry and advocacy, where people expose their own thinking effectively and make that thinking open to the influence of others.
>
> (2006, p. 8)

The *power* of a mental model is that it can enable thought, logic and action when it is accurate. The *limits* to a mental model are that if it is inaccurate, oversimplified or out of touch with the current reality, it can filter information poorly and restrict the effectiveness of actions based on that model.

Identify Your Group's Mental Models

A mental model is a representation in one's mind for how something works in the real world, and it provides a lens through which we perceive events, frame problems, create solutions and make decisions about our actions. You've probably heard the saying, "Where there's smoke, there's fire." This is a mental model of how things generally work—that smoke usually indicates that the source is a fire, although there are cases of particles in the air that do not originate from fires, such as those that come from aerosol cans. Usually mental models are useful, such as when they help us predict and quickly make sense of events impacting our lives. However, sometimes our mental models can become blind spots when they oversimplify or are just plain wrong. How can you tell what your mental models are? A good discussion with others that may have different viewpoints often reveals those blind spots.

We often ignore the step of exploring our mental models in our rush to find solutions or in **activity traps**—where we become so busy with activity that we forget and miss the aim of that activity (Odiorne, 1974). We will explore activity traps more in Chapter 15.

We must constantly remember our aim and repeat our question—"What is happening now?"—to focus on our goals, gauge progress and keep abreast of changing conditions. An activity trap is one habit of thought that can sabotage a change initiative. A habit of thought that gets the way of clear perception of conditions A and B (A is where we are now, B is our desired outcomes) is **observer bias**; the tendency to see what we expect to see, resulting in inaccurate interpretation of observation data. Other habits of thought that can sabotage our efforts include:

1. **Confirmation bias:** our inclination to selectively gather information that confirms our existing beliefs or ideas. It shows the influence of desire on our thinking.
2. **Too much information, too little meaning:** The large amount of information available often overwhelms people, making it difficult to pick out what is important and make sense of it. This can result in poor decisions.

Figure 9.6 Activity traps keep you so busy you forget your goal.

3. **Perceived need to act quickly:** people concerned about a problem in the community or organization may perceive a threat that needs an immediate solution. As a result, they want to move quickly without having collected data to use in order to assess and evaluate the project, or due deliberation among members of the project team to make solid decisions.
4. **Limits of memory:** while humans can remember large amounts of information, there is a distinct limit to the information you can hold in your mind (working memory) at the same time. This limits the information you can reflect on, interrelate, and use for making good decisions. Complex descriptions can create a burden on working memory, making it difficult to recall and use, unless diagrams or other methods are used to simplify storing and recalling the information.
5. **Desire to hold on to old patterns:** when we find something that has worked for us in the past, we often repeat it and sometimes get stuck.
6. Assuming or saying that a change **can't be made**.

Social issues can also derail our efforts. When team members don't know and trust each other, they may *alter* or *censor* their comments based on the expectations of the others. For that reason, the initial meeting experience or icebreaker is important, because it helps people get to know each other and trust each other so they can work together comfortably sharing their mental models and creating one that will effectively guide the change initiative.

HOW TO CARRY OUT THIS TECHNIQUE

Our tent (framework) needs to be firmly anchored in reality and to use a process with clear steps. To begin examining your mental models for how change works as a group:

1. Provide each person with markers and paper. Ask people as individuals, to draw or describe how community change works in the real world.
2. Then ask them to explain their model to others in a small group.
3. Ask the small groups to combine individual frameworks into a group framework for representing the reality of how things work. They then create a group model to share with the larger group. Alternatively, you, as facilitator, can then help them combine or identify a frame context.
4. Discuss and explore possible pitfalls such as the limits of memory capacity, biases, making decisions without enough information and rushing into decisions:
    a. Do the models seem to make a clear representation of reality?
    b. Does anyone see any possible biases in any of the models?
    c. Does anyone see any evidence of having too much (or little) information with insufficient meaning?
    d. Does anyone see any evidence of an urgent need to act quickly?
    e. Do any of the models shared seem too complicated? Is there any way to use a diagram to help people remember and use the information?
    f. Did anyone find it difficult to adopt a new pattern?
5. If you find any evidence of these pitfalls, ask what can be done about them.

This process works with the focus of any project (such as the causes of homelessness or food insecurity).

TRY IT!

Consider a change initiative in a small town to provide youth opportunities to engage in projects that are meaningful to them.

- Describe or draw your mental models/frameworks about how change will happen in this context.
- Explore and describe the power and limits of your model.

- Think about other models and new approaches; Play "What if . . ." and adopt different perspectives to test the relevance of the mental model against a changing environment to generate new model: For instance, "what if a large number of new families are moving to town to work at a new auto plant."
- Ask yourself what you can do to overcome inhibitors to change among your group members:
    - Biases.
    - Too much (or little) information with insufficient meaning.
    - The perceived need to act quickly.
    - The limits of memory.
    - The desire to hold on to old patterns.

Once you are happy with a mental model, go a step further. Describe how you will:
a. Implement the model.
b. Assess the model.
c. Continuously strengthen the model.

SUMMARY

This chapter examined mental models or frameworks for how change initiatives work in the real world, including the power and limits of models and inhibitors to change.

CITATIONS

Lynn, D. D., & Lofquist, W. A. (2007). *BreakAway*. Tucson, AZ: Development Publications.

Odiorne, G. S. (1974). *Management and the activity trap*. New York: Harper & Row.

Senge, P. M. (2006). *The fifth discipline: The art and practice of the learning organization*. New York: Doubleday/Currency.

Wind, Y. J., Crook, C., & Gunther, R. (2005). *The power of impossible thinking: Transform the business of your life and the life of your business*. Upper Saddle River, NJ: Pearson/Prentice Hall.

SPECTRUM OF ATTITUDES

10

Figure 10.0

WHAT'S IN THIS CHAPTER?

As a group, the change team members will hold many different attitudes. Understanding those attitudes will help team members understand their perspectives regarding those meant to benefit from the change, for instance, ask what are the perspectives of the members of an organization, employees, community members and the homeless in our community. Our attitudes determine our behavior and relationships with other people. A positive regard for beneficiaries of a change can lead to involvement in the change initiative, self-esteem and productivity.

Objectives

By the end of this chapter, you will be able to:

- Analyze your own attitude, and those of your team toward the beneficiaries of change.
- Describe what can be done to help change someone's perspective from wanting to do something good *to* or *for* someone to choosing to do something *with* someone.

A sense of **otherness** results from our different social identities created through social interaction with other people and our self-reflection on those interactions, derived from social, cultural, racial, physical capability, language and gender differences and life experiences. These differences result in valuable variations in ideas, perspectives and approaches to solving problems. Some of these differences may run counter to our own and cause tension in us as individuals and groups, but if we can consider these varied perspectives, examine them without rejecting them, and, as Palmer says, "hold tension in life-giving ways," (2011, p. 45) we may arrive at better and more inclusive decisions as a group.

A STORY ABOUT ATTITUDES TOWARD BENEFICIARIES OF CHANGE

From the beginning of the Homeless Coalition project, a Community Police Officer was assigned to work with the teams. When homeless people were later added to the team, there was tension, mostly coming from the homeless participants. After holding the group meeting with homeless people, two of them started attending our team meetings and were very active contributors. Lisa, a woman still living on the streets, had street smarts but her social skills were weak. She had a problem with anger management and came to public meetings often speaking with anger about the police. At one particular meeting, she loudly addressed the Community Police Officer, saying that the police were treating her people brutally.

The group froze because, although they knew there was truth in her statement, they were startled by her behavior. Later, Maurine was approached by a church member who said that Lisa did not belong at the meetings. Maurine responded to the lady's complaint about Lisa using the "spectrum of attitudes" graphic and saying that she *did* need to be included as a resource. Maurine agreed, however, that Lisa would need to learn how to interact with others who were different from her. Maurine added an item for discussion to the agenda for the next meeting: protocol for how we work together. During the discussion at the next meeting, Lisa commented that, "That police officer has never hurt me." She was able to halt her own stereotyping behavior without anyone mentioning it to her directly.

> *Protocol*: a system of rules and acceptable behavior used at meetings to define how people will work together.

Lesson Learned:

- Discussing acceptable behavior openly can help all team members work together.

VIEWING PEOPLE AS RESOURCES

We don't often like to admit it to ourselves, but often we see others as chess pieces on a board that must be countered by our own strategy. When we do this, we are seeing others as objects. Lofquist's *Spectrum of Attitudes* (see Figure 10.1) shows a new way of encountering others when he suggests that people who are most affected by the opportunity or problem of concern can turn out to be resources by assuming joint ownership of problem conditions, offering their perspectives and using their energies to work on appropriate solutions (Lofquist, 1989).

Viewing the homeless people as resources shifted the entire process. As a result, the project became more successful at utilizing all of the resources in the community. The teams had turned a corner when they realized that the homeless could become partners and resources in the change process. Soon the teams discovered other potential allies who could be resources like clergy, agency directors, government officials, business leaders and the police. They were onto something!

WHAT THIS TECHNIQUE IS ABOUT

Before reading the description of this technique, go to Appendix A and take the inventory, imagining that you are on the staff of a high school, and plan a change project at the school that will benefit your students. After you have taken and scored the inventory, come back and begin reading here. What style did you find yourself choosing?

Change, whether in businesses, nonprofits or communities, involves making plans that affect people. Lofquist (1989) notes that understanding people's behavior and relating to them constructively (p. 39) is key to making effective change plans. When one group makes plans that will affect another group (the beneficiaries of the plans), as if they know what is best for that group, they view them as objects. This is usually not effective and may produce resentment. When the beneficiary group is viewed as recipients, the first group views and acts as if they know what is best for the beneficiaries. The most effective approach or attitude is viewing the beneficiary group as resources and involving them. This attitude shows an appreciation for the value of others as well as respect for the beneficiary group and what they can do. This is summed up in Lofquist's Spectrum of Attitudes model as shown in Figure 10.1.

When we analyze how we see people using the Spectrum of Attitudes, we may be able to see the benefits of seeing everyone, including those that benefit from the change, as a **resource**, no matter where they fall on the continuum of power. This attitude requires a creative tension that is essential for making sense of things from others' perspectives. This habit of the heart needs to replace other, less productive habits, such as quickly stereotyping others and their ideas.

Figure 10.1 Lofquist's Spectrum of Attitudes (1989) adapted.

HOW TO CARRY OUT THIS TECHNIQUE

Use the inventory in Appendix A, copy it, then edit it, substituting the word *beneficiaries* with those who your project is aimed to benefit. Substitute the words *change team* with the actual name of your organization or project leadership team. Make copies to use at your next meeting.

EXAMINE THE SPECTRUM OF ATTITUDES WITH YOUR GROUP

Ask your project team to take the inventory. After the group has taken the inventory as individuals and scored it, discuss the Spectrum of Attitudes. Using the diagram in Figure 10.1, ask the group what they think the implications of the attitudes are. Often, they will come up with the following points on their own, but you can ask questions, to encourage them to come up with all of the points:

Style #1: Doing **to** *Others.*

- It is well known that showing kindness and doing good makes us feel good and is positive for our mental health.
- How much good it does for us depends on our attitude.
- If we do *to* them, it is as if they are objects and we know what is best for them.
- Beneficiaries of our acts will often know what our attitudes are and not feel respected.

Style #2: Doing **for** *Others.*

- One group does something good for others, but they may believe they know what is best for the others.
- The beneficiaries may be "allowed" to participate in the decision making because it may be "good" for them.

Style #3: Doing it **with** *others.*

- An attitude of respect is demonstrated toward the beneficiaries for what they can do.
- This attitude is conveyed to beneficiaries.
- The results can be greater self-esteem and productivity.

Set Up Your Protocol

Ask the team, including any clients or beneficiaries on the team, what rules and behaviors would help the meetings run smoothly. Guide them in setting up their own brief set of expectations for behaviors and rules.

TRY IT!

Imagine that you are working as a volunteer with a team on developing a teen center. Youth are engaged on the team as resources and participants. There are also adults on the team that hold negative stereotypes of adolescents. As a result of their perspectives, they tend to discount their contributions and "rescue" the youths, doing things for them. These behaviors do not help the youth to learn and grow, and they can damage the partnership with the youth.

    A pair of teens have been asked to research city zoning and present the results at the next meeting. An adult, thinking that the youth are unprepared, takes over the presentation.

What can be done to change the attitude of the adult so that the partnership with the youth is preserved? List the steps you would take.

SUMMARY

The analysis of the Spectrum of Attitudes will help those that lead and work on the change to determine their perspectives toward those meant to benefit from the change. Understanding and sometimes adjusting one's own attitude is important to the quality of our relationships with other people. In addition, when beneficiaries of a change are respected and involve change initiative team members, greater self-esteem and productivity can be a result.

CITATIONS

Lofquist, W. (1989). *The technology of prevention workbook*. Tucson, AZ: AYD Publications.
Palmer, P. J. (2011). *Healing the heart of democracy: The courage to create a politics worthy of the human spirit*. San Francisco, CA: Jossey-Bass.

11 WHAT'S HAPPENING NOW?

Figure 11.0

WHAT'S IN THIS CHAPTER?

When we notice something in our community or organization that doesn't seem right, usually we are seeing symptoms of a need or opportunity. What we seldom see is the actual cause. When we seek to remedy a situation without knowing the underlying cause, we are likely to choose the wrong strategies.

This chapter focuses on the *Elements of Change* (Lofquist, 1983) leading from where a project stands initially to the desired outcome(s).

Objectives

By the end of this chapter, you will be able to:

- Identify "what's happening now."
  - Examine symptoms of needs or opportunities.
  - Discuss possible causes.
- Identify the desired or ideal outcome(s)
- Determine how to assess project progress with data, including community-level archival data and data collected by the change team members.
- Identify big-picture indicators that can be seen as measurement(s) of outcome(s) of a change initiative.

A STORY ABOUT WHAT'S HAPPENING NOW AND DESIRED OUTCOMES

The Community Council of a high-rise public housing facility in an inner city was having serious problems with safety. The council decided to get some training on how to deal with it and invited Bill Lofquist, a community development facilitator, to lead a workshop for them. When asked "what's happening now," they described broken elevators in the high rises, drug dealing, criminal behavior among their youth and a lack of safety for children and families. Their ideal outcome was a neighborhood where elevators worked, stores were open for businesses and children and families felt safe to walk to parks or businesses. They were introduced to a simple way of gauging their progress called "looking for indicators"—in other words, ways to know if they were reaching their goals. An **indicator** is specific, concrete, observable evidence. Keeping this simple evaluation tool in mind, they kept recording indicators as they moved along their pathway.

Later, Bill returned for a follow-up meeting and asked if anything had changed for the better since they implemented their community development strategy. One leader said with a big smile, "Yes, now Domino's delivers!"

WHAT THIS TECHNIQUE IS ABOUT

Brainstorm "What's Happening Now"

Our first step in this part of the conversation is to identify "what's happening now." Shown in Figure 11.1 are headings you might use on easel paper, when stakeholders are describing the area of concern. While

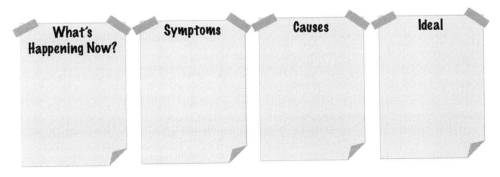

Figure 11.1 Easel paper headings for exploration of "What's happening now?".

the stakeholders describe each of the topics, the facilitator or a helper can record the thoughts so everyone can read them. On the first sheet is a general description of what's happening that is causing concern. The description should have enough detail that the change team can develop a profound understanding of the issue. Each statement related to "what's happening now" and ideal outcomes needs to be brief, clear, concrete, specific and focused on a single issue. In describing "what's happening now," focus on conditions. The description of "what's happening now" can address opportunities and threats, strengths and weaknesses.

> *Symptom*: an observable and describable sign of manifestation of some underlying condition or reality (Lynn & Lofquist, 2007, p. 23).

The second sheet is used to list **symptoms** of the problem or opportunity. Typically, when we have a problem, what we see is symptoms. If we work on addressing the symptoms, the problem may not be solved. Only by getting to the root cause of the problem can a solution be devised. So first we examine the problem deeply by discerning what are symptoms, and what *may* be causes. In medical terms, a symptom is an indication of a disease. So, too, a symptom can be an indication of a problem. A symptom is the result (direct or indirect) of a **cause**.

The third sheet lists possible causes or reasons behind the problem or issue listed by the group. These potential causes are, at this point, simply **hypotheses** that will need to be tested.

> *Hypothesis*: an assumption or supposition or guess that attempts to understand and describe the conditions underlying a symptom or group of symptoms (Lynn & Lofquist, 2007, p. 23).

ROOT CAUSES

There are many methods of seeking causes for problems. Causes might be individual causes, such as lack of skills or knowledge, motivations or tools. On the other hand, they might be social causes such as cultural, political or economic causes (Altman, Balcazar, Fawcett, Seekins, & Young, 1994). When the problem is a particularly thorny one, a possible approach to cause analysis is the "5 Whys." Make sure that your group includes people who are both affected by the problem and who can help achieve a solution. The more typical the brainstorm group is of those affected by the problem, the more likely it is for the actual causes to be uncovered. Solutions directed at actual causes are more likely to succeed than solutions addressing the symptoms (Wilson, Dell, & Anderson, 1993). (See Figure 11.2). Ask what the problem is. Then ask what caused it, asking "Why?" several times to get down to the actual cause. Keep in mind that community problems sometimes have multiple causes, so they may need more than one solution.

The fourth sheet is where we list the vision for an ideal situation or **desired outcomes**. More on visioning desired or ideal outcomes is found in Chapter 12.

"What's happening now" and desired outcomes are key elements of change, as shown in Figure 11.3.

Because it is important for change team members to "own" the problem and be committed to work toward the solution, it is useful to try to come to a consensus on each of the items. **Brainstorming** is a good start. Then you will want to discuss the ideas listed to make sure they are clear. **Consensus** means pooling opinions, listening to members of the group effectively, discussing ideas and coming to an agreement that everyone can live with, even if members don't get everything they might want (Kaner, 2014).

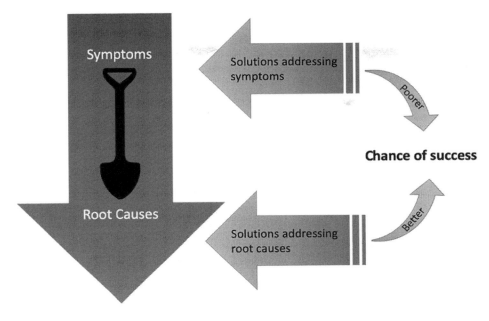

Figure 11.2 Digging for root causes results in more effective solutions.

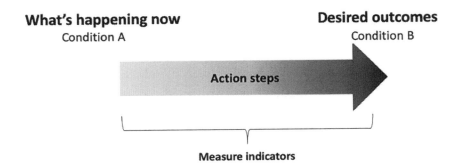

Figure 11.3 Elements of change.
Source: Adapted from Lynn and Lofquist (2007).

One method of coming to a decision is **multi-voting** to reduce a long list to a manageable few. Each member gets a number of votes equal to one half or one third of the sum of items listed. Members vote for the items they believe are best on the list, but only one vote per item. Items receiving votes from half or more of the group are underlined. Repeat the process, with members voting votes for the best of the remaining underlined items. The team continues voting until the list is reduced to a manageable number of items. Shown below is easel paper filled out for a project. Notice that the team reduced their focus to one aspect of "what's happening now," that being teen drug use because they believed it was a *high-priority, high-yield* problem.

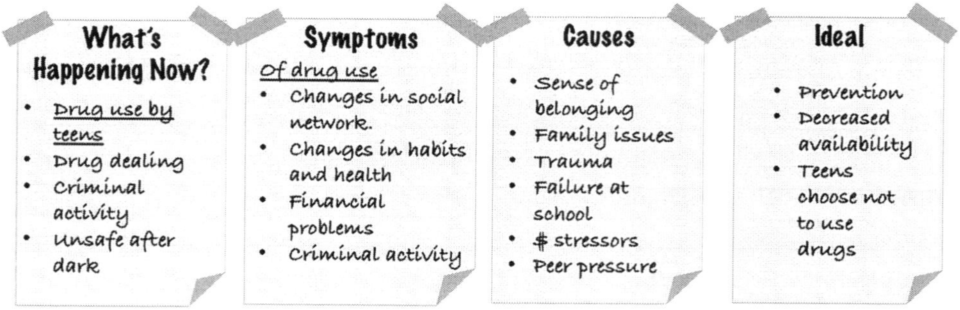

What's Happening Now?	Symptoms	Causes	Ideal
<u>Of drug use</u> • Drug use by teens • Drug dealing • Criminal activity • Unsafe after dark	<u>Of drug use</u> • Changes in social network. • Changes in habits and health • Financial problems • Criminal activity	• Sense of belonging • Family issues • Trauma • Failure at school • $ stressors • Peer pressure	• Prevention • Decreased availability • Teens choose not to use drugs

Figure 11.4 Example of brainstormed lists focused on drug use.

SWOT Analysis: Strengths and Weaknesses, Opportunities and Threats

Another way to look at "what's happening now" is a SWOT analysis of the elements of community related to the project focus. Strengths and weakness are commonly internal, while opportunities and threats frequently focus on the external environment. The planning team brainstorms these factors after completing the "what's happening now" brainstorm. The technique examines:

- *Strengths*: advantageous characteristics of the organization or project.
- *Weaknesses*: characteristics of the organization that place the organization or project at a disadvantage.
- *Opportunities*: factors in the environment that the organization or project could use to good advantage.
- *Threats*: factors in the environment that could cause problems for the organization or project.

An example of a SWOT analysis is shown in Figure 11.5.

The SWOT analysis can provide a different perspective and also provide the team information for planning strategies to build on strengths, strengthen weaknesses, take advantage of opportunities and minimize threats (Harrison, 2010). More on planning will be covered in Chapter 19.

CHOOSE HIGH-PRIORITY, HIGH-YIELD ISSUES

You will know you have a high-priority, high-yield problem by looking at the following:

- Frequency with which the problem occurs.
- Duration of the problem: Has it existed for a long time? Will it continue to exist in the future?
- Scope: How many people/products/services it affects?
- Severity: How severe is the problem? Is it disruptive to individuals? Community? Businesses?
- Perception: Does the community perceive the issue as a problem?

If the issue or problem is more frequent, is more severe and affects more people than other issues, then it becomes a priority to address.

Strengths	Weaknesses
• Law enforcement agencies work together on drugs • Resident diversity	• Lack of recreation, esp. on Sunday • Families with issues and trauma
Opportunities	**Threats**
• Public reporting of issues • Develop Parks and Recreation/Trails • Lighting • Strengthen family programs	• Crime and drugs • Dark areas • Unsafe after dark

Figure 11.5 Example SWOT analysis.

LOCATING AND ESTABLISHING INDICATORS

How will you gauge your progress and know if your project succeeds (Sholtes, Joiner, & Streibel, 2003)? How can you determine that changes have taken place? A good first step is to research other, similar change projects to see what they used to measure success. If none are found, brainstorm ways that would be persuasive to the community. Generating good indicators takes practice. If it is difficult to generate clear indicators, look again at the statements listed for "what's happening now" and ideal outcomes. Could they be clarified? Could they be more specific?

Community-level indicators of impact need not be complicated, but they may take some imagination. Look back at the symptoms listed by the team. Look at the list of symptoms and imagine what would indicate that the problem was solved—what are the **symptoms of success**? Remember the project to improve neighborhood safety in which a measure of increased neighborhood safety was "Domino's delivers."

Choosing the right indicators depends on a good grasp of what is important to your community and your change project. When selecting indicators for local projects, they should:

- Be relevant both to individual citizens and to local government.
- Reflect local circumstances.
- Be based on information that can be readily collected.
- Show trends over a reasonable period of time.
- Be meaningful both in their own right and in conjunction with other indicators.
- Be clear and easy to understand, in order to educate and inform.
- Provoke change (for example in policies, services or lifestyles).
- Lead to the setting of targets or thresholds (von Shirnding, 2002, p. 50).

When indicators are selected early in the process, they are useful to assess where you are at the start, and to evaluate your project's progress by comparing the initial data to data collected later. Indicators should also be limited in number so they can be collected within a reasonable timeframe. (See Chapter 38 on Evaluation.) Ideally indicators are also flexible, so they can be applied to future needs. You will want the data to be easy to explain, as well as reasonable and persuasive to community members. The data should be of good quality—credible and unbiased. Finally, based on looking at similar projects, you will want the data to be representative of the types of data used to measure your type of project to the extent possible. Use an Internet search to locate other projects similar to yours.

HOW TO CARRY OUT THIS TECHNIQUE

"What's Happening Now" Method 1 for Small Groups

One way to determine what's happening now is to have a conversation in which members describe what's happening now while the facilitator writes down the ideas on a sheet of easel paper, so everyone can see that the ideas are accurately captured. Next, the group should discuss what *should* be happening. Then brainstorm possible causes for what's happening now, recording those descriptions. Use the "5 Whys" as needed. The causes listed will be the focus of the solutions you will plan. Brainstorm possible indicators. This method usually works well with a smaller group.

"What's Happening Now" Method 2 for Large Groups

Large groups over 25 benefit from another approach:

- Before the meeting, place on each table a sheet of easel paper and a marker. Break the participants into groups of four by counting off. Ask each group to brainstorm and record descriptions of "what's happening now" in the community.
- After 10 minutes, have the group tape the easel paper to the wall so everyone can read the descriptions. Note the patterns of description that are repeated from group to group.
- Next, the group should discuss what *should* be happening.
- Then brainstorm possible causes for what's happening now, recording those descriptions. Use the "5 Whys" as needed.
- Try to get the group to agree on each of the items.
- Brainstorm possible indicators.

TRY IT!

Imagine that you are on the change team focusing on the broken elevators in the high-rise public housing.

1. Take a sheet of paper and draw lines dividing it into four columns.
2. Label them (1) What's Happening Now, (2) Symptoms, (3) Causes and (4) Ideal Outcome(s).
3. Brainstorm a thorough description for each column.
4. Now or after the meeting, do some research online to locate similar projects and find what kinds of indicators were used.
5. Evaluate the indicators using the following questions:
   a. Would the indicators be relevant both to citizens and to local government?
   b. Do the indicators reflect local circumstances?
   c. Are the indicators based on information that can be readily collected?
   d. Will the indicators be usable to measure project progress by showing trends over a reasonable period of time?

    e. Would the indicators be meaningful both in their own right and in conjunction with other indicators?
    f. Are the indicators clear and easy to understand?
    g. Could the indicators provoke change (for example, in policies, services or lifestyles)?
    h. Are the indicators directly related to the assessment of needs?
    i. Could the indicators assist in the setting of targets and strategies for getting to the project's ideal outcomes?
6. Make a recommendation for your indicators, making sure they would meet these criteria.

SUMMARY

Symptoms of a problem in our community or organization alert us that something isn't right. This chapter covered how to describe a need or opportunity, how to select a high-priority, high-yield need to address possible causes, ideal outcome(s) and indicators that can be used to measure the progress of a project.

CITATIONS

Altman, D., Balcazar, F., Fawcett, S., Seekins, T., & Young, J. (1994). *Public health advocacy: Creating community change to improve health.* Palo Alto, CA: Stanford Center for Research in Disease Prevention.

Harrison, J. P. (2010). Strategic planning and SWOT analysis. In J. P. Harrison (Ed.), *Essentials of strategic planning in healthcare* (2nd ed., pp. 91–97). Chicago, IL: Health Administration Press.

Kaner, S. (2014). *Facilitator's guide to participatory decision-making* (3rd ed.). San Francisco, CA: Jossey-Bass.

Lofquist, W. (1983). *Discovering the meaning of prevention: A practical approach to positive change.* Tucson, AZ: Development Publications.

Lynn, D. D., & Lofquist, W. A. (2007). *Break Away.* Tucson, AZ: Development Publications.

Sholtes, P. R., Joiner, B. L., & Streibel, B. J. (2003). *The team handbook* (3rd ed.). Madison, WI: Oriel Inc.

von Shirnding, Y. (2002). *Health in sustainable development planning: The role of indicators.* Geneva: WHO. Retrieved from www.who.int/wssd/resources/indicators/en/

Wilson, P. F., Dell, L. D., & Anderson, G. F. (1993). *Root cause analysis: A tool for total quality management.* Milwaukee, WI: ASQ Quality Press.

12 VISIONING

Figure 12.0

WHAT'S IN THIS CHAPTER?

Visioning is a critical step for any organization: you need to know where you are and where you are going. Some organizations let the future happen to them. Without a clear vision, organizations can lose sight of where they are going and continue working on activities with little chance of achieving anything.

A **vision** is a picture or idea that the organization has of its direction and what they want to accomplish in the future. A clear and vivid vision helps you and everyone in your organization pull in the same direction to pursue dreams and achieve goals. A vision can energize people, provide direction for planning and persuade funders that they want to support you.

Visioning is a way to gather the wisdom of the group before launching into action planning. The group is often smarter than the few (Surowiecki, 2005), especially when there are diverse perspectives. Visioning is one point at which the collective wisdom can benefit your change initiative.

Objectives

By the end of this chapter, you will be able to describe how to:

- Create a vision for desired outcomes.
- Brainstorm using a variety of techniques.
- Get the creative juices flowing when the group is stuck.

A STORY: SITUATIONAL BLINDNESS

Change brings ambiguity, and often fear. This fear can cause people to get stuck, or to look for a quick fix, rather than get to the root of the problem by addressing it. One solution to being stuck is to make a shift in thinking from right-brain to left or from left to right. The right-brain is the visual and creative part of the brain. This strategy was the key to this situation in the story which follows.

The Setting: a serene retreat center of lovely historical buildings amidst a beautiful arboretum. The retreat center is a religious nonprofit organization governed by a board of directors.

Key Actors: The community's ethos consists of a voluntary governance model which includes students-in-residence, administrators, teachers, hospitality staff and the board of directors. Recently an interim director had been appointed to address a crisis situation. A process facilitator was called in from the outside to assist the board with a re-visioning retreat.

Scene One: Although all appears to be well in this paradise, there is a worm in the apple. Trouble is bubbling underneath, but no one is talking about it. Recent financial difficulties had prompted the board to make some quick decisions that made the original problem even worse. Now the organization was suffering from "mission failure" and could potentially be closing. People were already losing their jobs, and the entire community was fearful, angry and anxious about the future.

Scene Two: A troubleshooter, who had successfully turned around other organizations, was asked to serve as the interim director. The retreat community members were suspicious of him since the appointment was made by the same board of directors that had made flawed decisions in the past. Trust was low and disappointment was high, so he had his work cut out for him from the beginning. They also invited their fundraising consultant, another outsider, to meet with the board a few days before the retreat was to occur. By chance, he had coffee with the facilitator one morning before the retreat, and they compared notes about the actual situation, minus the emotional overtones. He revealed that he was not able to raise any money because their loyal donors were no longer trusting the board. The process facilitator also spoke with a few senior visiting members of the residential community to ask them to attend the retreat as observers and helpers with the group process. These allies were able to offer objective information to the facilitator about "what is happening now" in the community.

Scene Three: On the morning of the retreat there were frozen smiles all around the dining hall. The usual friendly buzz of conversation was absent: people sat in subgroups and looked furtively at neighboring tables. The atmosphere was tense and yet expectant, too. Later the board members moved on to the location where the retreat would be held. As the process facilitator was unknown to any of the board members, no one knew what to expect from her. This gave her the advantage of surprise. The Chair had asked her to lead "a spiritual retreat" and had not communicated that to the board members. About halfway through the process, which was designed by using creative activities using story, song and symbols, many board members revolted against this style, saying it that it was a waste of their valuable time. They had *important* decisions to make, and they wanted to fire the facilitator and get back to business, as they saw it. But a senior visitor, who was widely respected by all, intervened and asked for time to reflect on the original request for the retreat. The Chair confirmed that the facilitator had been leading the retreat as she was asked to do it. That settled the matter, and the retreat went forward but with some grumbling in the background.

Scene Four: After the retreat had ended, the facilitator withdrew so that the board could finish its deliberations. When she returned several hours later to clear the room, she found two board members still sitting there in deep discussion. They looked up, smiling at her, and declared, "A miracle happened, and it is because you came." When she inquired what they meant by that, they replied. "We reaffirmed our mission, and now the work can go forward again." Somehow by turning aside from problem-solving and returning to the spiritual foundation of the institution, all talk of closing the retreat center or removing essential programs was dismissed. Eventually trust was restored with the board, and the donors came back, loyal as ever to the original mission. The retreat center was saved.

This is a cautionary tale for those who want a quick turnaround when the institution they love falters badly. The mission of a revered organization with a long history of stability was threatened, and the chain reaction from fear had become very difficult to manage. What to do when the organizational mission fails? The board members, who had a long history with the organization, were suffering from **situational blindness** due to their emotional condition. They did not see the situation clearly but rather made decisions influenced by strong emotions.

To stop the panic, the board Chair decided to call for a *process facilitator*, who is someone who can assist with approach to finding a renewed mission. When there is heightened anxiety and anger, it is essential to invite someone with a cooler head to assist with resolving the conflict. In this story, there were many other facilitators present—the interim director, fundraising consultant, and senior visitors—who all offered their clear, calm reassurance to the board. By inviting people who had not been engaged in the battle, much-needed objectivity was added, which is often in short supply during a meltdown of the mission. In addition, the process facilitator, coming in as a newcomer, was able to see symptoms that others could no longer see.

Let us examine the steps that were taken to resolve the situation and opened up new possibilities.

1. **Assessment of the situation.** This involved informal information gathering from sources close to the conflict. In this case the process facilitator privately interviewed the following key informants: resident students, faculty members, staff, the fundraising consultant, and the interim director. As a neutral player, she was able to find out more of what was actually happening behind the scenes by building trust with the informants and assuring them that their conversations would be kept confidential.
2. **The turnaround strategy.** Sometimes conditions look intractable but inserting a new player can make all the difference. The strategy used by the facilitator was the element of surprise. Knowing the attitude of some board members of competing for "being the smartest person in the room," she chose for the retreat format creative exercises and experiences that would introduce ambiguity through a shift to the right-brain. Since there was no decision-making to be done, the frustrated board members could only release their control, though unwillingly. The goal was to develop ideas for visioning by ignoring the known and moving into the unknown. During the retreat process, the

senior visitors were essential as advisors, keeping the board members on task because there was high resistance at the beginning.
3. **Restoring trust.** The work of the board quickly turned from competing with each other toward engaging in a cohesive visioning exercise where ideas were separated from the person who initiated them. Collectively, they began to see new avenues for the mission and then turned in a new direction together. Thus, they were able to come to agreement on renewing the mission statement and reaffirming the values of the institution. They regained their footing when trust was restored.

What are the core qualities of process facilitator? First and foremost, what is needed is openness. A questioning spirit allows for seeking new answers. In the midst of a conflict situation, a facilitator can keep the group grounded in times of stress/distress. Flexibility is also needed, since problems can arise unexpectedly and quickly and must be responded to with a cool head. When trouble arises, the facilitator must stay very steady. Other essential qualities are a hopeful and expectant attitude, patience, confidence, presence, authenticity, trustworthiness and a clear view of the goal. Nurturing also helps the group with processing emotions in a healthy way. Respecting each person and taking seriously the well-being of others is the core function of a process facilitator as the group moves into a new relationship with each other.

Lessons Learned:

- Change brings ambiguity and often fear, which can cause people to get stuck or to look for a quick fix rather than get to the root of the problem by addressing it directly.
- Strong emotions can lead to decisions that are not well thought out.
- There are times when things must be dug up and dealt with, even though there may be few tried and true paths to do so. This requires the facilitator to proceed mindfully, maintaining perspective, and attuning to the emotions of others to successfully interact with them. In addition, the facilitator needs self-awareness to be resilient in situations charged with emotion.
- One solution to being stuck is to make a shift in thinking from right-brain to left or from left to right. The right-brain is the visual and creative part of the brain. This strategy was the key to this situation in the story. Ambiguity or *brain-switching* is your best friend in the change process. Ignoring the fearful "known," the community can engage their creative side, color outside the lines (see Figure 12.1) and make a new path by walking.

WHAT THIS TECHNIQUE IS ABOUT

This technique is about creating a vision of your desired outcomes. A vision for your project's success is a clear and concise description of what the organization or community should look like after the completion of the project. Creativity is needed for visioning. You need a vision for your unique group situation, and not someone else's ideas that may not fit your organization or community.

The visioning process is a way to pull together the wisdom of the group before beginning to plan your strategies and actions. There are many models and techniques for how to go about visioning. One technique is to use focus questions to discuss and process different perspectives. This is useful because it questions the idea that there is only one way to proceed.

The completed vision communicates what the people involved want the community or organization to be (Green, Haines, & Halesbky, n.d.). It can be words or a picture of a future you choose to create. Agreement on a specific vision helps all people involved work toward the same end and helps provide greater cohesiveness to the project. It is important to a good vision to say what you will and will not work on. A vision that is too broad is doomed to failure because organizations and community groups have limited time and financial resources. A vision that is too broad also diffuses the efforts so that little gets done. A focused vision with all efforts expended in the same direction makes the desired outcome

Figure 12.1 Creativity requires being willing to "color outside the lines."

more attainable, and it can also help the project team see barriers more clearly so they can work to remove them.

SMALL-SCALE VISIONING

Organizational and community visioning can take place from very small-scale neighborhood projects to large-scale projects encompassing entire cities. A *small-scale* process may look like this:

1. Organize the visioning process meeting.
2. Identify and recruit representative participants.
3. Identify community (who will benefit?) and other boundaries (things your group will *not* address at this time).
4. Specify the planning and implementation period (e.g., the next five years).
5. Decide how to structure the process, and whether it should be short or long term.

6. Hold the visioning meeting and determine how the community envisions success with the problem or opportunity identified during the "what's happening now" step. One approach is to use focus questions:
   - Ask people to consider the following **focus questions:**
     - What do people want to *preserve* in the community?
     - What do people want to *change* in the community?
     - What do people want to *create* in the community?
   - Ask the individuals to share their thoughts and then merge their ideas in small groups of five to seven.
   - Ask the small groups to share ideas with the larger group.
7. Following the visioning meeting, find local allies or sponsors.
8. Prepare a budget and raise funds or locate/create resources (Okubo & National Civic League (U.S.), 2000).

LARGE-SCALE VISIONING

The visioning process for a *large-scale* project often needs a coordinating committee and follows roughly in this order:

1. Form a core coordinating committee.
2. Find local allies or sponsors.
3. Identify community (who will benefit?) and other boundaries (things your group will *not* do).
4. Specify the planning and implementation period (e.g., the next five years).
5. Give the process a name.
6. Decide how to structure the process, whether short or long term.
7. Prepare a budget and raise funds or locate/create resources for the meeting.
8. Publicize the visioning process.
9. Identify and recruit representative participants.
10. Organize the initial event.
11. Hold the visioning meeting.
12. Find local allies or sponsors for the change.
13. Prepare a budget and raise funds or locate/create resources for the change (Okubo, & National Civic League (U.S.), 2000).

A core coordinating committee is responsible for the up-front planning for a large-scale visioning process, including obtaining a facilitator to assist with the **initial event**. It is the job of the facilitator to help a group express their goals and determine their desired outcomes within the parameters set by the coordinating committee for the implementation period and the community boundaries, if applicable.

The facilitator begins the meeting with an explanation to participants about the purpose of the meeting, the concerns about "what's happening now" and any data that has been collected supporting those concerns. Finally, the facilitator explains the structure and process for the meeting, including what a vision is. While dreaming and brainstorming, invite people to see the bigger picture. Ultimately you will want the vision to be:

- Imaginable (easy to visualize).
- Desirable (outcome-oriented and appeals to stakeholders).
- Feasible (realistic and attainable).
- Flexible (general enough to allow different responses in light of future developments).
- Focused (clear enough to provide guidance for decision-making).
- Communicable (memorable, concise and easy to explain in five minutes) (adapted from Kotter, 2012, p. 74).

The vision may begin broadly, as in the following.

A Hunger-Free St. Michael Parish

A vision statement should also be stated in positive language, specify the *time period* in which the goal will be attained, focus on all the diverse *people in the community who will benefit* by an improved quality of life of some sort. Finally, when *indicators* are selected, add those to the desired outcome. For example:

Within five years, reduce food insecurity for all residents in the St. Michael Parish from 7.1% (very low food security) to the national average of 0.7% as measured by the Six-Item Short Form of the Food Security Survey.

HOW TO CARRY OUT THIS TECHNIQUE

Plan a meeting where visioning will be carried out. Invite stakeholders and interested community members. Create an agenda with strategies for creating the vision. Remember to keep it flexible.

Using a gardening metaphor, you would not simply toss some seeds onto untilled soil and expect to have them take root, would you? The first thing a good gardener does is **clear the space**. As the meeting facilitator, you have some weeding and tilling to do before you take any action. When we are planning to make significant changes to the social condition, there needs to be time set aside for deeply rooted reflection. Facilitation must be counter-cultural and provide strategies rooted in reflection practices before any action is taken. When planning a strategy or action, what is the first step? Think it out.

Before your meeting, turn off your phone, your computer, your radio or TV or any other device that might distract you from thinking! Begin by clearing your mind of any extraneous messages that could distract your thought process. Take some quiet time (five minutes) where ideas for organization's vision simply float to the surface of your mind. Next, visualize the change in your mind's eye, feel it, smell it, hear it. Make it as vivid in your mind as possible by sketching or writing your ideas down. Think about the following that will be shared with the group during the visioning session:

- *Who will benefit* from the project?
- A *time frame* (when will this vision be accomplished).
- *Boundaries* (things your group will *not* do).

> Remember that these ideas are the wisdom of one. At your meeting, you will gather the wisdom of the group (Figure 12.2).

Brainstorming: Gathering the Wisdom of the Group

Facilitate the visioning using some of the techniques listed here, or other, similar techniques. Given a description of who will benefit from the project, a time frame and boundaries (things your group will *not* do) the aim of the brainstorming process is to describe a vision of the desired outcomes of the project as fully as possible.

Most of us have used brainstorming at one time in our lives. We have explored the straightforward brainstorming technique (see Figure 12.3) for describing "what's happening now." This technique often works when envisioning ideal outcomes, however, sometimes, as in the story provided in this chapter, people need to use right-brain methods to free their creativity when they get stuck. This is particularly important with long-range, transformative change that might feel threatening when emotions run high.

Figure 12.2 Everyone may believe they have a good idea, but that is the wisdom of one person. Better ideas are often the result of a team effort.

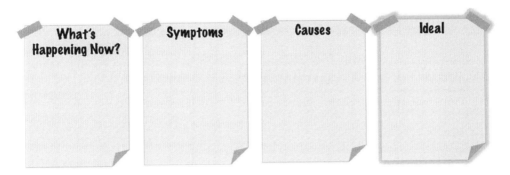

Figure 12.3 Easel paper headings for exploration of vision of ideal outcomes.

Conventional group problem-solving can often be sabotaged by lack of trust, worry about other people's expectations, feeling pressed for time, groupthink (where the desire for harmony reduces creativity or out-of-the-box thinking) (Csikszentmihalyi, 1996), forgetting your idea while listening to other people and watching other behaviors. Beginning with an analytical approach is useful because the change team needs to have a sound understanding of the problem that needs to be solved. However, continuing with an analytical approach may cause a group to get stuck or develop uninspired ideas that may lead to solutions that are untenable and bound to fail (Lumsdaine & Lumsdaine, 1993).

Brainstorming Methods

Begin all brainstorming with a clear definition of the opportunity or problem derived from defining what's happening now, the symptoms and causes. Also, share the description of *who will benefit* from the project, a *time frame* and *boundaries* (things your group will *not* do).

Prepare the group with these directions: (1) no negativity; (2) wild ideas are encouraged; (3) stay focused; (4) build on other ideas; (5) go for quantity; (6) computers and cell phones are turned off.

Headline news: Tell people, "Imagine your community 10 years from now. What would the headline news say about your community project?" You will need easel paper, markers, a timer and 10 minutes. Create small groups, ask them to brainstorm, and then to write their headline on easel paper to share with the larger group. Ask team members to close their eyes and really *see* the change in their mind's eye, feel it, smell it, hear it. Have them describe to each other how they feel about it.

Brainwriting: You will need index cards or Post-it notes, pens, a timer and 15 minutes. Each person in a group writes down an idea on a Post-it note or index card and passes it to the person on their right. The person receiving the card chooses to do one of three things:
   1. Use the other's idea as a jumping off point for a new idea.
   2. Use the other's idea to come up with a modification.
   3. Pass the card to the next person with no change.

Group brainwriting: Organizing people into several small groups, each of which brainstorms ideas one after the other until everyone involved has had a chance to contribute fully. Hand a description to the next group, for the ideas to be built upon, refined and finally prioritized. This will continue for three rounds. You will need note cards and pens, a timer and 10 minutes per round for a total of 30 minutes.

Design Charrette: A gathering of people for an intense period of brainstorming and design. It is often used in architecture and design but has far wider application. Faced with a problem or challenge, the participants pool their talents to produce plans to achieve a goal. You will need: pencils or markers and paper, rulers, tape, scissors, clay, toys such as blocks or other manipulable objects (use your imagination), a timer and 30–60 minutes. Ideas may be drawn, models may be built or other methods used to share ideas with the larger group.

Reverse brainstorm: Instead of asking how to make _____ (beneficiary group) more satisfied with the project _____, ask how to make them more *dissatisfied*. For instance, ask how can we make citizens more dissatisfied with the city council? Then reverse the reverse solutions to find ideas for the original problem. You will need: easel paper and markers, a timer and 20 minutes (10 minutes to brainstorm ways to make people dissatisfied, and 10 minutes to reverse the solutions).

There are many other methods of brainstorming that can be equally effective.

RECHARGING A GROUP THAT IS STUCK

Have you ever felt you or your team were really stuck? Maybe you have experienced artist's or writer's block when you had an important assignment due at work or school. How did you get around it? Where did you find your inspiration? What do you do for a creative recharge?

Most of us spend much of our adult lives working with linear and analytical thought. Even when given a task such as brainstorming, which requires creative thought, we sometimes continue to plod along using linear and analytical approaches. When your change team gets stuck, you might need to try something radical. Sit down and turn off your phone, your computer, or any other device that might distract you from your primary purpose—imagining!

Your goal is to use the visual or musical arts to encourage the brain's linear analytical mode to drop out. It's important to reassure people that they don't need to be an artist to do this exercise. You will need: pencils or markers and paper, a timer and 10–15 minutes.

1. If you are the facilitator, take a short break. Begin by clearing your mind of any extraneous messages that could distract your thought process. Take some daydream time (five minutes) where ideas simply float to the surface of your mind.

2. When the group reconvenes, ask the group to close their eyes and visualize the change in their mind's eye, then feel it, smell it, hear it.
3. Now the visions are written down (or sketched in images) on a piece of paper. Glancing at all the ideas, what do you see?
4. Ask your team to share their images or written ideas in small groups.
5. Then ask your team as a group to create an image, music or use other creative ways of expressing their vision of the ideal future for their project or organization.
6. Have small groups share their ideas with the whole group.
7. Look for patterns among the ideas. Find a way to combine the best ideas and work toward consensus.
8. Finally, do some group process reflection. How did this work for you? Did you find ideas forming in your minds?

OK, Now What?

Once your vision has been determined, and you have core team consensus, what do you do next? Keep your eyes on that prize by keeping the team focused on the vision:

- Create a sense of urgency about the change with the community.
- With your team, develop a short summary that captures in about 30 seconds what your team "sees" as the future of your community or organization (sometimes called an "elevator speech").
- Ensure that your change team can describe the vision in five minutes or less.
- Use your "vision speech" in the community often.
- Walk the talk—if the change requires behavior change, be sure your team models the new behavior in the community.
- Anticipate and address resistance to the change from the start. Address peoples' concerns and anxieties, openly and honestly. Start honest conversations, and give persuasive reasons to get people talking, thinking and acting.
- Build buy-in from all affected segments of the community.
- Apply your vision to all aspects of the change—from training to operations to staff performance reviews. Tie everything back to the vision.

TRY IT!

Imagine that you have been asked to facilitate a visioning session for a board like that for the retreat center. You are already into the fourth hour of the meeting, and you have no vision for the desired outcome. The board members are operating in panic mode because of looming financial problems and feel pressed for time. They want a quick solution. This is preventing their creative ideas from flowing. Describe the methods you would use to get them back on track, and why you selected them.

SUMMARY

In this chapter we focused on creating a vision for desired outcomes. Methods used included several possible methods for brainstorming. Sometimes groups get stuck for a variety of reasons, including fear, lack of trust, situational blindness and staying in the linear, analytical mode when the creative mode is needed. The facilitator needs to be flexible and aware of when this happens. It helps to have a co-facilitator or an invited observer to note things happening among participants that the facilitator may miss. Then the facilitator can adjust the agenda and the approach to visioning to get the creative juices flowing when the group bogs down. A facilitator never knows where a meeting or a project will go.

Poet Antonio Machado shall have the last word:

> Traveler, there is no path. The path is made by walking.

(2003, p. 8)

CITATIONS

Csikszentmihalyi, M. (1996). *Creativity: Flow and the psychology of discovery and invention*. London: HarperCollins Publishers.

Green, G., Haines, A., & Halesbky, S. (n.d.). *Building our future—A guide to community visioning* (Extension Publications No. G3708). Madison, WI: University of Wisconsin. Retrieved from https://learningstore.uwex.edu/Assets/pdfs/G3708.pdf

Kotter, J. P. (2012). *Leading change*. Cambridge, MA: Harvard Business Review Press.

Lumsdaine, E., & Lumsdaine, M. (1993). *Creative problem solving: Thinking skills for a changing world*. New York: McGraw-Hill.

Machado, A. (2003). *There is no road: Proverbs by Antonio Machado* (Companions for the Journey) (D. Maloney & M. Berg, Trans.). Buffalo, NY: White Pine Press. Retrieved from www.whitepine.org/noroad.pdf

Okubo, D., & National Civic League (U.S.). (2000). *The community visioning and strategic planning handbook*. Denver, CO: National Civic League Press. Retrieved from http://mrsc.org/getmedia/D9ADE917-2DF1-4EA2-9AA8-14D713F5CE98/VSPHandbook.aspx

Surowiecki, J. (2005). *The wisdom of crowds*. New York: Anchor/Doubleday.

CHANGE RESISTANCE AND READINESS   13

Figure 13.0

WHAT'S IN THIS CHAPTER?

A community is ready for change when they exhibit:

- Collective desire for change.
- Belief that the change is possible and that the benefits outweigh the risk.
- The existing community systems can accommodate the change.

If your community doesn't demonstrate those characteristics, don't despair. Start where they are and build readiness.

Change is primarily about people and their processes. A change project that accounts for people and how they deal with change will have the best chance of choosing strategies that will work. But how do you really know how ready the community is? Analyzing readiness is what this chapter is about.

Objectives

By the end of this chapter, you should be able to:

- Describe the differences between incremental and transformational changes and how they impact the change process.
- Analyze people readiness: resilience or resistance to change
- Analyze the community or organizational readiness to make the change.
- Determine how the Adoption Curve will affect your change strategy.
- Analyze how resistance affects the Change Cycle for your change plans.
- Select which strategies to use to address organization readiness, commitment and sustaining change based on your community readiness analysis.

A STORY ABOUT CHANGE READINESS: OPEN HOUSING IN WINSTON-SALEM, NORTH CAROLINA, 1968

Bill Lofquist tells the story of one of his many change experiments. This one concerned the issue of open housing around the time that the Civil Rights Act of 1968 was signed into law. The act included enforcement provisions prohibiting discrimination in the sale, rental and financing of housing. In a church in a Southern town, Bill and a Black elder led a Sunday School class that focused on the racial crisis in the South. Before they began the class, Bill and his co-leader brought their plan to the church board and sent letters of invitation to all church members to participate.

The class was to investigate if the President's Commission on Civil Disorders was correct when they stated that the cause of racial conflict was White racism. They examined racism in the form of prejudicial feeling in themselves, their church and the White community in Winston-Salem, North Carolina. They also looked at the level of readiness in their church to act decisively in the face of the crisis and their ability as a group to seek out resources available to accomplish the bold and tangible goal of making open housing a reality in Winston-Salem.

The class created three task forces to:

1. Determine the roadblocks to buying homes facing Black residents, such as real estate practices and the availability of mortgage loans.
2. Assess attitudes of White residents toward racial integration.
3. Identify specific Black families interested in pursuing adequate housing in segregated neighborhoods and encourage them.

During the course of the class, they invited community leaders each week to discuss topics such as racial intermarriage, the impacts of prejudice on Black education, employment and housing patterns, as well as Black and White Power movements. During the week, class members conducted surveys on the policies and practices of organizations to assess readiness throughout the community. They also took a bus tour of Black sections of the city led by a Black realtor. All of the information they gathered provided the class with a new understanding of values, expectations, norms, attitudes and housing practices in the South.

Not only had the task forces gathered information on readiness of their community, but other incidents gave the class an indication of the level of readiness of the community for integrated housing. People appeared to be afraid of the "radical ideas" discussed in the class. For instance, after the initial class meeting, about eight class members dropped out. Later, one church member confronted Bill and asked him, "What are you doing to our church?" The class leaders were also invited to the church board meeting to discuss the class because church members had become concerned about a (false) rumor that the class had bought a house and moved a Black family in. After the leaders' presentation, the board approved of the way the class was progressing.

Following the class, the members held an open meeting to which 75 citizens came. At the meeting, a group was formed called Winston-Salem Citizens for Fair Housing. They would investigate and assist when someone felt they were suffering discrimination in obtaining rental housing. They would offer assistance to real estate agents with challenges resulting from changing housing patterns. Finally, they would assist neighborhoods as housing patterns changed. This meeting was an indication that some citizens were ready for change.

The new citizens group was able to assist several individuals and neighborhoods. For instance, a Black social worker responded to an advertisement for an apartment but was told none were available, so she requested assistance. The plan was that when this happened, they would send a White person to the same complex immediately. There was a woman on Bill's staff who was the same age and earned the same salary. She was shown half a dozen apartments and offered the chance to rent one. The procedure was to have each of these people fill out an affidavit describing their experiences in detail. The arrangement was to notify one of the agencies in Washington, and they would have someone in town the next day to confront the manager with their offense. They would be directed to reconsider the offended person, and they were ordered to advertise for a period of time that they were an open housing renter. This helped to open apartment rentals without regard to race.

A neighborhood faced *panic-selling* among White residents when Black families started moving in. At one point, nearly 50 homes were on the market out of 200 in the neighborhood as a result of real estate people warning residents to sell before the neighborhood became predominantly Black. Mass meetings were held and personal visits to all residents calmed the panic, and finally a large neighborhood picnic was held. Change was on the move!

Lessons Learned:

- Consider the shared values, beliefs, expectations, assumptions and norms of groups of people.
- Assess readiness for change through surveys or interviews.
- Identify allies for planning by creating a list of groups, organizations and individuals who can be considered natural allies for working on the change. (Several of these individuals spoke to the class.)
- Work with those allies to lay the groundwork for decisions.
- Not everyone will be ready for change at the same time.

WHAT THIS TECHNIQUE IS ABOUT

Community or organizational readiness for change initiatives can be observed at several levels. For instance, when the initiative begins, are community members aware of a need for change? Do they understand the nature of the change proposed? Do they think it is a good idea? Are they willing to take action to invest resources or experiment with the change? Do they take actions to incorporate the change into ordinary, daily actions? Finally, do they value, commit to and "own" the change? (Conner & Patterson, 1982).

TYPES OF CHANGE

There are many types of changes. Some changes are **incremental**, such as a change in location for a Saturday community meal. Other changes are **transformative**, such as the Innocence Project (a nonprofit organization working to clear people who were wrongly convicted and to reforming the criminal justice system). In addition, not everyone deals with change the same. Readiness for fundamental, long-range change is far more critical than small, incremental, short-range changes. This chapter will focus on transformative changes.

> *Community readiness*: "a condition in which a significant portion of a community's leadership, resources, policies, energies, values and [community] . . . organizational missions are committed proactively to creating conditions that promote the wellbeing of its citizens."
>
> (Lofquist, 1996, p. 19)

Some changes, like mountains, are harder than others to summit. You simply walk up to some peaks like they were mere hills, while others require maximum exertion to reach the pinnacle. Incremental change is more like a hill. In Figure 13.1, incremental changes may be short range, or have a small scope. Examples of incremental changes include changes to technologies happening a little at a time in an organization. For instance, many schools and nonprofit organizations switched to online software office packages such as Google Docs from more expensive commercial software. Staff had many of the skills to use word processing, presentation software and spreadsheets already and applied them to the new online packages so the change went relatively smoothly for most people. Within organizations and committees, other examples of incremental changes might be newly elected officers or small changes to operations, strategies or missions.

Transformative change, on the other hand, such as changes in culture, values, attitudes or behaviors across an organization, requires much more exertion for the individuals involved. These are big picture, long-range changes. In our story, some members of the church were not yet ready for such a

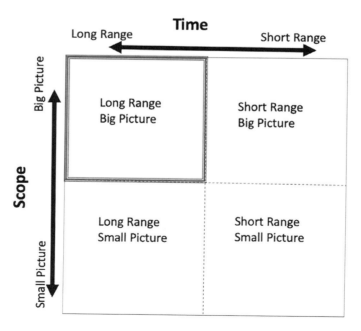

Figure 13.1 Readiness critical quadrant: Transformational change.

transformational change. The example of a transformative change given earlier, the Innocence Project, had a goal to reform criminal justice. This will take maximum exertion over a very long time.

INDIVIDUALS AND CHANGE

Change is not easy, and managers, volunteers and organizational boards who are enthusiastic about a change they would like to carry out may underestimate how much change people can take. As Rosabeth Moss Kanter (1985) observed, "Change is disturbing when it is done to us, exhilarating when done by us" (p. 63).

According to Prochaska's Transtheoretical Model of Behavior Change, a person generally moves from a place of not wanting to change at all (precontemplation), to thinking and learning about a change (contemplation), then preparation, adopting new changes (action) and finally working to maintain those positive changes over time (maintenance), as shown in Figure 13.2.

For many people, changes they initiate or *participate in planning* are easier to accept and commit to. Sources of resistance include mistrust, surprise or fear of the unknown, but when people are involved in creating the change, there are no surprises. As people move through the cycle (shown in Figure 13.2) from the present state to the future desired state, they first need to recognize that there is a concern, problem or opportunity with the present state. This should disrupt their acceptance of the existing state of affairs, or what's happening now. Some people **accept** the need for change more easily than others because they can see the benefits of the change, while others may push back or **resist**, as shown in Figure 13.3.

Resistance to change is often behind the comment "If it ain't broke, don't fix it." Engaging people early in the process, giving them a chance to weigh in, even getting them on a change team, helps them get used to the idea and accept the change because they have had an influence on the change and the change

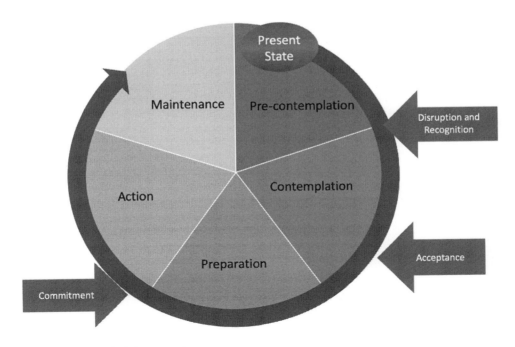

Figure 13.2 Ideal individual change cycle.

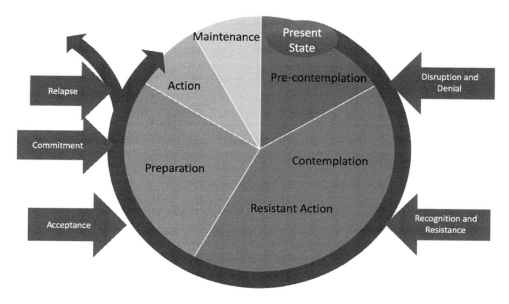

Figure 13.3 Individual change cycle with resistance.

process. People who resist change may not believe that the end product of change is worth the effort, and the change might seem impractical or unrealistic. Resistance can be caused by fear of losing something valuable, such as autonomy, security, control, mastery or relationships. People resisting change may go through a process similar to grieving. In her 1969 book *On Death and Dying*, Elisabeth Kübler-Ross developed a model to explain the grieving process in five stages: denial and isolation, anger, bargaining, depression and acceptance. Change in the community and the workplace is similar. People sense that they are losing their familiar way of doing things and go through predictable stages of emotion: denial, resistance, acceptance, exploration, commitment and ownership/integration. Since individuals are unique, they have their own predispositions to change (resilience) or to change resistance.

When change causes denial and resistance, then acceptance and commitment will be delayed. Changes can bring uncertainty resulting in stress, and we weigh our fears of loss more heavily than our anticipated gain (Beenen, 2016). Many of us have been through multiple changes in our lives. For instance, perhaps you have worked for organizations during acquisitions or divestitures and experienced restructuring, reorganization, and reassignments. Think about how you felt during these experiences. You may have noticed your own resistance to new ways of doing things. Stop reading and go to Appendix B in eResources to take the Personal Resilience Inventory to see how you deal with change. This may provide insight into strategies that might work for your change plans.

RESISTANCE

Resistance is natural and expected in a change process. Resistance is evidence that a person cares about an organization (Beenen, 2016) or community. When people resist change, the team should listen to their concerns and complaints, because sometimes they know things about the change, the community or organization that those on the team don't. For instance, those who resist may see a potential negative consequence of the change that the change team has overlooked. If the team listens and finds the threat credible, they can make plans to avoid or mitigate the risk of negative consequences.

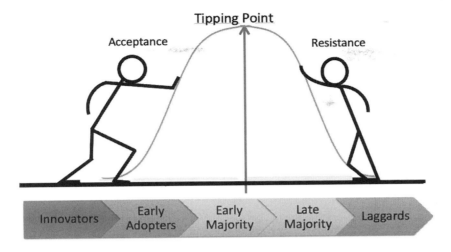

Figure 13.4 Change adoption timeline.
Source: Adapted from Rogers (2003, p. 281)

Change can cause fear of loss of something that people value. Generally, people consider a change and then decide to avoid negative consequences or to pursue positive consequences (Beenen, 2016). When people do not see the "big picture" of the purpose for a change and how it serves both their own needs as well as the greater good, they are likely to resist. They may also resist if they do not trust the process or the people involved to accomplish their goals.

In Figure 13.4, we see that people in an organization or community "get on board" with the change at different times, depending on their perspectives and motivations. *Resilient* people often get on board before the peak or tipping point when a critical mass of members of the organization or community have adopted the change. At critical mass, the change can begin to have a significant effect and get rolling (Gladwell, 2000). Those who *resist* may wait until well after the peak point at which most people have adopted the change. Later adopters often overcome their initial concerns about the innovation by discussing the issue with those who have already adopted the innovation. But realistically, there are some people who never get on board.

RESILIENCE

Resilience is defined by Margolis and Stoltz (2010) as "the capacity to respond quickly and constructively in a crisis" (p. 1). Innovators, early adopters and the early majority usually have these characteristics: (1) optimism about a change, (2) self-confidence that they can deal with change, (3) coping well with change, (4) good problem-solving skills, (5) acceptance that change is part of life, (6) a sense of purpose or meaning for their lives and (7) willingness to give and seek support from their colleagues, family and friends. Think back to your score on the Personal Resilience Inventory. How well would you be able to cope with change?

As Rosabeth Moss Kanter noted, change "is disturbing when done to us, exhilarating when done by us" (1985, p. 64). Another way of saying this is that we can cope with change better when we are involved in making it happen. This requires that we can see resources, strengths such as skills, and opportunities of the community or organization and believe that change is possible. People develop skills through work, paid or volunteer. As a facilitator, you will need to be alert for strengths such as the skills of people involved and encourage them by mentioning those strengths. As Mark Homan points out, "People, as individuals or as a community, move forward only through the use of their abilities" (1999, p. 43).

OPPOSITION

A small group opposed to the stream of African immigrants moving into a midwestern town attempted to counter a city council resolution to become a *welcoming community*. The welcoming community resolution was in response to several incidents of difficulty in the community between the immigrants and others. This resolution was meant to lead to "greater community support and understanding for refugees" including planning training, events, and programs that could ease friction between people who do not understand one another.

The opposition instead proposed a resolution to halt the resettlement of immigrants, citing poverty and the economic costs to the taxpayers. There are, in fact, costs such as additional ESL (English as a Second Language) teachers needed for the schools, and additional social services professionals. However, the additional economic development resulting from the immigrants was not discussed, nor was the number of new professionals with skills, credentials and higher education from outside the country such as professors, doctors and other medical personnel. Losing these professionals as a result of the opposition's counter proposal could hurt the whole community. A city council does not have the power to adopt such a proposal, but the opposition to the welcoming community resolution used several hours of city council time and delayed the start of potentially positive programs.

Those who do not get on board with a proposed change may actively resist change, push back and even sabotage the efforts of change agents. What do you do?

- Begin by understanding the perspective(s) held by those who oppose the change. What do they feel? We can acknowledge that resistance is normal and acceptable. We can have compassion for the fears that motivate the opposition.
- What do they value or believe? Are they members of an ethnic group, race or culture that is different from you? If so, learn more about the culture. Ask people you know what experience they have had with members of the opposition. Do some research to find newspaper articles or other media that sheds light on the perspectives held and tactics used in the past by these opponents.
- The next step is to listen in order to understand the opponent's points of view, keeping in mind that they may have some facts that are useful to learn. Some fact checking may be in order to be sure that the statements are true, just, and balanced. Be sure *your* facts are true, just and balanced, as well. Identify how the truth affects you and the community.
- What are the strategies used by the opposition? Research them and make them public.
- Respond to the opposition in an intelligent and rational manner.
- When a public meeting is to be held, make sure your organization sets the agenda and rules on speaking time, when possible.
- What are members of the opposition asking for? Is it possible and reasonable? Negotiate in good faith (see Appendix G in eResources for more on negotiation). Be willing to compromise where it will not harm your cause. Look for opportunities to work together, without capitulating to their position.

COMMUNITY READINESS

The readiness model for community change was developed by the Tri-Ethnic Center for Prevention Research at Colorado State University, and a set of practical tools were developed for assessing readiness. The readiness of a community for change depends, in part, on the issue. Readiness can also differ across segments of the community. It is crucial to understand the readiness of the community to plan effectively. Readiness includes these elements:

- Efforts and community member's **knowledge** of efforts to address the issue.
- Community **leadership support** of efforts to address the issue.
- **Community attitudes** toward the issue.

- Knowledge of the issue's **causes and consequences**.
- What **resources** are available to support the change effort (people, time, money, space, etc.) (Edwards, Jumper-Thurman, Plested, Oetting, & Swanson, 2000).

In an ideal world, community readiness would include several other components. Once these are in place, the change itself is nearly done. As agents of change, those people actively involved in making the change happen will need to move these building blocks into place. These include:

- Conceptual clarity about the issue.
- Appropriate policies enacted.
- Coordinated strategic planning about the issue.
- Collaborative work by community organizations toward resolving the issue.
- State and local collaboration toward resolving the issue.
- Coordinated efforts to evaluate the results of the change.
- Organized technical assistance to support change efforts.
- Funding or other resources committed to change efforts.
- Clear and effective models for the type of change your team is pursuing.
- Available data for planning.
- Recognized advocates and leaders for your change in the community.
- Demonstrated commitment by educational institutions in the area to support the change through training and continuing education for helping professionals (Lofquist, 1996, p. 16).

THE CHANGE TIMELINE

Figure 13.5 shows a change process timeline adapted from many experts in the change process (Connor, 1993; Kotter, 2012; Rogers, 2003; Plested, Edwards, & Jumper-Thurman, 2006). At the beginning, community or organization members are unaware of a need for change. That state of unawareness is

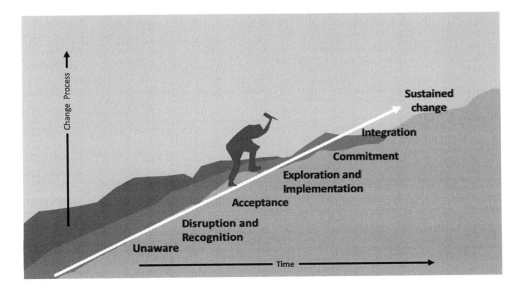

Figure 13.5 Change commitment timeline.

disrupted when they find out that there is a problem. When there is a significant change proposed, it is predictable that people will question or resist the need for change. Change is work and brings uncertainty. At this point, they may accept change, but they often resist a proposed change. If they accept that the change is necessary or valuable, then they will explore until they understand the change. At the next juncture, they make a commitment to making plans and implementing the change. The gains from the change need to be solidified so there is no backsliding. Ultimately, the change will be integrated into the way of doing things when there is wide ownership, and the change processes and model can be applied to other changes.

READINESS LEVELS

Use these descriptions when describing the readiness of the community for a change:

1. *Unaware*: The community is not aware of the problem, opportunity or need for change.
2. *Disruption and Recognition* (Denial or Resistance): The community recognizes that there is an issue, but denial or resistance to change is the action taken by individuals and groups when they perceive that a change that is proposed or occurring is a threat to them. They may express suspicion, skepticism or frustration.
3. *Recognition/Acceptance*: The community recognizes that there is an issue and accepts that change is inevitable. They may look forward to the change taking place.
4. *Exploration and Implementation*: Community members explore the idea of the proposed change, or they engage in planning and implementing the change.
5. *Commitment*: The community invests time, energy or money in making the change happen. They use resourcefulness to resolve issues that would hinder the achievement of the desired outcomes. They show ownership and commitment to the desired outcomes, even when it might be difficult to pursue them.
6. *Integration*: The community makes the change "part of the way they do things around here." The project team and community leadership work toward making the change stick through culture change, funding, policies and other methods. In sustaining the change, they make it part of the community culture so that it doesn't fade away.

MAKING PLANS

Once you have determined the levels of community readiness, you can begin making plans.

- *No Awareness*: Initially, stakeholders may or may not be aware of the need for change. If your community is at the level of no awareness, strategies include making contacts with community leaders, influencers, members and groups to share evidence of the need for change. Also, use the local media to raise awareness.
- *Disruption and Recognition*: At the moment of recognition, some people may readily recognize the need but may not yet accept it, or they may understand the need without knowing what can be done. Continue outreach through media, speaking or tables at local events such as parades, and listening at community showcases, school events or events sponsored by civic organizations, service clubs, churches or healthcare organizations, depending on the issue. Create posters and brochures to post and hand out. Focus on local incidents in media. All possible stakeholders and influencers should be trained to listen, build trust and bring back feedback to the change team from those who otherwise may be tempted to resist, push back or even sabotage the change initiative.
- *Acceptance*: To encourage acceptance, it is important to promote stakeholder buy-in and engagement. This is the point at which people will be *ready to make a change*. How is buy-in achieved?

1. *Communication*: *Listening* can provide the change team with the information they need to plan strategies and effectively implement the change process, as stakeholders are more likely to understand day-to-day issues than the change team. Listening and communication also generates *trust* and credibility among stakeholders when the change team is *transparent* and implements strategies clearly based on suggestions and feedback from the beneficiaries.
2. *Needs fulfilled*: When the change team has a clear understanding of the *needs* of the beneficiaries and the beneficiaries can clearly see their *gain* from the change process, they are more likely to buy in to the process.
3. *Positive perception*: A clear *understanding* of the proposed change and its benefits by all stakeholders often creates a positive perception which may lead to a commitment to the change. There are a number of other possible strategies that can lead stakeholders to the point where they are change ready (discussed later in this chapter).
4. *Change engagement*: When they are able to influence the change by voicing their concerns and engaging in planning, stakeholders are more likely to buy in to the change. It is important that participation is easy. For instance, if a meeting about homelessness were held in a place convenient to the beneficiaries, such as a public library where they are already spending their days, it is easier for them to participate.

- *Exploration and Implementation*: At this point, an individual may explore the idea of the proposed change, or they may engage in planning the change. Engaged change is one in which "stakeholders are involved in determining the course of the change process" (Strub & McClellan, 2016, p. 5). This harkens back to Lofquist's Spectrum of Attitudes, where he says that when beneficiaries of a change are engaged as resources, their engagement can lead to behaviors and attitudes resulting in greater productivity and self-esteem. In organizations, it can also result in greater cross-community or cross-organization input in the decision-making, and thus higher-quality decisions (1996).

  Project- and community-specific strategies during implementation can encourage later adopters to discuss the project with earlier adopters to allay their concerns. Strategies that can be used might include publicity such as newspaper articles, radio or TV interviews, open meetings or meetings with allies and other established groups to update them on project progress, in-service training for volunteers and professionals in fields related to the project. This is also a time to begin some project evaluation (see Chapter 38, Evaluation, for more information).
- *Commitment*: When the project reaches a community commitment phase, it is time to use the evaluation data to modify the project to make it better. It is also time to consider expansion and enhancement. Make sure appropriate local government policies are in place.
- *Integration*: Once the community takes full ownership of the project and integrates it into their everyday practice or life, your goal is to maintain the services and sustain the change, so there will be no relapse to the old ways of doing things. This might require ongoing and advanced training, diversified funding sources, policy changes and ongoing evaluation and modification as circumstances change.

HOW TO CARRY OUT THIS TECHNIQUE

Knowing your audience's readiness for change is a key element of effective change planning and management. Analysis of community readiness is often done through interviews (Oetting, Plested, Edwards, Jumper-Thurman, Kelly, & Beauvais, 2014) rather than surveys. (See Appendix D for a description of how to do an interview.) Interviews are useful for determining opinions, personal feelings, and perceptions. They allow an interviewer to ask probing questions and to clarify answers. They often achieve a higher **response rate** (the number of people who answered the survey divided by the number of people to whom the survey was sent) than surveys, which have become more difficult in recent years to get an adequate number returned because of survey fatigue caused by too many surveys. See Appendix C, in eResources for information on how to create, conduct and score a community readiness interview.

COLLECTING READINESS DATA

Create your interview questions. In your interview there should be questions related to each of the elements:

a. Community member's **knowledge** of efforts to address the issue.
b. Community **leadership support** of efforts to address the issue.
c. **Community attitudes** toward the issue.
d. Knowledge of the issue's **causes and consequences**.
e. Community **resources** that are available (Edwards et al., 2000).

Pilot test the interview questions and process. Choose your key respondents: brainstorm key respondents who can speak for each sector in the community that is touched by the issue. Select those who can best represent their sector. Contact each of your chosen respondents to ask if they are willing to be interviewed. If so, make an appointment. Train interviewers to introduce the interviews, conduct and record all interviews consistently.

ANALYZING QUALITATIVE DATA FROM INTERVIEWS OR SURVEYS

After interviews are complete, they can be scored. Create a way to rate or score the interviews. There are many methods for analyzing qualitative data. Qualitative data consist of words and observations, rather than numbers. One method that has been tested and validated is to:

- Review the data to identify levels and themes.
- "Code" the data by marking where the readiness levels and themes appear (by hand or by using qualitative analysis software). Qualitative analysis software is listed at the end of this chapter.
- Group together ideas and evidence about views on each theme.
- Explore the codes for patterns. (What themes show up most frequently? Not at all?)
- Calculate the average dimension scores for all of the interviews and an overall readiness score.

The analysis helps you to move from the interviews collected to an understanding of the community readiness for change.

Using the desired outcomes developed during visioning, you can begin to develop strategies for raising levels of community awareness:

- Formulate objectives.
- Target the audience.
- Create your message.
- Select the right communicator for the message (a respected role model).
- The method of communication.
- Create connections and relationships.

Planning strategies will be covered in Chapter 19 and communication in Chapter 31.

TRY IT!

Imagine that you are a member of a Homeless Coalition in your hometown.

1. First, write a clear description of the issue that can be used to describe it in 30 seconds or less.
2. Define your community (including the homeless).

3. Using the questions in Appendix C, select appropriate questions for your community readiness interviews. Write any questions that you think are needed, in addition to those selected. Try out your interview with someone and note how long it takes.
4. Describe key people to interview from the appropriate community sectors.
5. Use your descriptions from steps 1 to 3 to complete your interview introduction:

   Hello, my name is _____ from (your organization or affiliation). Thank you so much for agreeing to be interviewed for this project.

   We are interviewing key people to ask about (issue) in (community). The entire interview process, including people's names, will be kept strictly confidential. Data will be reported only in aggregated form.

   Just to clarify, when I mention (issue), I specifically mean: (define the issue).

   In addition, I would like you to answer specifically about the community of _____.

   (Give details you think are necessary about the community, such as town name and subgroup.)

   The interview will take about ___ minutes. (Use the average time from your pilot test.)

   I would like to audio (or video) record our interview, so that we can accurately report your answers. We will erase the recording after we transcribe it. Would that be okay with you?

SUMMARY

The change team can assess and plan strategies to deal with concerns of those people who resist change. Strategies might include persuading the resisting or opposing people that the change is in their best interest, and to channel their concern into exploration and integration of the change into their work or community lives. Other strategies include timely communications, facilitating involvement and providing support for those individuals who may otherwise lag behind in the change process.

CITATIONS

Beenen, G. (2016). Navigating change: From resistance to resilience. *Industrial Management*, 58(4), 17–21.

Connor, D. R. (1993). *Managing at the speed of change*. New York: Random House.

Conner, D. R., & Patterson, R. W. (1982). Building commitment to organizational change. *Training & Development Journal*, 36(4), 18–30.

Edwards, R. W., Jumper-Thurman, P., Plested, B. A., Oetting, E. R., & Swanson, L. (2000). Community readiness: Research to practice. *Journal of Community Psychology*, 28(3), 291–307.

Gladwell, M. (2000). *The tipping point: How little things can make a big difference*. New York: Little, Brown.

Homan, M. S. (1999). *Promoting community change: Making it happen in the real world*. Pacific Grove, CA: Brooks/Cole Publishing.

Kotter, J. P. (2012). *Leading change*. Cambridge, MA: Harvard Business Review Press.

Kübler-Ross, E. (2014). *On death and dying: What the dying have to teach doctors, nurses, clergy and their own families* (Reissue ed.). New York: Scribner.

Lofquist, W. A. (1996). *Technology of development*. Tucson, AZ: Development Publications.

Margolis, J., & Stoltz, P. (2010). How to bounce back from adversity. *Harvard Business Review*, 88(1–2), 87–92.

Moss Kanter, R. (1985). *Change masters*. New York: Free Press/Simon & Schuster.

Oetting E. R., Plested B., Edwards R. W., Thurman P. J., Kelly K. J., Beauvais F. (2014). *Community readiness for community change: Tri-Ethnic Center community readiness handbook*. Stanley L. (ed.), Fort Collins, CO: Tri-Ethnic Center for Prevention Research.

Plested, B. A., Edwards, R. W., & Jumper-Thurman, P. (2006). *Community readiness. A handbook for successful change*. Fort Collins, CO: Tri-Ethnic Center for Prevention Research. Retrieved from www.ndhealth.gov/injury/ND_Prevention_Tool_Kit/docs/Community_Readiness_Handbook.pdf

Rogers, E. M. (2003). *Diffusion of innovations* (5th ed.). New York, NY: Simon and Schuster.

Strub, M. M., & McClellan, S. S. (2016). Getting to a culture of assessment: Antecedents to change readiness. *Kentucky Libraries*, 80(4), 5–12. Retrieved from https://ir.library.louisville.edu/cgi/viewcontent.cgi?article=1307&context=faculty

Free Qualitative Analysis Software

HyperRESEARCH: runs on Mac and Windows. Retrieved from www.researchware.com
KH Coder: runs on MAC and Windows. Retrieved from http://khc.sourceforge.net/en/
QDA Miner Lite: runs on Windows. Retrieved from https://provalisresearch.com/
TAMS Analyzer: runs on Macintosh and Linux platforms. Retrieved from http://tamsys.sourceforge.net/

WONDERING AND HYPOTHESIS TESTING   14

Figure 14.0

WHAT'S IN THIS CHAPTER

Since good information is the key to problem-solving, we need to be sure that we are working with the best facts and figures possible. This chapter is about clarifying the issue or problem so that it can be addressed. When a community or business group comes together, they often know that there is an issue. But what do they know about it? This is a good place to start—finding out what they know. In this discussion, you might find that people have facts, but they might also derive inferences from those facts, they may speculate, and they may have opinions.

The next step is to clearly define the problem so that everyone knows what it means. We often use words that mean different things to different people, so this needs to be clear to everyone. For instance, an advocacy group for Native Alaskans was concerned about the incarceration rate in their community, but are they concerned about all members of the 229 tribes in Alaska? Or only those in their county, town or neighborhood? In order to measure their impact, the need and target population must be clear.

Next, analyzing the issue to identify probable contributing factors or causes will help you focus your efforts on a potentially effective solution. Finally, you will want to identify indicators to help you measure progress and test your hypothesis about the issue and solution.

Objectives

By the end of this chapter, you will be able to:

- Clearly define the need, opportunity or problem.
- Use the fishbone diagram to brainstorm possible causes for this data.
- Formulate a hypothesis that can be tested.
- Define observable and measurable indicators and then search for sources of evidence of those indicators.

A STORY ABOUT READING IN PRISON

Malcolm X was a powerful speaker, an American Muslim minister and human rights activist in the U.S. Civil Rights movement. It wasn't an easy road to get there from his troubled youth marked by foster homes and illegal activities following the death of his father and his mother's hospitalization.

Imagine Malcolm X in prison. While articulate in his personal conversation, he could barely write a letter home. Then he discovered the prison library and began the education he had failed to receive in the outside world. He described the value of the prison library:

> I have often reflected upon the new vistas that reading opened to me. I knew right there in prison that reading had changed forever the course of my life. As I see it today, the ability to read awoke in me some long dormant craving to be mentally alive.
>
> (X & Haley, 1973, p. 182)

Many inmates, like Malcolm X, learned to read in prison both for education and entertainment. They became ardent users of the library (Illinois State Library, n.d.) Besides awakening intellectual curiosity, reading can entertain (which can reduce conflict between inmates), and help inmates learn vocational skills that can help them get jobs and reduce the chance of returning to prison.

In the 3Rs Project—Reading Reduces Recidivism, a group of activists was concerned about the recidivism of prisoners that had completed their sentences and returned to the community. Recidivism is defined as an inmate having another sentence and/or incarceration following a prior incarceration. This might happen because the ex-offender did not find employment or reintegrate into society well, resulting in wasted human lives of the prisoners and huge costs to taxpayers. In the case of Malcolm X, and many other ex-offenders, access to effective prison libraries with educational programming changed their lives.

WHAT THIS TECHNIQUE IS ABOUT

This technique is about thinking carefully about an issue before selecting a solution. This requires the systematic examination of symptoms and possible contributing factors or causes before formulating hypotheses and testing them by taking action steps and making sure they lead successfully to the desired

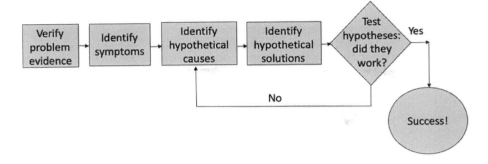

Figure 14.1 Testing hypotheses.

outcomes (Figure 14.1). Usually a problem presents in the form of symptoms, but symptoms may or may not indicate the actual cause for a condition. You will want to examine the evidence for the symptoms to make sure you really have a problem. Then you can begin to dig down to locate causes.

CLARIFYING THE PROBLEM

Let's take a look at the analysis process carried out by prison library advocates. The group came together around their concerns for reading skills of prisoners. At their first gathering the group began by finding out what members of the group knew about the issue. Group members shared the following information:

- In their midwestern state, the recidivism rate at the beginning of the project is near 45% within three years of release. There is ample evidence that education and reading can reduce recidivism and increase employment opportunities, especially for prisoners that had not finished school before incarceration. According to a study sponsored by the U.S. Bureau of Justice Assistance, inmates who participated in education programs had a 43% lower chance of returning to prison than those who did not (Davis et al., 2013).
- There is also a 13% better chance of post-release employment when inmates are literate and participate in educational programming, and libraries play an important role in supporting education.
- By law, every prison was to have a library to serve the institution's educational mission, to support prisoner's recreational, rehabilitation and legal reading needs. Yet, many prison libraries fail to meet all of these needs. There is significant recidivism when offenders enter and leave the prisons without learning to read or obtaining education and skills needed for employment in the community after release.
- Reading reduces behavior problems while in prison, because inmates are engaged in interesting or entertaining reading, rather than engaging in negative interactions with other inmates. However, there were few interesting and up-to-date books available in the 25 prisons of this state, and no budget for the prison to buy books, only for hiring librarians. In some of the prisons, there was also no librarian.

The group had a place to start, if they could verify that this information was accurate.

HYPOTHESIS

The *hypothesis* of the group was that if they could get books to the prisoners, then recidivism could be reduced. Initially, books were located and delivered by prison activists. This incremental change, however, was not a real long-term solution. Wardens were uncomfortable working with prison activists, and the activists had limited means to purchase books.

> *Hypothesis*: a proposed explanation made as a starting point for further investigation. In community or organizational change, the focus is on the conditions underlying the symptoms. It is usually stated in an "If . . . Then" form, and should be testable:
>
> **If** books are available to prisoners, and they read them, **then** recidivism will be reduced.

To solve the right problem, we need to ask the right questions, and to define the issues rigorously. By defining problems rigorously, we make them easier to solve and may save resources in doing so. Without rigor, organizations can miss opportunities, waste resources and pursue initiatives that won't address their concerns. We can begin defining the problem with the meeting discussion of what people think the problem is. Some key questions are:

- What is the issue? What facts do we have about it?
- What impact it is having?
- What are the consequences of not solving the problem? Why does the problem need to be solved?
- What are the emotions the problem is creating for those involved?
- Where and when does the problem need to be solved?

Next, we need to state the problem in a clear and straightforward manner. "The problem that we are trying to solve is: _____." Refine the problem to its simplest form but include adequate details and context. You are aiming for the most basic "source problem." Ask the group, "Why is this a problem?" If you come up with another problem, you may have just identified a deeper problem to solve.

Finally, we need to look at each word to make sure there is agreement among all members of your group and all the information used is based on evidence. For instance, if you use the word *hometown*, are you talking about the town someone grew up in, or the town they currently live in? Identify one issue or problem at a time.

> ### CHECKLIST FOR CLEAR PROBLEM STATEMENTS
> ❏ Avoids divisiveness, blame or emotionally loaded statements.
> ❏ Avoids identifying specific solutions.
> ❏ Defines the problem by behaviors and conditions that affect it.
> ❏ States specific measurable outcomes.
> ❏ Is supported by data.
> ❏ Reflects community concerns.
> ❏ States a solvable problem.
> ❏ Resolution would result in clear, meaningful improvements.

The prison activists defined the issue as "the prisoner's reading needs in the State of X prisons are not being met adequately to increase reading by 10%."

The third sheet in Figure 14.2 shows possible causes brainstormed by the team for prisoners not reading, keeping in mind that these are hypotheses that can be validated later by locating or collecting data. Causes included lack of funding for purchase of current library materials (except law books), space and library staff shortages, lack of interest or pushback from prison authorities resulting in low priorities for libraries, arbitrary censorship of books by authorities and damage or theft of items by prisoners.

What's Happening Now?	Symptoms	Causes	Ideal
• Prisoners not reading • Prisoners <u>enter</u> and <u>leave</u> the system illiterate • Few job opportunities for illiterate ex-offenders • High rates of recidivism	• Few books of interest available in state prison libraries • Out-of-date collections • No librarians in some prisons • Libraries low priority in prisons	• Budget, staff shortage • Lack of interest, pushback from prison authorities • Recidivism = lack of education • Arbitrary censorship • Space limitations • Damage, theft of items	• Recidivism will drop as much as 40% as a result of reading library books • Job opportunities will improve • Books will educate • Books will entertain, resulting in fewer negative behaviors

Figure 14.2 Prison library brainstorm.

CONTRIBUTING FACTORS

Contributing factors are conditions that can bring about a symptom. Getting to the most basic factors that cause conditions in a complex system such as a community, nonprofit organization or even a business, as mentioned in Chapter 9, is often called *Root Cause Analysis*. The goal of a careful analysis is to zero in on the most important contributing factors so you can choose the most effective action steps. Test the effectiveness of the action steps to see if they work and rethink the solutions if they don't.

THE FISHBONE DIAGRAM

There are many methods to help you dig down to the root cause. One useful method is the fishbone or Ishikawa diagram created by Kaoru Ishikawa. This method results from group research and brainstorming the contributing factors for a problem or issue. Write a clear definition of the issue or problem in a box on the right, under *effect*, and then draw an arrow from the left under *causes* to the box (Tague, 2005). The contributing factors or causes for the problem are then listed on the left as shown in Figure 14.3. Ask your group why the problem occurs, and what the contributing factors are. Write down the answers on the horizontal lines and then ask, "Why?" again. That is, why did the factors result in the consequence or problem? (Altman, Balcazar, Fawcett, Seekins, & Young, 1994). Do this at least five times or until your group agrees that all contributing factors or causes have been identified.

Brainstorm the major categories of contributing factors or causes of the problem. These categories vary depending on the organization or the community. For instance, Thomas Gilbert identified six factor categories related to job performance as: information, resources and incentives available to the person doing the job, and knowledge, capacity and motives of the person (Dean, 1994). A food service organization might use the four categories of surroundings, suppliers, systems and skill (Dudbridge, 2011). You can use generic terms to organize the factors into categories. For instance, when a community group is addressing social issues, they may use categories such as:

- Unemployment.
- Poverty.
- Rapid population change.
- Urbanization.
- Lack of education.
- Disruptive belief systems.
- Discrimination.

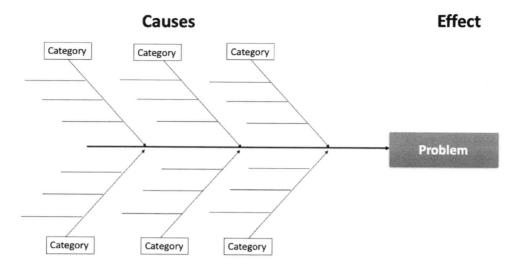

Figure 14.3 Fishbone diagram.
Source: Adapted from Ishikawa (1985)

- Lack of guidance for children.
- Environmental change/ecological issues.
- Substance abuse.
- Racial justice.
- Race unity/diversity.
- Equity in education.
- Homelessness.
- Crime prevention.
- Prison reform.
- Peace building.
- Community development.

The categories can be helpful for structuring the group brainstorm, but they are less important than the contributing factors or causes identified.

After identifying causes, indicators need to be identified. Indicators provide specific information about the level or state of something, and identifying the current state of something can serve as a baseline when later measuring progress. It is specific, observable and measurable, and when used for evaluation of your change initiative, it should show the progress made toward achieving a specific desired outcome. To identify an indicator:

- Describe what you want to measure.
- Focus on the action or change you wish to see.
- Quantify change in numerical terms, such as counts, proportions or percentages.
- Search existing information for matching your needs.

Using a fishbone diagram, the activists identified four categories (resources, environment, behaviors and incentives), and used these to examine the causes, as shown in Figure 14.4.

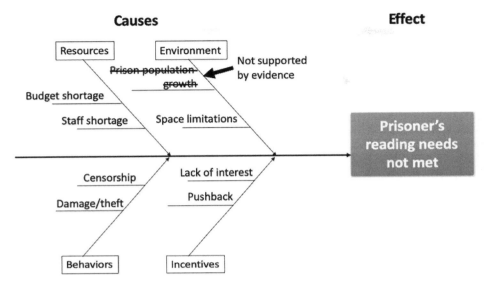

Figure 14.4 Activist's fishbone diagram.

Note that item under environment "Prison population growth" is crossed out. This is because when the activists conducted research on the possible contributing factors, they found this cause not to be true. The space limitations were not caused by population growth.

INDICATORS

The items that the activist group identified included the following possible contributing factors and indicators. Then they looked for concrete, observable evidence of contributing factors. The source for information on the indicator is shown in the third column of Table 14.1:
  Notice that some of the data found was national rather than local. When possible, use of *local data* is far preferable to that of national data, because efforts on a local issue will affect the local community and progress will be measured and evaluated locally, as shown in Figure 14.5.
  When selecting indicators, they should be:

- Relevant to assessing your project's progress.
- Limited in number but remaining open-ended and adaptable to future needs.
- Understandable, clear and unambiguous.
- Conceptually sound.
- Representative of research consensus on your type of project to the extent possible.
- Within the capabilities of your project team to locate or develop and collect data.
- Dependent on cost-effective data of known quality.
- If your project is local, the data should be primarily local in scope.

Properly identifying likely causes for a problem will help in identifying the most effective solutions. The group wondered which of the possible causes listed were actual causes and which contributed most to the

Table 14.1 Activists' indicators.

What They Want to Measure	Indicator	Source
Some inmates don't read because of illiteracy	Literacy rates among prison population	National Center for Educational Statistics
Some inmates don't read because recreational reading books are: o out of date, uninteresting o books are unavailable o often there is no librarian	Prisoner survey State prisons with no librarian	Unavailable
Uneducated people are economically and socially marginalized	Unemployment rates and earnings by educational attainment	Bureau of Labor Statistics
Prisoners who have not participated in educational programs often do not get/keep jobs and return to prison	Effectiveness of correctional education on recidivism	Bureau of Justice Assistance/RAND
Bored inmates engage in negative behaviors with other inmates	Negative behaviors are related to boredom	Rocheleau (2013); some information on Department of Justice, but no ongoing reports
Budget is constrained by growing number of prisoners	State corrections expenditures	Budget details unavailable directly from IDOC
Increasing prison population results in lack of space	Increased population not supported; population began to decline in 1996	Department of Justice
Budget shortage results in fewer library items purchased	Prison library budget	Illinois Public Media News (2018); budget details unavailable directly from IDOC

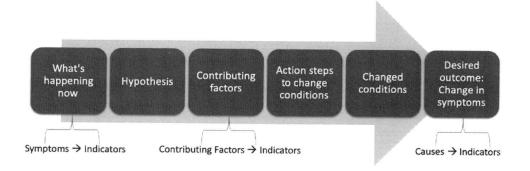

Figure 14.5 Gauging progress.

problem of prisoners not reading, so they could focus on the most potentially effective solutions. When preparing to gauge progress:

- It is important to identify indicators and find *sources* for information on those indicators.
- In addition, the information should be measured on an *ongoing* basis, so the project can have information at the beginning (what's happening now) and again at the end.

- The information is best if the data is *local*. In this case, data from sources such as the Department of Justice is frequently broken out by state.

SEARCHING FOR DATA ON INDICATORS

Searching for data may involve:

1. Networking with knowledgeable community members and authorities. They may know of sources of local data that can be used.
2. Searching the local public or academic library for information. Your librarian can assist you with your search.
3. Internet searches for existing data and ongoing data collection, preferably local data. City, state and national government websites are good sources for data.
   To limit your search to
   i. Go to a search engine like Google.com or Go Duck Go.
   ii. Enter the site, www.website.gov, and the *search term* into the search box
   iii. Look at the results, and then refine your search as needed. Don't give up easily. Sometimes it takes several tries to find just what you need. For more on searching, see Appendix D in eResources.

While searching for data on indicators, the group found a lack of information available for some of their contributing factors, and two factors were found to be untrue. The group noted that the current situation (what's happening now) may have multiple causes, but with limited resources, the group needs to address possible causes that would have the most impact. These causes can be considered hypotheses that could be tested.

If no existing information on your indicators exists, your team can collect information, for instance through a community survey. This will be covered in Chapter 18.

Library and Internet research is useful at several stages in your change initiative. In this case, it will help validate possible evidence for issues, validate hypothetical causes for your community issue and help you find existing data for your indicators. Data for indicators will give you a baseline, and then later help you determine if your hypothesis was accurate. Appendix D provides information to help you search for this information, with directions for searching and evaluation of the information you find.

HYPOTHESIS TESTING

The last sheet is a description of the ideal situation, sometimes called the desired outcomes. At this point, the group can discuss, "How would we know if we succeeded? Could success be measured?" The key outcome would be reduced recidivism—inmates would not reoffend and go back to prison. While each of the causes brainstormed by the group may have contributed, the group decided the hypothesis they would focus on would be that if they could get free books to the prisoners, perhaps recidivism could be reduced. After a period of time, the group could examine recidivism rates for their state (this key indicator is publicly available information) to see if reincarceration had dropped.

Like many community issues, testing hypotheses can be challenging. The difficulty with the prison reading hypothesis was that while it would be possible to see recidivism rates over time for the state, it would be hard to get information on how much the former inmates had actually read. How could the hypotheses be tested? Using the contributing factor indicators might be useful as substitute data. For instance, an increase in the use of the library for pleasure reading or study might be one way to measure increased reading. In addition, the group should be on the alert for indicators that they never thought of, and *secondary* or *indirect* results that occur following the implementation of action steps. In this project, a by-product of the project was the relationship between public and prison librarians.

ACTION STEPS

Based on the causes brainstormed and information located, you can move on to action steps.

If you remember our story from Chapter 3, action steps included local public librarians connecting with prison librarians. The librarians offered to share leftovers from quarterly book sales of books removed from circulation or those donated to the libraries for their "Friends of the Library" book sales. The local librarians brought the books to a collection site, where the prison librarians could come choose books that the prisoners would be interested in reading. This was a viable long-term change, because the local librarians did not compromise prison warden ethics, and there was a steady supply of books available from each quarterly Friends of the Library book sale. Since there were free books available that met prison library standards and interested the prisoners, wardens were able to hire librarians to process the books and lead some educational programs.

HOW TO CARRY OUT THIS TECHNIQUE

Clearly define the problem. Use the problem-statement checklist to evaluate your problem definition and revise if necessary.

Using the team brainstorm of "what's happening now," symptoms, possible causes and ideal outcomes, discuss and list possible contributing factors that bring about the symptoms to be addressed. One way to do this is to use the Ishikawa or fishbone diagram of possible causes.

Formulate a hypothesis to be tested.

Use an "If . . . Then" form.
Verify that the hypothesis is testable: that is, by carrying out the action steps, the conditions are changed, resulting in the desired outcomes which can be seen and measured.

Define specific, observable indicators of the contributing factors, and then carry out a search for sources of evidence for your list of possible causes. This may involve networking with knowledgeable community members and authorities, or library and Internet searches for existing data and ongoing data collection, preferably local data. If you find the contributing factor is not true, cross it off the list on the fishbone diagram or the list of indicators. Stay alert for other indicators that your team never thought of. If no evidence already exists, your team will need to collect information, for instance through a community survey.

As the action steps are carried out, gauge the progress of your project. Also, keep your eyes open for *secondary* or *indirect* results that occur following the implementation of action steps. These can be either positive or negative.

We will cover more on planning the action steps in Chapter 20.

TRY IT!

Use either an issue faced by your community, organization or business, or the issue provided in the following to practice analyzing causes using a fishbone diagram, and then identifying your hypothesis and how you might test it. Look for existing sources for indicators.

Issue: A community advocacy group on Alaska's Kenai Peninsula was concerned about the incarceration rate of Native peoples in their area. In Alaska, Native people constitute 15 percent of the total population, but a full 38 percent of the prison population. Follow the steps you would take to help the group analyze contributing factors for the issue and formulate a hypothesis.

- Define the problem clearly.
- Use the fishbone diagram to brainstorm possible causes for these numbers.

- Formulate a hypothesis that can be tested, including action steps.
- Define observable indicators, and then search for sources of evidence on those indicators.

SUMMARY

Using the "what's happening now" brainstorm, you can formulate a hypothesis that will be tested through the process of implementing action steps to move from the current state to the desired outcomes. This chapter covered how to clearly define the problem so that it can be solved. An important step before creating your action step strategies and tactics is to brainstorm or use a fishbone or Ishikawa diagram to identify contributing factors or causes of the issue. How to define observable indicators was covered, as well as how to search for already existing sources of evidence on your indicators.

CITATIONS

Altman, D., Balcazar, F., Fawcett, S., Seekins, T., & Young, J. (1994). *Public health advocacy: Creating community change to improve health.* Palo Alto, CA: Stanford Center for Research in Disease Prevention.

Davis, L. M., Bozick, R., Steele, J. L., Saunders, J., Miles, J. N. V., & The RAND Corporation. (2013). *Evaluating the effectiveness of correctional education: A meta-analysis of programs that provide education to incarcerated adults.* Retrieved from www.rand.org/pubs/research_reports/RR266.html

Dean, P. (Ed.). (1994). *Performance engineering at work.* Batavia, IL: International Board of Standards for Training.

Dudbridge, M. (2011). *Handbook of lean manufacturing in the food industry.* Hoboken, NJ: John Wiley & Sons.

Gilbert, T. F. (1978). *Human competence: Engineering worthy performance.* New York: McGraw-Hill.

Illinois Public Media News. (2018). Illinois prison system spent less than $300 on books last year. *Illinois Public Media News.* Retrieved from https://will.illinois.edu/news/story/illinois-prison-system-spent-less-than-300-on-books-last-year

Ishikawa, K. (1985). *What is total quality control? The Japanese way.* Englewood Cliffs, NJ: Prentice-Hall.

Rocheleau, A. M. (2013). An empirical exploration of the "pains of imprisonment" and the level of prison misconduct and violence. *Criminal Justice Review, 38,* 354–374. doi:10.1177/0734016813494764

Tague, N. R. (2005). *The quality toolbox* (2nd ed.). Milwaukee, WI: ASQ Quality Press.

X, M., & Haley, A. (1973). *The autobiography of Malcolm X* (1st Ballantine Books ed.). New York: Ballantine Books.

Data Sources Used in the Example

Davis, L. M., Bozick, R., Steele, J. L., Saunders, J., Miles, J. V., & RAND Corporation. (2013). *Evaluating the effectiveness of correctional education: A meta-analysis of programs that provide education to incarcerated adults.* Retrieved from www.rand.org/content/dam/rand/pubs/research_reports/RR200/RR266/RAND_RR266.pdf

Davis, L. M., Steele, J. L., Bozick, R., Williams, M. V., Turner, S., Miles, J. N. V., . . . Steinberg, P. S. (2014). *How effective is correctional education, and where do we go from here? The results of a comprehensive evaluation.* Santa Monica, CA: RAND Corporation. Retrieved from www.rand.org/pubs/research_reports/RR564.html. Also available in print form.

Illinois Public Media News. (2018). Illinois prison system spent less than $300 on books last year. *Illinois Public Media News.* Retrieved from https://will.illinois.edu/news/story/illinois-prison-system-spent-less-than-300-on-books-last-year

Illinois State Library. (n.d.). *Special libraries and special-needs patrons. Heritage project: 1839–2013*. Retrieved April 15, 2018, from www.cyberdriveillinois.com/departments/library/heritage_project/home/chapters/coming-of-age-the-1970s/special-libraries-and-special-needs-patrons/

Kyckelhahn, T. (2012, revised 2014). *State corrections expenditures, FY 1982–2010*. Washington, DC: Bureau of Justice Statistics. U.S. Department of Justice. Retrieved from www.bjs.gov/content/pub/pdf/scefy8210.pdf

National Center for Educational Statistics. (2016). *Highlights from the U.S. PIAAC survey of incarcerated adults: Their skills, work experience, education, and training* (Report NCES 2016-040). Washington, DC: U.S. Department of Education Office of Educational Research and Improvement.

Rocheleau, A. M. (2013). An empirical exploration of the "pains of imprisonment" and the level of prison misconduct and violence. *Criminal Justice Review, 38*, 354–374. doi:10.1177/0734016813494764

U.S. Bureau of Labor Statistics. (2018, March). *Employment projections*. Washington, DC: Office of Occupational Statistics and Employment Projections. Retrieved from www.bls.gov/emp/ep_chart_001.htm

PLANNING PERSPECTIVES

15

Figure 15.0

WHAT'S IN THIS CHAPTER?

An important initial step in planning change initiatives is to examine the type of change under consideration. The type of change might be a short range or long-range change, and the scope could be small, incremental changes or large, transformative changes. Figure 15.1 shows how time and scope are related to one another.

Objectives

By the end of this chapter, you will be able to:

- Define and analyze the "Arenas of Action" for your project.
- Analyze your project's focus and purpose to identify your planning perspectives

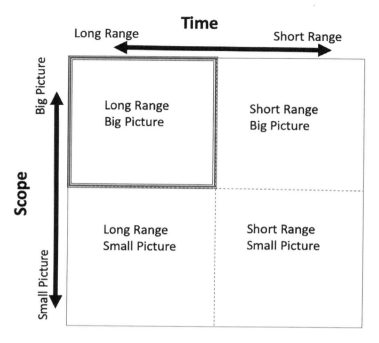

Figure 15.1 Planning perspectives.
Source: Adapted from Lynn and Lofquist (2007, p. 35).

A STORY ABOUT PLANNING PERSPECTIVES

Homeless Coalition organizers began their efforts to combat homelessness by focusing on the symptoms. Their first conception of how to help was a charitable impulse to distribute socks and toothbrushes. If the problem is conceived of as a nail, why not use a hammer? By meeting the immediate needs of homeless people, it appeared that the problem is nearly solved—or so they thought. One church even took a kindly approach of personal problem-solving and adopted a homeless woman; that led them down a path of intense engagement which absorbed their time and funding. Later on, the coalition members pursued making and distributing hygiene bags and woven plastic mats for sleeping on cold ground. As they moved along a continuum of community development, it became clear the solution was not simple. Was handling symptoms the best strategy for causing fundamental change?

William Lofquist, in his theory of community development, suggests that the starting point in any change process is the *goal of seeking well-being for the entire community*, then expanding expectations with creativity and new insights. By asking some good questions—*What caused the problem? Who can be part of the solution?*—you can avoid *activity traps* which are engaging actions that produce limited results. Socks and toothbrushes are useful but would not really solve the problem of homelessness. Returning to our metaphor of riding on a train, the Homeless Coalition had taken a detour and was not heading toward the ultimate destination which is reducing homelessness.

Meanwhile, the problem was growing more serious. Winter had come, and there was a need for emergency housing. The city manager opened up the Civic Center during a period of frigid winter to house people who were banned from Good Samaritan Shelter for unacceptable behavior. He could not bear watching them freezing on the street. This caused problems with the Chamber of Commerce and other groups who saw homeless people as a problem. How could the Homeless Coalition help?

A meeting was called including key city officials, the health department, social service agencies and the library director. Maurine, as the facilitator, was invited to lead this discussion. Her first task was to ask the question "What's happening now?" with the homeless in frigid winter. This question is asked over and over again during a change assessment to seek a deep description of conditions that can lead to a profound understanding. Conditions change!

> Those who promote positive change most effectively are not those who provide a new set of answers, but those who allow a new set of questions.
>
> (Lynn & Lofquist, 2007, p. 12)

WHAT THIS TECHNIQUE IS ABOUT

Development is about creating changes for enhancing growth or advancement in individual people or enhancing conditions in business, civic or community groups. These groups might include boards of nonprofit foundations and *ad hoc* groups that form to address a community need. Creating this change requires a clear sense of purpose and focus for generating conditions that promote well-being or performance of the group and of individuals in the group.

The pressures to solve community problems may lead to oversimplified thinking. Multiple *causes* may be reduced to just one or a few, and the resulting solutions may not be satisfactory. In addition, we may risk losing the opportunity to avoid tomorrow's problems and grasp its opportunities. Problems, opportunities and solutions are nearly always multidimensional. Accomplishing change may require incremental (small, short-term) changes or transformational (large-scale) changes in the goals, structure, processes, culture, beliefs, behaviors or strategies used by an organization or community. One approach commonly used in organizational design and development that may help avoid oversimplification is to examine two dimensions at a time using a grid. The grid discussed here is the Arenas of Action framework.

GRIDS AND UNITS OF CHANGE

Grids, like the planning perspectives grid in Figure 15.1, were first described by Robert Blake and Jane Mouton (1964) as a way for a group to move away from simple black-and-white thinking toward examining issues using what they called "two-sided thinking." Using the grid also helps a group consider what Blake and Mouton called "units of change." Will the change involve individuals or larger groups and conditions?

Imagine individuals going to a training course to learn a new, more effective method of doing a job. When the trainees return to work, it may be difficult to transfer what they learned to the job without the support of their supervisors and work teams. Lack of support is a barrier to using the new skills. The trainees fall back on previous patterns of behavior based on their workgroup and supervisors' expectations. On the other hand, if the work teams and supervisors learn and apply skills together as groups, it is far easier to make the transfer and apply the new behaviors to the work situation because they have similar knowledge and can support each other. A unit of change might be individuals, groups (such as work teams or neighborhoods), a whole organization or a larger social system.

FOCUS ON OUTCOMES AND CONDITIONS

Our attention to the *focus* and the *purpose* of the change will help us choose effective actions to create conditions to promote the well-being of the people involved. While the focus of change might benefit individuals, there are many benefits to focusing on **outcomes**, and on **conditions** creating barriers to achieving outcomes (and their causes), rather than on individuals. The focus on outcomes removes negative focus from individuals. That negative focus can otherwise increase their resistance to change. Instead, individuals can take responsibility for their behaviors and serve as resources: The perspectives of these individuals can inform the change team and help them understand barriers and conditions so they can be changed. They can take joint ownership of the problem being addressed and become allies working toward mutual goals. For those people directly benefiting from change, having taken positive roles and having had "successful experiences in planned change can be carried into other condition-improving activity" (Lofquist, 1983, pp. 25–26).

Analyzing the focus and purpose for a change can provide some direction to selecting actions addressing the issue. One tool to use is what Lynn and Lofquist (2007) call the "Arenas of Action" (see Figure 15.2).

Blake and Mouton (1976) describe many units of change from individual to organizational through the larger social system, placed on the continuum in logical order. These areas of focus might also include other constituents depending on the need. In Figure 15.3, the continuum goes from *Individuals* to *Conditions*. As the change involves relationships between people and the environment of the organization or community, the focus moves toward the Conditions pole.

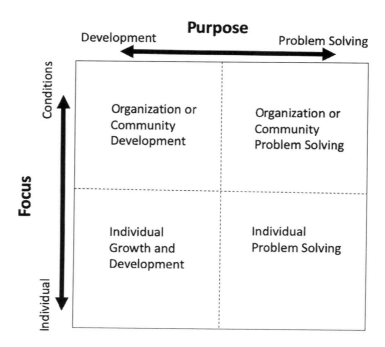

Figure 15.2 Arenas of action.
Source: Adapted from Lynn and Lofquist (2007, p. 8).

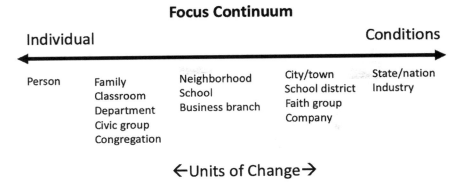

Figure 15.3 Focus continuum showing possible units of change.

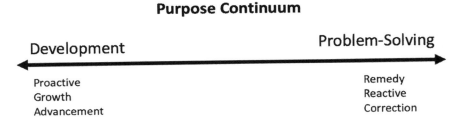

Figure 15.4 Purpose continuum.

PURPOSE

The purpose of any change strategy can be stated in several ways. The purpose continuum in Figure 15.4 ranges from *Development*, which is proactive and initiates change in anticipation of future needs, to *Problem-Solving*, which seeks to remedy a problem. On the development end, proactive efforts are made to create conditions and individual characteristics to improve the well-being of the community or organization before problems have occurred. At the other end, problem-solving is a reactive response to perceived problems.

It is possible that a goal has both proactive and reactive features, and so the purpose may be located somewhere between the two poles.

THE FOUR ACTION QUADRANTS

The two continua of Purpose and Focus define four quadrants or Arenas of Action (Figure 15.2).

Quadrant 1 is proactive development of the organization or community, through bringing about changes in specific conditions. Changes in this quadrant may bring about changes in the other quadrants. Strategies in this area might include community assessment, community planning, community education, training, organization design/development consultation, advocacy, legislation, policy development, holding celebrations, creating parks, museums, holding art exhibits and concerts.

Quadrant 2 is proactive individual growth and development through various means including community education, training, experiential learning, adventure learning, study groups, self-studying, learning communities, coaching and mentoring. These growth opportunities might take place through the school district, library, service clubs and arts councils. The focus of the learning may include technical skills, relationship skills, leadership skills or team-building skills.

Quadrant 3 is reactive organization or community problem-solving. When conditions have caused recognized problems in the community, some sort of problem-solving needs to take place. Problems of discrimination, low academic achievement and unemployment are examples of community problems in Quadrant 3. When this happens quickly, unprepared social service systems and schools may become overwhelmed. When many people are affected, these problems may lead to a sense of crisis. Unless root causes are addressed with the proposed community change, these problems may return.

Quadrant 4 is reactive individual problem-solving. This arena focuses on individual problem-solving and treatment. It may involve therapy for individuals or families, group therapy or assistance for individual students in classrooms.

HOW TO CARRY OUT THIS TECHNIQUE

1. Describe simply and clearly a situation and a change that might benefit one of your communities.
2. Using a graph of the Arenas of Action like the one shown in Figure 15.2, determine if the change is:
   a. A proactive development of the organization or community, through bringing about changes in specific conditions.
   b. Proactive individual growth and development for an individual.
   c. Reactive or remedial organization or community problem-solving.
   d. Reactive problem-solving for an individual.
3. Mark where you believe the change lies on the diagram with a dot. Remember that the mark can fall anywhere on the continuum, and not just on the ends of the poles.

AN EXAMPLE

A large influx of new immigrants to a formerly homogenous community brought significant differences in language, culture and religion which were not well understood by long-time residents. The community became divided. Many children had difficulty in school because they did not read and write in English, and their spoken English was not strong. Last year, immigrant students at the high school walked out of classes to protest discrimination. Students and parents recounted acts of harassment and bullying. Finally, an act of violence at the local mall caused shock, fear and anger on both sides of the community. The community was in crisis.

This kind of complex problem requires multiple strategies. The first focus is to help students succeed in school. This focus is individual, so it is in Quadrant 4, and it is also **community problem-solving**, so it is in Quadrant 3. Solutions can include creating new school programs to help children learn English. Students spend an academic year with an English language learner (ELL) teacher and an aide who speaks the language of the new immigrant children, before they join the mainstream.

Other solutions to other aspects of the problem, such as lack of mutual understanding, may include joint dialogue programs between the older and newer community residents, hosted by local mosques and churches, or the opening of a new museum featuring the culture of the immigrants and is likely to fall in Quadrant 1.

TRY IT!

Using the new immigrant story from this chapter, focus on the problems in the high school and identify where you think the solution falls within the Arenas of Action. Is it a problem requiring a remedy, or is it about community development that will prevent future problems? Is the focus on individual people or changing the conditions in the town? Mark the diagram with a dot where you believe the change lies on the two continuums. A solution is located at the end of the chapter.

SUMMARY

The Arenas of Action framework involves clearly defining the *purpose* of the desired change and the *focus* or the unit of change. Having a clear understanding of the reason for the change-oriented actions and the focus (individuals or conditions) will help a community group choose effective actions to create the conditions necessary to solve problems or promote the well-being of the people involved. The Arenas of Action technique also helps analyze a potential change while avoiding the problem of oversimplifying complex issues.

CITATIONS

Blake, R. R., & Mouton, J. S. (1964). *The managerial grid: Key orientations for achieving production through people*. Houston, TX: Gulf Pub. Co.

Blake, R. R., & Mouton, J. S. (1976). *Consultation*. Reading, MA: Addison-Wesley Pub. Co.

Lofquist, W. A. (1983). *Discovering the meaning of prevention: A practical approach to positive change*. Tucson, AZ: Development Publications.

Lynn, D., & Lofquist, W. A. (2007). *BreakAway: A framework for creating positive school communities*. Tucson, AZ: Development Publications.

16 FORCE FIELD ANALYSIS
Upsetting the Equilibrium

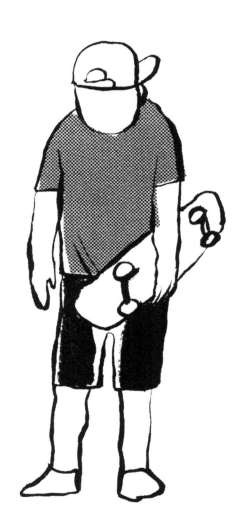

Figure 16.0

WHAT'S IN THIS CHAPTER?

This chapter is about another tool used or understanding the community context. An important step is to examine the forces driving or restraining your project. In this chapter, you will discover how to use Force Field Analysis to determine the push and pull factors in a community. This will provide valuable insights for planning, such as who needs to be aware of the plan and who is needed to help implement it effectively.

Objectives

By the end of this chapter, you will be able to:

- Analyze the driving and restraining forces that will affect your planning.
- Make plans to improve the probability of success by reducing the power of the forces opposing the change, or increasing the forces driving the change.

A STORY ABOUT ANALYSIS: A SKATEBOARDER'S SOLUTION

A city in the upper Midwest had a problem with skateboarders. Young people who enjoyed skateboarding looked in town for a place to skate with challenges and usability. No skate parks existed in the town at that time, and the youth chose a downtown shopping area where pavement texture was relatively consistent and there were interesting and challenging shapes to use for tricks. However, there was traffic, and customers entering stores had to dodge the youth. Many customers started shopping in the mall outside of town rather than in the downtown stores. This was not the ideal situation for either the youth or adults involved. Rather, both preferred that the youth go somewhere else where they could safely skateboard, and where traffic and shoppers did not block and endanger both the youthful skateboarders and the shoppers. The businesses also wanted to retain their customers.

The mayor and park board were willing to listen to the skateboarders, especially after a petition spearheaded by one skateboarder garnered 116 signatures. According to the mayor, a ninth-grade skateboarder made an appointment with him and explained the need and desired solution: a skate park. Concerns of the mayor and the Parks and Recreation Board include liability, costs and design.

WHAT THIS TECHNIQUE IS ABOUT

Force is usually thought of as a push or pull. Remember playing tug-of-war? Each team pulls on the rope, trying to pull the other team over a line. If both teams have the same number of people, with the same weight and strength, these two forces will be balanced, as shown in Figure 16.1. The pull that your team exerts is a positive force or driver for accomplishing your goal, and the pull of the other team is an obstacle or restraint to accomplishing your goal. If your team wants to pull the other team over the line, you will have to change this balance of forces.

The same can be said for introducing a change in an organization or community. The patterns of practices, attitudes, beliefs, customs, and behaviors are maintained by balancing forces. While there may be good reasons for a change (drivers), there will always be reasons that people may resist the change (restraining forces), such as comfort with the way things are, or fear of change. If your goal is to bring about some sort of change in the community, you will need to upset that balance or equilibrium and make the drivers stronger than the restraining forces. Kurt Lewin noted that "To bring about any change, the balance between the forces which maintain the social self-regulation at a given level has to be upset" (Lewin, 1948/1997, p. 47).

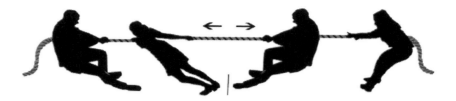

Figure 16.1 Push and pull forces.

From Lewin's work on Field Theory was developed Force Field Analysis (Crookston & Blaesser, 1962), a tool to help think through the push-pull forces, especially in social situations, to a proposed change. Once you have a good understanding of the things that push the change (drivers) or pull to prevent change (restraints), you can begin to think of ways to change the balance to allow a change to take place a technique Lewin called Force Field Analysis. Once you have an idea of where the forces are currently, you can strategize how to change them: to increase driving forces and reduce those that are restraining change (Thomas, 1985). Reducing the restraining forces may be more effective because this strategy is less threatening, more stable and predictable than strategies that increase driving forces and tension (Crookston & Blaesser, 1962). For instance, in the skateboard case, to reduce the restraining concerns about design, the youth could approach a professional skate park designer for their endorsement about the safety of the design. For cost concerns, the project team could seek donations.

This analysis technique has also been successfully used as a creative method for getting groups of people to collaborate in analyzing and planning change.

HOW TO CARRY OUT THIS TECHNIQUE

1. This technique begins with an understanding of what's happening now, as described in the previous section.
2. Describe where you want to be (the desired state). Write a brief description in the middle of the diagram in Figure 16.2.
3. In a group, brainstorm the forces that can **drive** the change (contributing factors—explored in Chapter 12 and 13). Write those on the left side of the diagram.
4. Then brainstorm forces (contributing factors) that **restrain** the change. Write those on the right side of the diagram.
5. Assign a score to each force, from 1 (weak) to 5 (strong). Place those numbers on the lines next to the descriptions of the forces in the arrows.
6. After you have carried out an analysis, you can decide as a team whether your project is realistic.
7. If you decide that the change is feasible, Force Field Analysis can help you to work out how to improve its probability of success by determining how to:
   – Reduce the power of the forces opposing the change.
   – Increase the forces driving the change.

AN EXAMPLE

Think about the skateboard scenario from earlier in this chapter. Shown in Figure 16.3 is the Force Field Analysis for this community problem and the desired solution after the youth presented his proposal to the mayor.

An analysis such as the one in Figure 16.3 can help a community group anticipate the forces for and against a project and prepare to strengthen the forces for the solution or weaken the forces against it.

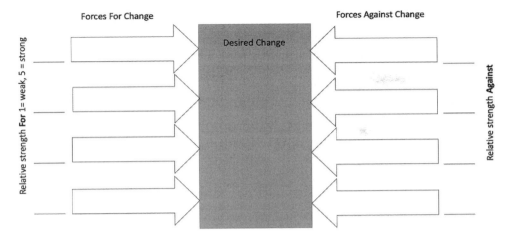

Figure 16.2 Force Field Analysis diagram.

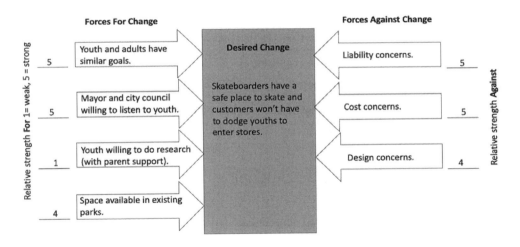

Figure 16.3 Skateboard park analysis.

Having anticipated these concerns, the skateboard group brought a design prepared after visiting many skate parks to learn about their designs and had facts and figures including the cost of the concrete. They had also identified possible locations in existing city parks. One of the biggest concerns from the city's perspective was liability. It was shown that, compared to football and basketball, skateboarding is relatively safe. The state's limited liability laws and the way the skate park was designed helped address the liability concerns of the Parks and Recreation Board.

Looking at the Force Field Analysis diagram:

- Can you see any forces for or against the solution that were not included?
- Given the description above, do you agree with the relative strengths listed?

Forces for the solution could include politics, legislation or public opinion. Forces against the solution might include a variety of things such as old structures, policies, systems, community members' fear of the solution, apathy or opposition. Next, analyze the forces to identify what can be changed. Using that information, you can create an action plan to change what can be changed, in order to make forces for the solution stronger than forces against.

TRY IT!

Exercise #1

Think back to the story called "Situational Blindness" about the retreat center. Financial difficulties had led to some quick decisions that made the financial situation worse and jeopardized the ability to carry out the mission of the retreat center. An interim director was appointed, but since he was hired by the previous board that had made the other failed decisions, he was not trusted. Fear abounded that the retreat center might have to close, and jobs would be lost. Board members attending the special retreat were anxious to see a quick turnaround. How would you diagram the forces for and against a return to the original mission? Use the diagram in Figure 16.4.

Exercise #2

Think of a situation you have experienced, where a change was needed. Describe the desired change. Then brainstorm your own list of forces for and against change and fill in your own chart. Then rate the strength of the forces from 1 to 5. Think through and explain the process you used and why you selected and rated the items as you did. Now think of strategies to shift the forces to favor the desired changes.

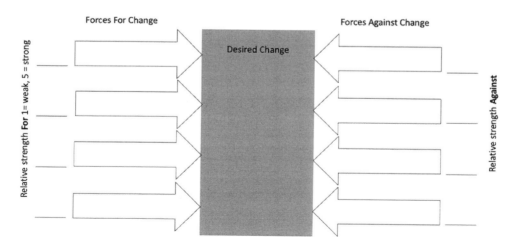

Figure 16.4 Retreat center Force Field Analysis.

SUMMARY

Kurt Lewin's Force Field Analysis tool was demonstrated here in graphic form to help you think through the push-pull forces to proposed change. While there may be good reasons for a change (drivers), there will always be reasons that people may resist the change (restraining forces), such as comfort with the way things are, or fear of change. With an understanding of these forces, you are better prepared to plan strategies for reducing the power of the forces opposing the change, or increasing the forces driving the change.

CITATIONS

Crookston, B. B., & Blaesser, W. W. (1962). An approach to planned change in a college setting. *The Personnel and Guidance Journal, 40*(7), 610–616. doi:10.1002/j.2164-4918.1962.tb02170.x

Lewin, K. (1997). *Resolving social conflicts and field theory in social science.* American Psychological Association. ISBN:9781557984159. (Original work published 1948.)

Thomas, J. (1985). Force Field Analysis: A new way to evaluate your strategy. *Long Range Planning, 18*(6), 54–59.

IDENTIFYING THE PLAY AND THE PLAYERS IN A COMMUNITY

Figure 17.0

WHAT'S IN THIS CHAPTER?

In a small community, it might be possible to know everyone well, and therefore you may be able to proceed with planning a community change without extensive data collection. However, you may also find that there is much more to learn about the community. If a larger community is going through demographic changes, or you are a new member of the community, then you could find yourself trying to implement strategies that may not work. Or worse, you might find yourself embroiled in controversy or tangled in a web that might have a long history.

An important step is to examine who will be affected by your plan, who are the key stakeholders and who can affect whether it is successful or not. Who is your community, and what are their characteristics? Who are the gatekeepers? What organizations should you engage with?

Objectives

By the end of this chapter, you will be able to:

- Identify and describe the players: community members, their cultures and values.
    - Determine who needs to be aware of the plan and who is needed to help implement it effectively.
    - Determine which individuals, agencies or organizations have influence in the community, and what their sphere of influence is.
    - Determine who are the key people and if they are community residents or if they work for community-based organizations.
    - Identify who is defined as "outside" the community and will not be affected by the change.
- Identify and describe the play: What's going on in the community.

A STORY: MAURINE PLAYS A *COLUMBO* ROLE IN A NEW PROJECT

In a professional setting, it would be easy for a highly skilled facilitator to enter the scene displaying your cards all at once. But the really savvy professional often has to play it like the old TV detective, *Columbo*. Try not to look too smart in the beginning because the other players are professionals, too. You first need to identify the players and then the play.

Setting: The Child Welfare System in a midwestern state.
Players: Six private child welfare agency directors, the director of the state agency, caseworkers and their supervisors, and a university evaluator of project outcomes.
The action:
Maurine was being interviewed for a new position as coordinator of a newly formed consortium for child welfare casework training, which was recently created with a major foundation grant. Six private agencies had been awarded a grant based on the idea that they would collaborate to provide training for new caseworkers. The state child welfare officials were concerned about high turnover among private agency caseworker new hires. One cause was lack of training, and this led private agency directors to seek another way to train them. The goals of the foundation grant were to provide training, study turnover and attempt to reduce it.

In the interview process there were staff members present who represented the six agencies plus the grant writer. Maurine was a candidate for coordinator since she was a seasoned facilitator with a long history of creating collaborations in human services and educational associations. She stated to the interviewers that she was not presenting herself as an expert in social work because she did not have that educational background or experience; her stated goal was to change the training system in child welfare. She noticed that the lead agency grant writer stared at her and looked rather grim. At first, she misread his face and intentions as disapproval, but later she learned that he was delighted with her presentation of her real credentials only. She got the job!

Not being an insider and wanting to assess the situation before designing her training program, Maurine asked herself an opening question—"What is the current training system for private agencies to train caseworkers?" She then issued an invitation to a panel of university experts and training directors to speak at a workshop to investigate the current status. Pretty quickly, her phone was ringing off the hook from agencies who wanted to send staff to the workshop. She eventually had to close off registration because the room would be too small to hold all the participants. What was causing all this excitement? It was just an assessment workshop!

On the day of the event there were two surprise (uninvited) visitors—the statewide agency director and his deputy director arrived unannounced. After the panel began speaking, it was apparent why these two important leaders had come. The answer to the question that the coordinator had raised was obvious—there was no training system in place for private agencies. Huge numbers of children were being taken into care and had overwhelmed the state agency. They handed off these cases in the thousands to agencies which had no capacity to train caseworkers. Turnover was high, and there were high-profile stories about neglect and abuse in the media. The two state officials had arrived to cover their own backs.

The facilitator had used the "Columbo" method of investigation by humbly asking questions and not assuming she knew the answers already. In doing so, she was able to *see the players and the play* right away. In addition, by the end of the day the entire group of attendees had participated in a community assessment of their training needs.

Lessons Learned:

- When entering a new situation, the wise facilitator will first notice and wonder (investigate and hypothesize) before taking any action.
- Starting off with a good question is a great way to begin.
- Humility will win friends among the other smart people you are working with. By respecting what they know as professionals, you can lead them to new understandings.

WHAT THIS TECHNIQUE IS ABOUT

This technique is about determining what is going on in the community, and who the people involved are. This information will help the facilitator and the change team find partners among other organizations and determine who are the beneficiaries of the change, who should be included from the community, and who is outside the community and should not be included (Flicker, Senturia, & Wong, 2006). Any strategies we use to make change happen will be more successful with an understanding of the community.

Within any county, city or town there are usually several overlapping groups, as shown in Figure 17.1. For instance, a professor at the local college may be a member of the education community, a member of the arts community when she participates in the local arts council classes, and a member of a faith community. She switches communities and roles as situations and tasks change. This dynamic can complicate our view of the players, while making it more accurate.

IDENTIFYING THE COMMUNITY, THEIR CULTURES AND VALUES

In our story, the explicit goal of the workshop was to assess the current private agency training for child welfare caseworkers before designing new training. The child welfare community included the six private child welfare agency directors, the director of the state agency, caseworkers, casework supervisors and a university evaluator of project outcomes. The workshop was also an opportunity for the coordinator to network and get to know the community members as well as their values and culture. The coordinator found during the workshop that this was not a community in the usual geographic sense; it was a community of interest spread across the state. During the workshop, she was able to observe the **players**: she could see the demographics and learn about some child welfare history within the state. While the panel was presenting, she was able to observe the values and culture of the community and find out who were the formal and informal community groups, subgroups and leaders. In addition, she learned about the **play**: Children were being taken into care by the state and an overwhelming number of cases were handed over to agencies which had no caseworker training.

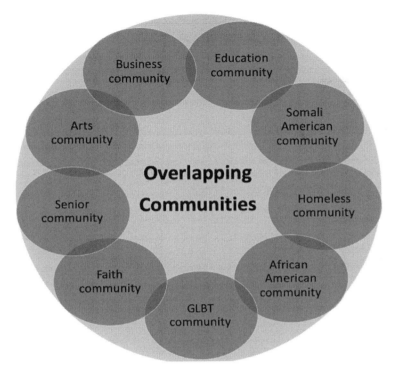

Figure 17.1 Overlapping communities.

Some things you might want to find out when conversing and networking include:

- How long have interviewees have been members of the community?
- How do they feel about the community?
- What do they think are some of this community's strengths?
- What are some improvements that could be made in the community?
- What makes them proud of their community?
- What can they tell you about the history of the community?
- What do they think lies in the future for the community?

> (adapted from the Center for Community Health and Development, n.d., https://ctb.ku.edu/en/table-of-contents/assessment/assessing-community-needs-and-resources/describe-the-community/tools)

Depending on the community needs and intended change, a change team and its partners might also want to identify some or all of the following:

- Community values and culture, including details of ethnic community values and culture.
- Demographics.
- History.
- Formal and informal leaders.
- Groups and subgroups.
- Physical community and infrastructure (roads, bridges, transportation, electricity, water, sewer and so on).

- Patterns of settlement, business, industry, institutions (such as schools, hospitals).
- Social services available.
- Economics, employment.
- Government, politics.
- Social structure.

This information is used as a *general* description of the community and provides a context for the change plan. The information provides sufficient familiarity with the community to allow informed conversations with community members and leaders, media, granting agencies and others. It also gives you context for planning. The change team will need to determine how to design strategies that are well suited to the community culture and values.

WHO NEEDS TO BE AWARE OF THE PLAN?

Target populations for the change are those who will benefit. They can be a good source of information, as well as partners that can help make the change happen. As shown in Figure 17.2, those beneficiaries directly affected by the change will first need to be aware of the change before they can accept and adopt it. In the story for this chapter, the direct beneficiaries of change were the case workers and indirectly, the children they work with. Other people that needed to be aware of the plan included stakeholders who might be helpful as change agents, such as school or public officials, parents, members of nonprofit organizations in the community and others. In the story, the private agency directors were stakeholders and change agents that would support the project.

Of those who need to be aware of the plan, you will want to identify who is needed to help implement it effectively. In the story, others that needed to be aware of the project to help implement it included private agency directors and the statewide agency director and deputy director. These people can bring the training to the awareness of the private caseworkers, support and encourage them as they undertake training and integrate it into their daily work.

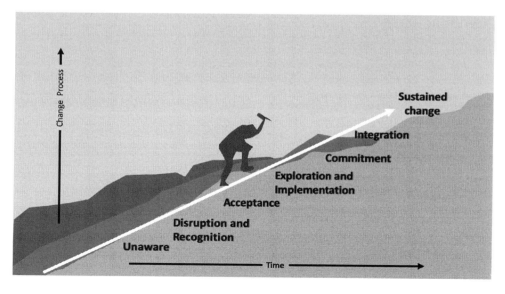

Figure 17.2 Steps in change adoption.

KEY MEMBERS

Identify key members of the community. Who can influence the people and the conditions that contribute to the problem or issue? These are the people or groups who can help address the issues your team is concerned about. These are sometimes, but not necessarily always, people currently in positions of power. They can also be empowered community members who can use their abilities to change the community for the better. Don't overlook retired people with a lifetime of skills and knowledge. These people might be good volunteers for your change effort, and they can assist in implementation efforts, such as making other people aware of the change or connecting your team to other organizations that can be useful partners.

WHO HAS INFLUENCE IN THE COMMUNITY?

Influence is the ability to have an effect on someone or something, including a community. Individuals, organizations and agencies can all influence community. An example would be a member of a committee considering buildings for a cold weather shelter for the homeless, who said, "Let me talk to a friend of mine who owns the old hotel building on Ninth Street. He might consider a proposal from us." As you network with them, find out about their sphere of influence. People with influence are empowered, often as a result of their current or past positions. These people may not currently be the elected or appointed leaders, but they often have many community connections, some of whom may be good contacts for you. Request an introduction because these people may also have knowledge or experience that is important to your change effort, and their opinion is widely respected. Ask your team who has been on the city council or school board or who puts together fundraisers, social activities or community showcases. These influencers can assist in implementation efforts, such as locating community resources and connecting your team to useful partners. This kind of influencer may also empower others to act on behalf of the planned change. There is another kind of influencer: a gatekeeper. This is someone who has the ability to control information or access to a decision maker or to information. Rather than helping you make connections they may be able to prevent contact. Get to know who they are and how to work with them.

Influencers can also be those with negative opinions that they are always willing to share. If these people are likely to resist the change, get them on board early, if you can. If you don't, they may work against you. If you do get them on board, they may contribute to making wise decisions on strategies because they can see the possible negative consequences to ideas.

WHO IS "OUTSIDE" THE COMMUNITY?

This part of your community description identifies where the change plan stops. While many of us would like to make the whole world a better place, it is not realistic. We need to define the community we will serve, including geographic or other boundaries. Because communities differ from each other, this helps simplify the planning process.

HOW TO GATHER THE INFORMATION

There are many methods of collecting this information in addition to the workshop in the story above. The data might be collected using:

- *Brainstorming*: With your change team, think about who needs to be aware of the plan, and who might be key community members with influence in the community. List people, nonprofit organizations and other organizations that are doing work in the area you are interested in. If there is a college or university nearby, include academics doing research and teaching in the discipline related to your interest.

- *Snowball networking and conversations*: Verify information from the brainstorm by talking to others in the community. When speaking to people, ask who else to contact to find out about the play and the players. In this way, your network can "snowball" or grow. This might include elected and appointed officials, clergy, police officials, school administrators and teachers, real estate agents, health professionals, beneficiaries of the proposed change and members of the community.
- *Windshield or walking surveys*: This method involves driving or walking around communities systematically observing community conditions to obtain objective information on the environment of the community, if that is part of the play. This is easier done in pairs, so one person is taking notes while the other person drives.
- *Public listening sessions*: Also called public forums or town meetings, these sessions engage community members, change agents or policy makers to share ideas.

IDENTIFYING THE PLAY

At this stage of the game, the facilitator needs to get some idea of *what is going on* in the community. If you are new to the area, three things you can do to get you started are to (1) scan local news, (2) attend meetings and (3) network and have conversations with local community members.

Look for local news media such as local radio stations or print or web news media and scan the information. When an issue concerns many people, you will want to look through comments to see the tenor of the posts. Also, you may find that there are several articles on the same topic over the course of the past year.

Attend open meetings such as local city council meetings, your congressional representative's "Town Hall" meetings and other meetings that may be relevant to your issue. Agendas for city councils meetings are often posted online at city web sites, so you can check to see when your topic will be discussed. If you intend to ask questions at the meeting, there is usually a time for this set aside on the agenda. Do your homework so you are well informed. At the meeting:

- Keep your question polite and brief, but avoid simple yes-or-no questions, or questions that require a commitment. Politicians, in particular, often resist making a commitment in a public forum.
- If you don't get to ask your question, stick around and speak to the representative or staff person.
- Bring business cards with your contact information to make it easier for the council person or representative to get back to you.
- If you heard someone express views similar to yours, network with them after the meeting. This is an opportunity to find out more about what is going on, locate potential partners or allies and add someone to your team.

THE COMMUNITY DESCRIPTION

Create a description of the community that you can use as a reference when talking to your team, community members, funders or the media. Don't stop there, though. Continue to gather information over time to hone and revise your description as your project continues and community changes. The description can take several forms, including graphs of data, photographs and written descriptions. Visual media can be persuasive when used to illustrate your points with policy makers, the media (newspapers, television or radio), social media and grant funders.

Following the *general description*, a change team will need to obtain *specific* assessment data (this will be covered in Chapter 18). In the story, the six private child welfare agencies were the partners that would assist with further specific data collection.

HOW TO CARRY OUT THIS TECHNIQUE

Create a general description of the affected community to use as a context for speaking with community members, media, grant funders and experts. Collect information about the community by using informal methods such as *snowball networking and conversations, windshield or walking surveys* and *public listening sessions*. Find out what people think of their community, including strengths, weaknesses, assets and problems. Use local data sources such as community web pages and news media. Attend meetings and network to find out about the *players*—key people in the community, economics, employment, government, politics—and the *play*—major issues in the community. Write up a general description of the community using words and other media such as photographs, tables and graphs.

TRY IT!

Imagine that you have been selected as a facilitator for a change initiative to create a welcoming community (see www.welcomingamerica.org) for new immigrants entering the town where you live or go to school now. Whether you have spent one year, 60 years or somewhere in the middle in a town, you never know it as well as you think. Create a general description including the play and the players, using the sources and methods described in this chapter. Use words, images (including tables and graphs, photographs or video) and, where relevant, audio recordings to tell your story. Be sure to include the following points:

- Who will be affected by your plan?
- Who are the key stakeholders?
- Who can affect whether it is successful or not?
- Who are members of your community, and what are their characteristics?
- Who are the influencers and gatekeepers?
- What organizations should you engage with?

SUMMARY

This chapter is about forming a general description of the community. An important step is to examine who will be affected by your plan, who the key stakeholders are and who can affect whether it is successful or not. Who is your community, and what are their characteristics? Who are the gatekeepers? What organizations should you engage with? In this chapter, you learned how to determine who needs to be aware of the plan and who is needed to help implement it effectively.

CITATIONS

Center for Community Health and Development. (n.d.). *Understanding and describing the community: Community description worksheet in Community Tool Box*. University of Kansas. Retrieved from https://ctb.ku.edu/en/table-of-contents/assessment/assessing-community-needs-and-resources/describe-the-community/tools

Flicker, S., Senturia, K., & Wong, K. (2006). Unit 2: Developing a CBPR partnership—Getting started. In *Developing and sustaining community-based participatory research partnerships: A skill-building curriculum*. The Examining Community-Institutional Partnerships for Prevention Research Group. Retrieved from www.cbprcurriculum.info

18 GETTING GROUNDED
Collecting Data Together

Figure 18.0

WHAT'S IN THIS CHAPTER?

Most likely your project is *local*, so the data should also be primarily local in scope. Much of the existing data and information is likely to be broader in scope. For instance, much of the data found by the prison library activists was national. To effectively measure progress of the initiative, they will need relevant and local information that is acceptable to the community. This chapter is about forming alliances or partnerships for data gathering for a community assessment and planning to address community needs.

Gathering local data is best done in partnership with the community. For instance, your organization, along with relevant community members and any external researchers you may have engaged, would work together, sharing expertise and decisions. This leads to joint ownership of solutions, and new knowledge and capacity-building. This process also leads to greater process knowledge as well as knowledge of the community issue and the results of community change efforts.

This approach is frequently used in public health, social work, education and psychology. It is generally called Community-Based *Participatory Research* (CBPR).

Objectives

By the end of this chapter, you will be able to:

- Describe the importance and principles of collecting data together.
- Identify research partners.
- Describe how to conduct participatory data gathering and evaluation.
- Share findings and decisions.

A STORY ABOUT DATA COLLECTION

The scene and demographics: located in a rural area, city of population 25,000 people, multicultural, diverse religious organizations, mixed race. A university is a major employer, city manager form of government, elected mayor is a volunteer.

Following several organizational meetings, the Homeless Coalition was getting up a head of steam and moving along the train track—Stage 1, Issue Awareness, and Stage 2, Socialization, had been accomplished, and now the teams were ready for Stage 3: Information Seeking. Mission clarification took quite a while because of different points of view on how to solve the problem, but finally the facilitator was able to help them agree on this mission statement:

Homeless Coalition's mission is to address issues of homelessness and poverty in our region.

After the initial visioning day, the facilitator had divided up the group of 15 volunteers into the five identified areas of interest. People could choose which team they wanted to join:

a. Knowledge and resources
b. Communication and advocacy
c. Emergency response
d. Long-term housing
e. Transportation

To keep the teams active and engaged, she challenged them to a 90-day sprint to the finish line. This technique was utilized to prevent the usual endless committee meetings that people find boring. The teams quickly became like racehorses competing to see who could get there fastest. But they needed some local data before they could even begin. The first questions they were always asked by community leaders and members were essentially these:

- How many homeless people live around here?
- Why can't we see them in large numbers?
- Who are they? Where are they living?
- What is the cause of their homelessness?
- How to count them?

As usual, perception forms our own reality, and there were different points of view on how to solve the problem of homelessness. For example, some teams saw the problem as a service-access issue where homeless people simply could not access services because of problems with transportation or because they were ignorant of the availability of the service. Others saw it through the lens of social injustice and racism. Some people even wanted to build tiny houses as a community for homeless people. Most of them felt that if you just fix the existing system, *then all shall be well.*

They all were basing their strategies for change on improving the existing service systems, and they considered themselves to be experts in their professional fields. However, they soon learned that homelessness is a *wicked problem* and that they were in for a longer search for answers than they had expected. A wicked problem is a form of social or cultural problem that is difficult to solve. In addition, all of the team members were socialized as middle class and had serious trouble translating their own life experience into the conditions lived by homeless people on the street.

The most pressing problems came from finding a way to count the homeless who were marginalized and not being served by the existing social service networks. There seemed to be an ever-changing landscape of homelessness. It was also difficult to define types of homeless people. Here is how they went about seeking answers to these urgent data questions.

- **Partnerships with community groups** such as the faith organizations, social services, public health, police and community activist groups led to alliances with the Coalition to study the problem.
- **National experts** on homelessness were consulted, and the promoters of the Tiny House Movement were invited to speak in public venues to educate the wider community.
- **Joint ownership of the problem was encouraged by seeking alliances** with the university, county health department, service agencies, Good Samaritan Homeless Shelter, the public library, faith communities and the police department. University Social Work interns were sponsored by the public library, and interns met homeless people who camped out in the library and networked them to existing social services.
- **Capacity building**—a Winter Outreach project was proposed to churches and city government to allow homeless people to stay overnight in church buildings in town. This idea was quickly rejected by the churches and the city government, who did not want homeless people hanging around town. Years later this idea was renewed when the location of the winter shelter would be placed in a trailer in an area where there was public housing. Location, location, location!
- **Knowledge sharing**—a Resource Guide was published in brochure form and distributed around the community.
- **Build process knowledge**—engaging with the homeless individuals and opening our eyes to the idea that they could become allies for changing community attitudes toward them.

Finally, the 90th day of our planning cycle came about, and the five teams were eager to present their findings to the whole group; but the facilitator threw a wrench into the works by asking them first to invite some homeless people to the meeting and allow them to speak first. The team leaders were very angry and said, "But WE are the experts!" They relented and offered one hour to listen to the homeless tell their stories. After that, the "experts" admitted that they really knew very little about what it means to be homeless. This proved to be a turning point, as homeless individuals were invited to join the teams and give a more realistic view of how they solve their problems.

LOCAL DATA COLLECTION

Another key leadership group that had been silent was the churches and other faith groups in the town. They engaged in charitable works like donating money or giving food to the homeless shelter, but it soon became apparent that most wanted to keep the homeless outside their doors. The facilitator engaged them at a group meeting of the Interfaith Council, asking them to reflect on this question: "What does it mean to be homeless in our region?" Stereotypes and biases were revealed, as well as feelings of guilt for not exhibiting true charity—like opening their doors to homeless people in frigid temperatures. PADS (Providing Advocacy, Dignity & Shelter) programs, which are commonly implemented by churches as temporary shelter in winter in urban environments, were rejected by the churches in this small rural area. Good Samaritan House, the shelter, which was started by the Interfaith Council two decades ago, was inadequate to meet the growing need, but the faith community had not caught up with these changing conditions.

The Homeless Coalition was now moving forward to find new solutions using local data gathering methods. By seeking new research partners with the university, especially the School of Social Work, they found a source for ongoing action research. University undergraduate social work students collected regional and national data from a variety of sources. Students were assigned in pairs to interview 15 homeless people and seek answers to their living conditions. These students then wrote papers, made presentations to the wider community and sent recommendations to the City Council.

External researchers were also engaged in projects such as the Civic Soul Project (a collaborative "town and gown" project between the local university and the town to create public discussions about important issues and make creative designs for social change) and a PhD doing his doctoral research on homelessness. By providing information in public programs, this research improved the climate for change since stereotyping of homeless individuals as grifters or bums was challenged by hard research data.

CONCLUSION

Getting detailed information about the shifting homeless population has been an ongoing problem. The studies done by social work students and the doctoral candidate were based on very small samples. Though illustrative of the problems experienced by homeless people, they did not produce enough significant data to answer these questions:

- How many homeless people live around here?
- Why can't we see them in large numbers?
- Who are they?
- Where are they living?

The next step would be to press for more demographic data from Good Samaritan House, where people come to eat at the soup kitchen daily. Volunteers at the soup kitchen can ask those who come for a meal where they are living. With this additional data, a more comprehensive picture will emerge over time about how many homeless people are in the area. It is difficult to take a complete census of people experiencing homelessness, where they are living and why they are homeless without a home address. People are living on the street and in the surrounding wooded areas.

WHAT THIS TECHNIQUE IS ABOUT

Community-based participatory data collection is an approach in which your team partners with other groups in the community, including the affected people, to gather local data about the issue in order to address it.

WHY COLLABORATE?

Most of us have heard that "many hands make light work," but collaboration can do much more. With partners and allies we can reduce duplication of effort and accomplish more with our limited resources than any group can accomplish on their own (Hacker, 2013). Sharing information, risks and rewards also increases the impact in the community. By pooling talents and skills of each partnership group, there is a greater skill set to work with (Horowitz et al., 2009). Through the process of sharing in the work, the skills and knowledge of each partner can grow, including knowledge of the partnership process. Creativity of a group of partners is greater because of the diversity of perspectives. Collaboration can increase the number of ideas generated and the speed with which those ideas are refined. Collaboration also expands the number of social connections the group can tap to help implement a community change. Finally, it can increase the energy to overcome resistance.

What factors lead to effective collaborations? Mattesich, Murray-Close and Monsey (2001) found that effective collaborations require six things (Figure 18.1): the right membership, a sense of purpose,

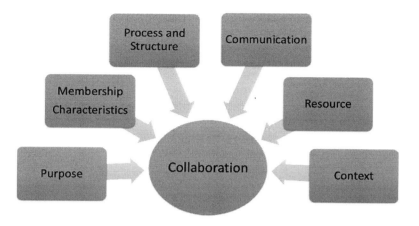

Figure 18.1 Six factors leading to effective collaborations.

resources, effective communication, a process and structure that works for the group and a favorable context.

Several years ago, Jeanne collected data as part of a team: it was an interfaith coalition effort to assess the community context and determine the greatest needs in the community using Community-Based Participatory Research. Several organizations were involved in the collaboration. These organizations had formed partnerships and created processes and structures that made the assessment run smoothly. The organizations recruited members with a diversity of skills needed to make the process effective, such as research (methods and statistics), communications (media relations, writing, social media, photography), community organizing and public health. Volunteers for the assessments and evaluations were trained and understood the purpose and how to collect the research.

They went into the neighborhoods in teams of two one Saturday morning and surveyed our community. The team found that economic and racial justice was high on the list of concerns across the board. Community meetings were announced, and this information was shared at meetings across town. Feedback from the community was collected on proposed projects to begin to address community concerns. So effective was the collaboration that it now extends statewide and is involved in health projects, affordable childcare and immigrant assistance, to name a few causes.

PRINCIPLES OF COLLECTING DATA TOGETHER

This approach to data collection or research includes the following principles:

- The approach recognizes *community identity*. Communities might be geographic, like neighborhoods, or dispersed like professional associations. What makes them communities are the emotional connections, shared norms, values and needs that members attempt to meet.
- *Builds on community strengths* and resources (Hacker et al., 2012). Resources might include knowledge, skills and assets of individual members, or groups, such as faith-based organizations. The social connections among members is also a resource.
- Focuses on *relevant local issues* and context to sort out the multiple contributing factors (such as the social, economic, cultural, geographical and climate factors) to the issues of concern.
- Commits to *long-term sustainability* of the process, partnerships and solutions.

- Promotes *equitable partnerships* that collaborate effectively, share power and empower all partners.
- Facilitates *partners' mutual capacity-building* (knowledge and skills) while collecting data and sharing decision-making.
- Partners collaborate to *share findings* with the broader community.

ACQUIRING RESEARCH PARTNERS

Using the general description written for your community, their cultures and values (Chapter 17), you are ready to get specific information about your concerns. To find and bring the right collaborators to the table to help you do this, the first place to begin is to:

- Determine who is needed to help effectively implement community data collection and create a change plan.
- Determine which individuals, agencies or organizations have influence in the community and what their sphere of influence is.
- Determine if key members are community residents or if they work for community-based organizations.
- Identify who the individuals or community-based organizations represent or report to.
- Identify who has the time, resources and flexibility to attend partnership meetings and take responsibility for action items.
- Identify who is defined as "outside" the community and should not be invited to participate (Flicker, Senturia, & Wong, 2006).

You will want a diverse group of partners in terms of in terms of "ethnicity, race, gender, social class, role, organizational or institutional affiliation, academic discipline, expertise, and role in the partnership" (Flicker et al., 2006, p. 35). Using the general community description, your group should brainstorm potential partners. A useful resource to use in this endeavor is *United Way's 211 Information and Referral System*, which contains information on nonprofit organizations for many communities. It might be necessary to do some research to find out if the agency, academic department or nonprofit organization has a mission conducive to a partnership with you, and if a partnership would benefit both partners. What can a partner provide, and how will they benefit? If it appears to be a good match, you (or someone on your team with a connection to that group, agency or organization) will contact the group and request a time to meet.

When contacting the potential partner, you will introduce yourself and the reason for the request for a face-to-face meeting. In Chapter 5 we mentioned writing a description of the community issue used to invite people to the first meeting. Similarly, you will want a brief description of the *partnership* to collect information on the community issue that explains the idea so that the listener can comprehend it in 30 seconds to a minute. Be sure to list ways in which each partner will benefit. If you had a referral from someone, you might mention their name if you think that might provide greater credibility for your invitation to collaborate.

Why a *face-to-face* meeting? Much of the meaning we derive from communication comes from body language and tone of voice, as well as words (Mehrabian, 1981). If all we have is email or telephone, we may be missing out on 55% of the message. Any collaboration requires trust and communication to work together effectively, so unless you already know your potential partner, you will want to have all the tools of communication to build the trust necessary for good collaboration. Be well prepared for the meeting, so you can act naturally.

Eye contact is a powerful part of body language, and you will want to meet their gaze more than half of the time throughout the conversation. When you first meet and greet them, meet their gaze for a few seconds, and then look away as you check your notes. This gives them a few seconds to look at the rest of your body language. Begin the conversation with some small talk looking for commonalities, and set your potential partner at ease, but don't spend so much time that they feel like it is a waste of time. The tone of your voice should be natural and not too rushed.

Transition to the purpose of the meeting by reiterating the project description and how each partner might benefit from participation. Your goal is to find out if their organization would be a good partner. Ask questions in a conversational way. Find out:

1. Some *background* about their work and issues that concern them.
2. Find out if they have any *experience with partnerships*. What was the experience like? If they have not participated in a partnership, ask what their approach would be.
3. Ask if they have an *interest* in working on such a partnership. Spend a few minutes exploring how both partners would benefit (Palermo et al., 2006).
4. Would they have *time to work on such a partnership*, including trust building among partners, seeking funding, creating infrastructure, doing the data collection and sharing the results with the community. They might also want to participate in planning, implementing and evaluating a project.

You want to bring together collaborators from across the community who will bring a diversity of skills and perspectives to the table and work well together. To work together, each of the members need to exhibit respect and trust toward other members and be able to compromise because they believe that collaboration is worth the potential costs (such as lost "turf") because the benefits will outweigh the costs (Linden, 2002).

SUSTAINING PARTNERSHIPS

Once you have the right membership, you will need a to agree to the purpose of the collaboration, a process and structure that works for the group (Mattesich et al., 2001).

The *purpose or vision of the collaboration* needs to be clear to and shared by all members, and unique from the purpose and goals of any of the participating organizations. Goals and objectives need to be concrete, measurable and achievable. (More about objectives will be covered in Chapter 21.) Each of the individual and organizational members have a stake and a sense of ownership in the vision and outcomes of the project.

The *process and structure* should be clear but remain flexible so that it can adapt to major changes in conditions, members and goals. Roles, responsibilities and policies should be developed jointly by members. In addition, multiple levels of organizations in each of the organizations should be involved in decision-making.

Sustaining partnerships begin with well-organized processes and structures that eliminate duplication of effort. In addition, open communication among partners and the community instills and helps maintain trust (Giachello et al., 2007). Another key is small but early individual or group successes and the satisfaction that comes with them. These successes motivate continuing on in the partnership until the larger successes roll in. Finally, when successes are *not* rolling in, there needs to be a reassessment and flexibility to adapt to changes and find new strategies that will be effective.

Other things needed for a successful collaboration include funding, a facilitator, good communication and a beneficial context.

Two key resources are *funding* and a *skilled facilitator*. The funding needs to be sufficient and consistent. While a grant may function as seed money to get the project started, funding must become self-sustaining over time. The facilitator needs interpersonal skills, organizing skills and a sense of ethics that all members regard as fair to all.

Effective *communication* is open and frequent, both within the group, and with stakeholders outside of the group. Formal communication plans should be documented so that they are implemented, but there should also be informal communication among group members.

Context includes a favorable social or political environment, a history of successful collaborations and the perceptions that the members of the collaborative are leaders in the community. An example is the Academy for Co-Teaching & Collaboration, which began with collaboration between a university and area school districts. The collaborators were viewed as leaders both locally, and eventually, nationally. Fifteen years after it began, the collaboration is still going strong, and three national conferences have been held to share ideas, methods and successes.

CONDUCTING PARTICIPATORY DATA GATHERING AND EVALUATION

To begin, locate and use local data, rather than reinvent the wheel by collecting data that is already publicly available. Local data may come from a mixture of local, county, state and federal data sources. These can include the following:

- The local municipality may be able to provide details on plans for area development. If the municipality has an updated comprehensive plan, it may be able to provide fairly accurate details on population characteristics, employment sectors and status, identified problems and plans to develop the area. It also is likely to provide citations and links to the sources of the data.
- State education websites can provide enrollment figures, gender and student performance.
- Hospitals may be able to provide data on admissions and health problems of the community.
- Local faith-based, non-governmental and government agencies may have recent studies conducted in the community.
- The municipal and county police may be able to provide crime statistics.
- The state government website may be able to provide numbers of registered voters by municipality
- The website of the U.S. Census Bureau from the last population census for the local area has details about the local area population. Detailed demographics for the local area can be found at the American Community Survey: census.gov/programs-surveys/acs. This data includes:

Age	Health insurance coverage
Housing	Income
Ancestry	Occupation
Work commute	Language spoken at home
Computer use	Marital status
Disability	Citizenship
Educational attainment	Race
Employment	School enrollment
Family	Gender
Fertility	Vehicles available
Food stamps benefit	Veteran status
	And other questions

DATA COLLECTION

Once you have exhausted sources of extant data, you can determine the data that remains to be collected. Information is collected about the facts that will influence decisions. This might include data that can help you to:

- Identify and define the community you seek to engage (defining the community was covered in Chapter 16)
- Learn about the community's culture and norms
- Identify possible additional partners

Even if you have a partner that is an expert researcher, all partners should share in the data collection. Any methodology that is appropriate to the issue and community can be used. Since those collecting data may not be professional researchers, the selected data collection methods need to be clear and easy to use. Provide training to all collecting data using interviews or observations so that all questions are asked in the same way or all observations are noted the same way. You might use:

- *Surveys*: Studies of communities using online or paper and pencil methods to gather data on needs, attitudes, impressions, opinions, etc., by polling a section of the population.
- *Photovoice*: A form of participatory research using video or photography and verbal (transcribed) accounts. It is especially useful where homelessness, poverty, language, culture or other circumstances become barriers to using language to collect data such as surveys or interviews.
- *Interviews*: A structured verbal conversation where questions are asked and answers are given to gather data on needs, attitudes, impressions, opinions, etc. Interviews may be completed face-to-face, on the telephone or using videoconferencing. Be sure to include key people in the community.
- *Focus groups*: group interviews of a small number of people whose responses to questions (such as a community's needs) is studied to determine the response that can be expected from a larger population. Participants can generate many ideas through interaction of group members.
- *Windshield or walking surveys*: driving or walking around communities systematically observing community conditions to obtain objective information. These should use observation checklists (for evaluating behaviors and things, like community parks, buildings, etc.)
- Other types of data collection:
    - Quantitative (numerical data analyzed using mathematical and statistical methods).
    - Qualitative methods such as reporting on community meeting results, especially when attendees discussed their priorities, preferences, etc.

If you plan to go door to door to do data collection, check with city administrators to make sure it is not illegal in the community. Also check on safety in the areas where you plan to collect data. Even when it is considered safe, it is best to go in pairs.

It is important that the process of data collection be shared among the partners as well as the data. In addition, once the data has been collected, interpreting what the numbers mean should be a shared process. More details on data collection can be found in Appendix E, and information on data analysis and interpretation in Appendix F.

What data are we collecting, and when? Generally, there are at least three times when data is collected, as seen in Figure 18.2: when the team gathers information on the strengths and resources of the community, when data is gathered on the current state (where we are now) and when data is gathered after the plan is implemented, to monitor the process and outcomes (where we want to be). The team may also evaluate the effectiveness of the partnerships as part of monitoring the process.

SHARING FINDINGS AND DECISIONS WITH THE TEAM

After collecting the data, your team will need to interpret what the data means. Your task is to take the data, analyze it and turn it into knowledge that can be used by the change team to improve the well-being of community members. You will also need to report the data to the team and community factually and accurately; but then you will need to explain what it means, and what you still don't know, and then make recommendations for action and for further research.

Numerical information may be persuasive, may be credible and can be analyzed using *statistical methods*. While some people shy away from statistics, they are very useful. If you're familiar with statistics and statistical procedures, and you have the resources in computer software and time, it's likely that you'll be able to do a formal study, using standard statistical procedures. On the other hand, analysis and interpretation is often best done as a team effort. Analysis of surveys may be possible for capable

Figure 18.2 Main data collection points in the change process.

novices, but if you are analyzing to predict or test hypotheses, it is useful to have skilled researchers such as academics or university graduate students in appropriate disciplines on your change team to assist with this process.

Many web-based survey services and university research offices will do some calculations for faculty and students, but it is important to understand what the statistical formulas will do and what the results mean. Even if a university researcher is on your change team or is a team partner, an understanding of quantitative and qualitative data analysis and interpretation will help you converse intelligently with them and understand why they interpret the results the way they do.

The process looks like this (shown in Figure 18.3):

1. *Study the data carefully*, using multiple ways of representing the data such as histograms, stem and leaf displays, bar or line graphs or tables. See Appendix E in eResources for detailed information on representing and analyzing data.
2. *Examine data from multiple perspectives*. Do you detect any patterns? Are they what you expect, or is there any deviation from the expected information? Do any of the patterns suggest that additional data needs to be collected? Would you find anything interesting if you separated the data into component parts?

Figure 18.3 Analysis and interpretation process.

3. *Daydream* and give it some time to percolate in the back of your mind. Don't rush this process. Insights about the meaning of the data may take more than two weeks to come to you.
4. Consider *alternative interpretations* of the data when trying to determine what it means.
5. *Evaluate* your findings. More on this process can be found in Appendix F, online.

SHARING THE FINDINGS WITH THE COMMUNITY

Plan and conduct a meeting to gain community feedback on your findings. This meeting will allow your change team to acquire community member feedback on priorities and preferences so that you can use your limited resources in the best possible way. Sharing the findings locally through meetings and local media to inform the community is fundamentally just and fair to all subjects and community members who participated or will be affected by the changes.

For academic partners, the study may be written and submitted to research journals. These methods of dissemination can lead to enhanced usefulness of the findings for each of the partners. In addition, community and academic partners may gain knowledge and proficiency through collaborative presenting and writing.

HOW TO CARRY OUT THIS TECHNIQUE

To carry out community-based participatory research, your team will need to obtain research partners to collaborate with. Together your team will identify the *purpose* of the research, what members need to be on the collaborative team and what knowledge, skills and contacts you need to be successful. Once you have invited these people or organizations to join, together you will lay out processes and structures necessary for effective work together, and you will decide how the group will communicate with the community and what resources are available, apply for grants (more information on grants and resources are available in Chapter 22) and determine what context is necessary for success.

Examine local data that are already available, and then use what you have learned to select your data collection method and create questions. Recruit and train community volunteers to assist with the data collection. Conduct data gathering to identify and define the community and their norms and values, and then analyze the data. Share the findings with the team so that together you can interpret and evaluate the findings. As a team, decide how you will communicate the findings with community members. You might use local media (newspapers, radio, television, social media) to invite community members to community meetings where you obtain their feedback on possible responses.

TRY IT!

Imagine that your community is a midsized town (about 60,000) located in the Midwest. It has been mostly homogeneous since the 1950s, with the exception of some diversity among the faculty and staff from the local university. Suddenly, your community has had an influx of immigrants, mostly from two African countries. The tension in the community high schools has ignited concern among a group of citizens.

1. Outline the steps you would take to carry out community-based participatory research to determine citizen concerns and priorities.
2. Who does your team need to collaborate with, and what skills do they need?
3. Keep in mind that volunteers will need to go to African neighborhoods that have different norms and values from each other. What skills should be included in volunteer training?
4. Through what methods will you collect data? How will it be analyzed and interpreted?
5. What information will you hope to find?
6. How will you share findings with the community?

SUMMARY

Because your projects are usually *local*, the data should also be local. To effectively plan and measure progress of the initiative, you will need relevant local information. This chapter covered forming partnerships to carry out data gathering for a community assessment and planning to address community needs. Partners and community members work together, sharing expertise and decisions. This leads to joint ownership of information, solutions, and new knowledge and capacity building. This process also leads to greater knowledge of the community issue and process knowledge as well.

RESOURCES

United Way's 2–1–1 Information and Referral Service, www.211.org/ ·
This web site contains information on nonprofit organizations for many communities.

CITATIONS

Flicker, S., Senturia, K., & Wong, K. (2006). Unit 2: Developing a CBPR partnership—Getting started. In *Developing and sustaining community-based participatory research partnerships: A skill-building curriculum*. The Examining Community-Institutional Partnerships for Prevention Research Group. Retrieved from https://ccph.memberclicks.net/assets/Documents/PapersReports/cbprcurriculum.pdf

Giachello, A. L. (author); Ashton, D., Kyler, P., Rodriguez, E. S., Shanker, R., & Umemoto, A. (Eds.). (2007). *Making community partnerships work: A toolkit*. White Plains, NY: March of Dimes Foundation. Retrieved from www.aapcho.org/wp/wp-content/uploads/2012/02/Giachello-MakingCommunityPartnershipsWorkToolkit.pdf

Hacker, K. A. (2013). *Community-based participatory research*. Thousand Oaks, CA: Sage Publications.

Hacker, K. A., Tendulkar, S. A., Bhuiya, N., Rideout, C., Trinh-Shevrin, C., Savage, C. P., . . . DiGirolamo, A. (2012). Community capacity building and sustainability: Outcomes of community-based participatory research. *Progress in Community Health Partnerships: Research, Education, and Action, 6*(3), 349–360. doi:10.1353/cpr.2012.0048

Horowitz, C. R., Robinson, M., & Seifer, S. (2009). Community-based participatory research from the margin to the mainstream: Are researchers prepared? *Circulation, 119*, 2633–2642. doi:10.1161/CIRCULATIONAHA.107.729863

Linden, R. M. (2002). *Working across boundaries: Making collaboration work in government and nonprofit organizations* (1st ed.). San Francisco, CA: Jossey-Bass.

Mattesich, P., Murray-Close, M., & Monsey, B. (2001). *Collaboration: What makes it work: A review of research literature on factors influencing successful collaboration*. Saint Paul, MN: Amherst H. Wilder Foundation.

Mehrabian, A. (1981). *Silent messages: Implicit communication of emotions and attitudes*. Belmont, CA: Wadsworth.

Palermo, A., McGranaghan, R., & Travers, R., (2006). Unit 3: Developing a CBPR partnership—Creating the "glue." In *Developing and sustaining community-based participatory research partnerships: A skill-building curriculum* (pp. 51–77). The Examining Community-Institutional Partnerships for Prevention Research Group. Retrieved from https://ccph.memberclicks.net/assets/Documents/Papers-Reports/cbprcurriculum.pdf

STAGE 4
Facilitation of Planning

The aim for you, as a facilitator, is to help groups get from where they are now to their desired condition. This stage will focus on techniques you can offer to help them use the information they have gathered to identify strategies that will help them move from current conditions (where they are now) to their desired outcomes (where they want to be).

In Stage 4 we will cover:

- Planning for change.
- Strategies and tactics.
- Fundraising plans.
- Effective learning objectives.
- Building alliances and collaboration.

Figure S4.0 Facilitation of Change Model Stage 4: Facilitation of Planning.

- Choreography of conversation.
- Setting the stage for productive meetings.
- Listening deeply.
- Observing the action.
- Asking good questions.
- What to do when things fall apart.

GETTING STARTED ON PLANNING FOR CHANGE

19

Figure 19.0

WHAT'S IN THIS CHAPTER?

Planning the actions that will get the team to their desired outcomes involves using the research your team has already done to select appropriate and realistic strategies and to create a plan of action, including specific tactics for implementation and measurements to determine if your team is achieving their objectives. As facilitator, you will guide your team through reviewing their research, doing a SWOT analysis and then selecting strategies and tactics.

Objectives

By the end of this chapter, you will be able to:

- Use your research as basis for planning strategies.
- Complete a SWOT analysis for your project.
- Describe two sources of design.
- Describe contents of a change plan.

A STORY: CONVERSATION FOR RACE UNITY

This story is set in a small midwestern college town, which has a diverse population of ethnicity and race, poised on the geographic border between the North and the South, On the northeast side of the city lives a residential community of mostly African Americans among 30 Black Christian churches. However, in the same locale there is also a large mosque with a diverse congregation drawn from Middle Eastern countries, those bordering the Mediterranean Sea, and some African American Muslims. It is not easy to explain the demographics of this border town by simply calling it Southern culture. Looking back at the town's not-so-distant history during the post-Civil War years, trains would stop at the downtown station to attach a Jim Crow car before moving south to Memphis. Racial tensions are still very evident in the layout of the city streets, thus isolating the racially segregated Black residential section. Few people, except for the Muslims, choose to cross this invisible racial barrier. However, some people have been attempting to make some changes in the town's culture by using a simple strategy of fostering interracial conversation.

Conversations about race are often mine fields which are usually avoided by not crossing the color line. "Whites" and "Blacks" mostly inhabit different social spaces. However, there was one brave woman in this town named Fern, an African American and a follower of the Baha'i faith, who wanted to propose a different idea for a change. She was intent on moving the whole community into a more sincere and direct conversation about race. This was not just a gesture of friendliness on her part; for Fern it was a matter of life and death unless the racial conversation could change. A few years before, Fern had received news of an incident in which her brother was confronted by the local police for having a weapon in his possession. When he was faced with officers with guns pointed at him, he calmed them down and informed them that he was an off-duty state trooper and authorized to carry a gun. But this was a tense and dangerous moment, like so many others, and Fern knew he could have been killed before the truth came out. They both wondered how the officers would have treated him if he had been White. So, she decided to ask her Baha'i community members to help her do something about it.

The Baha'i Community of Southern Illinois had heard about *Racial Taboo*, a film and discussion project that had been meeting for a year in a nearby community in Kentucky, which was initiated by another Baha'i community in Paducah. Fern reached out to them for advice and ideas for showing the film in her town. They offered to help her get started. Then Fern created an event and invited mainly African American leaders from the university, Christian churches and racial justice activists to a film preview at the public library, hoping to engage them in a common cause. Their cynical comments were: "We already know this," "This is not going to change anything," "We don't need to build friendships, we need justice or action." Fern was hurt and deeply disappointed by their resistant attitudes and was on the verge of giving up the idea. However, three community members asked to join with the Baha'i members to help them try again. A facilitator who volunteered her skills and the public library director offered her continued support. A Muslim woman also joined in, since the mosque was concerned with racial issues in their neighborhood. They decided to try again with this new group of allies.

The core organizers began by holding weekly potluck dinners at Fern's home with members of the Paducah Racial Taboo group. Based on their successful experience at creating and sustaining an interracial dialogue, they offered advice and kind support for the fledgling group. Bonding of the new group occurred over these intimate dinners that included times of prayer and reflection. Both food and prayer carried them through the rough road ahead toward getting the project off the ground.

Meanwhile, Scott, one of the Baha'i group leaders, began attending the monthly meetings of the Human Relations Commission (HRC), a body sponsored by city government. When he introduced the idea of holding respectful racial dialogues in the community to them, they were cautious at first. Then Eric, a White HRC member, began attending some of the core organizational meetings to learn more. When the idea came up later seeking an approval from the Commission, Eric challenged his fellow board members, saying, "If we don't do this [support the dialogues] we should be ashamed of ourselves." They unanimously endorsed the project, and Eric became a key contact between the Human Relations Commission and the Race Unity Group.

To jump-start the project, a second film preview was scheduled at the public library to which they invited a different leadership group. Seventy people showed up. The film was received with great enthusiasm. Based on the positive response, a community-wide film viewing of *Racial Taboo* was scheduled for the week following the annual Martin Luther King celebration. The film event, held at a community theater, was a sold-out event with 150 people attending, and some had to be turned away. After watching the film, there were facilitated discussion groups of 10 people each that met to discuss the film's content. It was announced that there would be a follow-up series of films about Black history shown weekly at other community locations to continue the conversation. The first venue was the Boys and Girls Club, which was chosen as one of the most racially integrated locations in town. Thirty people of all ages and races attended the first meeting. Later, the group met for five weeks at the African American Museum. At the close of the film series, a social event was offered by the Muslim community inviting the Race Unity Group to a potluck meal at the mosque called A Taste of Home. Each person brought a special dish and a cultural story to share. Some of the Muslims who hosted the event were also African Americans, including the Imam. Stereotypes were being broken, and a cross racial community was forming.

The focus and clear intention of the Race Unity Group was to change conditions and fixed attitudes toward race in the town. By using the film as a tool to open up a conversation, new situations were created in which every person's perspective became important for understanding and changing these conditions.

There were some identifiable steps that were taken toward reaching their goal of racial unity:

Step 1: Seeking Allies for Awareness-Building and Information-Sharing

New allies were forming into deeper relationships through *personal emissary work*. By joining with other civic groups in a common bond they were successful in forwarding the film project. Some examples are the Human Relations Commission, Public Library staff, African American Museum, Boys and Girls Club, MLK Celebration Committee and later the police department.

> *Personal emissary work*: An individual working on behalf of the project by personally taking messages, taking part in discussions, inviting stakeholders to meetings, requesting information and so on.

Step 2: Networking for Organizational and Community Resources

The African American Museum provided a safe environment for viewing the Black history film series. The content of the film was eye opening and disturbing for all viewers, both Black and White, about the American history they had never been taught. An added benefit was increasing the visibility of the museum and its educational resources to the wider community.

Step 3: Cooperative Creation of New Resources

As the project progressed, the name of the discussion was changed to "Continuing the Conversation," and the location moved to a Catholic student center on the university campus and later to the police department. Many new people joined the group and learned about a new way of listening reflectively to the stories told around the circle using a talking feather. The conversation deepened as more truth was being revealed about the difficulty of being Black in America. New friendships formed among different groups of people who before had very little meaningful contact with one another. The long-range, big-picture change was coming.

Lessons Learned:

- Because this had never been done before in this town, there was no prescribed structure to follow.
- Faith-based social action happens when people of faith work together, often with others outside their faith community, in order to achieve real and positive change within their local community, or in wider society.
- Reaching out beyond your comfort zone to engage personally with others can bring surprising results to any change process. Numbers of people affected by the conditions that are of concern can directly benefit.

WHAT THESE TECHNIQUES ARE ABOUT

The scope and time frame of the change you are planning may require that your planning process may be short range, or it may take longer and be more complex. This chapter will focus on long-range, big-picture plans (see Figure 19.1) that create transformational community change.

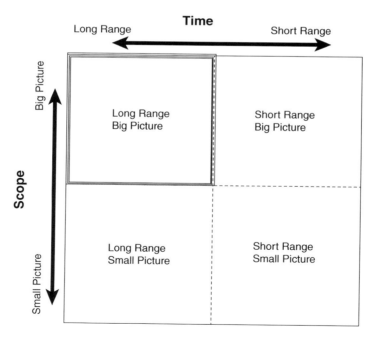

Figure 19.1 Planning perspectives.
Source: Adapted from Lofquist (1996, p. 6).

REVIEW YOUR RESEARCH

As Bernie Jones says, "planning is nothing more than systematically thinking through a situation in order to come up with a better decision" (1990, p. 1). Before you begin planning, you will want to review the situation as it currently stands, including the research your team has done so far. Examine your team's *spectrum of attitudes* toward others, in particular, to those who will benefit from the project. If your team views the beneficiaries as resources, now is an important time to involve them. Will their observations be included in planning the strategies for creating change? If so, invite them to the planning meetings, or hold listening sessions to obtain their perspectives. In the case of people such as the elderly, homeless or those with disabilities, it may be necessary to arrange for transportation. If this change involves women, they may need childcare arrangements for the meeting. Review your *vision* and your analysis of *what's happening now* with the symptoms and possible causes and the goals your team has set, along with indicators.

SWOT ANALYSIS

Using your vision and goals as your focus, do a SWOT analysis as a way of exploring both your current situation and possible strategies for accomplishing your goals. SWOT is an acronym for Strengths, Weaknesses, Opportunities and Threats (Jones, 1990). The matrix, shown in Figure 19.2, helps your team think about factors that are internal to your organization or community and external to your organization.

Internal factors might include the organization's people (staff and volunteers), their physical environment, financial resources such as access to money or in-kind donations (i.e., donations of the goods and

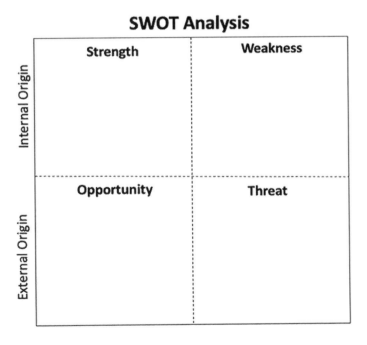

Figure 19.2 SWOT matrix.

services themselves rather than money to purchase them), the organization's experiences with similar projects and the processes used to accomplish organization goals. If any of these factors are strengths that can apply to the current project, list them under strengths. The same process applies for weaknesses (David & David, 2016). Be sure to include the perspectives of relevant people outside the group.

External factors are those outside the organization that are not under your control but still need to be considered. For instance, a community may notice a shift in demographics such as new immigrants settling in the area. This is a trend that is anticipated or actually taking place that may affect the current project. The team also needs to consider the economy, funding sources such as grants from foundations and possible or actual donors. The physical environment in the community may affect the project, as does legislation and regulations. Finally, local, regional, national, and international events might affect the project, and should be listed as opportunities or threats.

In Chapter 13 we discussed community *change readiness* and *resistance*. Use the data obtained from your community survey on *change readiness* to add this factor to your SWOT matrix. Finally, consider the *Force Field Analysis* factors (Chapter 16) for and against change. These factors and any other important information gathered during your community data collection should also be part of the SWOT analysis.

Use the completed SWOT matrix to identify the issues or problems you need to address or change to accomplish your goals, and then create your action plan. A SWOT analysis for the Conversation for Race Unity is found in Figure 19.3.

Race Unity SWOT Analysis

Internal Origin

Strength	Weakness
• Personal emissary work • Local faith-based leaders involved • Civic groups' interest • Support of Human Rights Commission • Effective networking • Funding available	• Initial disinterest of African American clergy • Community readiness appears low

External Origin

Opportunity	Threat
• Guidance of Paducah Racial Taboo group • Lack of existing structure allowed responsiveness and creativity • Positive response from university faculty and students who were African American	• Historical and present racial tensions of local area • Fixed attitudes toward race • Little racial mixing/socializing

Figure 19.3 SWOT analysis for conversation for race unity.

Use the factors identified in the SWOT analysis to brainstorm strategies for reaching the team's desired outcome. One approach is to match the strengths to opportunities. Another strategy is to reshape weaknesses or threats into strengths or opportunities. In this chapter's story, the team changed the weakness of the African American clergy's disinterest to an opportunity by finding a new audience among the African American university faculty and students.

PERSPECTIVES, PARADIGMS AND SOURCES OF DESIGN

Before setting off to write your plans, it is useful to acknowledge pressures that may shape your plan. There are many forces that can affect the design of change strategies (see Figure 19.4). These forces relate to the nature of an organization, its work, leadership and funding. For instance, an organization that must comply with laws and regulations related to child welfare, medicine and similar fields will find pressure to "go by the book" within a prescribed structure. On the other hand, in a crisis situation, there may be pressure to respond creatively to changing conditions and use a developmental process.

Both sets of pressures have benefits and drawbacks (see Figure 19.5). The prescribed structure is based on historical experience and accomplishments. However, it is guided by caution and may be unable to respond to evolving conditions. The developmental process may overlook experience of the past but may be more flexible and responsive. You may find a hint of these pressures showing up in the threats and

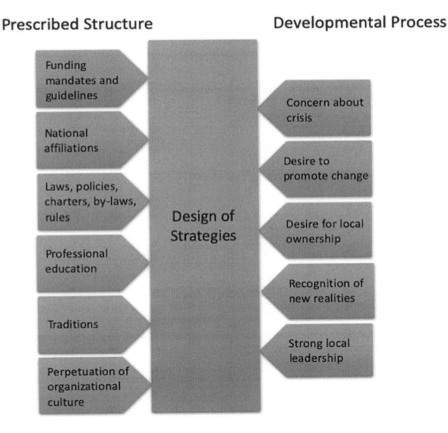

Figure 19.4 Design of change strategies.

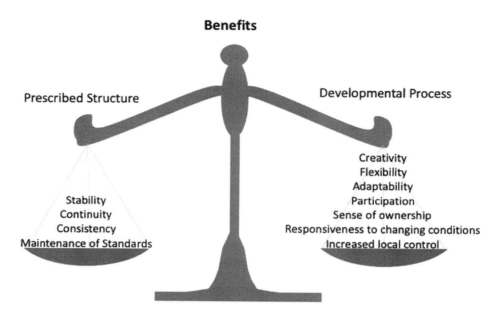

Figure 19.5 Benefits of approaches to design of change strategies.

opportunities of your SWOT analysis. It is useful to write down the pressures specifically, so they don't get overlooked.

PLANNING CHANGE STRATEGIES AND TACTICS

A *big-picture, long-range* change plan includes all of the following parts:

- Planning to manage resistance, motivate supporters and increase readiness (see Chapter 13).
- Developing a plan or interventions.
- Developing a fundraising plan. (Fundraising is covered in Chapter 22.)
- Planning implementation processes and training.
- Planning to sustain momentum.
- Evaluation plan.
- Planning to sustain change.

It is helpful to the change team and anyone else who will be involved in implementing the plans to document them in writing so that all actions can be coordinated.

HOW TO CARRY OUT THESE TECHNIQUES

A review of your research may help you determine the scope and time frame of the change you are planning. Determine if the scope is a big- or little-picture change and if it is a long- or short-range change.

Conduct a SWOT analysis. Use the data obtained from your community survey on *change readiness* to add the level of community change readiness to your SWOT matrix. Internal factors can include:
- The organization's people.
- The organization's physical environment.
- The organization's financial resources.
- The organization's experiences with similar projects.
- The processes used to accomplish organization's goals.

External factors can include:
- Trends: now and into the future in your community, whether state, national or international.
- The local economy.
- Funding sources (foundations, donors, legislatures).
- Demographics.
- The physical environment.
- Legislation and regulations.
- Local, national or international events.

Consider the Force Field Analysis factors for and against change and use those to determine Strengths, Weaknesses, Opportunities and Threats.

Determine if planning will need to address a prescribed structure in the design of change strategies, or if a developmental process will be used for the basis for planning.

As a team, brainstorm strategies to address the factors identified in the SWOT analysis.

- Look for ways to explore new solutions to issues of "Where are we now?" problems.
- Identify barriers or limitations that will limit your ability to achieve your community "desired outcomes," goals and objectives.
- Identify possibilities and directions that will be effective.

Based on the research data and the SWOT analysis, determine which of the parts of the change plan will be needed.

TRY IT!

The scenario: You are living in a friendly small town (population 1,200, in 472 households) in the semi-arid southwestern part of the United States, with 262 sunny days per year. The population began declining in the 1960s, and the U.S. Decennial Census saw precipitous declines in 1970, 1990 and 2000. The population declines resulted in businesses closing. The nearest large town is 70 miles away, so citizens are concerned with the distance they would need to travel for groceries, medical and dental care and other essential services if they were to lose the few remaining businesses and professionals. There are already several empty lots and empty commercial buildings in the business district. The loss of property tax base and some nearly worthless abandoned commercial buildings and homes have taken their toll on emergency services. Rodents and infrastructure failure have increased, while revenue and population declined.

The elementary and high school are rated excellent, but large numbers of young people leave after high school graduation as a result of lack of jobs. Some people commute 70 miles to the nearest city for employment. Those who find employment in town have a per capita income of only $15,000 and cannot afford a home.

Town traditions encourage individual motivation to do good and to take responsibility for what happens in town. As a result, it is a good place to raise children. It also means that the town park is always clean and safe, and the clean, wide sidewalks make this a walkable and family-friendly town.

A group of citizens, meeting in a corner of the town diner, discuss what can be done to prevent their town from dying. They have already optimistically determined that their top long-range goals are:

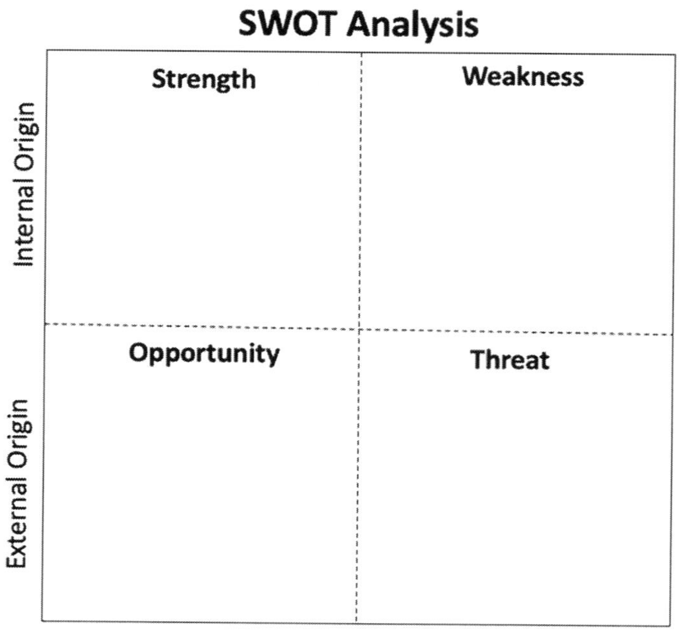

SWOT Analysis

	Strength	Weakness
Internal Origin		
External Origin	Opportunity	Threat

Figure 19.6 SWOT matrix.

- Within five years, the committee will encourage at least five entrepreneurs or businesses to develop or move into town.
- Within five years, employment of community residents will increase by 10% so that it allows them to make a better living, over a longer period of time, with choices available for full- and part-time workers.
- Within five years, at least 20% of obsolete housing or commercial buildings will be recycled by renovating to meet current trends or redeveloping them into a new use.
- Within five years, the community appeal will be increased through renovated buildings and parks to attract new families to move in.

Your task:

1. You have been elected facilitator for the discussion group. As they discuss the scenario in this section, you fill out a SWOT matrix (Figure 19.6).
2. Identify potential scenarios showing what could happen in the future if threats are ignored, and scenarios that could realistically happen if they are addressed.
3. Examine opportunities to determine if there is a way to make use of them.
4. Look over your SWOT analysis and creatively *brainstorm ideas* that may help accomplish the group's goals by using the items there. Remember, brainstormed ideas listed are not necessarily all viable ideas, but they may generate other viable ideas.

SUMMARY

In this chapter we covered using your research as the basis for planning strategies. This includes using a SWOT analysis as a way of systematically thinking through research and the overall situation that the team has to address. Part of examining the overall situation also includes determining if there is a prescribed structure that must be accommodated, or if the team needs to take a developmental approach where no structure exists. Where a big-picture, long-range plan needs to be created, the team may need to plan how to manage resistance and increase community readiness, determining what strategies are needed. Then the team will need to plan how the plan will be implemented, evaluated and sustained.

The remaining chapters in this stage addresses writing objectives and then strategies and tactics followed by:

- Process of planning, such as creating alliances and collaborations.
- Facilitating conversations while planning, listening, observing and asking good questions.

Specifics on types of actions that can be taken to improve a situation will be covered in Stage 5.

CITATIONS

David, F. R., & David, F. R. (2016). *Strategic management: A competitive advantage approach, concepts and cases* (global ed., 16th ed.). London: Pearson Higher Education.

Grimm, B. (Producer & Director) (2013). *Racial Taboo* [Motion picture]. United States: Wave Communications.

Jones, B. (1990). *Neighborhood planning: A guide for citizens and planners.* Chicago and Washington, DC: Planners Press, American Planning Association.

Lofquist, W. A. (1996). *Technology of development workbook.* Tucson, AZ: Development Publications.

20 WHERE ARE WE GOING AND HOW WILL WE GET THERE? STRATEGIES AND TACTICS

Figure 20.0

WHAT'S IN THIS CHAPTER?

This chapter will cover how your team can develop strategies including policies, communications, programs and practices necessary to create a sound, evidence-based plan to address problems identified in your assessment. A strategy describes *how* you are going to bring about a desired outcome. It is less specific than an action plan or tactic implemented as one or more specific tasks.

Objectives

By the end of this chapter, you will be able to:

■   Develop strategies and tactics and plan a timeline for implementation.

A STORY: HOW THE QUAKERS CHANGED DIRECTION ON THEIR VISION OF A RETREAT CENTER

In the story of the Quakers dreaming about a year-round retreat center, there was a hidden person of influence who I will call the Big Donor. Many organizations have such a person in the background guiding and perhaps controlling the outcome. In this case he was an elderly Quaker who had been a Methodist camp counselor in his youth. He had a wish to recreate that dream at the yearly meeting site, even though he might not have been doing this consciously. As a War Tax Resister, he was looking for a place to donate his retirement income so the government could not use it for military purposes. He kept pouring money into a special use fund in the yearly meeting budget and quietly endorsing its expenditure for architectural fees. Then he hired two architects to conduct a charette exercise to engage the entire yearly meeting (these are Quaker values) in designing the retreat center. The result was what could be called the Taj Mahal version with two beautiful new buildings with the latest LEED functions (Leadership in Energy and Environmental Design, a green building certification) at a cost of over a million dollars. The Quakers gulped at the price and ordered two professional feasibility studies. There was no way that the tiny annual budget could sustain such a large project, and the rural location did not make it a destination for other Quakers to rent it. This was an impasse. When Quakers are presented with a high price tag, they tend to quietly disappear rather than confront the issue head on. They loved the Big Donor for his generosity and did not want to appear ungrateful. This was another "elephant in the living room."

Actually, the Big Donor inadvertently solved the dilemma. There was an old farmhouse next door to the campus which had originally been in Quaker hands but was sold to a young couple from out of town. The Big Donor said to the Clerk of the Meeting (the facilitator), "If that property ever comes available, I want you to notify me immediately." A few months later, a trustee informed her that the property would soon be up for sale and the yearly meeting had two weeks to make the owner an offer. That happened right before the annual gathering, and the matter came up for consideration in the business session and was agreed upon with consensus. The Quakers can move pretty fast when they need to. The full price of $45,000 was agreed upon, and they bought the farmhouse immediately.

How is this an example of a change in strategy? By moving to meet a lesser goal of the donor, they found a way to have a smaller version of his dream. The farmhouse was renovated at a modest cost and increased the space for small retreat gathering throughout the year. It also become the much-longed-for permanent home for the Clear Creek Meeting, which could not use the old meetinghouse in winter because of high heating costs. One interesting fact was that during the charette exercise, their members had said they wanted to be able to see the old meetinghouse from their new site. The windows of the newly renovated farmhouse looked directly toward the old meeting house. Coincidence? No, just a good vision.

WHAT THIS TECHNIQUE IS ABOUT

A strategy explains how you will achieve the goal, and it usually includes the reasons it will lead to the goal. A tactic, on the other hand, is the specific actions you will take to fulfill the strategy. A tactic or action plan describes the who, what, when and how. As shown in Figure 20.1, tactics and strategy must be aligned with the vision and goal.

In the story just presented, the goal was a space that could accommodate year-round retreats. The original strategy was to build a new facility. The second strategy was to purchase the old farmhouse next door and renovate.

A good *strategy* will provide overall direction, without spelling out the details. Details are in the *tactics* (see Table 20.1). Strategies need to fit the resources available and take advantage of the opportunities that had been identified in a SWOT analysis. If barriers or community resistance to a change were identified, the strategy will describe how they will be addressed. The strategy should also indicate how it reaches the intended beneficiaries of the change. Finally, the strategy indicates how it fits the situation and will help accomplish the goal or desired outcome. No matter how much you might like a particular strategy or tactic, if it doesn't align with the goal, it won't work for your project. The Big Donor, in our story, loved the idea of the modern new building, but it was beyond the resources available. The participants in the yearly meeting knew that, and they resisted that strategy. Purchasing the old farmhouse and renovating it, however, was a strategy that aligned with the goal, so it was quickly accepted.

> *Strategy*: a description of the overall approach or direction to achieving a long-term goal. Does not spell out details.
> *Tactic*: specific actions comprising small steps and short time frames that support the strategy.

Often, an initiative will use several strategies to achieve its goals: reduce the power of the forces opposing the change, increase the forces driving the change, increase resources, eliminate barriers, modify the physical environment, provide information, training, programs or support. Each strategy will take several actions (tactics) to accomplish. In addition, strategy planning is ongoing throughout the project

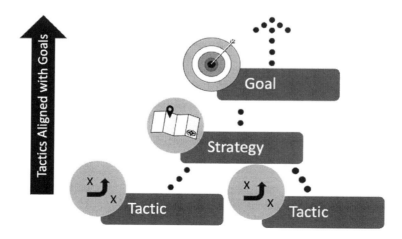

Figure 20.1 Alignment of tactic, strategy and goal.

Table 20.1 Differences between strategies and tactics.

Strategies	Tactics
General direction	Specific actions
Overall plan to achieve a goal	Small steps
How you will achieve long-term goals	Short time frames

because circumstances change, and sometimes an initial strategy does not work. Each new strategy can build on the previous one. If a letter writing scheme or attending city council meetings where you can speak to the issue doesn't work, escalate your approach by writing newspaper articles. Each escalation should appear reasonable, and not overblown or reactionary. They should also fit the situation so that they are neither too strong nor too weak to have an intended effect. Tactics can also change depending on how well your strategy is working.

Examples of Community Development Strategies

- Create effective communications to increase awareness and readiness.
- Use social media to recruit and involve community members.
- Create effective communication (information, training or programs) to implement and maintain change.
- Provide volunteer support to students at risk through private social media channels.
- Develop policies and procedures to affect change
- Develop leadership to continue the work of the organization into the future.
- Apply for grants and funding to support the work of the organization.

TACTICS

Tactics should be very explicit, specifying *who* will do *what*, *how* and by *when* (start and end dates) as shown in Figure 20.2.

If your strategy is to create effective communications to increase awareness and readiness, example tactics might look something like that appearing in Table 20.2.

How to Develop Strategies and Tactics

Review your analyses of the community, your Force Field Analysis, SWOT analysis and other data you have gathered so that you can create strategies and tactics that are appropriate for the audience, the community and the issues you are trying to address. List your goals formulated in the visioning process. Brainstorm strategies to accomplish your goals. After brainstorming ideas, select the strategies your team believes are most likely to help you attain your goal. For each selected strategy, brainstorm all of the steps or tasks necessary to carry out the strategy. Create detailed short-term plans listing who is responsible, what they will do and start and end dates. Each action should produce measurable results.

Two important things to include are: (1) creating short-term wins and (2) weakening or removing restraining forces and obstacles to change (identified during Force Field Analysis). Old structures (such as reporting structures), policies and systems sometimes create obstacles for change plans. Resistance, or lack of readiness, is also an obstacle to change (see Chapter 13 for strategies to overcome resistance or opposition). Stakeholders and volunteers need to be able to listen and communicate openly with

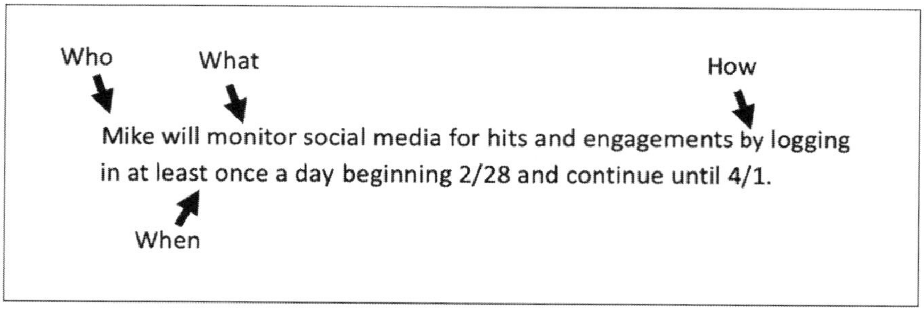

```
          Who        What                              How
           ↓          ↓                                 ↓
        Mike will monitor social media for hits and engagements by logging
        in at least once a day beginning 2/28 and continue until 4/1.
                      ↑
                    When
```

Figure 20.2 How to write a tactic.

Table 20.2 Tactics aligned with strategy and goal.

Goal	Within five years, reduce food insecurity for all residents in the St. Michael Parish from 7.1% (very low food security) to the national average of 0.7% as measured by the Six-Item Short Form of the Food Security Survey.
Strategy the overall approach or direction to achieving a long-term goal.	Create effective communications to increase awareness and community readiness for a community garden.
Tactics How the strategy will be carried out. Specify *who* will do *what*, *how* (if appropriate) and by *when* (start and end dates). Each action should produce measurable results.	Joe will determine what media channels are best for the organization and what messages work best for their audiences and make recommendations by the next board meeting. Bob will create video media for posting on social media to demonstrate the need for change by February 28. Laura will start and monitor a discussion about food security on St. Michael's community Facebook page beginning March 5, continuing until April 1. Carol will post video media on the chosen social media by March 5. Mike will monitor social media for hits and engagements. He will follow up any potential volunteers within 24 hours. Noreen will create business cards by February 8, to hand to potential beneficiaries so they know where to locate the community garden.

community members about issues so they can be addressed. Support and empower the volunteers' and staff's ability to make changes by listening and working with them to remove the barriers.

Create accountability by *monitoring changes continuously*. Make sure your indicators are used and results are reported. Create visible short-term milestones and celebrate when they are accomplished. Share the news with the community. Most community work takes a long time; some of it will never be done. Short-term wins help the community sustain faith in the progress toward change. Provide feedback to volunteers and staff that will reinforce timely actions and successes.

PROJECT TIMELINE

How can a team see the big picture for large projects, such as opening a winter warming shelter for the homeless, while planning? How can they keep track of the tactics during implementation, including

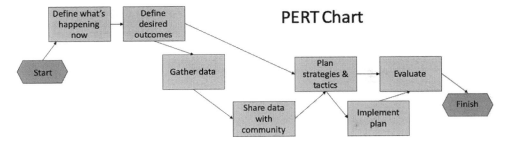

Figure 20.3 PERT chart.

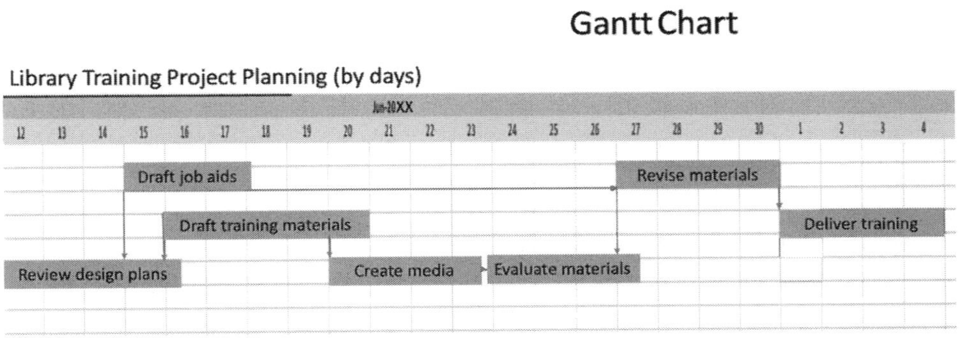

Gantt Chart

Figure 20.4 Gantt chart.

every milestone, task and subtask, and who is assigned to specific tasks and deadlines? One solution is a project plan with a timeline that helps all team members keep track of due dates for each tactic and milestone (important events such as when half of the people in an organization have completed training).

Project management software can help your team plan, organize, and estimate and manage resources. This software typically allows you to view the project as either a PERT chart or a Gantt chart, shown in Figures 20.3 and 20.4. Every milestone, task and subtask can be listed and assigned to a specific person with a deadline. A PERT (Program Evaluation and Review Technique) chart shows the dependence of each task on previous tasks. A Gantt chart shows the project tasks as a timeline.

A graphic depiction like this is helpful for team members trying to see the big picture and to keep on top of the tactics. Smaller change projects may not need anything so sophisticated. A simple task list with deadlines or a hand-drawn PERT or Gantt chart might suffice.

HOW TO CARRY OUT THIS TECHNIQUE

1. Review what's happening now and your desired outcome.
2. Review your research.
3. Review your Force Field Analysis and SWOT analysis (Barry, 1997).
4. Brainstorm strategies to accomplish your goals (desired outcomes), then select the strategies most likely to help you attain your team's goal. Be sure to include strategies to reduce forces against change and strengthen forces that drive change (Bryson, 2018).

5. For each strategy, brainstorm all of the steps or tasks necessary to carry out the strategy.
6. Create detailed statements for each strategy, including who is responsible, what they will do, and start and end dates. Use these statements to create a project timeline.
7. Make plans to remove obstacles to change.
8. Make sure to include plans to create and celebrate short-term wins.

TRY IT!

Scenario: As facilitator of a task force for Hunger-free St. Michael in the southeastern United States, you will formulate strategies and tactics for one goal formulated in the visioning process:

> Within five years, reduce food insecurity for all residents in the St. Michael Parish from 7.1% (very low food security) to the national average of 0.7% as measured by the Six-Item Short Form of the Food Security Survey.

1. Brainstorm *strategies* to accomplish your goals.
2. After brainstorming ideas, select the strategies you believe are most likely to help you attain your goal. Explain why those strategies were selected.
3. For one selected strategy, brainstorm all of the *tactics* (steps or tasks) necessary to carry out the strategy.
4. Create detailed short-term plans focusing on measurable results.
5. Include plans to raise awareness and deal with resistance as covered in Chapter 13.
6. Check to make sure tactics are aligned with the strategy, and strategy is aligned with the goal. Use the template provided in Table 20.3.

Table 20.3 Tactics aligned with strategy and goal for Hunger-free St. Michael.

Goal	Within five years, reduce food insecurity for all residents in the St. Michael Parish from 7.1% (very low food security) to the national average of 0.7% as measured by the Six-Item Short Form of the Food Security Survey.
Strategy The overall approach or direction to achieving a long-term goal.	
Tactics How the strategy will be carried out. Specify *who* will do *what*, *how* (if appropriate) and by *when* (start and end dates). Each action should produce measurable results.	

SUMMARY

This chapter covered developing strategies to address problems identified in your assessment to bring about a desired outcome. Then we covered creating an action plan of tactics supporting the strategy. Finally, we suggested using project management software to plan the timeline of the project.

RESOURCES

GanttProject (free desktop project management app): www.ganttproject.biz
MS Excel task list template: https://templates.office.com/en-us/Track-My-Tasks-TM10000093

CITATIONS

Barry, B. W. (1997). *Strategic planning workbook for non-profit organizations.* St. Paul, MN: Fieldstone Alliance.

Bryson, J. M. (2018). *Strategic planning for public and nonprofit organizations: A guide to strengthening and sustaining organizational achievement.* Hoboken, NJ: John Wiley & Sons.

21 EFFECTIVE LEARNING OBJECTIVES

Figure 21.0

WHAT'S IN THIS CHAPTER?

A majority of change initiatives will include some learning strategies. In order to effectively make change happen, learning objectives need to be clear to everyone as well as specific, realistic and measurable.

Objectives

By the end of this chapter, you will be able to:

- Describe why and how to create effective learning objectives for the program strategies (teaching, training, mentoring) for your change initiative.
- Write effective learning objectives.

A STORY: IF YOU DON'T KNOW WHERE YOU ARE GOING, ANY PATH WILL DO

In Chapter 17 we viewed the facilitator being hired as a training coordinator in the private sector of the child welfare system, a new field of endeavor for her where she had no content knowledge. She did not pretend to be an expert in this field; however, she had an important gift to offer—a fresh perspective on the problems they were encountering. What was the goal of the grant-funded project? To create a collaborative training system for some private child welfare agencies to prepare their newly hired caseworkers for the job.

Six agencies were to be engaged in this experimental model, and all of them were former orphanages that had been transformed into more modern service delivery systems for children in the child welfare system. The underlying concern of these agencies was the high turnover of caseworkers. The child welfare system was overloaded from too many cases, and there was intense pressure put on private agencies to perform well.

The new training coordinator had an early opportunity to view the scope of the problem as an objective observer. In a large public meeting for private agencies, the state's child welfare director made a broad statement, saying, "The social workers [i.e. caseworkers] are failing to do their jobs!" The facilitator/training coordinator asked for the microphone and retorted,

> Director, you realize, of course, that these are not social workers that are being hired. They are recent college graduates with a variety of degrees and no experience in child welfare. It is easy to blame the failure of an entire system on the lowest people on the totem pole.

Everyone in the room gasped and thought, "She can't say that—even if it is true!" Apparently, he was looking for a scapegoat to blame for the entire problem, and her statement revealed the underlying condition. The advantage of being an outsider allowed the facilitator to *speak truth to power*.

What were the observable symptoms of the problem?

> *Symptom*: an observable and describable sign of manifestation of some underlying condition or reality. This is not the same thing as a cause.

- A top-down system of management with caseworkers and their supervisors being treated as objects.
- A high turnover rate for newly hired caseworkers.
- Overloading cases on inexperienced caseworkers.
  What was the hypothesis for the project?
- Inadequate training for caseworkers was leading to high turnover.
- A collaborative training model would save money and improve overall value.

> *Hypothesis*: an assumption or supposition or guess that attempts to understand and describe the conditions underlying a symptom or group of symptoms. (Lynn & Lofquist, 2007, p. 23).

After noticing that there was no formal training for the private childcare agency caseworkers, the training coordinator was wondering what the core functions of a caseworker might be. Playing the role of Columbo again, she approached the supervisors of caseworkers and began to investigate how their system worked (or did not work). They were very pleased to serve as key informants because they were rarely treated as experts, even though they were doing the heavy lifting of managing large caseloads of damaged children and their families. The training coordinator invited the supervisors to a meeting and presented them with the opportunity to describe the core functions of casework. As it turned out, this was the first time they had been asked to be the experts contributing to the knowledge base of professional development. Hard to believe, but it was true. Using this base of knowledge, she created a set of objectives by which the success or failure of the training project would be evaluated. After the core functions of casework were defined, the project had a clear set of objectives to follow for designing the training program.

Lessons Learned:

- Sometimes facilitation requires taking risks and revealing uncomfortable truths.
- Look for the hidden leaders in any system; the people who do the job on the frontlines often know more than the folks at the top.
- Before you leap, look! Set clear objectives so that when you arrive at your final destination, you will know when to get off the train.

WHAT THIS TECHNIQUE IS ABOUT

This technique begins with the vision created by the change team early in the process. Revisit and reaffirm or revise your vision. Then move on to the high-priority, high-yield goals or desired outcomes selected and their indicators (Bryson, 2018). A desired outcome is an idea of the future or goal that a change team visualizes, plans and commits to work toward. They provide meaning, focus and motivation to your efforts but are sometimes quite broad. In Chapter 20, we saw that strategies are the overall approach or direction to achieving a long-term goal, and tactics specify *who* will do *what*, *how* and by *when* (start and end dates).

Objectives are similar to tactics, but they apply specifically to mentoring, teaching and training. They are specific, tangible and measurable and direct the teaching activities toward achieving the goals and visions of the change team and community. Objectives are usually narrow and specific like tactics. The major difference between learning objectives and tactics is that objectives are focused on what the audience will be able to do when the teaching, training or mentoring is done. There may be several objectives for each goal. Objectives help you and your team stay on track to accomplish the desired program outcomes.

> *Learning objective*: a clear, specific and measurable result of mentoring, teaching or training that a change team aims to achieve within a specific time frame and with available resources. Objectives are focused on what the audience will be able to do following the teaching. An objective is realistic and achievable. In general, objectives are more specific than goals and, as a result, easier to measure.

A well-written objective is important because it can have an effect on every other step of the change project. When you create an effective learning objective, you give your team and the beneficiaries of the change a greater chance of achieving the objective, and ultimately the goal, because they know exactly what they're working toward. Effective objectives are clear to everyone using them, specific, measurable and achievable, yet challenging, realistic and time-bound (Piskurich, 2011).

EXAMPLE: HUNGER-FREE ST. MICHAEL PARISH

A town hall meeting determined that food security was the number one concern for the parish. The change team is a local committee that focuses on teaching parish residents how to use new personal food practices. As shown in Table 21.1, the St. Michael Parish Hunger-free Committee listed their challenging

Table 21.1 Goals and objectives for St. Michael Parish Hunger-free Committee.

Goal

Within five years, reduce food insecurity for all residents in the St. Michael Parish from 7.1% (very low food security) to the national average of 0.7% as measured by the Six-Item Short Form of the Food Security Survey.

Objectives

1. During planting season, St Michael residents participating in the community garden will be able to use effective planting methods for vegetables they have chosen to plant as measured by a garden plot observation by year 2.
2. Residents will be able to evaluate food costs to decide what foods to grow and choose to plant more expensive vegetables by year 2 as measured by a garden plot observation.
3. Fifteen percent of food insecure residents of St Michael Parish will be able to carry out basic preservation and storage techniques for the food they grew this year. It will be measured by a post-harvest survey at the end of fall this year.
4. At least 20% of residents of St Michael Parish will be able to reduce reliance on prepackaged food by 50% within three years as measured by a survey in year 3.

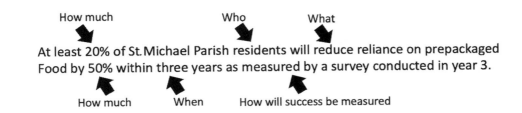

Figure 21.1 Components of learning objectives.

goal of reducing food insecurity. Under that, they listed learning objectives that will lead to accomplishing their goal of reducing food insecurity. Notice how the objectives indicate *who* will do something and *what* they will do to accomplish the goal, when the objective will be accomplished by and how well (or how much, or how many). In addition, several objectives indicate how they will be measured. At this point, the change team is thinking about evaluation of their efforts.

Food insecurity is a complex issue, and teaching new food practices is not enough. At the same time, state administrators and legislators are working on issues of state minimum wage changes, and staff from local social services offices are working on making sure all families in need are receiving the Supplemental Nutrition Assistance Program (SNAP) benefits.

HOW TO CARRY OUT THIS TECHNIQUE

To begin, list the high-priority, high-yield goal that was determined during the visioning meeting. Make sure the goal includes at least one indicator. Then below the goal, list objectives. Briefly state what will be done so that anyone would understand them in the same way, avoiding jargon or acronyms. Be sure to include who the learner is. To make the objective clear, include:

- **Who** will be able to do a specific task?
- **What** they will be able to do (Barry, 1997)?
- **When** they will be able to do it by?
- **How much, how many, or how well** will something be done?
- How will success be **measured**? (See Figure 21.1.)

SMART OBJECTIVES

You can use the SMART acronym to help you remember how to write your objectives (Doran, 1981):

- Specific—about **who** should accomplish the objective and how.
- Measurable—as far as possible telling us how well, how many or **how much** will be achieved and how it will be **measured**.
- Achievable but challenging—by your organization within the time available (**when**) but requires effort
- Realistic—in terms of your resources and capacities; and
- Time-bound—indicating by **when** you will achieve them.

TRY IT!

As facilitator for the southwestern town's sustainability committee, examine the goal from the group's visioning session and write at least three SMART objectives to support the goal (Table 21.2).

Table 21.2 Goals and objectives for sustainability committee.

Goal
Within two years, the committee will teach business basics to at least 20 potential local entrepreneurs.

Objectives

1.	
2.	
3.	

SUMMARY

In order to effectively make change happen, learning objectives need to be clear to everyone as well as specific, realistic and measurable. This chapter has covered why and how to create effective objectives for your change initiative.

CITATIONS

Barry, B. W. (1997). *Strategic planning workbook for non-profit organizations*. St. Paul, MN: Fieldstone Alliance.

Bryson, J. M. (2018). *Strategic planning for public and nonprofit organizations: A guide to strengthening and sustaining organizational achievement*. Hoboken, NJ: John Wiley & Sons.

Doran, G. T. (1981). There's a S.M.A.R.T. way to write management's goals and objectives. *Management Review, AMA Forum*, 70(11), 35–36.

Piskurich, G. M. (2011). *Rapid instructional design: Learning ID fast and right*. Hoboken, NJ: John Wiley & Sons.

NO TIN CUPS
Fundraising and Stewardship

22

Figure 22.0

WHAT'S IN THIS CHAPTER?

Whether your project is just an idea shared among a few friends, or an ongoing service carried out by an established organization, you will need resources to carry out your plans. How will you fund your planned strategies? There are many methods including sponsorships, individual giving, events, in-kind donations, fee-for-service and grants. It is fortunate that there are several methods, because it is far less risky to use several approaches than to count on a single approach, such as grants that might be available this year and not next year. Having a fundraising plan helps you define your fundraising goal (including both money and goods), key steps and measures you need to successfully reach that goal (Heyman, 2016).

People donate because they believe in the *mission* of your organization. If you passionately believe in the mission of your organization, *fundraising becomes an act of love* that takes commitment and courage to "take a stand for the just, equitable, and sustainable world we all dream of" (Heyman, 2016, p. xxviii). It is important when your organization receives resources or funding from donors to demonstrate honesty, accountability, trustworthiness and transparency of your organization to every person who has invested goods, time or money. It helps them to see that their donation makes a difference to a cause they believe in. If yours is an established organization, you may already demonstrate this stewardship through an annual giving/stewardship report sent to all major donors and posted on your website. You should also keep donors involved with your mission by asking them to come to your organization's events, volunteer, learn, and network; and they will continue to give.

> *Mission*: it is what you do; the core reason for your organization's existence, and from it comes your vision, goals and strategies for reaching those goals.

Objectives

By the end of this chapter, you will be able to:

- Enjoy the process of fundraising through building relationships with potential donors, while uncovering shared values and hearing the stories of what it is that motivates their generosity.
- List several means of raising funds.
- Select fundraising strategies appropriate for an organization.
- Create a fundraising plan.
- List steps you can take to demonstrate honesty, accountability, trustworthiness and transparency of your organization.

A STORY ABOUT FUNDING HOMES FOR VETERANS

In small southern towns like Merryville, when boys graduate from high school, only a few career paths are open. They can go to college, leave town for better job options or join the military. For guys with few prospects, the choice of putting on a nice uniform and getting some training seems like a good one—until they return home bringing the battlefield noise in their heads and perhaps flashbacks, nightmares, panic attacks, depression or rage. Family members are disturbed to find that their sons, brothers and husbands are not able to settle back into normal life. Relationships become frayed, and there is a wave of homelessness in the community. They have had bad experiences with the Veterans Administration and avoid it. In this town, the only other option is the nearby woods where they secretly "camp out" for most of the year. They go into town to beg on street corners when their money runs out. No longer are they honored heroes; now they are viewed as vagrants and beggars. Winter is coming, and more veterans will be coming into town from the woods. Where can they go to find a place to live if they have Post Traumatic Stress Disorder (PTSD)?

The mayor of Merryville has been frustrated in his efforts to clear the streets of beggars since a court ruling declared that they have a legal right to ask passersby for money. The merchant class is enraged because they feel that the presence of the homeless negatively affects their customers coming into stores and restaurants. The homeless shelter is not an option because it is crowded with families and individuals who have short-term housing needs. It is too noisy for a veteran with PTSD. Into this scene steps Mike, a veteran of the Vietnam War, who approaches the Rotary Club to request donations for hotel rooms in winter for vets. He also has an idea of building a community of tiny houses (small sheds) to house veterans. After the meeting, a club member, who is also a community activist, approaches Mike with an innovative idea. Since the downturn in college enrollments has impacted the older housing rental market in the town, there are plenty of vacant buildings. Why not try a pilot project to give vets an actual home? She coaches Mike in reaching out to some landlords who are sympathetic to the plight of vets to ask if they would house one or two with wraparound services offered to them from the nearby VA hospital. Then he reaches out to a local solar energy installer, who teaches skills to people to help them become independent contractors.

By starting small with a pilot project, it is possible to build on this success. Eventually, the community will see that these beggars on the street were actually people who served their country bravely in war. They deserve a home and a second chance at life.

Lessons Learned:

- Underutilized resources may be overlooked while reaching for other funding from donors or government sources.
- Be creative in your strategic planning efforts rather than falling back on the same old strategies.
- Starting with a pilot project and building a track record for success will promote eventual fundraising success.

WHAT THIS TECHNIQUE IS ABOUT

The lessons learned in the story just presented can provide you with the resources to make it possible to carry out the mission of your organization. Those lessons can also make fundraising successful as well as a satisfying job that can touch your heart.

CREATING A FUNDRAISING PLAN

A written, well-organized fundraising plan that works can help stabilize your organization so you can achieve your mission effectively. *Planning for raising funds needs to be part of the organization's strategic plan.* Some nonprofits, particularly smaller and new start-up charities, operate without a fundraising plan of any sort. If someone has a proposal for a campaign or event, these groups might put together a task force or committee and do anything they can in order to raise some funds. They may send out letters now and then, do some donor meetings, and when the bank account seems to be dwindling, they go into a panic and post alarm messages on their Facebook page or race around trying to find the money to keep the doors open. If you are operating without a plan, it is time to sit down and write one. Ideally, you'll have a plan each year. Some organizations will write a plan covering two to five years, and then they adjust it each year as necessary.

METHODS OF FUNDRAISING

Familiarize yourself with methods of fundraising outlined in this section, including sponsorships, individual giving, events, in-kind donations, fee-for-service and grants, and select the methods that work for your particular organization.

Sponsorships

Sponsorship is when a nonprofit organization partners with other organizations such as businesses in related fields to receive funds and in-kind donations. An example is when a surfing equipment store partners with a Clean Beaches initiative for a cleanup day. The process involves brainstorming for sources of support by possible interested organizations by the core team or board of directors. Then the team networks with possible sponsors to offer volunteers a premium that they would value. The sponsors generally expect recognition such as their logo printed on T-shirts or other premiums (such as beach balls) provided to the volunteers. The team then advertises to obtain volunteers. When the work is done, be sure to thank sponsors and provide publicity of the results to local newspapers, television, radio and social media.

Individual Giving

For most small grassroots organizations and small nonprofits (in the United States, they are those organizations with tax-exempt status under the U.S. Internal Revenue Code, section 501(c)(3)), individual fundraising will provide an important portion of your fundraising revenues. As your organization becomes more organized and established, important planning needs to take place: You will need a *fundraising plan* with a strong individual giving section.

The members of the board should be involved with fundraising. First, they need to donate. Then, they can brainstorm *who* else to ask for donations. They may know generous individuals or key people in corporations or businesses that have a track record of charitable giving. The board can help you research to find out more about people, such as their profession or involvement with other charities. Find out *when* it is a good time to ask. For instance, the first and last month of the school year is not a good time to approach teachers, and the months leading to tax day is not a good time to approach accountants.

Figure 22.1 shows the donor cycle for major gifts. Your board of directors should brainstorm to *identify* names of potential donors that they know may have a concern for what your organization does. Sort them into lists of "Most likely to donate," "Somewhat likely to donate" and "Unlikely to donate." Then they can *research* the potential donor's interests and affiliations. These can be found in local news media, the Internet, social media and informal conversations. If they look like good candidates for major gifts to your organization, the board members can approach those that they know.

From the first moment children sell candy bars or cookies to raise funds for schools, scouts and other causes, they are fundraising, but many of us never learn to *enjoy* fundraising, especially asking for individual giving. However, developing relationships and learning about people's passions can be both enjoyable and gratifying. To develop those relationships that lead to donations, spend most of the meeting time listening to your potential donors as they describe their hopes for the community, and the stories of what it is that *motivates* their generosity. Ask potential donors open-ended questions such as:

- What is important to you about being a member of this community?
- What is important to you when making decisions about your philanthropy?

Figure 22.1 Donor cycle.

Think about donors investing in the mission of your organization and the benefits donors will experience from their kindness.

Meet donors where their passions are to build authentic and meaningful relationships based on shared values. Donors appreciate those who understand their values and identities and make them feel included, so include them in donor events.

If the board members know these people well, then they may already know where their hearts are and the values they share. *Cultivate* relationships. When you are in their office or home, observe the things they surround themselves with. Do you notice anything that suggests their passions? Ask about them. When visiting the office of a major donor, John observed several images of sailboats. Asking about them revealed that his donor had a passion for sailing in lakes and preservation of the environment in those lakes. When John finds good articles on the topic, he sends them to him in a letter, even if it had nothing to do with his nonprofit. He also sends a birthday card.

Board members can describe to potential donors why *they* are involved with the organization and how they feel about donating.

Finally, you should *ask* potential donors to invest in the mission of your organization. Sometimes there are objections related to timing, the project, the organization or the amount. This is another moment for listening. The first objection isn't always the whole story, so it is important to listen and to read between the lines until the real concern is understood. Then, the meeting can become a joint problem-solving session.

Be prepared for someone to say "no" when you ask, and avoid anything that might seem like manipulation, which can destroy a relationship very quickly. Instead, focus on satisfying the donor's need to give, rather than your organization's financial goals. At the end, the potential donor should be thanked for their time whether they donated or not.

> *Donor stewardship*: the cultivation of a relationship between a nonprofit or charity and its donors, through which the charity seeks to express appreciation for a donor's gift and keep them as ongoing donors.

Once you have a relationship with donors that believe in your mission, continue to nurture the relationship by staying in touch, inviting them to events, sending newsletters and communicating using other methods. As you practice donor stewardship, and first-time donors are converted to recurring donors, you may find that young adults may be willing to continue to give online, but older adults are more likely to respond to appeals in letter form. Both groups give, but older people may give larger amounts. Relationships with younger adults, however, should also be nurtured, because they may give greater amounts as their incomes grow.

Build a Fundraising Network

Small or start-up organizations frequently operate with a single person responsible for fundraising. Shown in Figure 22.2 is your organization and its mission. Keeping your mission foremost, go to your *current supporters*, especially board members, large donors and those with large numbers of contacts. Build relationships and ask this group of committed supporters to help raise funds on your organization's behalf. These supporters can be donors, board members, volunteers, former clients or alumni, or simply supporters of the organization. They may help you simply because they believe in the mission of the organization, but it is a good idea to offer them some benefits in return for their efforts such as tickets to events, special lapel pins, regular seminars or meetings with community leaders, a special email newsletter, and recognition in your organization's annual report.

Then ask those supporters to contact their network who can fund your efforts, working outward until the fundraising goes *viral*. Provide resources to make their fundraising task easier and increase the likelihood that they will meet their donation goal. You might provide a few hours of training on how they

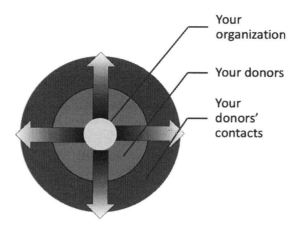

Figure 22.2 "Viral" fundraising model.

can use direct mail, email, social media or telephone to contact potential donors. Work with supporters to write the opening paragraph of emails or letters focused on the individual they are contacting. They should *not* be generic email or form letters; they should be tailored to each recipient. Ask supporters to request a face-to-face meeting where possible, especially if they will be contacting older potential donors. Other methods of soliciting donations are less personal and require larger budgets, such as using radio, television, billboards or social media. Ask your supporters to provide contacts so you can send thank-you notes to all donors. Keep your donor relationships strong by staying in contact with them and keeping them informed using social media (Mansfield, 2012), newsletters and your website.

Building a fundraising network takes time, sometimes as much as a few years, but it is well worth the effort.

Fundraising Events

Fundraising events can be a fun method of raising funds, but they also require work, advance planning and time. Typically, these kinds of events do not raise as much money as other methods, but they can be good sources for awareness and publicity. Keep in mind that the amount of donations that come in will need to exceed the cost of the event expenses, and written acknowledgment of contributions is required by the IRS for a taxpayer to deduct donations from their taxes.

In-Kind Donations

This kind of donation involves donating tangible or intangible goods, services or time rather than cash to an organization. These donations might be goods such as office equipment. Goods can be used, surplus, brand new or even loaned. Intangible goods might include a copyright or advertising. Services might include administrative support, transportation or help with publishing booklets by small businesses, corporations, colleges, individual professionals or tradespeople. An example of in-kind donation of time might be when a business donates the time of its employees to help a nonprofit or grassroots organization. Some small organizations are able to cobble together enough in-kind donations to meet most of their needs. The process involves a thorough knowledge of the organization's needs, brainstorming sources for the goods or services and networking or personal emissary work by all of the members of the team.

Fee-For-Service

A fee-for-service approach can help some organizations cover their expenses. There are several approaches: mandatory fees, voluntary donations, requested fees or a hybrid approach. To meet legal and IRS requirements, a *mandatory fee* is a predetermined amount that must be below the market rate (the amount charged by a for-profit organization). An organization providing a service provided for free can request *voluntary donations*. These donations tend to be small and may not cover the costs. Similarly, organizations may publish a list of the cost of providing a service and *request fees*, but expenses are not always covered and often need to be supplemented by donations. Each organization will need to choose which model might work for their clients, services and mission. If your organization is interested in a fee-for-service approach, you will need to examine any grants, laws or regulations that pertain to grants you have or are pursuing. Some grants prohibit collecting fees.

Grants

Grants are funds provided for a specific purpose by a governmental body or a foundation to help a nonprofit achieve their goals. Grants might help you conduct research, provide training or support other operating expenses. They might provide "seed money" to try to grow new conditions through new actions. Most grants are limited to geographical regions, type of programming or projects, so you will need to search for one that meets your needs. Also, grant writing is a complex process (see Figure 22.3), so partnering with a faculty member from a local university or hiring someone with grant writing expertise to help you write the grant is often money well spent. They may also have subscriptions to newsletters and other sources that post announcements of grant opportunities. When looking for someone to help you write a grant, seek someone with knowledge of your area. They should also be familiar with funding sources, evaluation and statistics and have the ability to network, collaborate and write (Gitlin & Lyons, 2014, p. 23).

Ideas that are fundable are often innovative, advance the field, have the potential to make an impact or address a critical gap in science or practice, and match the focus area or a funding agency (Gitlin & Lyons, 2014). This is the purpose of *seed money* given to innovative start-up projects and new projects within existing organizations for a maximum of three to five years. Many foundations hesitate to invest in a new organization without a track record, so pilot projects that demonstrate a project's feasibility can be key strategies. However, some foundations have grants specifically providing seed money.

ACCOUNTABILITY AND STEWARDSHIP

Nonprofit stewardship means responsibility planning and management of resources for nonprofit organizations including finances, governance, performance and mission (Behn, 2001; Ebrahim, 2009) as well as stewardship of donors. Reports on finances are used by: (1) administrators of a nonprofit organization in order to be compliant with all laws and be able to present an accurate picture of their organization's finances, (2) the board of directors for oversight to protect the organization's assets and make sure they are used to fulfill the mission of the organization and to make appropriate decisions, and (3) potential

Figure 22.3 Grant process.

donors to determine the financial health of an organization when considering whether they will donate. The process is shown in Figure 22.4.

A nonprofit is responsible for making sure that their *financial* resources are protected and used to advance the organization's mission. Since most of those resources are donated, the organization is then the guardian of the donor's trust and must be accountable to donors and the public through reporting, tracking funds, and communications.

The final type of stewardship is *donor stewardship*. This stewardship is the process of providing donors with care and service in an effort to retain them as supporters, and perhaps increase donations over time. Figure 22.5 shows that first-time donors giving small donations are often the bulk of your donors. Some of these may be impulse donors that don't know much about you. Often, the first gift is an emotional response to a disaster or an appeal. If you want one-time donors to become *recurring* donors, first send them a timely thank you, simply and sincerely, and let them know how their contribution helped others, highlighting the mission of your organization. Then, a short time later, you need to make the case for ongoing support. Recurring support helps your organization's sustainability and predictability of funding. With stewardship, they may move up to become recurring mid-level donors, and finally, to become major donors.

HOW TO CARRY OUT THESE TECHNIQUES

Create a Fundraising Plan

Write a fundraising goal based on the needs of the organization. Determine how much will it cost to carry out the strategies you have planned to accomplish your mission and use this to create a budget. Describe why you need that amount to accomplish your mission. Brainstorm and select the

Figure 22.4 Accountability and use of financial data for decision-making.

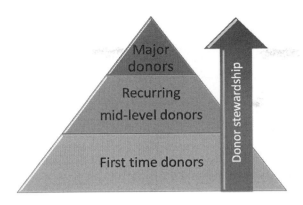

Figure 22.5 Donor pyramid.

strategies and tactics you will use to raise the full amount *well ahead of the point of need* (Hanberg, 2009). Create a detailed timeline for carrying out the strategies and tactics, including who is responsible for each action. Carry out your plan, evaluate your results and revise the plan where necessary to be more effective. If you successfully raise funds for your organization, you should consider filing for nonprofit status with your state and/or tax-exempt status with the federal government (U.S. IRS).

A fundraising plan does not need to be complicated. It takes creativity, and it needs to be organized.

1. Write a *goal* based on the needs of the organization.
2. Determine how much will it cost to carry out the strategies in your strategic plan.
3. Describe why you need *that amount* to accomplish your mission.
4. Brainstorm and select the *strategies and tactics* you will use to raise the full amount.
5. Create a *detailed timeline* for carrying out the strategies and tactics, including who is responsible for each action. This should include:
   a. *When* and *who* to ask for funding.
   b. What grant funding will be available.
   c. Fundraising events that will be held.
   d. Donor stewardship and communication plans.
6. Include the fundraising plan in the organization's strategic plan.
7. Involve board members, volunteers and members in fundraising. If you are the director or facilitator, you will burn yourself out if you try to do it all yourself.

FUNDRAISING STRATEGIES

Conduct Meetings Seeking Donations

Larger nonprofit organizations may begin a fundraising campaign by raising *awareness* with radio, television and even billboards. Smaller organizations may use email newsletters. Begin by building relationships when you are seeking sponsorships, individual giving or in-kind donations. Contact potential donors with an individualized letter or telephone call to set up an appointment. Relax and create a comfortable environment. When the meeting begins, thank the donor for meeting with you.

Tell the potential donor why you are involved with your organization and share your excitement. Tell them why this organization is excellent. People want to back winners. Ask open-ended questions such as:

- What do you enjoy about this community?
- What do you want to see happen in the future?

Listen carefully, focus and maintain comfortable eye contact (see Chapter 26 for more on listening). Identify common interests and values. Find out what the *donor wants*. Ask for a contribution: *"Please consider a gift. . . ", "As a leader in this community, please consider making a gift."* Pause for them to consider your request and respond. Manage objections: Find out if it is an objection to the cause, organization, project, amount or timing.

- Accept the objection, and make sure you properly understand it. Listen for the background, detail and emotion behind it.
- Accept the person. It can be scary to bring up an objection. Build trust by learning more about the donor.
- Gently work with the potential donor toward a possible solution.

Ask the potential donor to give until it feels good. Don't ask a donor to give if you aren't willing to give. Board members are expected to make donations first. Make a donation before asking others to do it. Invite the donor for a visit to the facility to view the work in progress (if you have a facility or some way to make to project visible to others)

Thank them whether they commit to a gift or not. Ask if they know of anyone else that you might contact for donations. Always follow up and keep promises.

Build a Fundraising Network

Go to your current committed supporters such as board members and large donors and ask for help in raising funds. When board members join the board, they should be made aware that making donations and helping with fundraising is part of the job. Offer them some benefits in return for their efforts, such as tickets to events, special lapel pins, regular seminars or meetings with community leaders, a special email newsletter, and recognition in your organization's annual report. Provide resources and training to make their fundraising task easier and increase the likelihood that they'll meet their donation goal. Ask board members and supporters to contact those contacts of *theirs* that can fund your efforts. Help them write individualized letters or email if they will be used.

Events

Begin by deciding on the purpose of the event: is the event purpose to build relationships, publicity or to raise money? Create a detailed budget for the event, including all expenses such as staff, catering, entertainment, security, and anything else needed. Make sure income from the event will exceed the cost of the event. Invite major donors, business leaders or local celebrities who support your mission to host your event to help you generate donations. Decide and carry out the following:

- Who will be invited to the event?
- Who will set up the event?
- What will be on the agenda?
- How you will market the event and sell tickets?

Go through the event details, and practice so everything goes smoothly. Hold the event, implementing all plans. Send thank-you letters to all donors and volunteers.

In-Kind Donations

When you receive in-kind donations, you will need to record the item received with the fair market value and the date. A donation can be valued by determining the price that would be paid on the open market. For instance, if an organization were serving the homeless and they received a number of donated used winter coats from a resale shop, they might go to several resale shops to determine the average charge for a used winter coat. For donations of time, they can use salary surveys for the average salary of someone with the skill level needed for the service in the geographical area to determine the value of the in-kind donation. (See the Resources section at the end of this chapter for a list of salary survey websites.)

If receiving in-kind donations is part of your funding process, it is useful to draft policies to help manage your donors' expectations for what kind of donations will be accepted, A written policy is also useful to staff and board members who might be asking for or receiving contributions. The policy can state what kinds of gifts are accepted and not accepted, how they are valued, how large gifts or gifts such as real estate will be handled (noting if Realtors, title companies or lawyers should be consulted). Forms for gifts or in-kind donations can ease the work of staff or board members accepting donations. (See the Resources section at the end of this chapter for a list of websites with form examples and templates.)

Fee-For-Service

Determine if there is a market demand for the services you plan to offer and then determine what kind of fee structure to use:

- Mandatory.
- Voluntary.
- Membership.
- Combination.

Plan how to meet regulatory and professional standards. Research tax implications and make sure there is *no conflict with grants* that forbid your organization from charging fees. Determine what the overhead and administrative costs will be and how they will be covered. Select your key performance indicators and plan for ongoing evaluation of success and continuous improvement of services.

Grants

Determine why you want a grant. What will a grant allow that is not happening now? Search for grants that meet your needs. Read the grant requirements thoroughly. Look for a grant writer at local universities that can partner with you to help write the grant. Look for someone with expertise in locating funding sources, evaluation, descriptive and inferential statistics, ability to network, collaboration, thinking creatively and critically, and writing ability.

Begin by writing an abstract of your idea. It needs to be persuasive and intriguing to grant reviewers, but don't use a hard sell. Explain what you intend to do, why the work is important, what has already been done and how your organization is going to do the work. State the problem, the broad, long-term objectives and specific objective, explaining the project's relevance to the mission of the granting agency. The abstract:

- Describes the project.
- Shows the significance, innovation and approach of your nonprofit's service, product or research.

- Is used as a guide to the rest of the grant application,
- Is used to decide where to assign your application.

After identifying and describing a need or idea that might be funded by a grant, you will need to search for a funding agency. Grant opportunities may be offered by federal government agencies, private foundations, professional organizations and private industry. Two good search sources are Grants.gov and the Foundation Directory Online. If you are searching for seed money in the Foundation Directory, simply select "Seed Money" under "Type of Support" in the search form. Effective grant writers are aware of other sources of information as well. Scan these sources frequently because the grant environment changes constantly, and new opportunities often become available.

This "seed" for your fundraising efforts could also come from hidden sources of money if you have a really good concept to present to potential donors. When Maurine was employed by the child welfare organization, she was hired under a three-year foundation grant. However, she was not told that she had to raise $100,000 herself in the second year to keep the project going. Undaunted by this rather shocking news, she approached another major foundation to ask for the money. When she met with their program officer, she was told in no uncertain terms that "we do not fund training." Maurine then said that the project was not about the usual training system support; rather, she intended to use the training of caseworkers as a strategy to change the entire system of child welfare. With one successful year of the project under her belt, she could point to some initial achievements and a really good concept for change. They handed over the check for $100K!

On another occasion with the Angel in the Night story, she used that concept to persuade the university's Dean and the Development Department to share its public relations budget with the project. This was a high-risk request because the play project was becoming very expensive, and the play had not even been written. Yet, the officers somehow trusted that the "town and gown" collaboration with potential donors would pay off in the long run. New donors came forth from the surrounding community after the project ended, and the university received national press attention when the play project unfolded. They received a greater payoff than otherwise possible. Sometimes boldness and a good idea can pay big fundraising dividends from hidden sources.

When you locate a funding source, read the Request for Proposal (RFP) or Funding Opportunity Announcement (FOA) thoroughly to make sure there is a good match to your need. The name and contact information for a program officer is found in the RFP. Contact them and request a visit to discuss the project you have in mind and the RFP requirements. This conversation will help you write a more effective grant proposal (Gitlin & Lyons, 2014).

Read the RFP instructions, suggested outline and evaluation criteria and *follow them carefully* when writing. Before you begin writing, learn everything about the sponsoring agency. Search for copies of funded grant applications. Examine them closely for how the application was written, including the format and structure.

Involve your whole team or board in writing parts of the grant, including:

- Cover page.
- Abstract.
- Table of contents.
- Abstract/Introduction.
- Project goals and objectives.
- Review of literature.
- Description of the proposed project.
- How you will carry out the project (methodology).
- Personnel.
- Budget.
- Current and pending support.
- Evaluation plans.

- Dissemination plans.
- Supplementary materials such as vitas and letters of support.
- Project timeline including all activities, personnel and responsibilities.

Since some grant applications are complex, the whole core team may be involved in writing different sections, including: the items listed here and supplementary materials such as vitas of those working on the grant and letters of support. If you have done a needs assessment or pilot study, it can provide data that will strengthen an application.

When constructing a budget, review the RFP budget section to determine what their requirements are and what they will and will not fund. For instance, some grant agencies will not fund computers, travel or equipment. Create a realistic timeline for the project including all activities, personnel and responsibilities. This will help you calculate salary costs.

After all sections have been written, the entire grant should be reviewed and edited for consistent wording. Other things that the editor should look for is clarity which can be improved by avoiding trendy words, jargon, abbreviations and redundant writing. Also, the narrative needs clearly defined constructs, variables and other key terms.

After submitting a grant application, it will be reviewed for a number of criteria, including evidence of need, relevance, plan of operation or methodology, quality of personnel, cost-effectiveness of the budget, evaluation plan and adequacy of resources. All of the proposals submitted for a particular grant are reviewed and ranked. Then the funding is granted to approved projects in order of rank until all of the funds are gone. Finally, they make their decisions known to the applicants. Throughout the period of the grant, you will need to keep rigorous documentation of the grant work, including expenditures and evaluations to be used for reports to the funding agency.

Demonstrating Accountability and Stewardship

Plan and manage the resources of your organization including finances and governance. Clearly communicate the *use* of contributions and for distributing donor contributions for their *intended purposes*. To maintain your donors' trust, your organization must be transparent and accountable to the public, showing that the resources are protected and used to advance your organization's mission (Brinckerhoff, 2004). Reporting in your annual impact report (to major donors and posted online) should include a financial summary of gifts raised and growth in net assets, powerful stories describing the impact donors make on those served, and an honor roll of donors.

Communications should also include policies posted online, such as your discretionary spending policy and gift acceptance policy. Financial reports should be available by request and thy should also be reviewed quarterly by the organization's board of directors. (See Appendix H for examples of financial statements.) Communications with donors and others should carry a message of accountability and transparency, including your annual report, a quarterly newsletter, donor summaries for tax season and your IRS form 990.

Accountability is also demonstrated through an organization's governance. The board of directors is responsible for the mission, leadership, strategy and financial health of the organization. They should:

- Disclose conflicts of interest and place the organization's interests over personal ones.
- Act to advance the organization's mission while adhering to internal organizational policies for making decisions (Ebrahim, 2016).
- Set organization mission, strategic directions and policies.
- Ensure that the organization fulfills obligations to the law, members, donors, staff, clients and the public.
- Review the budget and financial reports quarterly to protect organization assets, make decisions and monitor financial results. See Appendix H for more on governance and financial statements.

Performance assessment and evaluation of how well your organization accomplished its mission can be carried out by conducting regular evaluations that measure:

- Efficiency and effectiveness of accomplishing the organization's mission.
- Compliance with all laws and regulations that apply.
- Short-term assessment of outputs.
- Long-term strategic assessment of impacts.
- Use of evaluations for learning which focuses attention and resources on how to solve social problems.

Donor stewardship is demonstrated by identifying levels of donor giving (one-time, recurring, major) and determining what forms of gratitude will be used for each level of giving. You will also need to decide on the stewardship techniques you will use. Select from among the list of donor communications in Table 22.1.

Table 22.1 Donor communications.

Donor Communications	
Acknowledgments and thank-you letters	Thank-you phone call
	Thank-you call from CEO
	Handwritten thank-you note with a photo of a client/shelter animal, signed by development director
	Thank-you story from client/recipient
Stewardship communications	Impact letter: "This is what your donation has already done!"
	Send email with video update of impact
	Quarterly newsletter
	Donor interest survey
	Celebrate donor-versary
	Birthday card
	Holiday cards
	Annual report (major donors)
Invitations	Invitation to VIP event
	Invitation to tour facility
	Invite to coffee with the ____ (donor appreciation events)
Recognition	Community recognition
	Recognition by organization's board of directors
	Website donation e-wall
Appeals	Giving Tuesday email/mailing
	Annual appeal
	Holiday wish list mailing
Tax statement	Mail donor summaries for tax season

Communications

People give because they believe in your mission, so keep all fundraising communications focused on the good your organization does through its mission. There are several ways to build relationships, communicate gratitude and honor your donors:

- Send a personalized thank-you expressing true gratitude for each donation focused on the donor and the difference he or she is making.
- Include stories or quotes from recipients (or pictures if you are serving animals or the environment). Reinforce your mission and stay focused on your mission rather than solicitation.
- Create giving societies with perks for larger donations.
- Host donor appreciation events.
- Send articles of interest to donors.
- Create volunteer opportunities for those who wish to get more involved.
- Document your plan, describing who will do what when. You can use a form such as the one shown in Table 22.2.

Carry out your plan and listen to your donors to keep improving on your stewardship.

Software to Assist With Fundraising

Having the right tools to demonstrate accountability, transparency and stewardship will keep your organization's goals and mission alive and will keep your donors engaged in your cause. Software is available, both commercially and for free, to help you with fundraising and other aspects of your organization's work. Customer Relations Management (CRM) software can help you remember information about your donors, such as the donor's intentions. It can also provide communication and reporting tools that help strengthen donor relationships. (See the Resources section under "Free Software for Fundraising" for a list of software.)

TRY IT!

Imagine that you are the chair of the board of directors for a nonprofit serving the homeless called Hope's Place. The mission of Hope's Place is to assist people in finding housing so they can then seek jobs. You are going to facilitate a planning session on fundraising for the next five years. This planning may take

Table 22.2 Donor stewardship plan template.

| **Donor Stewardship Plan:** Organization Name_____ Year_____ ||||||||
Activity	Responsible Staff	Date	Gift #1	Recurring	Major	No Gift

up to three meetings. Create agendas for these meetings that include plans for fundraising (sponsorships, individual giving, events, in-kind donations or fee-for-service), and grant seeking. One meeting should focus explicitly on planning how to demonstrate accountability and stewardship.

SUMMARY

Meet donors where their passions are, to build authentic and meaningful relationships. Uncover shared values: Donors appreciate those who understand their values and identities and make them feel included. Focus on the joy that comes from hearing the stories of what it is that motivates generosity. Think about donors investing in the mission of your organization and the benefits donors will experience from their generosity.

Organizations small and large need resources to carry out their plans, so fundraising is a key part of their strategic plan. This chapter covered fundraising plans and methods. It also covered how to demonstrate the honesty, accountability, trustworthiness and transparency of your organization.

RESOURCES

Salary Surveys
Often used for creating a budget.
www.salary.com
www.payscale.com
https://hr-survey.com/SalarySurvey.htm

Donation Forms and Web Pages

Donation request letters and form templates from Fundly: https://blog.fundly.com/donation-form-templates

Sample fundraising letters from Lovetoknow: https://charity.lovetoknow.com/Sample_Letters_Asking_for_Donations

Examples of nonprofit donation web pages: https://wiredimpact.com/blog/great-nonprofit-donation-pages

Free Software for Fundraising

Snowballfundraising. (2017). *Top 10 free fundraising software providers for nonprofits*. Retrieved from https://snowballfundraising.com/free-fundraising-software

Sources for Grant Searches

Search for Federal Grants: www.grants.gov
Foundation Directory Online: http://foundationcenter.org/products/foundation-directory-online

Websites for More Information

BoardSource. (n.d.). *Beyond cash: A guide on how nonprofit boards can tap pro bono and in-kind resources*. Retrieved from https://my.taprootfoundation.org/docs/BEYOND-CASH-Guide-for-Nonprofit-Boards.pdf

Community Tool Box. (n.d.). *Soliciting contributions and in-kind support*. Retrieved from https://ctb.ku.edu/en/table-of-contents/sustain/long-term-sustainability/solicit-contributions/main

Council for Advancement and Support of Education. (n.d.). *Gift agreements*. Retrieved from www.case.org/Publications_and_Products/Fundraising_Fundamentals_Intro/Fundraising_Fundamentals_section_10/Fundraising_Fundamentals_section_104.html

Cravens, J. (2016). *Pro-bono/in-kind/donated services for mission-based organizations: When, why and how?* Retrieved from Energize, Inc.: www.energizeinc.com/a-z/article-internal/11990

IRS. (2016). *Charitable contributions*. Retrieved from www.irs.gov/pub/irs-pdf/p1771.pdf

Kester, K. S. (2014). *Charitable Allies: Can my donor take a tax deduction for in-kind donations?* Retrieved from https://charitableallies.org/news/in-kind-donations/

Miller, L. (2014). *Gifts in-kind: The A, B, and C's of properly recording*. Herbein+Company, Inc. Retrieved from www.herbein.com/blog/gifts-in-kind-the-a-b-and-cs-of-properly-recording

National Council of Nonprofits. (n.d.). *Gift acceptance policies*. Retrieved from www.councilofnonprofits.org/tools-resources/gift-acceptance-policies

National Council of Nonprofits. (n.d.). *Gift acknowledgements: Saying "thank you" to donors*. Retrieved from www.councilofnonprofits.org/tools-resources/saying-thank-you-to-donors

NCVO. (n.d.). *Knowhow nonprofit: How to do resource-raising*. Retrieved from https://knowhow.ncvo.org.uk/how-to/resource-raising-why-bother

Poderis, T. (n.d.). *Raise-Funds: In-kind gifts: How to acknowledge and recognize them*. Retrieved from www.raise-funds.com/in-kind-gifts-how-to-acknowledge-and-recognize-them/

Strengthening Nonprofits. (n.d.). *Planning for, securing, and documenting in-kind donations*. Retrieved from www.strengtheningnonprofits.org/resources/e-learning/online/inkinddonations/Print.aspx

CITATIONS

Behn, R. D. (2001). *Rethinking democratic accountability*. Washington, DC: Brookings Institution Press.

Brinckerhoff, P. C. (2004). *Nonprofit stewardship: A better way to lead your mission-based organization*. St Paul, MN: Wilder Foundation.

Ebrahim, A. (2009). Placing the normative logics of accountability in "thick" perspective. *American Behavioral Scientist, 52*(6), 885–904.

Ebrahim, A. (2016). The many faces of nonprofit accountability. In D. O. Renz (Ed.), *The Jossey-Bass handbook of nonprofit leadership and management (essential texts for nonprofit and public leadership and management)* (4th ed., pp. 102–124). Hoboken, NJ: John Wiley & Sons.

Gitlin, L. N., & Lyons, K. J. (2014). *Successful grant writing: Strategies for health and human services professional* (4th ed.). New York: Springer.

Hanberg, E. (2009). *The little book of gold: Fundraising for small (and very small) nonprofits*. Scotts Valley, CA: CreateSpace.

Heyman, D. R. (2016). *Nonprofit fundraising 101: A practical guide with easy to implement ideas & tips from industry experts*. Hoboken, NJ: John Wiley & Sons.

Mansfield, H. (2012). *Social media for social good: A how-to guide for nonprofits*. New York: McGraw-Hill.

23 BUILDING ALLIANCES AND COLLABORATION

Figure 23.0

WHAT'S IN THIS CHAPTER?

Community change seldom takes place as a result of a small group working alone. The group often has greater success when they build partnerships with stakeholders and other outside individuals and organizations that can influence or assist with the change process. Nonprofit organizations typically work within tight budgets that make continued operation difficult. Strategic alliances are a way to reduce costs, and to share resources, equipment, physical facilities and programs in a way that reduces duplication and supports all stakeholders. This takes team and personal emissary work, as well as efforts to bridge cultural, social and community values.

A strategic alliance does one or more of the following:

1. Promotes the core goals of the organizations.
2. Advances the development of a core competency or other resource.
3. Blocks or overcomes a threat.
4. Creates or maintains opportunities for the organization.
5. Mitigates a risk to the organization.

Objectives

By the end of this chapter, you will be able to:

- Build alliances with outside organizations.
- Build the collaborative community using effective methods of working together.
- Bridge cultural, social and community values.

A STORY ABOUT OPENING DIALOGUE

In the Avenue of the Righteous story in this chapter, a rabbi noticed an article in the newspaper about the death of a Righteous Gentile who had risked his life to save the Jews from the Holocaust. His life and deeds had passed without notice by the Chicago area Jews. The rabbi asked himself why his deeds had been forgotten. To make sure another Chicago area rescuer was not forgotten, he would need allies from the Christian, Jewish and Baha'i congregations to help identify non-Jewish rescuers of the Holocaust and bring together the resources to honor them.

Here is an example of how a facilitator used the opening dialogue for initiating a project to establish immediate solidarity between traditional adversaries who were seated at the same table for the first time.

Members of the Avenue of the Righteous and the Foundation for the Righteous have invited Chicago area Polish and Jewish leaders to the table for a discussion of how they could work together on a joint project to honor Polish rescuers. These two cultural groups rarely met, except in formal intellectual discussions to discuss who was responsible for the Holocaust. Not much movement had been made on that difficult topic because when the survivors of the Holocaust left Poland, the Jews had settled in one section of Chicago and the Poles in another section. Their enmity had grown stronger in their new land of America as they avoided each other. Ordinary Jews and Poles tended not to relate to each other even though they lived in the same city, and over the decades they continued to blame the other for the Holocaust. How to bring them into a partnership for a major citywide project to honor Poles who had rescued Jews during the war? That would be the challenge facing the facilitator of this initial meeting.

She began with a question—"Why are you here?" The Polish consul general opened with a personal story. He was born in the post-war years in Poland, and his school curriculum never mentioned the Holocaust. He said that he first heard about it during his postgraduate studies. Then an American psychology professor who had fought in World War II said that he had never heard about the Trail of Tears until he was in his graduate program. Both recognized a common bond of wanting to tell the truth even it if was hard to face, and this interchange between them bonded the entire group. Each person followed up with a personal story and revealed why they were willing to open a bitter subject from the past to air it out. Despite past differences, the foundation had been laid for a successful project.

In this story, the facilitator chose a reflective opening question using an emotional tone to evoke the participants' sensory responses. By offering an open-ended question, rather than a more focused one, she prompted the first speaker, the consul general, to give an authentic response. As a public official representing his country, he could have resorted to "officialese," but he had come to the meeting for a different reason. The facilitator also modeled a sincere desire to hear his response by adopting an attitude of deep listening; she did not interrupt or direct him. By sitting silently and keeping eye contact, she evoked a "feeling" response rather than a spoken one. Dialogue methods like this can be effective starting points for action.

> *Deep listening:* Deep listening involves listening to learn, and for understanding, rather than agreement, and asking good questions to explore the learning. Deep listening can occur on the intrapersonal (listening to yourself), interpersonal and group levels.

WHAT THIS TECHNIQUE IS ABOUT

Three goals of a collaboration should be:

- Strong organizational commitment and substantial investment by all parties.
- Significant initiatives.
- Significant community impact.

ALLIANCES WITH OUTSIDE ORGANIZATIONS

Many nonprofits begin as a grassroots unincorporated association. Much of what is described in this book is for this type of organization. Organizations can plan and implement programs and activities informally, with financial activity being conducted by one or more individuals within the group. Later, when they have grown and are receiving donations, they may incorporate within their state as a nonprofit organization. Still later, they may apply for tax-exempt status from the Internal Revenue Service so that they can accept tax-deductible donations (Hopkins, 1989). (See Appendix H, online, for information on nonprofit and tax-exempt statuses.)

Determine what your team needs and wants to have as a community impact. How will they carry out their strategies and tactics? Begin to outline what your group can accomplish on their own, and what will need assistance. Do they need to network with allies to build awareness (see Figure 23.1), and share information with another organization? Do they need to extend organizational resources by working with other, similar organizations? Or is there a need for cooperative creation of new resources (Lofquist, 1989, p. 59)?

Figure 23.1 Levels of networking with other organizations.
Source: Adapted from Lofquist (1989, p. 59).

The next step is to determine if there are already groups in the community working on similar issues. Members of your group with significant history in the community probably have an extensive network of friends and acquaintances in other community organizations. As a group, use this knowledge to brainstorm a list of individuals and organizations with similar interests and missions that could partner with your group. City Hall, the Chamber of Commerce, the Yellow Pages and web searches may be sources you can check for information on community organizations that might be potential allies. You will want to locate information on the organization's missions, projects and finances.

Your team should discuss how integrated you want the allied organizations to be (see Figure 23.2). Associations of allies work together on projects to achieve a common purpose, but they are integrated to a lesser degree than those that offer joint programming or referral relationship. The most integrated is a collaboration that shares staff and services (The Bridgespan Group, 2015).

Part of due diligence needed before making a decision about working with other organizations is doing your homework and learning about an organization to uncover any potential issues before joining forces. Explore the possible strategic alignment and fit between the other organizations and outline ways in which each group would benefit from working together to achieve your goals and theirs (Burtch, 2013). Research the potential allies as a team to determine if the other organization is struggling financially, or if it is stable. Does the other organization have a reputation for competition with other organizations or internal trust issues? If so, steer clear. Due diligence investigations such as this can help uncover potential red flags before they impact your organization. See the Resources section in this chapter for places to find out about nonprofits and tax-exempt organizations.

> *Due diligence:* the examination of an organization's (nonprofit or for profit) records done before creating an alliance, especially one that involves shared services, staff or funding. Locate information on strategy and results, leadership, financials, organization and operations where possible.

Finally, select a *few* to approach. Don't inflate the new alliance with too many members right at the start. The more there are, the slower it will go, but make sure you have people with the right skills and

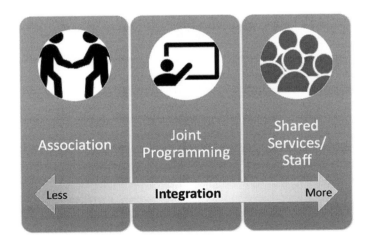

Figure 23.2 Allies integration.
Source: Adapted from the Bridgespan Group (2015).

knowledge as well as credibility. For instance, you may need to include a legal advisor if you plan on fundraising as an alliance. Describe the importance of each of the allies chosen.

Revisit the original summary of your group's purpose discussed in Chapter 5. Is it still up to date? Revise it if necessary, and prepare answers to these questions:

- What is the history of the condition or issue of concern?
- What information do we have about the situation?
- When reviewing data, what numbers, words or phrases stand out?
- What are the actual conditions we are trying to achieve?
- What resources do we have to achieve those conditions?
- Why should the collaboration be formed? What are the purpose and goals?
- Is there strategic alignment and fit between your organization and theirs and ways in which each group would benefit from working together to create value and achieve your goals and theirs?
- How many people should be involved? How much time is expected? What leadership will be involved?

> *Strategic alliance:* a relationship between two or more organizations that can create significant and sustainable value.

Once your summary is up to date, divide the work of contacting the chosen individuals or organizations among members of your core group. If someone has a personal relationship with an individual in the organization, it is easier to begin a conversation about a possible alliance. Keep in mind that personal emissary work comes easily to some people and not to others. When members of your team talk to individuals from other organizations, ask them to explore the strategic fit, and discuss openly whether the organization can commit to the type of alliance you envision. Finally, invite them to collaborate with your group or organization if they seem receptive to an alliance.

> *Personal emissary work*: an individual working on behalf of the project by personally taking messages, taking part in discussions, inviting stakeholders to meetings, requesting information and so on.

BRIDGE CULTURAL, SOCIAL AND COMMUNITY VALUES

Effective collaboration requires that people relate well to each other and enjoy fair exchanges and a sense of equality with one another. In addition, people need autonomy and a sense that the future is predictable (Rock, 2008). When all of these factors are in place, collaboration with others can be a rewarding experience.

When bringing allies together, the result may be a group of diverse people, as in the Avenue of the Righteous project described earlier in this chapter. As mentioned in Chapter 8, this may present difficulty in becoming an effective team when:

- People have never met, so they do not have relationships.
- They come from different parts of the community with different backgrounds, cultures, values and perspectives.
- They may have different levels of wealth or authority, which may intimidate some people, leading to a sense of unequal status.

The task of a facilitator during the initial meeting is to reduce the threats of unequal status and uncertainty, when members of each of the collaborating organizations come together to discuss their goals and how they will work together. It may be useful at this meeting to melt the ice and create a common bond within the group as the facilitator did in the story above. The icebreaker or opening experience needs to be nonjudgmental so all the collaborators feel free sharing personal aspects of themselves via stories, photos and other means. That is why the facilitator asked an open-ended question as her icebreaker, listened for understanding and used the similarity of the stories told by the consul general and the professor and their desire to tell their truth as way of creating bridges between persons of differing cultural backgrounds. As a result of the activities of that first meeting, members need to arrive at a sense of equality, fairness and relatedness. They also need to leave the meeting with a sense of certainty that the future of the alliance will be beneficial to the community and rewarding for the members.

The depth and clarity of a facilitator's cultural and social lens can make or break diverse collaborators' ability to learn to work together. When the differences are very profound, it may be useful to invite cultural liaisons to the first meeting if the facilitator does not have extensive experience with different cultures.

BUILD THE COMMUNITY AND METHODS OF COLLABORATING

Now that you've got your collaborators working with you and offering the benefits you each need, you need to maintain your alliances. To maintain alliances, it is important to build relationships between the organizations and to hammer out methods of collaborating. You will want to cultivate trust between the key internal contacts in your organization and your alliance partners through regular contact, clear and open communication and encouraging collaborative behavior. Discuss how you will work together and leverage the differences between the organizations to create value. True grassroots organizations usually start with no rules or hierarchies, and they prosper in the short term because they are organic and self-organizing. Over time, they will come to benefit from some top-down, authoritative structure. That's when it gets tricky—making the organization more efficient without stifling its creative energies.

Creating structure in a collaborative arrangement of allies can prevent a world of woes. To begin this process, the collaborators should determine clear strategies, processes and structures for working together that are directly linked to the shared goals and measures of success for the alliance. Document these things in a written **agreement** or compact. The agreement defines the alliance's purpose (or mission), functions and rules for its conduct or leadership:

- **Mission and purpose.** These have already been established, but the group may need to clarify or spend time discussing the wording and details including the scope, timeline and milestones. Build in opportunities for short-term successes and celebrations. Determine how success will be measured.
- **Alliance leadership and decision-making process.** Everyone must decide on who will take the leadership role and what exactly they will do. Will the leader be chosen from among the members? Will decisions be made by consensus (discussion until agreement) or some sort of voting system? How will decisions be recorded, and how will absent members be notified? How will you provide feedback to hold members accountable?
- **Values and assumptions.** If a member organization has a concern about the way things will be done, now is the time to discuss and make these official. For instance, one organization is concerned that allies should not compete with one another on who will bring in the most literacy clients for tutoring. They can discuss this and make non-competition a written value.
- **Ethics policy.** If a conflict of interest arises, how should the alliance resolve that issue? Do the policies of each member organization apply to the alliance's actions? What will you do in case of a conflict in policies?

Use this agreement as a guide during conflicts and decision-making. This step will save the alliance grief in the long run and should be done early in the process. All members of the collaboration should read it, sign and receive a copy for their reference.

With input from each of the collaborators or allies, develop evaluation measures on how the alliance is working, and how it is progressing on accomplishing goals of the alliance. Do members collaborate effectively? Don't wait until the end to evaluate. This should be used as a formative evaluation that can improve the effectiveness of the collaboration by asking "What can be improved?" and making midstream corrections.

> *Formative evaluation*: the process of examining an alliance, project, program, or process to determine what's working, what's not and why, so that mid-course corrections can be made.

Often it is desirable for small alliances to appoint *liaisons* between the groups who attend key meetings of the other organization who can report back to your organization. However, regular whole group meetings are also useful to maintain relationships and trust. As Deborah Tannen noted, "talk is the glue that holds relationships together" (Tannen, 2007, p. 85). When the community environment changes (for instance, there are shifts in community demographics that affect your projects and partnerships), trust will allow the collaborators to have the honest discussions necessary if a change in direction is to take place.

> *Liaison:* someone who will maintain communication for awareness and collaboration between organizations. A cultural liaison has knowledge of the culture and language of a particular group of people.

ALLIANCES WITH OUTSIDE PEOPLE

Making alliances with individuals is sometimes desired to obtain the assistance of people with expertise, connections or resources to carry out the work of the organization. Besides determining that individuals have the expertise needed, it is important to interview them and make sure they will mesh with the organization. Traits to look for include: (1) interest in and passion for your cause; (2) taking responsibility for the outcomes; (3) respectful of board members, staff and volunteers; (4) creative problem solver; (5) willing to learn from others in your organization. These are also useful traits for members of your board of directors.

HOW TO CARRY OUT THIS TECHNIQUE

Ask your group to determine what your team needs and wants to carry out their strategies and tactics.

Identify what your group can accomplish on their own, and what help will be needed. As a group, use your knowledge of organizations and people in the community to brainstorm a list of individuals and organizations that could partner with your group. Explore strategic alignment between another organization and your organization. Using that information, select organizations you may want to partner with (Steinhilber, 2008). Revisit and revise your organization's summary, describing how each organization would benefit from working together to achieve your goals and theirs.

Ask someone in your group to contact an individual in the organization to discuss an alliance using information in the summary. Once you have reached agreement, schedule a meeting with all allies.

At the initial meeting, work to build trust and bridge cultural, social and community values. Establish between the members:

- Equality between members.
- Fairness in the exchanges among members.
- Relationships between members.
- Certainty in the future benefits of the alliance.

Ensure that all allies will work together to determine a clear purpose, shared goals, direction, processes and structures for working together and evaluating the collaboration. Clear purpose and shared goals need to include scope of your collaborations and timelines. Create clear processes and structures for discussion, working, problem-solving together and delegating the work.

Maintain regular clear and open contact between members. Appoint liaisons where necessary.

Continually evaluate effectiveness of the collaboration process and outcomes and make course corrections.

TRY IT!

Imagine that you are a member of a grassroots organization (an organization created by the people in a given community to organize collective action to affect change in the local area) working to create a homeless shelter in extreme northern Wisconsin where people could sleep out of the winter cold for the night, have a shower and get a warm meal.

- With a budget of $500, what can your group accomplish on their own?
- List some allies with whom you could partner. You can begin with the United Way 211 directory (http://www.211.org/) and the resources listed at the end of this chapter.
- Describe the strategic alignment between your organization and theirs.
- Describe how each organization would benefit from working together to achieve your goals and theirs.
- Create an agenda for the first meeting.
- Describe how you will evaluate the collaboration process and outcomes.

SUMMARY

Community change requires effort, and a small group working alone often can accomplish more when they join forces with other nonprofit organizations, for-profit organizations, educational institutions or governmental agencies. Building collaborative partnerships with stakeholders and other outside individuals and organizations can powerfully influence the change process. Strategic alliances can assist your organization to reduce costs and to share resources, equipment, physical facilities and programs to reduce duplication and support stakeholders of both organizations. This takes team research and personal emissary work as well as efforts to bridge cultural, social and community values. Finally, it requires that the collaborative group devise and document how they will work together.

RESOURCES

When doing research on potential allies, you can check:

- Printed or published materials by the organization with information such as mission statement, annual reports, brochures and newsletters.

- Newspaper, magazine, journal and online articles about the organization.
- Biographies, resumes or LinkedIn information of executive director and other organization leaders.
- Form 990 (the Internal Revenue Service tax form required for organizations with annual receipts of over $200K) provides a formal public view of the organization's financial condition, strengths, weaknesses, and income sources. All U.S. tax-exempt nonprofits make public their three most recent Form 990 or 990-PF annual returns. They can be searched at several websites including:
    - Foundation Center: http://foundationcenter.org/find-funding/990-finder
    - Guidestar: www.guidestar.org/Home.aspx
    - Economic Research Institute: www.erieri.com/form990finder
    - ProPublica: https://projects.propublica.org/nonprofits/
- IRS status certifying that the organization is eligible to receive tax-deductible charitable contributions, found at the Internal Revenue Service website (www.irs.gov). Select the "Charities and Non-Profits" tab located at the top of the web page. This will take you to the web page that contains tax information and for charities and other nonprofit organizations. You will find the organization's name, its location and its deductibility code.

CITATIONS

The Bridgespan Group. (2015). *Partnerships and collaboration*. Retrieved from www.bridgespan.org/insights/library/nonprofit-management-tools-and-trends/strategic-alliances

Burtch, B. W. (2013). *Win-Win for the greater good*. San Rafael, CA: Bruce W. Burtch Inc.

Hopkins, B. (1989). *Starting and managing a nonprofit organization*. New York: John Wiley & Sons.

Lofquist, W. (1989). *The technology of prevention workbook*. Tucson, AZ: AYD Publications.

Rock, D. (2008). SCARF: A brain-based model for collaborating with and influencing others. *NeuroLeadership Journal, 1*(1), 44.

Steinhilber, S. (2008). *Strategic alliances: Three ways to make them work*. Watertown, MA: Harvard Business Review Press.

CHOREOGRAPHY OF CONVERSATION   24

Figure 24.0

WHAT'S IN THIS CHAPTER?

One of the core skills for advancing any social change action is the ability to manage the conversation among teams or in large group settings. Imagine yourself leading a discussion about your chosen issue or concern with a diverse, recently formed community group. At the outset, you might have a particular goal or envisioned outcome in mind. As one of the initial organizers, your first thought will probably be, "How can I get all of these folks to work together?" This is the starting point for the process of change. A facilitator can make the work of a change team easier by choreographing the conversation to ensure clear communication and avoid miscommunications or hard feelings.

Objectives

By the end of this chapter, you will be able to:

- Observe others facilitating a group discussion to learn to facilitate more effectively.
- Identify communication styles of group members.
- Choreograph the conversation by provoking or directing the conversation and keeping team members on task.
- Restart the conversation again when the team gets stuck.

Let's begin to address this skill set of facilitating conversations in groups with another story to show how managing or mismanaging an initial meeting can affect the change process.

To explain how group facilitation works in a real-world context with real people who have their own individual ideas of how things should go, we need a graphic way of looking at it. For this purpose, I am borrowing a metaphor from the dance world which I am calling the **choreography of conversation**. The definition of choreography is the practice of designing choreographic sequences of steps and movements in dance. There are similarities to the beginning of a project when a group of activists come onto the dance floor without a clear idea of how to coordinate steps with (speak to) one another. Often the beginnings are fractured by a mixed set of steps with no choreography. But who will guide the conversation?

In order to avoid the predictable conflicts that arise in group process when each person is dancing to a different tune, it is important to have a Dance-master (i.e. the facilitator role) who can oversee the dance design and the performance. A facilitator can help keep the tempo and create a pattern of fair listening and speaking so that people do not inadvertently (or on purpose) step on each other's toes. Extending the metaphor of a group meeting as a dance floor, you might observe people taking on different roles like these—the wallflower who is not participating, the prima ballerina who grabs the center stage and holds on, or that girl doing the rumba by herself in the corner when everyone else has agreed to dance the minuet.

What are the qualities of a Dance-master? Here are just a few—calmness, openness, flexibility, nurturing, and taking seriously the well-being of others. Being willing to allow for ambiguity or waiting in silence. Staying grounded in times of stress/distress in the organization. Primarily, the group facilitator must develop the ability to remain unmoved in the heat of the moment. When the going gets rough, the Dance-master must step in and ask the group, "What is happening right now?" By stopping the action, the facilitator calls for the group members to pay careful attention to the dynamics of the conversation. Is someone stepping on others' toes? Some dancers did not come to the dance to cooperate but to call their own tune (i.e. further a private agenda). The Dance-master must then instruct them on the value of listening, the basics of civility and waiting for their turn. Here is a story that exemplifies these qualities of facilitation in a group conversation.

A STORY ABOUT COMMUNICATION: MR. MAYOR ATTENDS A RACE UNITY GROUP MEETING

A small mixed group of African Americans and others were meeting at a community center to discuss issues of racial bias in their town. Arriving late and with a bit of drama, the mayor of the town slowly entered the room and joined the discussion. It did not take long for him to begin dominating the group with his proclamations of how *they* (the African Americans) should be stepping up to solve racial issues in the town. Fern, a visitor from a nearby town, began to speak. She did not know she was speaking to the mayor. He kept interrupting her and indicating that he knew best. Fern tried valiantly to be heard, but he kept on stepping on her words. Just then, the facilitator said, "What is happening now?" She described what had just occurred and called the group to pay attention by saying, "An African American woman is trying to speak and cannot be heard." Suddenly the room went into an ambiguous silence. Then Fern was able to finish her comment. The mayor looked surprised but also went silent and afterwards began to listen to all the members of the group when they were speaking; he no longer took control of the conversation with his own speech.

WHAT THIS TECHNIQUE IS ABOUT

Let's evaluate some aspects of group facilitation which were present in this example, though not visible to most members of the group. We will take it one dance step at a time so you can become aware of the skills that were being used in this setting.

Step 1: Which Dance Step Is Appropriate?

As a group conversation begins, it is important to understand the context. Was this to be a formal board meeting, with an agenda and with a person conducting the meeting using parliamentary procedure, or was it an informal gathering of equals? Will decisions be made by motions and voting, or by coming to consensus? The form of facilitation you choose will depend on how the meeting is functioning. In this story, the setting is a community center where a group of people have been meeting informally for several months as equals. There is no hierarchy or fixed leadership role, and the program revolves around a selected topic. The facilitation model in this context should be based on helping each person having an equal chance to speak.

Step 2: Who Leads? Who Follows?

Within an informal context there is an unwritten agreement that all members are of equal rank in their relationship to one another. However, the mayor violated this rule by holding fast to his right to speak over everyone else. In fact, he was acting like a prima ballerina, outranking the others and keeping them from having their fair chance to speak. He overrode communication by many people with his own declarations about how they should be listening to his advice. The implication was that he had the higher rank, and that they were not "doing it right." There was a quiet revolt going on in the room with other members who wanted their turn to speak.

Step 3: Cutting In

Cutting in is an acceptable way to change partners with a tap on the shoulder that allows someone new to have a turn at dancing. This could be used as a metaphor for the skill of *interruption*. When the facilitator asked the question "What is happening now?" she was cutting in and pointing out subtly that the mayor was hogging the floor. A facilitator must be courageous enough to interrupt unwanted behaviors such as grandstanding, over-talking or not listening. In this scene she "stopped the music" to find out what was going on in the group conversation. The mayor suddenly found himself in the uncomfortable position of seeing that he was preventing Fern from having her turn. He stopped talking and began listening. After the interruption by the facilitator, other group members also rejoined the conversation.

"Cutting in" can be used as a method of changing the conversation's direction by any member of the group. The way to do it is like a light tap on the shoulder. It is important that it be offered not as an accusation but as redirection. Avoid direct eye contact with the offending person and speak to the entire group. Do not say "you" or appear to be blaming the offender. Simply stop the music and offer an observation about what is going on. Then everyone will place their attention on what is happening in the group conversation to observe what is not working and needs to be changed.

THE ARTS OF OBSERVATION AND REFLECTION

To observe the behavior of others, we first need to know ourselves so that we can observe objectively. According to Merrill and Reid (1981), two factors contribute to objectivity: (1) as we observe human behaviors, we have to remember that our own feelings and attitudes get in the way of our objectivity; (2) we need to try to determine how our own behavior compares to that of others (p. 35). In other words, we need to look at our own behavior objectively, rather than subjectively, so we can remain neutral. Merrill and Reid (1981) noted that:

1. By focusing on what we see and hear, we can objectively describe behavior.
2. By observing and describing enough behavior, we will be able to anticipate or predict a person's future behavior.
3. By learning to predict well, we can exercise some control over how we respond to the behavior that we are describing and predicting (p. 36).

Even when we get good at predicting behaviors of another person, it is important to remember that people are flexible and can adapt their behavior to the circumstances in which they find themselves. In fact, people will sometimes combine characteristics of multiple communications styles when necessary. You can also practice that kind of flexibility in facilitating and communicating with the people in the room.

During a meeting, observe what is happening while the dance of conversation is going on and mentally evaluate the outcomes. What are we looking for while we are observing?

- Is the discussion on topic? Or does it need to be refocused?
- What is the energy level? Is it energetic, or is it slowing down and in need of pushing forward or re-energizing?
- Does there appear to be a sense of safety to people in the room? Who is participating? Who is not? Do you see any wallflowers? Are some people talking too much, or dominating the conversation? Do some people need encouragement to share their ideas?
- What nonverbal cues (visual social distance) are you seeing? Do you see physical distance between team members? Are you reading emotional tone in physical bodies or gestures (interest, excitement, boredom, tension, anger or fear)? Do you see people making eye contact with each other or not? Does anyone look apathetic?
- Is there conflict that needs to be smoothed over?
- Are the ideas expressed clear, or should follow-up questions be asked to clarify? If the ideas are good, be sure to make an encouraging comment or praise the person. If the comment is off topic, find the good or relevant in what the person said.
- What are participant's communication styles?
- Are there any *distractions*, including physical, emotional and intellectual distractions, to be removed? Do you need to close the door or curtains to keep people focused?

Observation also includes periods of silence while coming to an understanding and reflecting on certain actions or reactions in the group. The Dance-master/facilitator plays a key reflective role in the planning and implementation phases of any group process. Reflection can take many forms. What is generally involved is slowing down and thinking ahead, or looking back with a calm mind. Here are a few techniques of reflection that are tried and true.

- *Knowing when to speak and when not to speak.*
    - Careful consideration of our own speech patterns in concert with the patterns of others can lead to a fruitful dialogue. Restraint of speech is also useful when we notice that we feel triggered (feel an emotional reaction) by a comment someone made. Stop and reflect for a moment before reacting. There might be a *meta-message* that we are missing.

- *Noticing and wondering.*
  - The facilitator had noticed that one person was commanding the attention of all and wondered if this was shutting down the group communication.
- *Listening instead of defending or rebutting.*
  - Group members in the story began to listen to each other more deeply when they felt that they would be heard. No longer did they have to interrupt for a chance to speak.
- *Asking simple questions.*
  - The facilitator asked, "What is happening now?" and refocused the conversation by prompting a reflection on the group process. The mayor became reflective or thoughtful when he recognized that he was preventing Fern from having her turn at speaking. He had been unaware that he was stepping on her toes because he was used to directing a meeting instead of being an equal participant.

> *Meta-message:* a message that can be implied or inferred from the reading "between the lines" of a message. The message behind what someone is saying.

KEEPING IN STEP (TAKING CUES FROM THE DANCE-MASTER)

Before the dance can even begin, there must be a time to create the choreographic design. What will be the size of the group, which steps will be used, how to keep the pace or rhythm and synchronize all the dance movements? The expression "keeping in step" is useful for situations when some of the dancers lose their focus and draw the others into side steps. There are many cues to be considered. *Verbal cues* are short phrases or single words that inform the dancers about the next move or help them to remain in the proper sequence. As we have seen in our story, when one of the dancers is out of step, it can stop the entire production. *Visual cues* are also helpful when a facilitator uses a whiteboard or easel pad to track ideas that are under discussion. Keep in mind that some participants are visually oriented, and others are auditory participants, so try to offer multiple cues (visual as well as verbal) to satisfy the information processing preferences of everyone in the room.

Here is one example which demonstrates this difficulty with those who dance to a different tune than the one that is being called by the Dance-master:

A small religious community has called a meeting to discuss renovating their building. Several persons are leading the discussion, and no single person has been designated as the facilitator. The conversation goes a bit like this, "I can appreciate that Sue thinks the fireplace is beautiful and worthy of being fixed, but I do not really like the way it looks." "Why are we spending money on material things for our own comfort when the environment is failing, and climate change is pending?" "Can't our building be beautiful as well as utilitarian?" Obviously, there are divergent points of view in this discussion, which is perfectly average in any group; however, with effective facilitation there can be a deliberative focus that moves this conversation forward instead of backward. The problem is that the group members are out of step with each other.

What can the designated group facilitator do to help people at a meeting find common ground?

Step 1: Identify the common goal. Why have they gathered, and what outcome are they seeking? In this case they share an idea that the building needs to be renovated to make it more ADA accessible for aging members and to beautify it so that it is both utilitarian and attractive. Write the common goal or focus question in big letters on a piece of easel paper where all can see it. Read it out loud and ask the group to agree on the wording. Keep referring back to the focus question whenever someone leads the group "out of step."

Step 2: **Invite individuals to answer the question on a piece of paper.** How is the building serving us now? Then the facilitator can write their responses on easel paper so all can see them. Read them aloud after they are scribed to assist auditory and visual learners alike.

Step 3: **List agreements on a separate sheet of paper to mark consensus items that can be tracked as the discussion moves forward.** This keeps newcomers to the conversation from retreading old ground. Those people who participate get to make the decisions without being second-guessed by latecomers or those who are only minimally participating. This reduces the frustration of "nothing ever gets done."

Step 4: **Use a "Parking Lot" page to write down new ideas that are not part of the current focus but could be considered at a later time.** For example, a member might suggest something outside the scope of the current discussion or a blue-sky idea like "Let's build a new building." Look for the central flow of decisions and keep the creative souls from leading people down another path too soon. Respect their offerings by saying, "Thanks. We will put this idea in the parking lot for consideration at another time."

COMMUNICATION STYLES

In trying to develop an awareness of ways of talking, people often ask me what a particular expression or conversational habit "really means." I always answer that no phrase or device has only one meaning. Like the practice of overlapping—beginning to talk when someone else is already speaking—what looks on the surface like the same way of talking can have varied meanings and effects. A listener may talk along with a speaker to provide support (what Deborah Tannen calls cooperative overlapping), or to change the topic (Tannen, 2007). Even changing the topic can have a range of meanings. It can show lack of interest, it can be an attempt to dominate the conversation, or it can be a kind of "mutual revelation device," matching the speaker's experience with the listener's (Tannen, 2007, p. 295). Even mutual revelation can be done with different motives; either in the spirit of connection, to establish rapport and emphasize sameness, or in a spirit of competition, to top a story and frame oneself as important.

There are many styles of communication, and these reflect the speaker's gender, intellectual strengths and their reading of the drift of the conversation. People whose strength is analysis might prefer specifics, hard facts and data. Others want to see the big picture before they get into the details. They might also like to think outside the box and challenge convention. Other people like process, timelines and step-by-step, thoroughly conceived plans. Then there are those who are good listeners, who are excellent at maintaining the health of relationships. All of these communication styles (shown in Figure 24.1) and their corresponding skills are important in accomplishing the goals of a change initiative.

What is important for a facilitator is to be able to observe and understand the communications styles of the attendees in order to read and respond to their meta-messages, at the same time leaving them feeling understood and excited about the possibilities for their change initiative. The key is to first understand your own particular communication style. Look at Table 24.1. Which best describes your "default" communication style, the one you fall back on? If you look at the list and think that you are, say Expressive (intuition-oriented), you know that Drivers (action-oriented) and Analytical-oriented people may become frustrated, unless you can include process, timelines, real data and hard numbers.

We all unconsciously vary our communications depending on the situation using a process called mirroring, but we can communicate even better. When you recognize these communications styles among your participants, some tips for communicating with someone with a *Driver* style, try to avoid chit chat. Instead, discuss progress to goals and focus on actions and solutions. For someone with an *Expressive* style, speak briefly and to the point. Set clear goals for the meeting, address problems and objections in terms of results, and conclude with a summary, providing details only on request. For someone with an *Amiable* style, leave time for small talk about people (family and children) before or after the meeting.

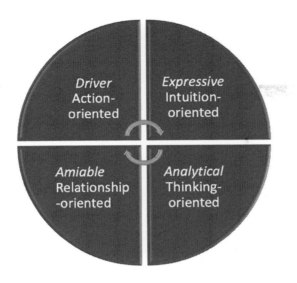

Figure 24.1 Communication styles.
Source: Adapted from Merrill and Reid (1981).

Table 24.1 Communication styles adapted from Merrill and Reid (1981).

Communication Style	Behavior
Driver Action-oriented	Prefers results, process, detail, timelines and practical plans. Sometimes becomes frustrated with "broad view" people.
Expressive Intuition-oriented	Prefers the broad view first. Prefers communicating the essentials briefly. May become frustrated with "excessive attention to detail." Enjoys generating ideas.
Amiable Relationship-oriented	Listens well. Prizes relationships and learning what makes others "tick." May become impatient conversations that miss relationship signals in favor of analysis.
Analytical Thinking-oriented	Prefers actual data, numbers and statistics. Can become frustrated with emotion-oriented discussions.

Use relevant stories about people to illustrate points. Finally, for someone with an *Analytical* style, prepare for the meeting with facts and figures. Allow time for this person to analyze and expect questions.

The goal for the facilitator is not to do a lot of talking, but to successfully direct the conversation and keep team members on task. You want to keep the rhythm or the pace of the meeting—synchronizing the dancers. To do this, practice flexibility and match your communication style to those who need to hear you.

HOW TO BREAK UP TENSIONS IN THE GROUP—INTRODUCING NEW STEPS

Take action *immediately* to address conflict at a team or community meeting. For example, at a recent town hall meeting on becoming a welcoming community, one angry man stood in line to make a statement about the immigrant issues in town. He related a difficult situation at the grocery store that made him feel very uncomfortable. He concluded by saying, "I just don't get it. It is getting harder these days to be a white male around here." He sat down, crossed his arms and looked up with challenge in his face. What should the facilitator say?

He paused a moment to gather his thoughts and then he began with compassion. He kindly asked the man, "How did that situation make you feel?"

The man replied, "Unwelcome in my own town."

The facilitator replied, "That must have felt terrible. A welcoming community is for you, too. When anyone does not feel welcome, they implicitly feel unwelcome. How can we turn this situation around, so *everyone* feels welcome?"

The man's body language changed in that moment. He had been heard and understood. He uncrossed his arms and looked up attentively. "I'm not sure, but I am willing to listen," he replied.

If the tension is caused by overlapping conversation, simply interrupting the conversations and pointing out what is happening may be sufficient, as in the case in the story about Fern and the mayor. Keep in mind that some conversational overlap is supportive. Rather than *stepping on someone's toes*, supportive "cooperative overlapping" (Tannen, 2007) is speaking just a few words of elaboration or encouragement. On the other hand, talking over another person, which causes tension in the meeting, may reveal a serious problem.

Take a break if needed. Ask team members to think of possible solutions. Depending on the severity of the conflict, a 10-minute break may be sufficient. If the conflict is severe, reconvene in a week when all team members have had a chance to think about what may have caused the conflict and possible solutions. Connect individually or as a group with team members to identify the possible cause of the conflict and their ideas for solutions.

Regular communication with team members can help a facilitator stay ahead of possible conflicts and diffuse them before the meeting.

HOW TO CARRY OUT THIS TECHNIQUE

1. Determine context of the meeting: formal or informal.
2. Observe what is going on in the room.
    a. Is the discussion focused on the topic?
    b. Is the energy level of the conversation energetic or slowing down?
    c. Do some people need encouragement to share their ideas?
    d. Are some people dominating the conversation?
    e. What nonverbal cues do you notice? Are people engaged or withdrawing?
    f. Are participants making eye contact? Or avoiding eye contact?
    g. It the emotional tone of the body language interested or apathetic? Excited or bored? Calm or tense? Are they showing trust or fear?
    h. Are there any distractions, including physical, emotional and intellectual distractions, to be removed?
3. Facilitate open discussion of ideas:
    a. Push toward new ideas and move discussion forward as needed.
    b. Ask participants follow-up questions for clarification.
    c. Encourage *everyone* to participate. Gently move on to prevent one person from talking too much or dominating the discussion.
4. Smooth over conflict, but don't ignore it. Assess the severity of the tension or conflict.
    a. If there are emotions involved, listen carefully and compassionately.
    b. If the problem is simply differing ideas, help them find common ground.
        - Provide writing paper and ask them to answer focus questions on the whiteboard or easel paper.

Table 24.2 Responding to people with different communication styles.

Communication Style	Behavior	Response
Driver Action-oriented	Prefers process, detail, timelines and well-thought-out plans. May become impatient with "big picture" people.	Discuss progress to goals. Avoid chitchat. Focus on actions and solutions.
Expressive Intuition-oriented	Prefers the big picture first. When speaking, is brief and to the point. May become impatient with detail-oriented conversations. Has many ideas and enjoys brainstorming.	Speak briefly and to the point. Set clear goals for the meeting. Address problems and objections in terms of results. Conclude with a summary. Provide details only on request.
Amiable Relationship-oriented	Good listener. Values relationships and learning how others think and feel. May become frustrated with analytical conversations that miss relationship cues.	Leave time for small talk about people (family, children) before or after the meeting. Use relevant stories about people to illustrate points.
Analytical Thinking-oriented	Prefers real data, hard numbers. May become impatient with feeling-oriented talk.	Prepare for the meeting with facts and figures. Allow for time to analyze. Expect questions.

- List agreements to the board to mark consensus points on a whiteboard or easel paper.
- Create a "Parking Lot" easel sheet to "park" ideas to consider at a later time.

c. It the problem causes mild tension, cut in, avoiding eye contact with the offending person. Speak to the whole group, while asking something like "What just happened, here?" Offer considerate redirection.

d. If the problem is more severe, call a break time, asking all to assess the cause and bring back possible solutions. The problem may only need a 10-minute break. If the problem is more severe, reconvene the meeting again in a week.

e. Observe communication styles of attendees and respond in kind:

TRY IT!

Exercise #1: Describe How You Would Facilitate

Imagine that you are the facilitator for a grassroots community change group working on the issue of youth hanging out downtown, disrupting pedestrian traffic. This concerns the businesspeople and store managers. A few young people have been observed smoking marijuana. As a result, the police are concerned. Along with teachers and parents, young people have been invited. You are conducting an assessment of "what's happening now." Most adults have been actively interacting, and the businesspeople have been particularly vocal, but there have been no comments from young people.

- Is it important to hear from the young people? Why or why not?
- What do you do if you wish to get their input? Describe your facilitation strategies.

FACILITATION OBSERVATION PRACTICE

1. Is the discussion on topic? Or does it need to be refocused?
Needs to be refocused on topic
1   2   3   4   5
What is the facilitator doing about this? _____

2. What is the energy level? Is it energetic, or is it slowing down and in need of pushing forward, or re-energizing?
Slowing down Energetic
1   2   3   4   5
What is the facilitator doing about this? _____

3. Is everyone participating, or do they need encouragement to share their ideas?
Some need encouragement Everyone participating
1   2   3   4   5
What is the facilitator doing about this? _____

4. Are some people talking too much, or dominating the conversation?
Some people are dominating No one is dominating
1   2   3   4   5
What is the facilitator doing about this? _____

5. What nonverbal cues (visual social distance) are you seeing?
Team members distancing themselves Team members normal distance
1   2   3   4   5
Avoiding eye contact Making eye contact with each other
1   2   3   4   5
Emotional tone in physical bodies or gestures:
Apathy Interest
1   2   3   4   5
Boredom Excitement
1   2   3   4   5
Frustration Satisfaction
1   2   3   4   5
Tension/Anger Calm
1   2   3   4   5
Fear Trust 1   2   3   4   5
What is the facilitator doing about these behaviors? _____
_____

6. Are the ideas expressed clearly, or should follow-up questions be asked to clarify?
Follow-up questions needed Clear ideas
1   2   3   4   5
Is the facilitator asking clarifying questions? _____

7. What are participant's communication styles?
Driver: (List names) _____
Expressive: (List names _____
Amiable: (List names) _____
Analytical: (List names) _____

8. Are there any distractions, including physical, emotional and intellectual distractions, to be removed?
Physical: No Yes (Please describe) _____
Emotional: No Yes (Please describe) _____
Intellectual: No Yes (Please describe) _____

Exercise #2: Practice Observing a Meeting

1. Use a copy of the facilitation observation form, observe a meeting being facilitated by someone else, what is happening and how the facilitator is managing it. You can learn from both well-facilitated meetings and those that are not as well facilitated. (A copy of this form is available online.)

SUMMARY

This chapter covered how to observe a discussion; how to identify communication styles of group members; how to choreograph conversation, provoke or direct the conversation and keep team members on task; and how to start the ball rolling again when the team gets stuck.

CITATIONS

Merrill, D. W., & Reid, R. H. (1981). *Personal styles & effective performance.* Boca Raton, FL: CRC Press.

Tannen, D. (2007). *You just don't understand: Women and men in conversation.* New York: William Morrow.

25 SETTING THE STAGE FOR PRODUCTIVE MEETINGS

Figure 25.0

WHAT'S IN THIS CHAPTER?

A facilitator needs to do some advance planning to conduct a good meeting, including planning the process, framework, agenda and ground rules. To carry on a focused discussion, it is important to think ahead about what methods can be used to: (1) create a sense of safety so that all voices can be heard; and (2) remove distractions, including physical, emotional and intellectual distractions.

Objectives

By the end of this chapter, you will be able to:

- Plan for accommodations for those who will be attending.
- Plan for arrangements and time for participants to socialize.
- Plan how you will engage attendees while maintaining a sense of safety so they will feel safe to comment.
- Plan for the team to create their own "ground rules" or create a set of ground rules for community meetings.
- Plan an agenda, including icebreaker, reports, community comments and conclusions.
- Plan for recording minutes and key points.
- Plan for the room set-up.
- Plan for removing distractions and staying on task.

A STORY ABOUT PRODUCTIVE AND UNPRODUCTIVE MEETINGS: GUN VIOLENCE IN OUR TOWN

Small towns, especially college towns, are no strangers to violence. Large numbers of young people gathering to drink at house parties can sometimes lead to dangerous outcomes. But the night that the shooting started was quite different for our town. Over 200 college students were at a party at a small house in a residential neighborhood where middle-class folks also lived. Two men came from out of town to settle a vendetta and started shooting wildly into the house party. Next door lived a local musician who moved rapidly onto his front porch and grabbed two young women dragging them to safety into his house. They survived, but he died from a gunshot wound from a single bullet. The popularity of this musician drew greater attention than usual to this gun event. Also, this incident happened on the "nice side of town."

A small activist group led an effort initially, but the results were mixed. An organizing grassroots meeting was called by the neighborhood association which was well attended; however, there was no effective facilitation of the meeting, and the group quickly descended into acrimony about what to do next. What could have been a starting point for community action turned out to be a false start.

What happened next? There was a huge public outcry that the chief of police and the mayor were not doing enough to counter the rising tide of gun violence. A town meeting at the Civic Center was called for by the neighborhood association where the shooting had occurred, and 175 people came to find out what they could do to change this situation. With such a large group of emotionally charged people, the scene could have disintegrated quickly, but someone had the wisdom and foresight to invite a professional facilitator from the university to lead the meeting. He skillfully guided the conversation so that each person who wished to speak was given an opportunity. A pencil and paper process also gave everyone a chance to write down ideas that were later coalesced onto large sheets of easel paper and posted on the wall. The facilitator then invited everyone to approach a poster-size message on the wall and select their issues of highest priority. Following the meeting, the city government and the police chief announced that they would be adjusting their approach to public safety to meet the stated needs of the community.

WHAT THIS TECHNIQUE IS ABOUT

This technique is about effective facilitation: planning, opening, conducting and concluding your meetings so that they will be productive. What follows are a few of many ideas that can be used to keep a meeting productive, like the town hall meeting in the story just described.

PLAN TO ACCOMMODATE ATTENDEES

A diverse group representing all sectors of the community is desirable for good community development efforts, including those from immigrant groups and retired citizens that will be affected by the planned change. As mentioned in Chapter 5, you will want to plan your space to accommodate any intercultural participants, elders and disabled members of the community. For participants that speak English as a second language or have significant cultural differences, you should consider the following:

- Work to gain trust of those attending.
- Find out about the cultural norms, for instance, to determine if separate seating or even separate meetings must be available for men and women (Espy, 2017).
- Practice reflection on your presuppositions/assumptions with a strong cultural basis.
- Detailed directions on language and culture may be helpful for co-facilitators.
- Compare your impressions to other people's (preferably a cultural liaison) and written sources to check validity of interpretations of participant comments.
- The agenda can be projected on a screen, or copies can be made for attendees to follow. Because written materials are often understood before the spoken word, this practice can help attendees for whom the meeting is in their second language.
- Printed materials may also be translated (verbally or in writing) for those with emerging second language literacy.

Older facilitators have often learned to be sensitive to needs of older participants. The following are suggestions that may help older or disabled attendees:

- Place elders near the front so they can hear or see well.
- Increased illumination and contrast of text in projected presentation material can help to improve readability. Try to avoid glare or poor lighting.
- Use 12- to 14-point type for printed materials.
- Keep meetings short (less than 1.5 hours).
- Use a quiet room and reduce reverberations in the room caused by bare walls and floors.
- Speak clearly. Avoid covering your mouth or speaking while writing on a whiteboard.
- Accessibility of the meeting room should be considered: are curb cuts, ramps and/or elevators available for older or disabled attendees? If not, try to move the meeting to a more accessible location.

PLAN TO SOCIALIZE

People bond and get more done when they interact and share positive time together. Socialization creates a sense of safety. Small talk can lead to the big talk of the meeting. This includes mingling and sharing food. Plan to include some time for this. For a longer (all day) meeting, plan a potluck or catered lunch. For a shorter meeting, having coffee, tea and cookies as people gather before the meeting might help people socialize.

PLAN A TEAM CULTURE DISCUSSION

If this is an initial meeting or there have been non-productive meetings in the past, plan a discussion about how you want the team to work together, including the *process* and *framework*. This framework is part of a team culture. What does the group want it to be, and how can they make it happen? One key factor to discuss is how to maintain mutual respect. Ask the group to brainstorm key words for the following questions:

- What kind of team culture do we have now? (What's happening now?)
- What team culture do we *want*? (What is our desired outcome?)
- What can we do (specific action plans) to build a strong team culture?
- What agreements will help us create this culture? What *ground rules* are needed? (e.g., it is *safe* to speak honestly in the meetings, all ideas are welcome during brainstorms, cell phones turned off during the meeting or everyone will arrive on time so we can leave on time).

PLAN THE AGENDA

Prepare an agenda for the meeting. For ongoing team meetings, create an agenda and send it out to the participants, asking for corrections and additions. Then make copies for everyone. Having the agendas ahead of time gives people a chance to think about the meeting issues.

PLAN TO RECORD KEY INFORMATION

Meeting minutes are routinely recorded, but to keep the meeting on task, it helps to have information posted on whiteboards or easel paper: Using five sheets of easel paper, write the following headers: *Purpose* (goal or desired outcome) *Agreements*, *Actions*, *Decisions* and *Parking Lot*. Take markers and masking tape to the meeting so you can post the sheets and record meeting information.

PLAN FOR INTERACTIVE ACTIVITIES

Plan activities to *engage* participants and accomplish the purpose of the meeting. Structure activities using optimal working groups (size, mix, etc.). We have found groups between four and six people to work well. If any materials are necessary, gather them together to take to the meeting. These activities might include icebreakers, brainstorming and other activities needed for a meeting that is productive.

ROOM SET-UP

Plan how you will set up the room to accomplish the desired outcomes of the meeting (see Figure 26.1).

- A *round table* set-up is useful for discussion-oriented meetings.
- A *U-shaped* set-up for meetings is useful where you want the participants to see and interact with each other when needed. This or a boardroom set-up is useful for regular team meetings, depending on the size of the team.
- Set up chairs *in a circle* with you in the center for meetings intended as open and participatory.
- A theater-style setting with *chairs in rows* is good for establishing a speaker as the main focus. This set-up works well for community meetings when the main purpose is reporting information rather than seeking discussion. Add a table at the front of the room for a *panel of speakers* to sit up front if several people will be reporting or discussing information.

PREPARE YOURSELF

Immediately before the meeting, take some time, maybe five minutes, to complete what you are doing. Then take another five minutes to calm your mind and center yourself so you have no preoccupations or concerns interfering with your ability to remain neutral, observe accurately and facilitate well. As facili-

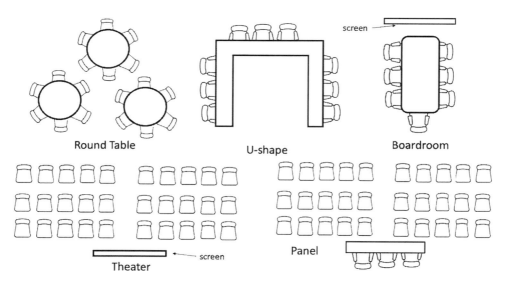

Figure 25.1 Meeting room arrangements.

tator, you will need to model mutual respect. This can be done by keeping eye contact, listening carefully and allowing for silence and ambiguity when necessary.

OPENING THE MEETING

Arrive early and greet everyone who arrives at the meeting. Once everyone is there, if anyone is new to the group, welcome them and have everyone introduce themselves. If it is a very large group of attendees, introductions might be done in small groups at tables. A meeting will go more smoothly when people feel like they know one another at least a little. One thing that can be done to set a positive tone is to ask people one thing about your change initiative that they are proud of since the last meeting.

An agenda is usually shared next with a call for any additional agenda items. Identify the *Purpose* or goal(s) of the meeting and write it on a sheet of paper or other media visible to everyone. The other posted sheets are be labeled *Agreements, Actions, Decisions* and *Parking Lot*. Typically, after the icebreaker and agenda, the meeting will move to the first agenda item. While reports and discussion are occurring, you will begin observing the people and action.

DURING THE MEETING

Observing

Begin a productive meeting by clearing your mind and planning before any process begins. Then, during the meeting, observe continuously what is happening while the dance of conversation is going on and mentally assess the outcomes and determine when to speak.

STAY ON TASK

Carry out activities that will engage the participants and get the work of the meeting done. If you need ideas, try brainstorming. If you are working on change plans, break into small groups to do planning.

Sometimes a team gets off task because of physical, emotional or intellectual distractions (Rogelberg, 2018). *Physical distractions* might include noise in the hallway, uncomfortable temperatures, poor lighting, a heavily decorated room, technology, late arrivals and those who are not prepared for the meeting. Also, when someone in the room is fidgeting, looking at a clock or watch, or playing with their pen, it can be distracting for others. A quick and pointed look at them might stop this, but many brilliant community members and businesspeople who might be on your team may fidget because of ADHD or similar disorders. A better option is to provide fidget toys such as Koosh™ balls. Flagging energy can also become a physical distraction when people are arriving after a full day of work. Socialization time with refreshments at the beginning sometimes re-energizes people. Arrange the room beforehand to eliminate as many of these distractions as possible.

Intellectual distractions happen when a team member diverts his or her attention to another mentally demanding task. If this is happening because of cell phones or other technology, gently call attention to the problem if it is widespread and ask the participants what can be done. Asking participants to turn off or silence cell phones is appropriate, but keep in mind that cell phones are often used as controllers or remote microphones for hearing aids, so hearing-impaired attendees may need them to hear.

Emotional distractions might include issues related to team members' private lives, the meeting topics, team members' perspectives, or interactions among team members.

Your job as a facilitator is to address emotional issues before they escalate. You can defuse a debate by encouraging more dialogue by others in the meeting. In the event of a conflict as mentioned in the previous chapter, you can also listen to each side and identify common ground to bring the opposing parties together. In the event that common ground can't be found, you could say: "it appears that you are coming from different sides, but the issue is clearly important to both of you. Let's try to focus our attention on finding a solution that works for both of you." Avoid embarrassing anyone during the meeting. They may never return.

Look for the relevant points in what someone is saying. If there are none, label the sidetracks, record the idea on the "parking lot" easel page for consideration at a later time, and then gently redirect the conversation. Then, start the ball rolling again. Try one of the following methods:

- Thank you for that observation. Let's park that in the "parking lot" for now and come back to it (Butler, 2019).
- Let me interrupt for a minute. Hold that thought. [Point to the meeting goal on the easel paper.] Let's get back to our focus for the meeting.
- Speaking of . . . we need to move on to. . .
- That reminds me of. . .
- Well, we need to. . .
- What you're saying relates to. . .
- For a side conversation, "Is this something the whole group needs to hear?" [If it is, focus the meeting on that discussion for a few moments. If it is not, kindly ask that the discussion be handled later.]

CONCLUDE THE MEETING: AGREEMENTS, ACTIONS AND DECISIONS

Throughout the meeting record all agreements, actions and decisions on easel paper or other visible media so everyone can see them. For any actions to be taken, record what will be done, when it will be done and who is responsible for getting it done. At the conclusion of the meeting, summarize the agreements, actions and decisions, and then note the date and location for the next meeting.

HOW TO CARRY OUT THIS TECHNIQUE

Planning

1. Plan physical accommodations for attendees (especially elders and people with disabilities) and interpreters and written materials for those from cultures different from yours.
2. Plan time for socialization.

3. If this is an early change team meeting, plan for a "team culture" discussion.
4. Plan an agenda and send it out ahead of time for corrections and additions.
5. Plan to record meeting minutes and the following information on a whiteboard or easel paper:
   - Meeting purpose.
   - Agreements.
   - Actions.
   - Decisions.
   - Parking Lot (ideas for later consideration).
6. Plan how the room will be set up to accomplish intended outcomes.
7. Prepare yourself by spending a few minutes clearing your mind.

Open the Meeting

1. Arrive early.
2. Greet people as they arrive.
3. Hand out agenda.
4. Conduct icebreaker.

During the Meeting

1. Remove physical, intellectual or emotional distractions.
2. Conduct engaging activities that will further the purpose of the meeting.
3. Observe the conversation and assist the team with accomplishing the meeting purposes.
4. Follow agenda while staying on task.

Meeting Conclusion

1. Review agreements, action items and decisions.
2. Note the location, time and date of the next meeting.

TRY IT!

Imagine that you have been selected to facilitate a meeting where the planning team for Hunger-free St. Michael will report the results of their community readiness survey. Write a checklist to prepare for the meeting. Include the following:

- Plans for accommodations.
- Plans for socialization.
- Plan how you will engage attendees while maintaining a sense of safety so community members will feel safe to comment. Include your ground rules.
- Plan agenda, including icebreaker, report, community comments and conclusion.
- Plans for recording minutes and key points.
- Plan for room set-up.
- Plans for removing distractions and staying on task.

SUMMARY

A facilitator needs to do some planning to conduct a meeting that stays on task and accomplishes its purpose. Plan the process, agenda and ground rules that will maintain a sense of safety. Keep the conversation focused and make sure that all voices are heard, and no distractions interfere with the discussion.

CITATIONS

Butler, A. S. (2019). *Mission critical meetings: 81 practical facilitation techniques*. Tucson, AZ: Wheatmark, Inc.

Espy, L. (2017). *Bad meetings happen to good people: How to run meetings that are effective, focused, and produce results*. Memphis, TN: Blue Room Press.

Rogelberg, S. G. (2018). *The surprising science of meetings: How you can lead your team to peak performance*. Oxford, England: Oxford University Press.

26 LISTENING DEEPLY

Figure 26.0

WHAT'S IN THIS CHAPTER?

When facilitators listen to the discussion in the meeting, they should be fully present without trying to control it or judge it. Some would say that presence *is* deep listening. It is "being open beyond one's preconceptions" (Senge, Scharmer, Jaworski, & Flowers, 2004, p. 13). Then they can listen deeply, maintain open, calm, receptive attention and *not* plan what to say next. Facilitators are there to make the process easier, rather than push a particular point of view, so freed from that compulsion, they can listen more intuitively and reflect to the group meanings that might otherwise be missed. This chapter will provide direction on listening deeply.

    Deep listening involves attentive listening from a caring and receptive place inside us to learn, and for understanding, rather than agreement, and asking good questions to explore the learning. It involves a temporary suspension of judgment, whether the information you hear is neutral, pleasant or unpleasant. Deep listening can occur across differences and diversity, on the intrapersonal (listening to yourself), interpersonal and group levels. If you have ever had someone listen to you will all their attention, you would describe it as supportive, empathetic, generous and accurate. And most important, you would say you felt *heard*.

Objectives

By the end of this chapter, you will be able to:

- Examine your own fears or concerns you have about a meeting topic.
- Determine before the meeting what can you do to revert back to a calm and receptive state of mind if you feel an emotional reaction to the discussion
- Determine how you will remove barriers to deep listening, including physical, intellectual and emotional barriers.
- Create and foster a sense of connectedness between each of the participants and yourself so they feel safe to speak out.

A STORY ABOUT LISTENING

Returning to the story of the Racial Unity Group, for many months Maurine took a central role in managing the conversation in order to help the attendees learn deep listening skills. What is deep listening? Usually people are only offering half of their attention to a speaker. They might be planning a rebuttal, arguing internally with the point being taken, or simply creating their own response. When the subject being discussed is race, there can be many potential pitfalls in the ensuing conversation.

In the weekly Race Unity meetings, the group members could just drop in and did not have to be there all the time. This fluidity of attendance and the absence of a set agenda meant that great care needed to be taken to protect from the effects of speech indicating unconscious bias or inadvertent racial language that could be taken as offensive.

Maurine introduced the Native American tradition of the "talking feather" to teach them a practice of deep listening. It was used in tribal circles to ensure that the speaker received a fair and just hearing and that only the person holding the feather could speak. The others agreed to listen deeply. The "talking feather," which was passed around the circle, allowed for each person to be heard fully without interruption. The ground rule was that no cross talk or debate was allowed about what someone had said. This was so important since the stories told by people of color were sensitive because of abuse they had received from White people, which made them leery about sharing them with people they hardly knew. Often when they had told these stories in mixed racial groups, they were not believed, or the facts were discounted.

For example, Helene talked about an incident in a local laundromat where she was threatened by a White male who called her a monkey and told her to go back to Africa. The group listened deeply to her story and did not ask any questions; thus, they created a safe space for her to tell it. She said later that for the first time in her life that she felt she was heard and believed. Accepting that such incidents are commonplace is hard for many White people. Our privilege might be as simple as being allowed to be in public spaces without being threatened. At Race Unity, many stories of abuse were shared and believed. This changed the culture of the group.

Lessons Learned:

- Accepting ambiguity is a rare trait. That means being willing to allow space to hear something new and to let go of our internal judge which decides too quickly about what is right or wrong.
- The first step to developing listening skills is to tell the voice in your head to be quiet. Reserve judgment until you have heard the entire story.
- Reflect internally on what you have heard. In a word—wait! You might hear something you never heard before, and it could change your mind.

WHAT THIS TECHNIQUE IS ABOUT

Removing the Barriers to Listening

Many things get in the way of deep listening: talking, not understanding what a person is saying; biases; physical, visual, mental, emotional and auditory distractions; interruptions and expectations. As a facilitator, you will want to eliminate those barriers within the meeting room and within yourself.

Talking and Not Understanding

If chattering is our normal practice in conversation, during facilitation you need a different approach. Speak briefly, if you need to, and watch your listeners. When your attendees are speaking, listen fully without interrupting. It is acceptable to seek clarification after they are finished if there is something that you didn't understand.

Biases

Preconceived notions of ideas or of other people in the room can shut down listening. If biases have entered the room, gently usher them out again by showing respect for ideas, all the people attending, their life experience and knowledge. Rein in your thoughts and hear everyone out.

Distractions and Interruptions

Face the person who is speaking and maintain eye contact without staring. Ensure that others in the room are listening, also. If there is emotion on the part of the speaker, it can be hard to listen. Reassure them that they are safe to speak and that you are listening. If the emotion is on your part, take a deep breath and calm yourself. Then focus all of your attention on the speaker. If the distraction is noise, look for the source and try to eliminate it, so the speaker can continue without interruption.

Expectations

It is a mistake to think others think the same as you. Expect that what is said comes from something true in that person, even when it is expressed poorly or with frustration or other emotion. A diverse team will challenge your thinking with their diverse perspectives and help make better decisions (Rock & Grant, 2016). Embrace that diversity so your team can make better change plans.

Components of deep listening include presence, eye contact and nonverbal feedback. Ask questions and create a sense of connection as shown in the diagram provided in Figure 26.1.

Presence

Presence means being psychologically present and focused in a situation, with a sense of connectedness between participants and the facilitator. Presence begins before the meeting starts, when you take time to calm the chatter in your mind. You want to facilitate with a receptive frame of mind. Often community change initiatives begin with situations that cause discomfort and fear, such as gun violence, racism or homelessness. The focused discussions that will take place around these issues can be emotional; however, fears and defensiveness can sabotage communications.

You want to start by being open and receptive, and if you feel triggered emotionally, you want to revert back to a receptive state of mind to listen to difficult conversations. Before the meeting, spend

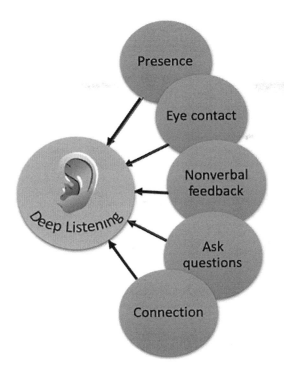

Figure 26.1 Components of deep listening.

some time thinking about what fears you have about the meeting topic and what you can do to ease a shift back to a state of mind that is calm and receptive. This process is deep listening at the *intrapersonal* level when you practice self-awareness through listening to yourself. You may also try meditation to help you clear your mind before the meeting.

At the *interpersonal* level, you will focus on listening deeply to one person. Avoid thinking about how you will reply and simply listen in silence with an open mind and open heart, discerning what the person really means. Encouraging the speaker can be done nonverbally through nodding and smiling when appropriate. Be confident that the words to respond will come to you when they are needed. We also listen deeply to many people in the group, one at a time, and groups can listen deeply to one person as the Race Unity group did with Helene.

Eye Contact

Eye contact happens when two people simultaneously look at each other's eyes. Eye contact is a form of nonverbal communication that can have a powerful influence on social behavior, but it may differ by culture. There are times when avoiding eye contact as a facilitator is appropriate, such as when giving bad news or pointing out a behavior, as in the story told in Chapter 23 about the mayor talking over Fern. However, when speaking, eye contact can help in building trust and engaging an audience. And when listening, eye contact can show your interest.

A useful approach with most Western audiences is to turn to the person speaking with your head and body. Facing your body to the other person can tell them that you are listening, engaged, and ready to communicate. Look at them gently, and give them your complete attention, while nodding occasionally. Break eye contact every once in a while, and then look back again as you listen. This break in eye contact prevents the conversation from seeming too intense or unsettling to the speaker. These eye contact tips are useful with *most* of those from Western cultures, but there are several cultural differences, even within each country.

When you have members of different cultures in a meeting you are facilitating, it is important to remember that individuals are shaped, but not circumscribed or limited, by their cultural background. However, it is best to be aware of the cultural differences and try to understand those from other cultural backgrounds. For instance, there are cultural differences about what eye contact is appropriate. Western cultures generally see eye-to-eye contact as positive, as indicated in the tips outlined in this chapter. However, it is a bit more complex than that. In the U.S., African Americans use more eye contact when talking and less when listening. The reverse behavior is often seen with Anglo Americans. This can cause some sense of unease between races in the United States. Arabic cultures make prolonged eye contact. For them it shows interest and truthfulness, but it may feel too intense to many Americans. However, people from Japan, Africa, Latin America and the Caribbean region tend to show respect by avoiding eye contact.

Nonverbal Feedback

Nonverbal feedback can include facial expressions, the tone and pitch of the voice, gestures displayed through hand motions, body language (kinesics) and the physical distance between the communicators (proxemics). Nonverbal communication provides clues and additional information to meaning beyond the words that are spoken. For instance, you can nod and smile to provide encouraging feedback. You might lean slightly toward the person or tip your head slightly showing you are listening. Think about what it feels to be the other person, and nod while looking sympathetic when someone tells a sad or difficult anecdote. The meaning of nonverbal feedback depends on the people, their cultures and context.

Another form of nonverbal feedback is mirroring. Mirroring is subconsciously imitating the gestures, speech patterns, or attitudes of another. Mirroring can be powerful if you have a trusting relationship with the other person. When you feel a connection with the other person, chances are you are already mirroring their behaviors naturally, especially positive nonverbal behaviors, without even trying. If you don't feel rapport with and connection to them, neither will they feel rapport. Establish the connection first. When you think about what it feels to be the other, you should feel the connection begin. Then, mirroring will be authentic and natural. These mirroring expressions can help to show empathy in emotional situations.

Nonverbals such as gestures are specific to a culture, so their meaning can become confusing when communicating across cultures. For instance, an acceptable gesture in your own culture may be offensive to people from another culture. For instance, the thumbs-up gesture is largely positive in the U.S., but in Greece, Italy and some Middle Eastern countries, it is like giving someone an obscene gesture with the middle finger. In addition, how much gesturing is used varies from culture to culture. People from some cultures gesture energetically; others are more restrained. People from restrained cultures often feel animated cultures lack civility and restraint. People from animated cultures, on the other hand, may feel that those from restrained cultures are apathetic or lack emotion. The best rule is to learn something about the cultures of people attending your meetings so you can navigate the minefields of nonverbal behavior. (Note: it is recommended that if you plan to become a professional facilitator that you take a Cross Cultural Communication course since there are many subtle differences in communication such as those mentioned here.)

Ask Questions

There are no perfect questions, just the right questions for the person, time and place. The two kinds of questions that can be used effectively when listening, are *clarifying* questions and *open-ended* questions for more information. Clarifying questions ensure that you understand what the speaker has said. This can reassure the speaker that you are genuinely interested in what they have to say and are attempting to understand accurately. Clarifying questions are neutral and nonjudgmental. You can also summarize what they said and seek feedback about its accuracy. Good open-ended questions start with "when," "where," "how" or "why." Much more information about open-ended questions will be covered in Chapter 27.

Connection

Psychologists from Maslow (1943) to Baumeister (Baumeister & Leary, 1995) have noted that a sense of social connection is a fundamental human need. Creating belonging among members of the change team and making the meeting space feel safe and accepting for people to speak their truths may be the most important component of deep listening (Chapman, 2012). In the story for this chapter, Helene felt connected to others in the room and safe enough and to tell the troubling tale of what happened in the laundromat. Her belonging was not threatened by speaking out. Since a focused discussion allows group members to interact and affect each other's ideas during discussions on change, all members of the team need to have a sense of connection for group deep listening.

As this discussion demonstrates, all of the components of deep listening are closely related, and it is difficult to talk about one component without mentioning another.

HOW TO CARRY OUT THIS TECHNIQUE

1. Begin before the meeting by spending time thinking about what fears or concerns you have about the meeting topic, and what you can do if you feel "triggered" to shift back to a calm and receptive state of mind.
2. Remove barriers to deep listening from the meeting space, including physical, intellectual and emotional barriers.
3. Be fully present and focused. Create a sense of connectedness between each of the participants and yourself.
4. Maintain good eye contact with each of the team members as they speak.
5. Use nonverbal feedback to indicate that you are listening and interested, as long as you are comfortable that it has a similar meaning for all attendees.
6. Ask clarifying and open-ended questions.
7. Foster connection between all of the team members so they sense that they can speak out and still belong.

TRY IT!

Imagine that you are the facilitator for a community discussion of gentrification in a medium-sized city on the West Coast. Invited to the team are a number of those affected by gentrification, longtime residents that feel they are about to be priced out of their neighborhood with all of its long-time connections. The question to be discussed is this: is it possible to create inclusive cities and neighborhoods that can meet the needs of all city-dwellers? If so, how? Discuss the following:

- What fears or concerns do you have about the topic? If you feel an emotional reaction to the discussion, what can you do to revert back to a calm and receptive state of mind?
- What will you do to remove barriers to deep listening, including physical, intellectual and emotional barriers?
- What will you do to create a sense of connectedness between each of the participants and yourself?
- How will you foster connection between all of the participants, so they feel safe to speak out?

SUMMARY

When facilitators listen to discussion in a meeting, they should be fully present and listen with open, calm, receptive attention, and without trying to control or judge the comments. Deep listening is about removing barriers, listening intuitively to learn, and for understanding, rather than agreement, asking questions and reflecting to the group meanings that might otherwise be missed.

CITATIONS

Baumeister, R. F., & Leary, M. R. (1995). The need to belong: Desire for interpersonal attachments as a fundamental human motivation. *Psychological Bulletin, 117*(3), 497–529. doi:10.1037/0033-2909.117.3.497

Chapman, S. G. (2012). *The five keys to mindful communication: Using deep listening and mindful speech to strengthen relationships, heal conflicts, and accomplish your goals.* Boulder, CO: Shambhala.

Maslow, A. H. (1943). A theory of human motivation. *Psychological Review, 50*(4), 370–396. doi:10.1037/h0054346

Rock, D., & Grant, H. (2016, November 4). Why diverse teams are smarter. *Harvard Business Review.* Retrieved from https://hbr.org/2016/11/why-diverse-teams-are-smarter

Senge, P. M., Scharmer, O. C., Jaworski, J., & Flowers, B. S. (2004). *Presence: Human purpose and the field of the future.* New York: Crown Business.

OBSERVING THE ACTION

27

Figure 27.0

WHAT'S IN THIS CHAPTER?

Once a meeting has begun, there are several facilitation tasks that benefit from observation. After setting the ground rules and the focus of the meeting, facilitators will need to get things flowing, using introductions and icebreakers. During the meeting, they will need to keep the energy flowing and to engage and include the participants. At several points they will need to summarize progress. Facilitators need to monitor discussions and nonverbal behaviors to determine if it is necessary to intervene. Using the open, calm, receptive attention learned in the previous chapter, facilitators observe the gestures and body language of the participants at the meeting and use that knowledge to either calm the group or energize it to accomplish the aims of the meeting.

Objectives

By the end of this chapter, you will be able to:

- Observe participants at the beginning of the meeting to determine the best way to get things flowing, such as using introductions and icebreakers.
- Observe during the meeting to know how to keep the energy flowing with a particular group (Wilkinson, 2012).
- Observe to see who is engaged and who is not, in order to include and involve all participants.
- Observe to determine when to summarize progress.
- Monitor discussions to determine if intervention is necessary.

A STORY ABOUT OBSERVATION OF PARTICIPANTS

This story was told by a facilitator who was able to observe and notice while her colleague was presenting.

> At a large conference for drug prevention training, my co-trainer was making his presentation to people sitting at round tables. They were teachers mainly, and most were fully engaging in the conversation, except for one. She sat quietly and did not face the presenter. I noted that she was wearing a beautiful shawl that seemed to keep her wrapped and somehow quietly nestled in her own world. I sat next to her and commented, "you are a little nesting bird." She looked at me with a puzzled expression. I pointed out that the shawl looked like a nest and that she had a napkin of seeds in front of her. She was not offended by my gentle observation. She never participated vocally on any of the three days of training.
>
> On the last day she entered the room dressed in beautiful African-style clothing with a headdress. As she stood in the closing circle for our final conversation, she bowed to me as if to ask. "Shall I speak now?" I bowed to her and she told a beautiful folk tale. She had chosen her moment to speak and knew that I had opened the door for her wisdom to be shared intimately in the circle at just the right moment.
>
> (Personal communication)

Had the co-facilitator *not* noticed the woman quietly sitting through the training, the entire group may have been deprived of her wisdom on the topic. It is not easy to observe effectively at the same time as you present or direct activities. In this anecdote, it is the facilitator who was *not* presenting that was able to observe and notice the patterns of behavior among the participants.

WHAT THIS TECHNIQUE IS ABOUT

This technique is about watching and noticing individual and group behaviors, intervening only when necessary, so that you can initiate and maintain an upbeat and productive flow of interactions while objectively keeping focus on the desired outcomes. It is not possible to see everything that goes on in a meeting. As Courtright notes, "whenever we observe communication behavior, we are sampling a small smidgen from an infinitely large universe of possibilities" (2014, p. 5). However, you will need to see enough to make the work of the change team move along through useful meeting outcomes. If, by observing nonverbal behaviors, you can get a clue of an individual's emotional state, then you can be better prepared with the most appropriate response (Atre, 2016).

Are all the participants engaged? Participant engagement occurs when they make a psychological investment in the change planning process. They are focused, ask questions and make contributions of thoughts and ideas.

Much of the observation done during facilitation is of nonverbal behaviors such as:

- Facial expressions.
- Eye contact.
- Gestures.
- Postures and body movements.
- Appearance.

Observe the group actively and frequently throughout the meeting.

COMMUNICATION ACROSS CULTURES

Diversity and intercultural communication have been an important topic in business for many years. In community change initiatives, intercultural communication may have even greater importance because diverse community members are often involved in change projects. While observing participants, it is important to keep in mind that nonverbal behaviors can vary across cultures, just like language (Castelli & Galfano, 2016). However, as Darwin (1872/2009) noted, there are some nearly universal nonverbal behaviors: facial expressions indicating happiness, sadness, anger and fear appear to be similar among most cultures.

Individuals are unique, so "it is important to be cautious and prudent when making cultural generalizations" (Samovar, Porter, McDonald, & Roy, 2012, p. 21). Generalizations are approximations—not hard rules—but can provide some help in interpreting communications across cultures, as long as you remember that they are not absolutes. Customary meaning for eye gaze and contact, or lack of it, is usually culturally specific. The meanings are similar in the U.S. and Europe (especially Spain, France and Germany). Generally, maintaining eye contact indicates interest and honesty. In the Middle East, eye contact with members of the same gender is common, but it is less common and considered less appropriate between members of opposite genders. In many African, Asian and Latin American cultures, prolonged eye contact can be taken as an affront or a challenge. It is deemed more polite to have only intermittent, brief eye contact, especially between people of different social strata.

Some gestures (movements of the hands and body) are somewhat similar across cultures, such as waving, pointing or using fingers to indicate numbers. Other gestures are unique to individual cultures. Postures and body movements have been found to be important for nonverbal communication of emotion and somewhat similar across cultures. We often look to posture to determine a participant's engagement (degree of attention or involvement) or, conversely, their level of disengagement. Postures and body movements are subtle and dependent on the situation, type of room, furniture and presence of others of the opposite sex.

HOW TO CARRY OUT OBSERVATIONS OF PARTICIPANTS

There are many points during a meeting when facilitator actions require observing reactions by participants. These include when the facilitator:

- Sets the stage.
- Proposes or invites suggestions for ground rules.
- Invites comments on agenda items.
- Conducts positive/negative polls.
- Gets the process flowing.
- Engages participants.
- Include participants.
- Summarizes progress.

When you see signs of engagement, interest or agreement, you should feel free to continue on. However, if you hear or see things like heads shaking "no," silence, negative comments, leaning away from speaker or crossing arms, then you need to actively manage the situation. Some responses might be to offer a general invitation to the group to express opposing feelings or further comments. You might also make a verbal note of some people being silent or appearing uncomfortable and ask for further comments. Use eye contact, which will invite a potential comment. Look for body language which indicates willingness to contribute if called upon.

Ahead of meetings you can place empty note cards on the tables to allow people to respond silently or write their questions down anonymously. Periodically ask for cards to be passed in so you can respond and answer questions. We have found this to work well in intercultural discussions. Finally, you can ask for any negative feedback directly. Be sure to record comments on easel paper to show validation.

If someone is dominating the conversation, gently cut in, thank the person for their comments and then ask to hear what others think.

If you see nonverbal behaviors indicating negative feedback, ask for any negative feedback directly. Respond with empathy if the comment is emotional. Be sure to record it on easel paper to show validation.

PRACTICE OBSERVING

Do you tend to rush from task to task, or do you take time to absorb what is happening? Accurate observation takes empathy and practice, and it starts with slowing down and watching. Notice individual actions and group interaction patterns. Human behavior is complex and varies from culture to culture, so don't expect to gauge someone's behavior too quickly.

If you are feeling pressed for time, or are preoccupied with your own thoughts, you will be distracted from observing other people. Instead, put your own needs aside and concentrate on the other person. Watch what they are doing and how they are interacting with others in their groups. On the other hand, you want to be *unobtrusive*. Don't stare: people will wonder what's up if you watch too intently. Even if you are entirely focused on someone or some group, make sure you glance away when appropriate.

Many professions, like teaching or counseling, require observation and interpretation of behaviors. Good observation takes practice. If you are not already good at this kind of observation, then you can practice, beginning with colleagues, friends or family, or even people at a coffee shop. You might hold a book or magazine while you observe. Glance at from time to time and avoid gazing too intently.

1. Look for gestures and body language—these make up as much as 60% of face-to-face communication:
    - Does the person make eye contact? If not, the person may be uncomfortable.
    - Does the person lean away or back while talking? If so, that can indicate the person is stressed, nervous or afraid.
    - Does the person cross his or her arms? That may mean the person is feeling uncomfortable, either with a situation or the temperature of the room.
    - Does the person hunch over or have bad posture? The person may not feel confident.
    - Does the person tap his or her fingers or feet, or jiggle his or her leg? The person may be feeling anxious or impatient.
2. Write down what you observe about people so you can begin to notice patterns.
3. Next, begin wondering. Imagine that you are the person you have been observing. What would you be thinking or feeling if you exhibited the particular behavior that you observed? Write down your interpretation.
4. Finally, check your interpretation. If you have been observing a family member, ask them what they were thinking or feeling. As you practice, you should notice your interpretations becoming more accurate.

The same process applies to observing small groups, but observe also who is talking to whom. Are people talking over other people's comments? Are group members making eye contact? Do you note any physical tensions or emotions? When a facilitator observes positive behaviors, verbal or nonverbal, then it is acceptable to proceed. Negative behaviors, on the other hand, require the facilitator to actively manage the meeting, to get it back on track and make sure that participants are understanding and accepting the direction that the meeting is taking. Using empathy, the facilitator can imagine what the behaviors might indicate. Remember to interpret communications cautiously and tentatively (Wood, 2010). Then he or she can decide what to do.

A facilitator's tone, posture and volume can be perceived differently by different people, and not everyone responds to comments in the same way, so facilitators need a full toolbox of options. Some respond well to a direct invitation to comment on a point of discussion, while others prefer to think about it and comment in their own time. Still others may be embarrassed if they are "called out."

Table 27.1 Facilitator responses to participant behaviors.

Facilitator Tasks	Participant Observed Behaviors		Possible Facilitator Responses (to negative behaviors)
	Positive	Negative (requires active management)	
Set the stage	Signs of agreement or understanding such as nodding Leaning toward speaker	Heads shaking "no" Silence Negative comments Leaning away from speaker, crossing arms	
Propose ground rules Invite suggestions Conduct a positive or negative poll	Signs of agreement and understanding (nodding or positive comments) Positive comments Leaning toward speaker	Heads shaking "no" Silence Negative comments Leaning away from speaker, crossing arms	
Get the process flowing	Smiles, laughter, eye contact, conversation, heads nodding, turn taking or balanced participation	Silence Leaning away from others, crossing arms	
Engage participants	No notice taken of you, focus, listening, asking questions, making connections between ideas, working and contributing.	Silence Leaning away from others, crossing arms	
Include participants	Participant appears to be reflecting	No contribution Leaning away from speaker, crossing arms Someone dominates the conversation.	
Summarize progress	Signs of agreement/ understanding such as nodding Learning toward speaker	Heads shaking "no" Silence Negative comments Leaning away from speaker, crossing arms	

TRY IT!

Exercise #1

Keeping in mind the exercises from Chapter 24, attend a meeting with trusted colleagues (when you are *not* facilitating) and observe at least one colleague, looking for gestures and body language. Write down what you observe. Using empathy, imagine what the behaviors might indicate. Then ask your colleague what they were thinking or feeling. Keep practicing until what you imagine that you see becomes fairly accurate.

Exercise #2

Imagine that you are asked to facilitate a meeting of a local charity (your choice). Think ahead about observing participants during various points during the meeting related to facilitator tasks. If you observe positive behaviors such as nodding, smiling and leaning toward the speaker, you will know that you are free to proceed with the agenda. If you observe negative behaviors such as participants leaning away from the speaker or crossing arms, you will need to pause to manage the situation. Use empathy to try to imagine the reasons for those behaviors and then fill in the column in Table 27.1 with suggested responses.

SUMMARY

Observing, noticing and wondering will improve the quality of your facilitation. Once a meeting has begun, several tasks are carried out: (1) set the stage by going over the purpose of the meeting, the agenda and ground rules and seeking agreement; (2) get the process flowing, using introductions and icebreakers to engender familiarity and trust; (3) engage participants; (4) include the participants who are quiet; (5) summarize progress at several points during the meeting. Throughout the meeting, monitor discussions and intervene when absolutely necessary. In Chapter 29, we will discuss what to do when you note other types of negative behaviors in the meeting.

CITATIONS

Atre, S. (2016). *Observing nonverbal behavior: An exhaustive guide to the essential skill of "social intelligence."* New Delhi: Educreation Publishing.

Castelli, L., & Galfano, G. (2016). Nonverbal behavior and intergroup communication. In H. Giles, A. Maass, H. Giles, & A. Maass (Eds.), *Advances in intergroup communication* (pp. 137–154). New York: Peter Lang.

Courtright, J. A. (2014). *Observing and analyzing communication behavior.* New York: Peter Lang.

Darwin, C. (2009). *The expression of the emotions in man and animals* (4th ed.). New York: Oxford University Press. (Original work published 1872.)

Samovar, L. A., Porter, R. E., McDonald, E. R., & Roy, C. S. (2012). *Communication between cultures* (8th ed.). Belmont, CA: Wadsworth Pub.

Wilkinson, M. (2012). *The secrets of facilitation: The SMART guide to getting results with groups* (2nd ed.). San Francisco, CA: Jossey-Bass.

Wood, J. (2010). *Interpersonal communication: Everyday encounters.* Boston, MA: Wadsworth-Cengage Learning.

ASKING GOOD QUESTIONS

28

Figure 28.0

WHAT'S IN THIS CHAPTER?

As a facilitator, your job is to help participants create their own answers to their community challenges or opportunities. One of the chief techniques to engage and energize your team members is the use of good questions. A good question is both answerable and challenging. It can elicit facts and inspire analysis, synthesis, interpretation and critical thinking. *Asking questions* keeps the focus on the team, provokes thoughtful discussion and guides the flow of the discussion. This chapter provides techniques for formulating essential questions that are critical drivers of the discussion that lies at the heart of an issue, while they sidestep the pitfalls of broad or universal questions that leave people in stunned silence or narrow questions that allow for only single-word answers.

This chapter will help you formulate questions that:

1. Are both answerable and challenging.
2. Elicit facts, inspire analysis, synthesis, interpretation and/or critical thinking.
3. Help to unlock hidden value, unleash creativity and passion that will move your change initiative toward the future.

A STORY ABOUT ASKING QUESTIONS

Setting: a large US city
Timeframe: mid-1990s
Scene: a board meeting of the Elizabeth Fry Prison Reform Association [fictional name]
Organizational mission: to oversee the conditions of prisoners and prisons in the state correctional system
Characters: Ruth G. (community activist), Jim D. (founder of the Fry Association), Judge Smith (who has a drug diversion courtroom), Bernice W. (founder of Families First), judges and private attorneys, former prisoners.
Agent of change: Maurine, drug prevention specialist

At times, a friendship with a key ally can open the door to social change opportunities leading to unexpected outcomes. Here is an example of "seizing an opportunity" when it is offered without actually knowing why.

When Ruth G. invited her friend Maurine to attend the annual dinner of the Elizabeth Fry Prison Reform Association, Maurine had expected only to accompany her friend, but Ruth had other intentions. The organization was founded in the 20th century by a philanthropist named Jim D., who was the "grandfather" of the organization and an old friend of Ruth. When introducing Maurine to Jim, she revealed her hidden agenda, by saying to him right away, "You should invite Maurine to serve on the board." Jim studied her face and without knowing any other background information, he said yes immediately. He knew that Ruth was offering him an opportunity, so he took the risk of accepting Maurine, who was an unknown to him. However, Maurine was flummoxed. "What is Ruth up to now?" she asked herself.

At her first board meeting when she entered the room, she viewed the scene. First of all, she **noticed** that she was the only woman on the board and that most of the men were judges and lawyers. Fortunately, her father had been a judge, so she was somewhat familiar with this legal culture, mostly inhabited by men. Jim warmly greeted her and asked her to introduce herself to the others. At that point in her career she was serving as a drug prevention specialist in a human service agency which focused primarily on youth development. Her professional focus was not on the end of the spectrum of punishment for crimes committed by youth, but rather on the need for early intervention with families in order to prevent the crimes. She brought a completely new perspective to the scene. **Wondering** silently to herself, she posed a question: "*What new perspective on prisons can I offer to this board?* [first question]."

She spent several meetings just listening to their conversations about bail-bond issues and the construction of new prisons in the rural areas of the state, where jobs were few and the money from prison construction could be the "new industry" that would save their economies. Her next step was to go on prison visitations with the staff to learn firsthand about **what was happening now.** On one such visit she saw a long line of Black young men being ferried from one side of the prison to another, and she thought, "They should be in high school and not in prison." She made the connection between the new "Three Strikes You're Out" laws that could put a novice criminal into prison for three nonviolent drug offenses and the need for more prisons. It appeared to her to be a vicious cycle of racism, poverty and poor education leading to an entire generation of African American youth becoming branded as felons.

Then Maurine started to speak up board meetings about **what was happening now** in her urban/suburban/rural community and how she was working with families, schools and local government officials where drug offenses were rising. She posed a question to the board; "*Instead of punishing young people for breaking the law, why don't we intervene earlier with their families to prevent them from coming into prisons?*" That was a real conversation stopper! The former prisoners in the room nodded with approval. Judge Smith spoke up and said he resented the "Three Strikes" law because it took away his ability to judge cases individually. He also invited Maurine to visit his courtroom where he practiced diversion of young people into drug treatment rather than immediately sending them to prison. She had found her allies on the board.

Whenever her schedule would allow it, she went on prison visits to learn more about the different prison populations and the conditions of prisoners. On a visit to the women's prison, she met an innovative warden who allowed the mothers to invite their children to a week-long summer camp inside the prison, which had a grassy campus space for setting up tents. This project was quickly quashed by government officials when they learned about it from news reports; they felt she was coddling prisoners. I was impressed that the female warden had made the connection between healthy child development and the future prison population. Studies show that children of prisoners often feel depressed, shame and stigma (Allard & Greene, 2011; Brookes, 2018; Martin, 2017; Saunders, 2018). She had also heard that children of prisoners believe that it will be their fate to go to prison and to display delinquent behavior in the absence of their parents, and they may turn to gangs for support.

Maurine was taking action to connect the dots for the prison reform board. If they were actually interested in reform, they needed to start at another point—with families. She asked Jim if she could invite a specialist in child development to speak to the board. He readily agreed. Bernice W. was the founder of Families First, which had the mission of healthy child development in communities. When she entered the board room, she embraced Jim and explained that he had stood up for her at her wedding. "Small world" connections like this one can help bond the group! Her presentation was well regarded, and as a result, she agreed to collaborate with the prison board to write a major foundation grant for a drug prevention program for the children of prisoners.

Intuitively and with careful investigation, Maurine had found a pathway forward by seeking answers and humbly asking new questions. She was acting like the TV detective Columbo, who always ended each conversation with this phrase, "Just one more thing . . ."

Over time Maurine asked several powerful questions:

- What is the correlation between having a parent in prison and a child going to prison?
- How does healthy youth development in families influence patterns of drug use in youth?
- What is the impact of new laws such as *Three Strikes You're Out* for young offenders who have committed nonviolent drug crimes?
- What is the economic connection between building more prisons and arresting more youth and putting them in prison?

WHAT THIS TECHNIQUE IS ABOUT

Why Do People Ask Questions?

- To obtain information.
- To create relationships with rapport
- To express interest in an idea or person.
- To clarify information.
- To make sure you understand something someone said accurately.
- To challenge thinking and encourage further thought and discussion of an idea.

Questions are one of the key tools a good facilitator has to help his or her team assess situations, determine their desired state and gather data, including indicators they will use to monitor and evaluate their efforts, plan strategies and implement them.

Questioning and Teamwork

Effective questions can have a powerful impact on creating relationships with rapport by expressing interest in a person and their ideas. According to Will Wise (2017), this process begins by setting an intention as shown in Figure 28.1. Before the meeting begins, a facilitator can determine that they intend to create an environment where the team can do their best work and find meaning by contributing to the group's work. Repeat this intention a few times until it is ingrained in your mind.

To create rapport, use your curiosity (Kimsey-House, Kimsey-House, Sandhal, & Whitworth, 2018). Notice something about the person, wonder and ask them open-ended questions about it. These usually begin with what or how. Be sure to be open, authentic and sincere, and avoid trying to prove something in the conversation. Other approaches include:

- *Comment on something pleasant*, such as weather or snacks provided at the meeting.
- *Ask for information*, such as directions to the restroom.
- *Offer assistance*, such as help carrying a plate of cookies.
- *Ask for an opinion*, such as what a person thought about a report you both heard.
- *Mention a mutual acquaintance*. "How long have you known Mayor Johnson?"
- *Offer a compliment*, such as "I thought the web site looked very attractive after you updated it."

Listen deeply, as we discussed in Chapter 26. Reflect on the conversation as you listen to make sure the conversation is moving forward, but don't let the team rush to a premature conclusion. Ask meaningful questions and get everyone to comment before they come to a conclusion or settle on a single response. Use the "Notice, wonder and ask" method to ask about what the team member is sharing. Watch gestures, body language and actions, and listen for emotions. If you see or hear barriers to the conversation being erected, you might stop the conversation and ask, "What's happening now?" or "I'm trying to imagine what you are feeling. I think it's (angry, frustrated, embarrassed, happy), would that be right?" Allow time for people to think, even if the silence becomes a bit uncomfortable. Maintain empathic

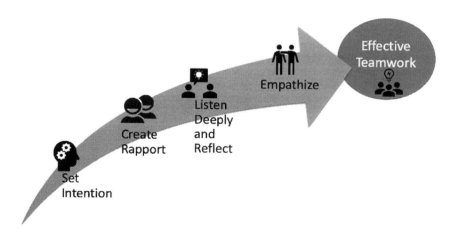

Figure 28.1 Using questions to establish relationships.

eye contact. Sometimes keeping the team in discomfort for a time, as in the story told in Chapter 12, is necessary for a team to overcome problems such as situational blindness, but ultimately your goal is to keep the team in harmony so they can continue to work together. Occasionally, you may need to keep the team in disharmony or discomfort to move past a point at which the team is stuck. (See the story in Chapter 12 for an example of this.)

Asking Questions

There is no one best kind of question. The right question to ask depends on where the team is in the facilitation and change process. It is useful to start by asking close-ended questions and progressing to open questions as attendees relax. Open-ended questions are usually neutral, invite creativity and are good at engaging participants and generating conversation.

Types of Questions

- *Close-ended questions*: invite a short, focused answer, sometimes one word such as *Yes* or *No*. An example of a useful starting question is, "Is homelessness a problem in our town?"
- *Open-ended questions*: require a person to pause and think. The answer requires explanation. "What would happen if. . .?"
- *Recall questions*: require the listener to recall some information from memory. "What percent of this community suffers food insecurity?"
- *Process questions*: require more thought and analysis and/or a sharing of opinion. "What new perspective on prisons can we offer to this community?"
- *Rhetorical questions*: are used to promote thought. "Who would not hope to have a safe and stable place to return home to?"
- A *leading question* (also called suggestive interrogation): points the respondent's answer in a certain direction. For instance, asking before a potential donor has made a commitment to donate, "How soon would you be able to contribute?" is a leading question. Try to *avoid* this type of question by stating questions neutrally.

You need to sidestep the pitfalls of broad questions that leave people in stunned silence because they don't know where to begin, like "*What is the cause of homelessness?*" If you want to provoke further thought, avoid close-ended questions that allow for only single-word answers. Powerful questions are generally open-ended and may have the effect of:

- Grabbing your attention and drawing you in.
- Inspiring curiosity and learning.
- Putting focus on what has meaning and possibility.
- Requiring introspection and reflection.
- Causing team members to question their assumptions and re-evaluate their thinking.
- Putting a stop to confusion and evasion.
- Creating initiative.
- Generating innovation or action.

QUESTIONS THROUGH THE CHANGE PROCESS

In the beginning of the change process, the facilitator usually describes the focus, and then the discussion moves to **stage 1**, describing the present state (see the stage labeled 1 in Figure 28.1) using the questions "What's happening now?" This can be followed up with "How does it look to you?" or "How do you feel about it?" To clarify statements that someone makes, you might ask "What do you mean?" or "Please say more" or "What is missing here?"

In **stage 2**, you want to elicit the desired outcomes by asking "What do you want to happen?" or "What is your desired outcome?" The initial question can be followed up by asking it another way: "How would you know you have reached it?" or "What would it look like?" Focus questions such as those described in Chapter 11 work well:

- What do people want to *preserve* in the community?
- What do people want to *change* in the community?
- What do people want to *create* in the community?

In **stage 3**, you will gather data about causes and contributing factors so you can create hypotheses about how to improve the conditions causing the situation. To determine why a situation exists, you will need to differentiate between the symptoms and the causes. You might ask, "What are the symptoms of this situation?" and "What are the root causes of the symptoms?" As you determine possible causes, remember to help your team dig for root causes, using a fishbone diagram. Ask "*Why*" at least five times, as you dig deeper looking for root causes. Addressing symptoms with your change initiative is like giving socks and toothbrushes to homeless people. It simply does not address the root causes of homelessness, which are complex and may be different for different groups of people.

You also want to identify or create indicators of the desired outcomes. Ask the team "How will we measure success?" Identify community measures that already exist and will be measured on an ongoing basis, or create your own methods of measuring success, such as improvements in satisfaction surveys or counts of people doing something, such as an increase in the number of people participating in a community gardening project. An indicator is specific, observable and measurable, and when used for evaluation

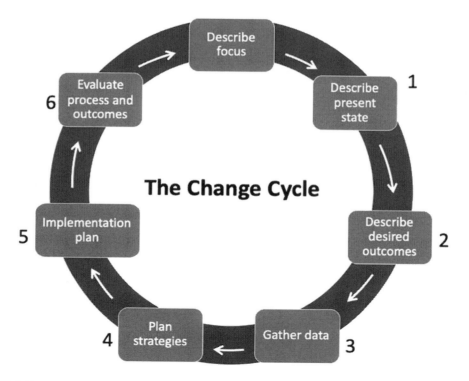

Figure 28.2 The change cycle.

of your change initiative, it should show the progress made toward achieving a specific desired outcome. To identify an indicator:

- Ask the team, "What do you want to measure to know if you are succeeding?" Ask them to focus on the action or change they wish to see.
- Ask them, "Can you quantify the change in numerical terms, such as counts, proportions, or percentages?"
- Finally, ask the team members, "Is there any evidence that shows that this proposed solution (hypotheses) will work?"

Your team will need to look for examples where similar solutions led to outcomes that they want to achieve. They may also find useful indicators when they search. They may need to search existing information online, in research and practitioner journals (usually found in academic libraries) or from government sources for ideas matching their needs.

In **stage 4**, the team will plan strategies and tactics for carrying out the mission of the organization. Some ideas for strategies have been captured in the hypotheses explored in the data gathering. To explore additional options, the facilitator might ask, "How do you think the situation can be improved?" List several possible solution options. As strategies are explored, you might probe the team members by asking "How do you suppose this will work out?" and "What are the chances of success?" Include fundraising in the strategic plan, so there are sufficient resources to accomplish the goals of the plan.

In **stage 5**, your team will outline the implementation plan including the tasks (tactics), dates each tactic will be completed, who is responsible for each tactic and what resources will be needed. The next step will be to carry out the plan.

In **stage 6**, you will evaluate the ongoing work of the organization and revise strategies as needed to carry out the organization's mission. Questions and probes you might use include:

- "Are our strategies working?"
- "What do you think this data means?"
- "How would you summarize our efforts so far?"
- "If you could do it over again, would you do anything differently?"
- "How can we make sure the organization remembers what we learned from this?"

A Few of Our Favorite Questions
What is happening now?
What does it look like?
How will you know when you have succeeded?
What caused the challenge we face?
What information do you need to help you decide on strategies?
How can we create new resources?
Who are potential allies to enhance our resources?
What will happen if we do this?
What if you don't do anything?
How will this effort fit with the values of the community?
Who is responsible for this action step?
What support do they need to get the job done?
If you could do it over again, would you do anything differently?
What do you think this data means?
What will we take away from this?
Can you say more about that?
What are we missing here?

DELIVERING QUESTIONS

Good questions use the language of the participants and addresses them using "you." Questions that can build an image in the minds of the participants and are action-oriented can get participants thinking. A phrase like "Imagine that you are facilitating . . ." will put the participants in the scenario. "What do you do to begin creating relationships when participants begin walking through the door?" will invite people to use their creativity and knowledge to respond.

Use Silence

Ask your question, and then pause. Pauses in speech can help to emphasize points and give team members a few moments to gather their thoughts before continuing. It is tempting to fill in the silence if no one speaks up right away. Resist! Count up to 30 before stepping in and rephrasing the question. Pause again after a first response. This can encourage the speaker to continue with their answer in more detail. Pauses of at least three seconds have been proven to be effective.

Encourage Participation

You can encourage people to respond by asking questions of individual members of the group. You can also redirect a question from an active member of the group to one who is less inclined to answer; however, you want to encourage but not force quieter members of the group to speak. Another method is to have individuals write a response on paper and then discuss their answers with one or more people around them. This often gives quieter people the courage to speak up.

Responding to Answers

After participants respond to questions, it will be your turn to respond. Wilkinson (2004) notes that there are several ways for a facilitator to respond, depending on the nature of the answers.

- *Replay* the answer to be sure you understood. "It sounds like you are saying . . . Is that right?"
- A *direct probe* can be used to challenge a statement. "Why do you think that won't work?"
- An *indirect probe* can be used to clarify. "Would that idea work because. . .?"
- A *leading question* (yes, there is a place for leading questions) can be used to pursue further ideas. "Are there other possible causes for these symptoms in the area of. . .?"
- A *redirecting question* can be used to get a discussion on task. "That's an interesting possibility. Can we put it on the "Parking Lot" sheet so we don't forget it? Then we need to get back to our task . . ."
- A *prompt* question can be used to help keep the group focused. "We have covered possible causes in areas of . . . What about in the area of public policy?"
- *Drill down* to determine *why* someone disagrees with others in the group. "You might be right. Help me understand why you think this idea will never work." Continue to ask "why" until the point is clear.
- When you or others disagree, *validate* the portion of their statement that has some merit. "I can agree that . . ." Then challenge the statement by asking an "objection" question.
- *Challenge*: state an objection by asking a question that gives the person the opportunity to resolve the objection. "If we do it that way, how can we. . .?"
- *Suggest an idea*: "What if we . . ." If the participants like the idea, ask "What do you see as the benefits?" This question is used only when team members are missing an important idea.

HOW TO CARRY OUT THIS TECHNIQUE

Questions and Teamwork

- Set your intention before the meeting: What do you want to achieve in this meeting?
- Before or at the beginning of the meeting, establish rapport. *Notice, wonder and ask* participants open-ended questions about something you notice about them.
- Listen deeply to team member answers, whether they are speaking to you individually or to the group.
- Reflect on what group members say and restate some points already mentioned.
- Maintain an appropriate pace for the conversation:
  - Make sure the conversation is moving forward.
  - Don't let the team rush to a premature conclusion: Ask meaningful questions and get everyone to comment before they conclude or settle on a response.
  - "Notice, wonder and ask" team members about what they are sharing.
- When you see or hear barriers to the conversation being erected:
  - Stop the conversation to ask, "What's happening now?"
  - If emotions are running high, you might say: "I'm trying to imagine what you are feeling. I think it's (angry, frustrated, embarrassed, happy), would that be right?"
  - Allow time for people to think, even if the silence becomes a bit uncomfortable (Sobel & Panas, 2012).
  - Maintain empathic eye contact.

Questions Throughout the Planning Cycle

- In stage 1, focus questions and probes on *"What's happening now?"* and list clearly the symptoms of the present state.
- In stage 2, elicit the desired outcomes by asking *"What do you want to happen?"* or *"What is your desired outcome?"*
- In stage 3, focus on gathering data about causes and contributing factors by asking questions such as *"What are the symptoms of this situation?"* and *"What might cause the symptoms?"*
  - When doing a fishbone analysis for possible causes, ask "Why?" at least five times to get to the root causes.
  - When describing indicators, ask the team questions like *"How can your success be effectively measured?"* Ask them to focus on the action or change they wish to see.
- In stage 4, 5, and 6, as outdent team members begin to suggest possible strategies or solutions, ask *"Is there any evidence that shows that this proposed solution (hypotheses) will work?"* The team should look for examples where similar solutions led to outcomes that they want to achieve.

TRY IT!

Imagine that you are facilitating the planning for projects supporting children in an inner-city school. Create a cheat sheet of questions to use through the planning cycle, as in Table 28.1.

SUMMARY

One of the techniques for engaging your team members is to ask good questions. A good question is answerable and challenging. It can elicit facts and lead your team members to and through analysis, synthesis, interpretation and critical thinking. Asking questions builds rapport, keeps the focus on the

Table 28.1 Possible questions and probes.

Cheat sheet of possible questions and probes to use through the change planning process		
Stage	Purpose	Questions
Before the meeting	Creating relationships	
1	Describing the present state	
2	Envisioning desired outcomes	
3	Gathering data (assessment)	
4	Planning strategies	
5	Implementation plan	
6	Evaluation	
Any time	Clarification Elaboration	

team, rather than on the facilitator, and elicits reflective discussion. Questions and probes can unlock creativity and passion that will move your change initiative forward toward the desired future throughout the planning cycle. This chapter provided techniques for formulating essential questions that can drive conversation and get to the heart of the issue while they sidestep the pitfalls of overly broad questions that people can't begin to answer or narrow, closed questions that allow for only single-word answers.

CITATIONS

Kimsey-House, K., Kimsey-House, H., Sandhal, P., & Whitworth, L. (2018). *Co-active coaching: The proven framework for transformative conversations at work and in life* (4th ed.). Boston, MA: Nicholas Brealey Publishing.

Sobel, A., & Panas, J. (2012). *Power questions: Build relationships, win new business, and influence others.* New York: John Wiley & Sons.

Wilkinson, M. (2004). *The secrets of facilitation: The S.M.A.R.T. guide to getting results with groups.* San Francisco, CA: Jossey-Bass-Wiley.

Wise, W. (2017). *Ask powerful questions: Create conversations that matter* (2nd ed.). West Columbia, SC: CreateSpace Independent Publishing Platform.

Citations for Studies Cited in the Story

Allard, P., & Greene, J. (2011). *Children on the outside: Voicing the pain and human costs of parental incarceration.* Justice Strategies Report. Retrieved from https://justicestrategies.org/sites/default/files/publications/JS-COIP-1-13-11.pdf

Brookes, L. (2018). Why we need to listen to children of prisoners. *European Journal of Education, 53*(3), 271–274. doi:10.1111/ejed.12278

Martin, E. (2017, March). Hidden consequences: The Impact of incarceration on dependent children. *NIJ Journal*, 278. Retrieve from https://nij.gov/journals/278/Pages/impact-of-incarceration-on-dependent-children.a

Saunders, V. (2018). What does your dad do for a living? Children of prisoners and their experiences of stigma. *Children and Youth Services Review*, 90, 21–27. doi:10.1016/j.childyouth.2018.05.012

29. TROUBLE ON THE TEAM

Figure 29.0

WHAT'S IN THIS CHAPTER?

At the beginning of this book we retold the story of David and Goliath, where a small boy had the confidence and skill to confront the giant when the others ran away. He acted without fear. The core teaching of this book is how you, as a facilitator, can learn how to intervene to move the action forward in difficult situations. In spite of our best intentions, meetings sometimes degenerate for a variety of reasons, including distractions, talkative members, people with an ax to grind and fear of conflict. When humans face a conflict, we choose either "fight or flight," and most people choose to walk away rather than fight. This chapter provides techniques for dealing with discouragement and disorder that come from the failure to face and resolve the conflict because of fear.

Objectives

By the end of this chapter, you will be able to:

1. Identify types of team trouble that can occur.
2. Describe methods of facilitated resolution.
3. Describe poor communication situational blindness and solutions to this type of team trouble.

A STORY ABOUT AN ELEPHANT IN THE LIVING ROOM

Here is a story of how one person was able to acknowledge the unspoken truth in the room at an international conference which eventually resolved a large conflict.

Two adventure-trainers were preparing to lead a rock-climbing experience for their corporate clients as a team-building exercise. While setting up the course, halfway up the mountain one man suddenly fell and was severely injured. As a result of the fall he was permanently disabled and could not continue his career. This marked a groundbreaking moment for both of the friends and the end of life as they knew it. Together they made a life-changing decision to share their expertise in team building in the form of teaching cooperative play to children around the world as a form of peacemaking. They invited their friends to join them in this new adventure, not knowing where it would take them, and many joined them as volunteers. The peace project, operating on a shoestring of donations and grants, slowly expanded to several countries around the world with assistance from their international volunteer network of cooperative players. As the organization grew, it became apparent that a corporate structure would be needed to sustain it. At this point the disabled partner withdrew, leaving only one director who had the essential business expertise to create an expanded worldwide organization in order to keep it grounded and protected.

What happened next? The personality of the second founder took over the organization. He was creative, smart and tireless in his efforts, but he was a **top-down leader in his decision-making style.** Since the organization was spread across the world, there was very little contact between the unit leaders. Even though the board members traveled occasionally to visit sites, there was no cohesive organizational management. Thus, the director's centralized control was dominating the board and local leaders. Communication became diffuse and confused, resulting eventually in rumblings of discontent in the ranks. Though there were many side conversations by email between leaders, no one had the opportunity to confront the problem because they never saw each other face to face in a group.

The organization, though brilliantly begun, was eroding. A sudden gap in funding resulted in the loss of their office space, and for a few years there was a potential scenario of organizational failure. The director knew he had to take action, so when funding became available again he invited two facilitators to lead an international conference of representatives from all of the global peace teams.

When the unit leaders from six different countries began to arrive at the conference center, they had opportunities for informal interaction in the hallways, and in these private talks they compared notes.

Things were not going well for any of them. They recognized that the director was about to make some really bad decisions that would affect all of them, yet no one was willing to raise the issue. Here are some behaviors that they exhibited which are typical for groups in conflict.

LET'S ASK THE KEY QUESTION AGAIN—WHAT'S HAPPENING NOW?

In this conflict situation some typical human emotional responses are visible—if you choose to see them. However, most often people are looking away when there is trouble. Here is an explanation of each of these conflict avoidance behaviors apparent in this story.

Appeasement: When trying to appease an opponent, you are making concessions in order to avoid conflict. This can appear to be a weak position of attempting to bribe someone to change their ways. As a result, a more powerful opponent can sense your fear and then look for ways to undermine your position.

Scapegoating: This occurs when a person(s) is receiving the blame for all that goes wrong, and thus other contributing factors are being ignored. This is usually a way of deflecting the true issues by shifting the blame to a scapegoat. Thus, the group can avoid taking responsibility by placing their anger on someone else.

Shunning: Turning away from an associate or friend with whom you have a dispute is a typical response to conflict in interpersonal relationships. When we are unwilling to confront an issue, it often feels safer to ignore the person with whom we are having a problem. This is a highly destructive form of conflict avoidance because the person being shunned can feel that they have been erased and left out of the group entirely. Trust is eroded and people start to leave in anger.

Sweeping the conflict under the rug: People believe that if we don't see the problem or don't acknowledge it, then it will just go away. Except it never does. Ignoring the issues only magnifies them when they eventually emerge down the line in another context. The only way around a conflict is to go through it. Otherwise, you keep tripping over the lumpy rug.

Taking sides: The creation of factions can lead to even greater conflict. As a result, more people are drawn into the conflict and become biased in their positions or opinions. Creating allies in this context can be a very negative choice because it often leads to thinking that the other side is the enemy.

Leaving the group: When the kitchen gets too hot, some people just leave. This can also be a short-term stress reliever for the group, but the side effect from walking away is wounded people with unrelieved guilt or shame issues. The conflict remains unresolved.

These are all examples of "**blind-spotting**," which means that either an individual or the entire group is refusing to see and act upon the clear evidence of conflict right in front of their eyes. Instead of acting, they hide their emotions and hope for the storm to blow over. This behavior often occurs when a conflict situation has become so intractable that it appears easier to ignore the symptoms than to seek a solution.

BACK TO OUR STORY

Here is how an effective intervention into the conflict changed the outcome.

Team building and training in community development was on the conference agenda, and when the leadership group gathered, there was a shift of consciousness that was unplanned. Together at last, the local leaders began to compare notes in private conversations about how the organization was functioning. No one had the courage to bring up the uncomfortable subject in front of the entire group; they were just whispering about it with each other in the corridors. The facilitator knew the time was ripe for some honest conversation.

At one point during the formal training session, the facilitator decided to raise the hidden issue by saying, "It sounds like there is an elephant in the living room." She was being metaphorical, of course, and was surprised by the startled reaction of the Indian participants. They were looking for a real live elephant. She reassured them that this turn of phrase relates to a problem as big as an elephant that no one will address openly. One person was not afraid. A team leader raised some pointed questions to the international director about the loss of volunteer support over the years. She observed that many good people had stopped coming from America to help them, and she wondered why.

She actually knew the answer to her inquiry: the director's autocratic control was keeping them away. He had occupied the center stage and felt threatened by his old friends who were more open in their criticism of his leadership style. Trust between them had been broken, and they had withdrawn their volunteer support. Drawing a curtain over this difficult discussion, let's just say that eventually there was a decentralization of the power structure, and the founding director stepped down to become a board member. Another unit leader who had a cooperative and collective leadership style was named as the worldwide program director. This one change led to a renewal of leadership and a surge of growth in peace programs to 40 different countries.

Lessons Learned:

- There is no way around conflict; you must go through it to resolve it. Acting to confront a problem directly is wiser than allowing it to grow out of sight with more serious consequences down the road.
- If you can spot the game, then you can change it. Clues to the problem are usually evident in the behavior of the players. Looking for solutions is much wiser than avoidance.
- As the old motto goes, "in the kingdom of the blind, the one-eyed man is king." One person who is willing to see and speak the truth is the key to resolving most conflicts.
- Facilitation is often the best strategy for altering the situation even when it appears intractable.

WHAT THESE TECHNIQUES ARE ABOUT

What Is the Role of Conflict in Community Development?

Conflict, both interpersonal and organizational, is usually the "elephant in the living room" that no one wants to talk about. Most people run from conflict which sends them in the wrong direction. Conflict, when handled effectively, can serve as a source of generative energy that can lead to new growth of an organization. Remember how Mount St. Helens blew its top off in a shocking event, but the later outcome was vibrant new growth after the detritus had settled. Conflicts can be very useful if we know how to use them.

Conversely, lack of conflict may also be a sign of trouble. When a team arrives prematurely at consensus by failing to critically evaluate options, the result may be poor decision-making. This phenomenon is called groupthink. Groupthink is thought to be caused by group insulation, homogeneity (McCauley, 1989; Macleod, 2011), collective confirmation bias or community fear, although further research needs to be done to verify these causes. Group members may also fear that disagreement leads to conflict, and they wish to avoid those consequences (Hartwig, 2010).

HOW TO ADDRESS THE PROBLEM OF CONFLICT IN A HEALTHY WAY

This chapter will take you through a step-by-step process to show that there is a pathway which can remove a block on the track. The facilitator's role becomes vitally important when there is conflict. If you cannot find a neutral person to fill this role, then a member of the group must assume an objective stance to manage the conflict. Someone is needed who can stand outside of the dispute and avoid taking sides while serving as the group's coach, listener or guide. I call this person the "midwife" because the role is similar to helping with childbirth during labor. The facilitator needs to keep a cool head and an observant eye.

The first step in addressing a conflict is *noticing* what is going on in yourself as well as in others. Watch the behavior patterns of the players and write down your observations (as dispassionately as possible). Try not to characterize either side of the conflict as positive or negative, right or wrong. Raise the question—"What's happening now?" This can serve as a useful starting point for addressing the conflict.

Next comes *wondering* about what you observe. Keep in the back of your mind the acronym WRGOH?—What's really going on here (Senge, 2014). Do you have any hypotheses about the conflict and its sources? Might there be a person not in the room who is influencing behaviors of one or more present? What might serve as a potential opening in the wall? Who might be willing to change sides or seek a "third way" solution? Be open to the outcome; do not predict the outcome. Adopt an attitude of liminality, meaning waiting on the threshold. Don't step over it. Allow the group's movement to direct the action. You might be surprised by the unexpected outcome which leads the group in a new and positive direction.

Processing is the next step. Invite all sides of the conflict to communicate with each other in a healthy, nonjudgmental way. Take some time to teach listening skills or at least model them by being a fair listener as their facilitator. It might be necessary for the facilitator to meet separately with each side in order to hear them out before putting them at the table for a face-to-face conversation. Emotions often run high and people need time to simmer down before they can see their opponent more clearly. "Keep your powder dry" means being prepared for the struggle, but do not enter into the emotional distress of the parties yourself.

Speaking truth to power. Speak the truth without blaming either side. Take your position firmly as their facilitator and hold the conversation within boundaries that are both fair and productive. Always keep in mind that organizational storms do blow over eventually, and the next stage will be to set group norms. At that point the work will be reframed or re-engineered based on a new, collective understanding of how to move forward (Shapiro, 2015).

WHAT ARE SOME TYPICAL ISSUES THAT CAN CAUSE CONFLICT?

In the story in this chapter, a frank discussion of the problem needed to take place, and then a plan of action created to transition the organization from an organization in the founding stage, run by the founder, to a more mature structure. Interventions to help make the transition may come from the founder, the board or from others involved in the organization.

- *Founder's syndrome*: Dynamic organizations, both nonprofit and for profit, begin with one or more people with a vision, determination, energy and support (McLaughlin & Backlund Nelson, 2008). As the organization matures, its needs change. A study of founder-led and nonprofits not led by the founder indicates that founders and non-founders hold different perspectives, and founders can hold organizations back by holding onto the leader role (Block & Rosenberg, 2002). A founder may continue to make all the decisions, become inflexible and fail to allow skilled professionals the autonomy to do their jobs. The organization may become less productive and have a smaller budget, and boards may meet less frequently than organizations that are not founder-led, allowing the founder to make more decisions. In the worst cases, the founder may reject ideas without justification and make business decisions based on personal preferences and unsound judgment, rather than observable data. When this kind of behavior takes place, it may be time for the founder to step down.
- *Team conflict*: It seems that even in optimal circumstances, conflict is inevitable. It is a part of life that can have both positive and negative effects. It can take a number of forms, from mild differences of opinion to shouting matches. If not resolved in a timely fashion, team conflict can lead to long-term antagonism that reduces the productivity of an organization. However, conflict on teams

is not always problematic. Some conflict can lead to new ideas and better ways of carrying out the mission of the organization. It can also highlight organizational challenges or weaknesses. When this happens, solutions can be sought that can leave the organization stronger in the long run.

Conflict can result from differences in perspectives caused by different values, skill sets, goals and expectations. These differences may have their basis in educational, cultural or generational differences. They may also come from poor communication skills. To complicate things further, the apparent cause of the conflict isn't always what is at the heart of the problem. Whatever the cause, those people involved in the conflict may feel uncertain or even threatened. Threats might include:

- Threats to relationships.
- Threats to a sense of belonging.
- Threats to identity or ego.
- Threats to our values.
- Threats to physical safety.
- Unknown fear (Hamilton, 2013).

HOW TO CARRY OUT THESE TECHNIQUES

When people feel threatened, they might respond by: (1) accommodation (giving the opposing side what they want), (2) avoidance (delaying or ignoring the conflict in the hope that it will resolve itself) or (3) competition (seeking to win while the other side loses). How people respond depends on factors including temperament, culture and context. Often, the response is a *mix* of these styles accompanied by strong feelings. None of these styles result in truly satisfactory results, because they create a sense of separation from others, and loss of trust.

As facilitator, you can help address the conflict by bringing compassion and objectivity to the forefront. First, gently interrupt the dispute, asking **"What's really going on here?"**

RESOLUTIONS

Ask if the dispute could be resolved through a one-on-one meeting between the two people involved. This is the first step as shown in Figure 29.1. Organizations that provide training in conflict resolution to their staff have the advantage of knowing a protocol for resolving differences with each other: The parties discuss the problem from both points of view, brainstorm solutions and decide together on a course of action.

If the exchange is very heated, you will want to interrupt before heightened tensions lead to team members making personal attacks or aggressive gestures. At this point, the facilitator may need to use a *facilitated resolution* process (step 2). First, call a break, asking people to become aware of their feelings. The facilitator can reframe the disagreement. Sometimes strong feelings indicate a boundary that has been crossed, or an issue that they care deeply about. Then ask them to practice speaking their truth, without any blame or misinterpretation, during the time until the next meeting. Ask them to commit to not name-call or characterize the other's behavior. Set a time to reconvene with just the two parties.

During the time until the next meeting, it may be useful for you to have a private conversation with each of the parties to better understand their perspectives and reduce their anxiety. Not all people can easily express their points of view in public because of their own cultural norms, respect for elders or past life experiences (Hamilton, 2013). A private meeting may help them feel more comfortable expressing their needs or desires in the current scenario. Also, you will find out if each of the people are able to see the situation from the perspective of the other persons. Some people are very flexible and can look at the situation from multiple perspectives, while other people cannot. During that private meeting, you might

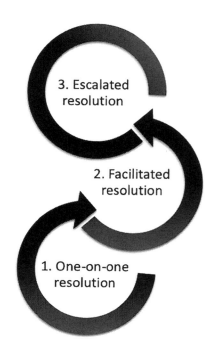

Figure 29.1 Conflict resolution methods.

also suggest they locate and bring copies to the next meeting of policies, regulations or other documents that may shed light on the issue.

When the meeting reconvenes, ask the people involved in the conflict to truly listen to the other person as they restate their points calmly, respectfully, without blame or interruption. "I" statements can be used to state their feelings, beliefs or values. There are multiple perspectives on most things, and there is no guarantee that both parties can understand the other's perspective, but the use of "I" statements allows people to exchange perspectives more effectively. Your job, as facilitator, is to remain neutral, and to improve the empathy and dialogue between both parties. Begin by acknowledging the validity in both perspectives and then identify the issues. Ask each party questions to clarify the details and identify the respective interests and objectives of each party. Look for common ground, and state what it is. Ask the parties for acceptable objective *criteria* or standards for judging that they have chosen a good solution and help them reach an agreement. Next, ask for solution options that would meet everyone's needs. Discuss the options and adjust them until both sides can agree.

Should you find that there is no agreement, it might be useful to *escalate* (step 3) the situation and bring in a trained mediator to assist. Either have the mediator work with the two people involved, or involve the whole team if the problem involves several people. Call a team meeting and explain the problem from the point of view of a neutral third party. Ask each of the team members engaged in the conflict to add anything missing to your description of the situation. Ask other members of the team to contribute their thoughts on the situation with a brief and objective statement, with team and organization goals, policies and procedures as their frame of reference. Come to a group decision and document it.

SITUATIONAL BLINDNESS

Situational blindness is the opposite of situational awareness. Situational awareness is the perception and comprehension of our immediate environment and all of the events happening in it. For teams, shared

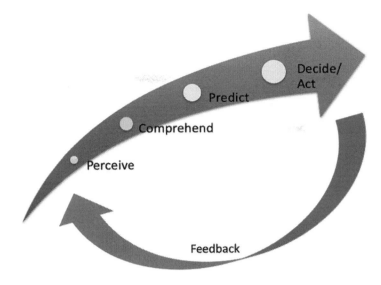

Figure 29.2 Situational awareness.

situational awareness is key for productive work. It requires unity of effort that comes from clear goals, direction, shared experience and continuous monitoring of themselves and their peers in relation to the dynamic environment surrounding the organization. One problem causing lack of situational awareness is attentiveness or lack of it. "We pay attention to what we are told to attend to, or what we're looking for, or what we already know . . . what we see is amazingly limited" (Chabris & Simons, 2011).

Shown in Figure 29.2, situational awareness requires that information about the one's self and peers, and about the internal and external factors of the organization is perceived and comprehended. Information about the internal factors might include personnel capabilities (staff and volunteers) or finances. External factors might include location, legislation, regulations, community readiness and sociocultural changes. These factors were examined by the team in the course of doing the SWOT analysis and the Force Field Analysis. This information needs to be understood and interpreted accurately for it to be used to predict or anticipate the future and make decisions about what strategic directions to take. Through feedback, you can assess the accuracy of your process and improve it over time.

Problems on the team may come from a few different sources: (1) lack of shared situational awareness as a result of poor communication of information, or a blame culture causing lack of accountability or fear of making mistakes; (2) lack of direction caused by poor leadership resulting in nothing getting done until someone pulls the plug on the project; (3) no shared experience on how to get a task accomplished as a result of lack of training or selecting people for the project without adequate skills and knowledge.

To overcome these issues, the team must develop effective communication, a collaborative method of working together, and effective leadership through training, mentoring or coaching. The quality of the decision can usually be traced to the quality of the discussion, so the role of facilitator or chair becomes critical. Create a positive environment in which to research the situation and discuss your options. Several of the methods already discussed in this book can help in making sound decisions that avoid groupthink, including the fishbone diagram and Force Field Analysis.

To get to the heart of the problem and make the best decisions possible, team members should ask themselves these questions when discussing ideas.

- Are we drawing the right conclusion?
- Why did we assume this?

- Are our conclusions based on facts?
- Why do we think this is the right thing to do?
- Can we do this in a different way (Argyris, 1982)?

The facilitator can foster open discussion and encourage all members to contribute their thoughts. Group norms should be established that speaking one's mind openly and occasional disagreement is a healthy part of effective decision-making because that means that different perspectives are being offered on the issue. Team members should avoid quickly criticizing or insulting others' ideas. However, subgroups can be established to critically evaluate important plans, their assumptions and consequences. When offering their critiques, the subgroup's comments should be offered with a spirit of collaboration and encouragement.

POOR COMMUNICATION

Good communication involves sending and receiving clear messages, checking that listeners understand and/or responding to inquiries for clarification. To communicate effectively, you need to know the people to whom you are speaking or writing, so they can understand. Conversely, *poor* communication among team members during or outside of meetings can result in confusion, conflict and hurt feelings. These results are caused by one or more of the following:

- Presenting one's own ideas as if they are the only feasible ideas, and not considering other alternatives.
- Talking too much and not listening to other people's ideas. During meetings, team members may interrupt or talk over one another.
- Disparaging other people's ideas.
- Focusing on people instead of problems. Getting emotional and belittling other people.
- Disregarding or invalidating feelings of others on the team.
- Responding with sarcasm or indirect resistance to comments of others.
- From other team members, you may get consistent silence as a result of communications taking the forms listed here.

Learning to communicate effectively is a matter of recognizing poor communication and practicing more effective methods.

TRY IT!

The Scenario

Rising rents in a college town have increased stress on students trying to find appropriate housing. Differing points of view on this situation include local residents who want stable housing, high income people who want fancier places to live, and students who want low rent. The mayor has called a town meeting to open a dialogue on this difficult subject. Imagine that you are the leader of the student activist group. You have been asked to speak on their behalf. It appears that you may have the following issues to address:

- In the Town Hall there will be open dialogue between all groups who have different points of view. Meetings in the past have been marked by situational blindness and emotionally fraught communications, that have stalled progress. This worries the student activist group.
- The student activist group is in a creative rut. They are going in circles regarding the potential of a single solution, and not identifying additional potential solutions to bring to the town hall meeting.

WHAT YOU NEED TO DO

Keep in mind the chapters on listening deeply (Chapter 26) and asking good questions (Chapter 28), then reflect on what's likely to happen. Determine what method you, as the leader/facilitator of the student group, can offer to open a path toward working together. What is the best course of action, and who is the best person to be a spokesperson? Use the online team troubles checklist (available online in eResources for this chapter) to ensure that you are considering all available points when writing your answer.

Describe in your own words:

1. Each issue causing difficulty.
2. A path forward that could be used to address these issues in the next meeting.

SUMMARY

Avoiding and resolving team troubles are challenging goals. They require that you help team members find project activities interesting, support their independence and goal setting, help them progress through data collection, analysis, planning and implementation, and clearly communicate feedback when they are successfully doing so. Finally, help team members to feel accepted and cared for by the team to support their creativity and contributions to the discussion. A facilitator can also encourage the team members to become more goal and intrinsically motivated. This chapter addressed how to resolve team conflict and to avoid situational blindness, groupthink and decision difficulty. It also addressed the consequences of lack of team identity, poor communication, lack of creativity and, finally, lack of effective leadership.

CITATIONS

Argyris, C. (1982). The executive mind and double-loop learning. *Organizational Dynamics, 11*(2), 5–22.

Block, S. R., & Rosenberg, S. A. (2002, June). Toward an understanding of founder's syndrome: An assessment of power and privilege among founders of nonprofit organizations. *Nonprofit Management and Leadership, 12*(4), 353–368.

Chabris, C. F., & Simons, D. J. (2011). *The invisible gorilla: How our intuitions deceive us* (Reprint ed.). New York: Harmony. (Original work published 2010.)

Hamilton, D. M. (2013). *Everything is workable*. Boston, MA: Shambala.

Hartwig, R. (2010). Facilitating problem solving: A case study using the devil's advocacy technique. *Group Facilitation*, 17–31. Retrieved from https://brainmass.com/file/274163/Research+Article+-+DA.pdf

Macleod, L. (2011). Avoiding groupthink: A manager's challenge. *Nursing Management, 42*(10).

McCauley, C. (1989). The nature of social influence in groupthink: Compliance and internalization. *Journal of Personality and Social Psychology, 57*(2), 250–260. doi:10.1037/0022-3514.57.2.250

McLaughlin, T., & Backlund Nelson, A. (2008). *Moving beyond founder's syndrome to nonprofit success*. Washington, DC: BoardSource. Retrieved from https://boardsource.org/product/moving-beyond-founders-syndrome-nonprofit-success/

Senge, P. M. (2014). *The fifth discipline fieldbook: Strategies and tools for building a learning organization*. New York, NY: Crown Business.

Shapiro, M. (2015). *HBR guide to leading teams*. Brighton, MA: Harvard Business Review Press.

STAGE 5
Community Development

This section provides information for developing and managing key elements of a community initiative customized for the context of your community. Using an assessment of local indicators, community readiness assessment, cause analysis (fishbone diagram) and Force Field Analysis, the next step is to research "best practices" that your team could adapt to local circumstances to address the issue or objective. After choosing appropriate community change strategies and planning to adapt to the local situation, you will need to implement your plan. This requires skills for monitoring and management of strategies as well as the skills for developing effective communications, programs or other interventions.

Figure S5.0 Facilitation of Change Model Stage 5: Community development.

CHOOSING AND DEVELOPING A SOLUTION

30

Figure 30.0

WHAT'S IN THIS CHAPTER?

In choosing or developing a solution for your community, you will begin with the analyses you have completed and then search for promising practices or interventions used by other communities that show potential for your own community. You can find good information by *researching* in libraries and on the Internet. Ideas might also be found by *networking* with state and national professional or advocacy groups, state and federal agencies, public and private funding groups, academics in the field and community members. If no potential practices can be found, you can use past experience and analysis and theory to identify promising solutions. As a team, compare *promising practices* or *interventions* and then choose one or more practices that you think will work. Assess possible risk factors so you can plan to reduce risks as much as possible and make sure that the project can be repeated in the future. Pay close attention to adapting interventions to local personal, moral, legal and social standards as well as local cultures and sub-communities.

Objectives

By the end of this chapter, you will be able to:

- Search for promising practices or interventions.
- Use networking to locate promising practices or interventions.
- Identify attributes of promising practices.
- Select practices or interventions for your community by matching causes to solutions.

A STORY: A NEW LIBRARIAN COMES TO TOWN

A small town like Carbondale (population 25,902) really treasures its public library. Imagine the excitement when the news was spreading that a new library director was hired. Right after she arrived, people heard new ideas springing forth from her connections with the wider community.

What is essential and energizing about Diana Brawley Sussman's approach to library work is that she sees it as a place for creative intervention for social change. Diana was not a novice to library work. As she describes herself,

> I learned public librarianship in a large city library. Then I put those tools to use in a special library, which had national, statewide, and regional layers to it. This taught me to think like a big city librarian, and to apply that thinking to libraries in unique settings with smaller budgets.

In addition, Diana already knew the community before she took the job. "Carbondale is my hometown, so I have an innate understanding of this community. Carbondale is a little city, but being a university town with urban sensibilities, it requires a big-city approach to community services on a small city budget,"

In our interview to capture this story, Diana stated:

> Libraries have always been innovative, adaptive, responsive organizations. That's why we're still around! The librarians who taught me how to be a librarian had this same vision in the 1990s. They'd been practicing this socially responsive and engaged style of librarianship since the 1960s or 70s, and it didn't start there. The very idea of pooling resources to educate, enlighten, and serve the public in an equitable manner requires librarians (and their staff and Boards) to imagine a place for creative intervention and for social change.

She has geared much of the library's programming toward promoting a culture of inclusiveness, fostering dialogues of mutual understanding. Most libraries are centers of learning, but with Diana in charge, the public library in Carbondale became a center of social action. For example, like most librarians, she noticed how many homeless people were among her patrons and wondered how the library could be helpful to them. To affect change on homelessness, she worked with other concerned community leaders on intervention activities by offering public education, outreach to faith communities, and civic dialogues. With these connections firmly established, she invited interns from the university's School of Social Work to serve in the library as a source of support and connection for homeless people and others with social service needs (Esch, 2017).

When she learned about the international Compassionate Cities program, which promotes a social justice environment of fairness and compassion for everyone, she joined several community partners in an effort to engage the entire city in this cause. This initiative led to the City Council passing a "Compassionate and Nonviolent Community Resolution," committing to this vision. As stated by Karen Armstrong, founder of the global movement in The Charter for Compassion:

> A compassionate city is an uncomfortable city! A city that is uncomfortable when anyone is homeless or hungry. Uncomfortable if every child isn't loved and given rich opportunities to grow and thrive. Uncomfortable when as a community we don't treat our neighbors as we would wish to be treated. Karen Armstrong, The Charter for Compassion.
>
> (compassionatecities.org)

Diana also helped to create and continue a collaborative project called Nonviolent Carbondale (www.nonviolentcarbondale.org) which has hosted hundreds of programs about social issues. Having performed at one of those programs, author John Dear was inspired to found a nationwide Nonviolent Cities Project with Carbondale as the model (Pace e Bene Nonviolence Service, n.d.). There are now 50 Nonviolent Cities projects in the United States and Canada (https://paceebene.org/nonviolent-cities). Eventually, the city passed a resolution: "Be it resolved that the Mayor and the Carbondale City Council affirm the Charter for Compassion, declare Carbondale a participant in a long-term campaign to become, strive toward, and sustain a Compassionate Nonviolent Community." As we stated in the introduction to this book, big social movements often begin with small actions; in this case, it began with a small-town librarian who had a big dream.

WHAT THIS TECHNIQUE IS ABOUT

Social issues are complex, and as this story shows, most community change efforts need to use multiple strategies such as programs (education), civic dialogues (communication), internships for students to provide social services for clients (support) and, finally, government actions on policy changes.

To select interventions, you need to examine the cause analysis done previously and make sure the intervention matches or solves the cause or it will not work. Then look for promising interventions that might be adapted for your community through library and online research and networking. Your team will need to analyze the solutions they found and decide which solutions will work the best for your community and how to adapt the solutions to local conditions.

HOW TO CARRY OUT THIS TECHNIQUE

Who Should Be Involved?

Use a collaborative approach to address opportunities or problems. Include community stakeholders, professionals in the area of the issue, members of your organization and community influencers.

Searching for Promising Practices or Interventions

Each member of the core team should search for possible practices or interventions that look promising. Begin your search for practices and interventions at the library or on the Internet. Organizations and individuals that receive grants must file reports, and many go on to publish articles about their projects. For instance, a search to locate information on effective interventions for homeless youth was conducted at a university library, and a couple of good sources were located. Notice during your search if a source is a peer-reviewed journal article. This should ensure that the article is trustworthy. Similar scholarly search results can be found using Google Scholar, but you may find that there is sometimes no link to the article. For more detail on a particular project, locate and contact the authors or people associated with the practices or interventions in which you are interested. Ask the authors *what worked* and *what did not work* in their project. Discuss the article and the characteristics of their community such as cultures, ages of clients, etc., to see how it compares to your context.

The difficulty of getting articles published in scholarly journals often prevents successful smaller projects carried out by non-academic teams from being published; however, many of these projects have web pages. Simply doing a search on the topic of your project may turn up many of these websites, but they may not have enough information for you to use their practices or interventions for your project; so you may need to contact the people who created the website directly.

Another method of locating promising practices or interventions is *networking* with others. Talk to everyone you know in:

- State and national professional or advocacy groups.
- State and federal agencies.
- Public and private funders.
- Academics in the field and community members.

When you go to professional conferences, attend relevant sessions and then take advantage of networking opportunities to discuss the practices or interventions in depth with presenters.

Be sure to investigate a variety of interventions. It is often more difficult and costly to create something that never existed before, but it may be worth considering when nothing you find looks like a good fit to your community.

Attributes of Promising Practices or Interventions

When looking for promising practices or interventions for your community, look for descriptions of practices, interventions or programs that are *credible*, *objective*, *clear* and able to be *reproduced* and implemented with appropriate modifications in other settings. In a field filled with advocacy groups, policy makers and activists, it is important to locate information that is trustworthy and independent of ideologies.

- Descriptions should be *comprehensive* enough to include the detailed actions of the intervention or practice, the resulting human behaviors as well as the context(s) so that your team can evaluate the extent to which the conclusions drawn are transferable to your settings, situations and people.
- The practice or intervention has been recommended as *effective* by other nonprofit providers, federal and state funders of services, or experts in the field.
- The practice or intervention description is *results-oriented*, including evaluation data demonstrating the ways in which the clients benefited from the program. The program should directly impact at least one of the indicators used to evaluate it. Look for practices and interventions that changed at least one outcome by 20% or more.
- Project evaluation is described.

> *Credibility*: the extent to which the information is recognized as reliable. In this case we are concerned with the description of a community intervention or practice that is described in sufficient detail so that it can be repeated; it provides objective, evidence-based information on the results showing **how well the intervention or practice worked** for the community in which it was used and **what did not work**.

TEAM DECISION PROCESS

Begin by asking "What's happening now?" and then form a vision for the solution. State the goals and objectives concisely and with indicators. With these goals and objectives in mind, move on to selecting strategies to achieve the objectives.

In the process of choosing strategies to address community change, it is best to work with a team because the cumulative knowledge and wisdom of the group far outstrips the knowledge and wisdom of any one individual on the team. Individuals have seen different strategies used in community change, so together those solutions can be compared and discussed. In addition, the team can avoid making illogical decisions by asking each other:

- Are we drawing the right conclusions?
- Why did we assume this?
- Is our conclusion accurately based on facts or the data we have collected on our community needs, readiness and characteristics?
- Why do we think this is the best thing to do?
- Is there a different way to do this?

Each intervention strategy decision should be made with all the wisdom the team can muster, using the knowledge, experience, understanding, common sense and insights of everyone on the team, not just the loudest voices, or based on the opinions of those on the team holding the most power in the community. The process of selecting solutions looks like Figure 30.1.

In Chapters 10 and 11, we discussed how to determine what's happening now and visioning. The gap between what is happening now and your desired goal may reveal many causes, including environmental (natural and social) and individual factors. Keeping in mind the analyses you did earlier on the causes (see Chapter 14), focus on the causes, not symptoms. Then *prioritize* the causes you will address (Van Tiem, Moseley, & Dessinger, 2012). Usually an organization is prevented from addressing all the causes of the problems they are trying to solve because of resource limitations, or because some causes are beyond the scope of the organization to address them, so prioritizing what they will address is necessary. The team should conduct a review of publications and web sites to find solutions that worked for other communities and consider if they would meet the needs of your community. Match causes to potential solutions (individual or clusters of solutions) that should address the issues and then customize the solution(s) to fit your community's needs and level of readiness. While there are many causes and solutions, this book will focus on five solutions:

- Communications.
- Programs (learning).
- Policies.
- Physical environment.
- Support.

Figure 30.1 Selecting solutions.

GAIN CONSENSUS FOR GROUP COMMITMENT

Using a collaborative approach, list potential interventions. In a process recommended by Van Tiem et al. (2012), individuals can select 10 to 15 potential interventions which match the cause of the problem or an opportunity, of which they prioritize 5–6. These prioritized lists are shared and discussed with the team and then interventions are selected to implement. The final selection might use a consensus process or take a multi-voting approach. In the multi-voting approach, each team member has a few votes about a third of the total possibilities. Each team member cast their votes as they wish, either by spreading them out among the possibilities or placing them all on one intervention.

Base the selection of solutions on an understanding of the community context, situation, readiness, causes and clients. Draw on expertise including:

- Clients.
- Stakeholders.
- Practitioners (those who will implement the interventions).
- Team members.
- One or more people who will sponsor the project (in business, this is commonly called a champion).

ANALYZE COSTS AND BENEFITS

Does money spent now on community change or social services by nonprofits return more to the economy in the future? Clearly, it does, and to continue receiving funding, it is important to demonstrate to a skeptical community that the cost of the interventions or services your team provides will result in significant economic or other benefits. Include in your team deliberation the cost and value of each of the interventions your team is contemplating, as well as long and short-term effectiveness, the human resources and organizational support required to develop and implement the intervention(s) (Van Tiem et al., 2012, p. 2010). One way to compare what it *costs* to design, develop, implement and support the changes resulting from each possible intervention, and the value or *benefits* of various interventions is to carry out a *cost-benefit analysis*. Basically, you subtract all of the costs from all of the benefits you anticipate from an intervention. The idea is to find interventions where the benefits are in excess of the costs (Johansson & Kristrom, 2016).

In order to conduct a formal cost-benefit analysis, the team will need to determine the cost of the intervention, and the financial value of the results.

1. Review the causes of the opportunity or problem, the goals and objectives of the intervention.
2. List alternative interventions, each of which match the causes.
3. Brainstorm costs for each intervention.
4. Brainstorm benefits for each intervention.
5. Select measurement(s) and measure all costs for development and delivery of each intervention, and all benefits resulting from the intervention for a selected period of time. Some costs that should be considered include:
    a. Salaries for staff members working on your project.
    b. Specific materials, supplies, and equipment for your project.
    c. Travel to perform work on your project.
    d. Subcontracts that provide support exclusively to your project.
    e. Overhead costs (a percentage of your organization's costs such as space rental, general supplies, and the costs of furniture, fixtures, and equipment).
    f. Potential costs of not doing the project.
    g. Potential costs if the project fails.
6. Convert all costs and benefits into your local currency (such as today's U.S. dollars).
7. Compare costs and benefits over a relevant time period for each of the alternative interventions.

8. Narrow down the list of alternatives to only those in which benefits are in excess of the costs.
9. Make sure the list of interventions will match and address the causes. Select the best alternative and adopt the recommended intervention.

Some nonprofit agencies vigilantly track the outcomes of the interventions or social services they provide. They can describe what happens to their clients, and how the improvements in their lives (such as staying warm for the night, feeding their family, finding a job or housing) provide benefits both to individuals and to society. However, many charities find it formidable to quantify the benefits of interventions or community change. Even businesses find intangible benefits challenging to calculate.

It would be a mistake not to consider how much it can cost a community if a solution is not implemented. For example, as much as 25% of people experiencing homelessness may also suffer mental illness. This includes many of the people who frequent public libraries. A public library without staff trained to work with mentally ill patrons can suffer the consequences (Dowd, 2018). In one case, a fire that was started by a homeless patron caused half a million dollars in damages and closed the library for two to three months. While this example is somewhat extreme, it illustrates the point about tangible costs and intangible costs. It is easy to calculate the tangible costs of repairs (half a million), but how can one calculate the intangible costs to the community of not having a library? If your team considered training staff to work with people experiencing mental illness, you would want to consider the potential costs of not doing the project in your calculations.

MATCHING SOLUTIONS TO CAUSES

Community opportunities or problems are complex and usually have more than one cause. There should be a solution in your intervention for each cause, or the intervention will not work. Shown in Table 30.1 are causes and solutions stated generally. In your plan, you will state your cause and your solution specifically and include the strategies and tactics you will use to implement them. See Chapter 20 for more information on strategies and tactics.

In the case of the people experiencing homelessness in the library story, the causes and solutions can be analyzed and prioritized as shown in Table 30.2.

DESIGN AND DEVELOPMENT

Design and development are about the creation of solutions, including tangible products, processes or services. The solution selection decisions need to be carried out by creating the solution before implementation. The design and development process is shown in Figure 30.2. The team prepares by reviewing data and analyses they have completed to date, and then design and describe their planned solution.

The review of previously collected data and analyses includes:

- What's happening now.
- Causes.
- Desired state.
- Community readiness and possible resistance.
- Forces for and against change.
- Objectives.
- Combined resources available with allies.

After completing reviews, the team will describe the solution in a design document (a template of which is shown in Table 30.3) as thoroughly as possible for those developing the solution to be able to do so satisfactorily. As a change intervention is developed, there needs to be a focus on the people that will be affected (Varkey & Antonio, 2010).

Table 30.1 Match solutions to causes.

Causes Identified through cause analysis (fishbone diagram). *If the cause is:*		Potential Solutions *Then a matching solution would be:*
Environmental factors	Barriers	Remove barriers (physical, social, policy, etc.)
	Lack of information	Communications or programs (learning) providing needed information
	Lack of feedback	Communications or programs (learning) encouraging feedback
	Lack of support	Provide support/assistance (emotional, tangible, informational, companionship or other resources). Policy changes to create supportive social networks and services
	Lack of resources	Provide: ■ Programs (learning) on how to obtain resources ■ Resources, or ■ Tools to obtain resources
	Lack of tools	Provide tools
	Inadequate equity, consequences, rewards or incentives	Communications or programs (learning) encouraging feedback, consequences, rewards or incentives Policy change to promote justice, fairness, opportunities
Individual factors	Lack of skills or knowledge	Communications or programs (learning) to teach needed skills, knowledge and empowerment
	Lack of capacity	Change in physical environment Provide support or tools that improve individual capacity
	Lack of motivation/expectations	Communications or programs encouraging feedback, consequences, rewards or incentives Support to encourage motivation and change expectations

Information for the development plan was covered in previous chapters, up until timetables.

The *budget* should include all work hours for paid staff involved to create the intervention. In the example, one of the interventions was training. To create a budget, add the costs of creating and reproduce training media (text materials such as handouts, job-aids, visual media for the project). Calculate the following for design of training:

Example budget details for training:

Design

- Media writing, design and duplication.
- Administrative costs.
- Overhead: equipment, logistics, space.
- Staff salary and benefits.

For delivery of training (implementation), the following must be calculated:

- Instructor salary and benefits.
- Travel and living costs.

Table 30.2 Causes and solutions example.

Priority	Probable Causes	Potential Solutions
1	Homeless people congregating at the library resulting in conflict with other patrons from issues such as snoring, body odor, panhandling, too many bags, mental illness-caused difficult behaviors in the library.	Staff learn to work compassionately with the homeless people to solve problems by connecting them with needed resources and using empathy-driven enforcement.
2	Library staff lack knowledge and confidence to work compassionately with the homeless people.	Library staff inclusiveness policy. Library staff inclusiveness education.
3	Growing diversity with lack of recognition resulting lack of inclusiveness in the community.	■ Promoting a culture of inclusiveness through public education, outreach to faith communities and community dialogue. ■ Creating a collaborative project called Nonviolent Carbondale. ■ Persuading the City Council to pass a "Compassionate and Nonviolent Community Resolution," committing to a long-term campaign to realize this vision.
4	Lack of information, support resources and connection for homeless people.	Interns from the local university's School of Social Work placed at the library to support homeless people by connecting them with social services.

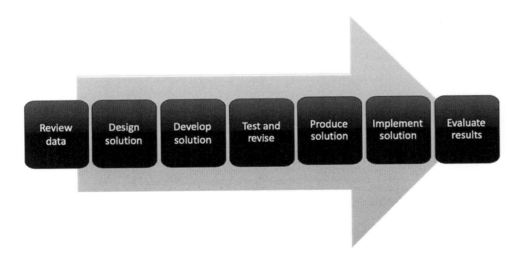

Figure 30.2 Design and development process.

- Lost opportunity costs.
- Administrative costs.
- Overhead: equipment, logistics, space.

Lost opportunity cost related to people is the value of decreased productivity, because an individual staff member is absent from a job when they are attending training or other change initiative activity. Any time

Table 30.3 Intervention design document template.

Intervention Design

Purpose:

Client needs (what's happening now):

Client description
Demographics and general characteristics:
Knowledge of the topic:
Readiness and attitudes towards the topic:
Client context:

Goal (desired state) and objectives:

Deliverables (the tangible or intangible goods or services produced as a result of a project):

Timetable:

Constraints (limitations or restrictions, such as how fast a project should be done or the maximum cost):

Key indicators:

Budget:

---

an individual is not carrying out the usual tasks of their job because they are doing something else (such as training), an organization bears the cost of a lost opportunity. This can also apply to volunteers but is more difficult to calculate when no pay or benefits are involved. Lost opportunity cost can also relate to the lost opportunity if the money is spent on another project rather than the one the team is considering.

Similarly, a budget for creating *any* change initiative needs to be broken down in detail.

Some projects require extensive *development*, while others require little time and effort, depending on what resources are available and the nature of the community. In either case, the community and organizational leaders must be committed to the project; as seen in the story, the library director was committed to the solutions, as was the city council. The project also needs to be both feasible in terms of budgets and human resources and sustainable over the long term (as long as necessary). Implementation follows development and needs to follow the intervention plans faithfully (Moseley & Hastings, 2005).

Sustainability will be covered in detail in Chapter 36.

EVALUATION

Every community change project that is carried out should be evaluated in the field to provide trustworthy information (Lincoln & Guba, 1985) that can improve the interventions and to provide evidence to donors and funders that the work of your organization is effective. Evaluating interventions addressing complex social issues is a complicated process (Schorr, 1997). More on evaluation will be covered in Chapter 38.

TRY IT!

Imagine that your community has many people experiencing homelessness congregating in the public library. You are part of a community advisory group for the library. Your concern is that community members will avoid the library because of concern about the difficulties and discomfort caused when there are confrontations with homeless people or snoring, body odor, panhandling, too many bags, or mental illness-caused difficult behaviors.

Table 30.4 Causes and solutions analysis template.

Priority	Probable Causes	Potential Solutions

Table 30.5 Intervention design template.

Intervention Design

Purpose:

Client needs (what's happening now):

Client description
Demographics and general characteristics:
Knowledge of the topic:
Readiness and attitudes towards the topic:
Client context:

Goal (desired state) and objectives:

Deliverables:

Timetable:

Constraints:

Key indicators:

Budget:

1. Using the form in Table 30.4, brainstorm probable causes and potential solutions.
2. Create an intervention design document for your high priority solution, using the form in Table 30.5.

SUMMARY

In this chapter we examined the process of choosing or developing intervention solutions for your community, beginning with a review of the analyses you have completed, and then searching for promising practices or interventions used by other communities that may work for your own community. We also covered how to compare interventions in terms of cost and benefits and prioritize which issues you will address first. Next, we discussed how your team would select one or more practices that will work. It is important to assess possible risk factors and ways to manage and reduce the risks. Finally, your team will adapt the intervention for local needs, to local personal, moral, legal and social standards; as well as local cultures and sub-communities.

CITATIONS

Dowd, R. J. (2018). *The librarian's guide to homelessness: An empathy-driven approach to solving problems, preventing conflict, and serving everyone.* Chicago: American Library Association.

Esch, K. J. (2017, August 1). Carbondale Public Library director named state's Librarian of the Year. *The Southern Illinoisan*. Retrieved from https://thesouthern.com/news/local/communities/carbondale/carbondale-public-library-director-named-state-s-librarian-of-the/article_74846a87–85ae-585d-8855–288fe31d0ca0.html

Johansson, P., & Kristrom, B. (2016). *Cost-benefit analysis for project appraisal*. Cambridge, UK: Cambridge University Press.

Lincoln, Y. S., & Guba, E. G. (1985). *Naturalistic inquiry*. Newbury Park, CA: Sage Publications.

Moseley, J. L., & Hastings, N. B. (2005, April). Implementation: The forgotten link on the intervention chain. *Performance Improvement*, 44(4), 8–14. doi:10.1002/pfi.4140440405

Nonviolent Carbondale. (n.d.). Retrieved from www.nonviolentcarbondale.org

Pace e Bene Nonviolence Service. (n.d.). *Nonviolent cities project*. Retrieved from https://paceebene.org/nonviolent-cities

Schorr, L. (1997). *Common purpose: Strengthening families and neighborhoods to rebuild America* (1st Anchor Books ed.). New York: Anchor Books, Doubleday.

Van Tiem, D., Moseley, J., & Dessinger, J. (2012). *Fundamentals of performance technology: Optimizing results through people, process and organizations* (3rd ed.). San Francisco, CA: Pfeiffer.

Varkey, P., & Antonio, K. (2010). Change management for effective quality improvement: A primer. *American Journal of Medical Quality*, 25(4), 268–273.

COMMUNICATION

31

Figure 31.0

WHAT'S IN THIS CHAPTER?

Providing information and instruction are often key components of change initiatives, even when other approaches are also used. Communications can include issue awareness campaigns, promoting interest and participation in the change initiative by community members, and training of staff, volunteers or clients. First, you need to raise community awareness of the initiative, then understanding, acceptance and commitment to implement the change in the community. Communications might take place through word of mouth, news or promotional stories online, in print and other media. Your team will want to create a comprehensive plan to communicate your message to the community. Good communications are created using a clear understanding of the purpose, audience, message and the methods used to get the message out. Finally, when the communications are implemented, you will want to monitor their effectiveness and improve them where possible.

Objectives

By the end of this chapter, you will be able to:

- Create an issue awareness campaign, promoting interest and participation using:
    - Personal communications (personal emissary work and word of mouth).
    - Promotional stories shared with news media.
    - Promotional stories on the web.
    - Promotional stories in print and visually.
    - Promotional stories in social and other media.
- Plan community meetings, news and promotional stories online reporting results.
- Follow guidelines to create effective communications using visual, verbal and print messages.

A STORY ABOUT COMMUNICATION AS A STRATEGY

In the story about the formation of the Race Unity group, we met a Muslim woman named Sumera, who crossed over the town's boundary of segregation to make friends with African Americans in the weekly discussion group. As you may recall, the mosque was located in the Black neighborhood far from the center of town. The Muslims had followed their tradition of generous giving by building a water feature in the park without branding it or claiming credit, and their African American neighbors knew about it. They also knew some Muslims who were African American, like the imam who also ran a social service agency for kids in the neighborhood.

In the middle of the neighborhood was a community building called the Hayes Center, which was built under the Model Cities Program in the 1960s. Over time, the building had fallen into disrepair as funding was withdrawn by the city government. Sumera approached Maurine to ask, "Why doesn't the Christian community keep up this building?" That was a loaded question, and she was not aware of the background. Maurine explained that the churches were all in competition with each other with the exception of two Baptist churches. No single pastor had the ability to hold sway on this issue, and so they remained in their own camps looking with suspicion on the other pastors. It seemed to be a stalemate because of invisible cultural differences. What did they have in common?

Sumera had the financial ability to solve the problem of restoring the center with one large check, but Maurine warned her that without buy-in and participation from the local leadership, the project would ultimately fail to be sustainable. She recommended a strategy called *personal emissary work* (Lofquist, personal communication, March 18, 2016). In other words, she suggested going in person to engage each of the pastors in looking at the situation and asking how they would solve the problem. Using this method, Sumera was able to connect the mosque with the immediate community and the pastors with each other over a shared concern for the future of the Center.

What were the shared cultural aspects between the varied Christian churches and the Muslims? What were the driving forces that could lead to change? Crime was rising in the neighborhood, particularly gun violence. Two young men had recently gotten into a gun battle in the parking lot of the Center, and one was killed. A concerned and angry grandmother called out for change and organized the mothers into an advocacy group called Women for Change. The NAACP also became alarmed at the crime rate. Why was the Center not being used as a central place for organizing? The reason was hidden competition between the constituencies. Sumera had an idea to share; Why not create a joint fundraiser? In a few weeks, hundreds of people gathered at a middle school auditorium to hear a new vision for the community center at a fundraising dinner. Sumera provided the food and stood to the side, allowing the pastors to take the center stage. She was proceeding as the "guide on the side rather than the sage on the stage."

From that point on, the activities of the Center increased and so did the financial support. A state senator opened an office in the Center for constituent service. The Women for Change group offered activities and started a voter registration campaign. The NAACP and the police department offered training sessions for community members.

Lessons Learned:

- Mutual decisions, mutually arrived at, are longer lasting.
- Stakeholders form alliances and go forward together.
- Consider cultural differences and plan for their inclusion in the change strategy.
- Expect to encounter resistance.

WHAT THIS TECHNIQUE IS ABOUT

Methods of communicating and *promoting issue awareness, interest and participation* include personal communications including emissary work and word of mouth. Information can also be shared via news media, stories shared online, in print and visuals and in social and other media. When reporting results, you can use community meetings, news and promotional stories online.

When creating communications in any media, determine what your goals and objectives are and who the members of the target audience will be. You will need to know what their needs and gratifications are, what will result in an emotional connection with them, and any barriers that might exist to effective communication. You may also need to know what technologies they favor, such as radio, newspaper or social media (Mahoney & Tang, 2017). As an organization, aim for accountability (by being responsible for your actions) and transparency (making it easy for others to see the actions of the organization) in your communications.

As a team, you will create a comprehensive plan of communications to raise awareness and encourage participation.

- State your goal and objectives using the SMART format discussed in Chapter 21. Ask yourself:
  – What would you like your audience to learn, know, support or do?
  – What are the next steps you expect your audience to take?
- Describe indicators that will best show success. Describe how you will collect data on your indicators.
- Describe your audience, your message and the methods and timing used to get the message out. Consider how your team can use emissary work, word of mouth, social media, visual, verbal and print messages.
- Finally, describe how you will evaluate your communications intervention using your indicators.

Guidelines for creating communications using emissary work, word-of-mouth communications, public behaviors that others will want to emulate, social media, visual, verbal and print messages will be covered next.

HOW TO CARRY OUT THESE TECHNIQUES

Guidelines for Emissary Work

Emissary work is a form of quiet, informal peer-to-peer dialogue, for the purpose of preventing or solving problems, or for laying the groundwork for a decision or change. To carry out this work, you would:

1. Seek out those you believe will be key decision-makers and hold small meetings (either formal or informal) with them in advance of a larger meeting at which a decision will be made.
2. Explain the proposal or idea that you are planning to bring to the larger meeting and obtain the reaction of the person(s) you are meeting with. If the reaction is even somewhat positive, ask for suggestions to improve the idea or improve the chances that the idea will be accepted.
3. Following the small meetings with decision-makers, use suggestions to revise your proposal or your presentation. Alternatively, if your idea is not acceptable, you will understand why.

In the story, Sumera used personal emissary work when she sought out decision makers, met with them and persuaded them to join her in a joint fundraising effort that helped the Center and also increased activity at the Center.

GUIDELINES FOR WORD-OF-MOUTH PROMOTION

Word-of-mouth communication is highly effective at spreading the word about community change news or events, whether it is done face-to-face or using social media. It is more effective than advertising or social media at getting people to try new products, services or behaviors because it is more persuasive and targeted (Berger, 2016). It is more persuasive than advertising because while we tend to distrust the truthfulness of advertising, we trust our friends to tell us things candidly and objectively. It is more targeted because our friends pass on information that they believe that will interest us.

Local change initiatives often have little budget for advertising, but using word of mouth to spread the message about the initiative can have a powerful impact. Messages passed on by trusted friends to interested others can be very effective (Bughin, Doogan, & Vetvik, 2010). Individuals will pass on information that is relevant to the listener, often from personal experience. As shown in Figure 31.1, the message is more credible and persuasive than an advertisement which does not come from a personal friend and is dispersed rather than targeted, the way word of mouth is.

Jonah Berger (2014) says that word-of-mouth promotional comments are goal driven and self-serving. He goes on to describe identifiable drivers of word-of-mouth promotion:

- *Social currency*: people want to talk about things that are interesting or surprising which make them look good.
- *Triggers*: everyday conversations consist of things that come to mind, so you want your message to come to mind. Use messages that can be suggested or triggered by things people see in the

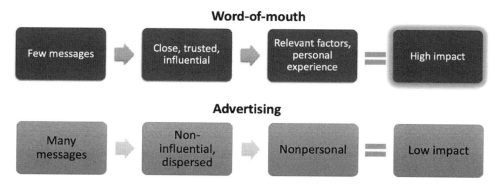

Figure 31.1 Relative impact of word of mouth versus advertising.

environment. Ideas that are foremost in people's minds are likely to be on the tips of their tongues, so people are likely to share them.
- Information that arouses *emotions* is likely to be shared.
- *Public* and observable behaviors, or their evidence: if a behavior is easy to see, people are more likely to imitate it.
- *Practical information*: people like to share ideas that are useful (saves time, saves money or improves health).
- People enjoy telling *stories* (Berger, 2016).

To promote your change without a budget, you will want to craft messages that take advantage of these drivers. You do not need to use messages for all six drivers; choose one or more drivers as needed.

For **social currency**, locate surprising statistics or scientific findings related to your mission. For instance, if you want to promote a youth mental health initiative, you might describe startling information like this from a report by the U.S. Surgeon General on the mental health conditions of children and adolescents. Don't rely exclusively on data. Be sure to include stories or testimonials and images of people (still or video) helped by your initiative.

> One in every 10 (10%) children and adolescents in the United States experience severe mental illness that causes some level of functional impairment, but less than 1 of 5 (20%) of those children have received effective treatment (U.S. Department of Health and Human Services; U.S. Department of Education; U.S. Department of Justice, 2000). That comes out to only 2% of the youth and children in the United States that need mental health treatment will receive it, even though this is one of the wealthiest countries in the world (WorldAtlas, 2019).
>
> Tina, a bright, but shy seventh grader. She had friends and social skills, but a clique of girls started picking on her and excluding her from activities. The girls were good at hiding their behavior from adults at school, so the teachers didn't notice what was happening. After weeks of harassment, Tina's self-confidence started slipping. She started thinking of harming herself. Today however, she is a confident college student after help from the Springfield Youth and Family Counselling Services.

Example of a Message with a social currency

For **triggers**, think of things people are likely to see around them that can remind them of your message. For the youth mental health initiative, you might say:

> Next time you see young people with their eyes glued to their cell phones, ask yourself what that might mean for their mental health. Some social media sites are not healthy environments for adolescents when bullying, cliques and sexual experimentation are involved.

Example of a Message with a trigger

People often talk about information that arouses **emotions** of fear, anger, outrage, awe, happiness or amusement. These emotions cause people to take action. Emotions such as sadness are shared less often. Messages that are resonant with people's values may be more memorable, arouse more emotion and will be shared more often (Valenzuela, Piña, & Ramírez, 2017). A human-interest approach "brings a human face or an emotional angle to the presentation of an event, issue, or problem" (Semetko & Valkenburg, 2000, p. 95). Craft your message so that it relates to people's values and arouses emotions, possibly using

Figure 31.2 Picture of Tina to be included in message example that appeals to emotion.

a human interest setting to create a sense of personal connection to the people that will be helped. For instance, if your initiative is concerned with youth and bullying, you might create a message like this:

Example of a Message that appeals to emotion

> Tina is a bright, but shy seventh grader. She had friends and social skills, but a clique of girls started picking on her, and excluding her from activities. The girls were good at hiding their behavior from adults at school, so the teachers didn't notice what was happening. After weeks of harassment, Tina's self-confidence started slipping. She didn't feel safe at school and started to fake illness. This began to affect her grades, she felt depressed and withdrawn emotionally from her family. Her parents were concerned. What could they do? On Wednesday September 27, Dr. Joy Mendez will be at Family Night at the Round Lake library, where she will hold an interactive workshop for youth and their parents on how to deal with bullies.

GUIDELINES FOR PUBLIC BEHAVIORS THAT OTHERS WILL EMULATE

The things people do that can be seen may lead others to imitate them, such as participating in bike rides to raise funds for a cause. Many such events include T-shirts that can be worn afterwards showing evidence of participation. Imitation is a natural human behavior, because watching what others do provides us with valuable information. For instance, when you are on vacation in a location where you are not familiar with the reputation of restaurants, you might look for a parking lot with several cars. This suggests that the food may be better than a restaurant with only one or two cars in the parking lot (Berger, 2016). Generally, donating or volunteering are private behaviors. Your goal is to *make those behaviors visible to others* so they can choose to participate as well. You can do that by holding public events (such as rallies, parades, bike rides, or walks) and providing lasting evidence of participation such as wearables (T-shirts, hats or bracelets), useful items such as tote bags or a place on social media for participants to review the event and share images.

GUIDELINES FOR SHARING IDEAS AND STORIES

People are likely to share ideas that are useful or **practical**. Using brochures, social media, news media interviews or articles, and videos on your website, you can share tips related to your initiative, and encourage readers to share them using Facebook, Twitter or Instagram. Keep the tips coming, so readers will come back again and again. For instance, a youth mental health organization website might post practical tips for parents on what to say and do to protect their children when using social media.

People enjoy telling **stories**. To tell great stories, you need to collect them. Make sure all staff and volunteers listen to clients and collect stories about the impact your organization has had for them. Good stories help connect your organization with the audience. When you share the stories, be sure to place them in the context of your organization and the problems they solve for the community, and make sure the purpose for telling the story is clear. While you want to demonstrate credibility, it is important to focus on the people that are being helped more than statistics. Tell about the people, the conflicts or challenges they faced, the choices they made and the outcomes. Use visuals or a video where possible to help tell the story. If the person is vulnerable or a child, disguise the name and shield the face. Stories like this can be used on your website, on social media, in the news media and in your brochures.

GUIDELINES FOR STORIES IN THE LOCAL NEWS MEDIA

To get a story in the local media, sometimes a simple press release is enough, but at other times you may need to convince a reporter that it is newsworthy. They will need to know why it is news, why now and who would be interested. The reporter might be pleased to have a "scoop" if it is a remarkable story offered exclusively to them. If you can tie your story to a national story, there might be a heightened level of interest. There is enough bad news in the media, so a "good news" story, showing how your organization is part of the solution, may be a welcome addition to the newspaper or news hour.

As you write your story, write your message concisely, focusing on its absolute core, so readers know your point, your priority and why it matters. Consider how you can make the story more interesting to readers, listeners or viewers. Conflict or controversy can add interest to the story. Is there anything unusual or unexpected about your story? Is there something about it that is a first? The biggest? The oldest? Does it involve celebrities or prominent people? Use the human interest angle and provide pictures or video of an individual that has benefited from your change initiative. It is acceptable for the story to use

 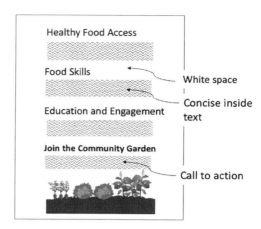

Figure 31.3 Brochure design.

several quotes; the person served should be able to tell their own story. Use vivid and image-building words. Use emotive language that evokes our audience's response—enthusiasm, humor, happiness or sadness—but avoid sensationalism.

If you are promoting an event, be sure to include the key information:

- *Who* should attend?
- *Why* should they attend?
- *What* will happen?
- *Where* and *when* will the event take place?

GUIDELINES FOR COMMUNICATIONS IN PRINT AND VISUALS

Brochures can help organizations quickly draw the attention of prospective participants, donors or volunteers. They can be distributed at events, placed in brochure racks or sent in email.

Determine the audience for your brochure. Are you writing it for funders? Donors? Potential clients? Media? What is the purpose of your brochure? To persuade? Inform? What message do you want to convey?

Select *images* that attract attention and enhance the ability of the brochure to deliver your message. Images include illustrations, graphs, tables and photographs. Well-chosen graphics attract attention, explain the content and make the brochure more interesting to read, but too many can be distracting.

The *cover* of your brochure is a key element of the brochure, since it must motivate the reader to look inside and read more. A well-chosen title, colors and graphic can attract the attention you need.

The *text inside* will need to be very concise; you will need to select information and images carefully. Try to be brief and accurate. Write in short sentences with active voice. Use positive language and try to make your brochure helpful. Use bulleted lists when possible. Like creating stories for word of mouth or social media, brochures should be written with simplicity, unexpectedness, concreteness, credibility, emotions and stories (Heath & Heath, 2007). Testimonials from satisfied clients in the brochure can increase its credibility.

Add a call to action at the *end* of your brochure. Your call to action should be explicitly tied to the audience that you have identified and your indicators. Ask your readers to visit your facility, make a phone call, visit a website for more details, or take some other kind of action. Provide all the details necessary to take action and *make it easy* for them to do so.

Group related elements to organize the brochure, and separate unrelated ideas with white space. Align elements to please the eye and emphasize the connection of the elements, as shown in Figure 31.3. When laying out the brochure, leave some space, free from text or graphics, to reduce clutter. This is called "white space," and it helps readers separate important points in the brochure. White spaces separate paragraphs of text, graphics and other portions of a document and keeps the reader reading the document (Williams, 2014), and find what they are interested in reading. Keep your design relatively simple. Using too many fonts, type styles (italics, bold lettering, shadow) and color will make your brochure look unprofessional. Pick colors and elements to harmonize and provide visual unity and consistency. Use contrast to emphasize important points by using large or bold elements.

GUIDELINES FOR COMMUNICATION IN SOCIAL AND OTHER MEDIA

When creating communications in social media, determine first who members of the target audience are, what technologies they use, what their needs and gratifications are. This will guide you in creating a sense of community. A sense of community involves membership and a shared emotional connection to your cause and to other members (McMillan & Chavis, 1986). Within the social media community, members find needs fulfilled as they influence each other and your organization.

To create this sense of engagement and community, select a social media within which to create a group, or create your own app if your group has access to someone with that skill. Then establish your criteria for membership, such as donors or program participants. You want the members to feel that they are part of a special group, so allow them to create their own profiles and to connect with each other. To get the conversation going, provide new content each week so you can maintain interest. For instance, identify feature stories about members of the group to share (with their permission) or hold contests, games or give away token gifts for participation. Prompt members to participate in dialogue that **raises awareness** about the organization's activities and encourage participation by asking questions when things are slow and let conversations flow from the members when there is lots of activity. Make sure members are getting relationship needs met. Monitor your social media, but don't control it. Instead, listen carefully to what members are saying, and identify their needs. Make it easy for members to **participate** in the work of your organization by providing tangible actions tied to your mission. Finally, in everything you say as a representative of your organization, be authentic and transparent.

GUIDELINES FOR REPORTING RESULTS

Reporting results can be carried out through community meetings, sharing news with the news media and promotional stories online. Since sharing with news media was discussed earlier in this chapter, this section focuses on community meetings. Community meetings bring together a cross-section of the community with a variety of viewpoints. It can allow an exchange of information and ideas, but it will succeed only if it is well organized and run.

Start planning the meeting early enough to set a goal, an agenda, and a time, date and place. If your community is in a place that is subject to bad weather, it is also wise to designate a snow date. You will need to reserve the space and invite participants, being as inclusive as possible of the diversity in the community. Send information in a press release to local radio, television and newspapers. You might also ask everyone on your board to invite at least two friends.

At the meeting, as a facilitator you want to be sure to stick to the agenda. If you plan to use media such as presentation software to convey your report, be sure it is short, simple, legible and engaging (Reynolds, 2008, p. ix). It needs to be short, so you can allow time for discussion. It needs to be simple and legible so that viewers can clearly understand the slides. Avoid a "data dump." This is your opportunity to convey a meaningful message to your community. Don't clutter it up by putting too many words on a slide. If you do, participants will be reading the slide (if it is legible from their seat in the room) instead of listening to you. Finally, you should engage the audience, by telling your story while bringing your energy and passion for your mission to the presentation. Then invite their responses.

After the meeting you should provide the results of your meeting on your website, on social media or through news media.

OTHER METHODS

Other methods of getting the word out include newsletters and outreach programs to schools, faith-based and other organizations and community leaders. Special events and open houses can also be used to get your word out. Make any communications local and as short and succinct as possible to achieve the goals.

EVALUATING COMMUNICATIONS

When the communications are implemented, you will want to monitor their effectiveness and improve them where possible. Ultimately, we want to know if the communications are altering perceptions or behavior, but this is not always possible. What we can do is:

- Track responses to communications such as inquiries through email, social media or phone calls.
- Track any responses to completed communications events, presentations or reports.
- Track any solicited and/or unsolicited feedback coming from audiences or stakeholders

After collecting evaluation data, examine it to see if the audience received the message and understood it and how you can tell. If not, how can you improve the message? How can you make the message more compelling? Was the timing appropriate?

Some things you might look at when you include *news media* in your communications plan are how much coverage you received, and if the tone of that coverage is positive or negative. Which media outlets were most responsive in giving your initiative coverage? Where in those media was the coverage? What's the audience of those placements? Did they include the visuals you provided? Did the coverage reflect your key messages? Did they quote your spokespeople? Was your initiative the focus of the article, or a side note?

Social media such as Facebook and Instagram allows a team to examine page metrics to see how people are engaging with your page, which posts have the most engagement, which pieces of the digital content (images, videos, stories) were opened and consumed and when your audience is on your page. If you have large numbers of people using your page, you may also see demographic data such as age, gender and location. Another method of collecting evaluation data is to post a quick survey to solicit their feedback.

TRY IT!

Imagine that you are a member of a team that is facilitating a public health project in a community of 50,000 people to train vaccine-supportive parents to use dialogue to engage their peers, online and in person, in discussions about vaccines. This project is sponsored by state and county public health officials. A recent outbreak of measles in a nearby town has concerned medical experts. Even though support for vaccines is 87% in this community, the remaining 13% are vulnerable to such an outbreak. About 1% to 3% have their minds made up and will not change them, but 10% to 12% of parents of young children are hesitant or confused by the huge amount of misinformation on the Internet. Parents hesitant to vaccinate tend to underestimate the risks of diseases and overestimate the risks of vaccines

Table 31.1 Communication planning template.

Communication goal	
Communication objective(s) (SMART) ■ What would you like your audience to become aware of/learn/know/support/do? ■ What are the next steps you expect your audience to take?	
Communication indicators ■ How many people will be doing/knowing/supporting what? ■ What indicators will best show success?	
Audience	
Messages or content	
Method of communication	
Evaluation ■ How will you collect data on your indicators? ■ How will you analyze the data? (By whom? By when?)	

and feel that medical staff do not always take their concerns seriously or explain the science in ways that are easily understood. These are the parents that the project aims to reach and persuade.

You will need to raise awareness of parents of young children and invite their participation. Using the form in Table 31.1, create a comprehensive plan of communications raise awareness and encourage participation.

- State your goal and objectives using the SMART format discussed in Chapter 21.
- Describe indicators that will best show success. Describe how will you collect data to inform your indicators.
- Describe your audience, your message and the methods used to get the message out. Consider how your team can use emissary work, word of mouth, public behaviors, social media and visual, verbal and print messages.
- Finally, describe how you will evaluate your communications intervention.

SUMMARY

Communications can include an issue awareness campaign, thereby promoting interest and participation in the change initiative by community members. It is important in the awareness campaign to promote understanding, acceptance and commitment to implement the change in the community. In this chapter we covered communications through personal emissary work, word of mouth, news or promotional stories online, in print or other media. Your team will want to create a comprehensive plan to communicate your message to the community. Effective communications plans are developed using the purpose, audience, message and the methods used to get the message out. Finally, when the communications are implemented, you will want to monitor their effectiveness and improve them where possible.

CITATIONS

Berger, J. (2014). Word of mouth and interpersonal communication: A review and directions for future research. *Journal of Consumer Psychology, 24*(4), 586. doi:10.1016/j.jcps.2014.05.002

Berger, J. (2016). *Contagious: Why things catch on.* New York: Simon & Schuster.

Bughin, J., Doogan, J., & Vetvik, O. J. (2010, April 1). A new way to measure word-of-mouth marketing. *McKinsey Quarterly.* Retrieved from www.mckinsey.com/business-functions/marketing-and-sales/our-insights/a-new-way-to-measure-word-of-mouth-marketing

Heath, C., & Heath, D. (2007). *Made to stick: Why some ideas survive and others die.* New York: Random House.

Mahoney, L. M., & Tang, T. (2017). *Strategic social media: From marketing to social change.* Malden, MA: Wiley-Blackwell.

McMillan, D. W., & Chavis, D. M. (1986). Sense of community: A definition and theory. *Journal of Community Psychology, 14*(1), 6–23.

Reynolds, G. (2008). *Presentation Zen: Simple ideas on presentation design and delivery.* Berkeley, CA: New Riders.

Semetko, H. A., & Valkenburg, P. M. (2000, June). Framing European politics: A content analysis of press and television news. *Journal of Communication, 50*(2), 93–109. doi:10.1111/j.1460-2466.2000.tb02843.x

U.S. Department of Health and Human Services, U.S. Department of Education, and U.S. Department of Justice. (2000). *Report of the surgeon general's conference on children's mental health: A national action agenda.* Washington, DC: U.S. Department of Health and Human Services. Retrieved from www.ncbi.nlm.nih.gov/books/NBK44233/

Valenzuela, S., Piña, M., & Ramírez, J. (2017). Behavioral effects of framing on social media users: How conflict, economic, human interest, and morality frames drive news sharing. *Journal of Communication, 67*(5), 803–826. doi:10.1111/jcom.12325

Williams, R. (2014). *The non-designer's design book* (4th ed.). Berkeley, CA: PeachPit Press.

WorldAtlas. (2019, June 28). *The richest countries in the world.* Retrieved from www.worldatlas.com/articles/the-richest-countries-in-the-world.html

PROGRAMS

32

Figure 32.0

WHAT'S IN THIS CHAPTER?

A program broadly defined is a method planned in advance for achieving particular objectives. A program defined this way is often several interventions that work together. For instance, some self-help programs are intended to lead to new attitudes and behaviors, increase social support; and create supportive environments, policies and resources. A curriculum of training courses leading to defined skills or knowledge is clearly a type of program, but there are many others, many of which overlap with other types of interventions. We will look at policies in Chapter 33, modifying the environment in Chapter 34 and support in Chapter 35. The focus of this chapter will be on creating learning interventions.

Objectives

By the end of this chapter, you will be able to:

- Use goals and objectives previously defined, and analyze what needs to be taught.
- Select appropriate instructional strategies to create a simple training program.
- Create a job-aid to support learning.
- Select appropriate strategies to create a coaching or mentoring program.

In designing a program for mentoring, teaching or training others to use new skills, a plan is developed for each high-priority learning experience that will produce a set of valued outcomes for individuals, organizations or the community. These programs can then be delivered to individuals, schools, faith-based and other organizations through invited speakers from your team, special events or training sessions. This chapter will provide information on basic steps for developing learning, mentoring or coaching programs.

A STORY ABOUT PROGRAM INTERVENTION: RENEW

As any regular rail-rider will tell you, sometimes the train gets stalled on the track, and you might be stuck looking out the window for hours. It takes patience to get through periods when apparently nothing is happening; yet something might be hidden in the landscape that will be revealed later. This is one such story.

After successfully completing the three-year child welfare grant-funded training project, Maurine was looking for more secure employment. She was approached with an offer to become the assistant director of an international mental health self-help organization called *ReNEW* (fictional name). The small international organization had a director and several support staff members but was led mostly by volunteers who had benefited from the self-help method using cognitive behavioral training. Since this newly created leadership role was undefined, Maurine felt it could provide her with an opportunity for creativity. However, after accepting the job, she assessed that the 70-year-old agency had a great past with no vision for the future. The executive director was silent and did not offer any advice about where Maurine should begin her work. The culture of the organization was marked by fearfulness about change. For months after starting her new role, she just kept looking out the window and wondering how she could get their train moving again. She wisely used the open space in time to reflect on how she might motivate the *very conservative* board of directors to consider new ideas. It was up to her to make the first move.

Her first action step was to build trust relationships with individual board members when they came to the international office for committee meetings. When she was introduced to the volunteers, they subtly asked, "Are you one of us?" She chose to reveal her own struggles with depression, and that quickly created an opening to develop a bond of trust. One of the most important cognitive mottos from the *ReNEW* Method was *Choose Humor Over Anger and Fear*. That principle worked out well with the facilitator's characteristic style of facilitation since she loved to share gentle humor to motivate people. Sometimes she caught people by surprise with a joke, and that lightened up the group process as people chuckled at her silliness. This also brought her down to a humble level and removed fears of her being an *expert* by board members. She began to find acceptance.

Quietly, without mentioning it aloud, she began a SWOT analysis (Table 32.1) of the organization. (See Chapter 19 for more on SWOT analysis.) She was "thinking it out" before acting. By moving quietly at first, she did not immediately contribute to their fears about the future of their beloved organization. This gave her a starting point for developing strategies for changing the organization and its market.

Now it was time for Maurine to make her first move. She reviewed the existing website, which had been created by a student intern, and critiqued it by inviting a friend, a web designer, to come to the next board meeting. She was careful not to call this visitor a "consultant" so that board members would not immediately fear spending money. The conversation was about how a new website was essential

Table 32.1 SWOT analysis for *ReNEW*.

Strength	Weakness
■ *ReNEW* Method really works! ■ Adept group leaders have recovered their mental stability and developed leadership skills ■ Endorsements from psychiatry and social work professionals (track record) ■ Loyal donors who gave bequests	■ Poor communication between leaders/groups ■ No marketing strategy ■ Weak website design ■ Risk-averse board leadership ■ Executive director had little desire for change and did not want to collaborate

Opportunity	Threat
■ Possibility of expanding markets ■ Potential collaboration with other self-help organizations ■ Expansion of self-help service over the Internet using the website	■ Competition from other groups ■ Increasing use of social media by younger people for support ■ Geographic barriers

for marketing the *ReNEW* Method on the World Wide Web. Suddenly, the board president asked the web designer to estimate how much it would cost to create a new website. When she heard the cost, she declared, "We need to do this now!" She further said, "I do not want to see *ReNEW* die and have its assets become a trust, as has happened to other failed nonprofits." Her argument inspired the board into making a significant financial decision, and they hired the web designer on the spot!

The next step would be to develop a communications team to work with the consultant. Fortunately, a leader from Los Angeles who had some marketing experience and was enthusiastic about helping with the website volunteered. The Los Angeles leader recruited others who were willing to learn, and they became internal consultants to the web designer. The board president respected the "know-how" of the communication team and developed a mutually beneficial working relationship. This is an example of how teams can play a significant role in program planning and execution of plans.

The second step taken by Maurine was encouraging a visioning process. Although the leaders were well grounded in the past history of the organization, they needed a vision for the future to portray to their worldwide members and reach new markets. At the following board meeting one month later, she engaged a group of about 20 leaders in a visioning exercise. Not only did they project their vision into the future, they also affirmed their commitment to the traditions of the *ReNEW* Method. Two sides of the same coin: future and past.

The new website became part of an overarching marketing plan to reach out to new audiences across the world by initiating collaboration with groups in countries not yet affiliated with the organization. An innovative website allowed for the creation of support chat rooms that broke the barrier of geography. Telephone groups were also formed to support people who were unable to use the Internet services. The website helped to tell the success stories of people who had previously been disabled by mental illness and their reentry into normal life using the ReNEW Method. The marketing plan, alliances and new support group plan was a win-win for the organization by attracting new donors and greater respect from mental health professionals.

All was going swimmingly with volunteers enthusiastically implementing their vision of a renewed organization, until the train reached a blockage on the track. The conductor/facilitator looked around to see what was standing in the way of progress. An internal threat was slowly revealed when Maurine began to reach out to other similar self-help organizations to offer collaboration. She noted that the executive director was reluctant to meet with other groups and was even stubbornly ignoring their offers to work together. She also observed that this elderly leader who had once been very effective was losing her leadership capacity and hiding it. What to do? Maurine quietly informed several senior board members of her observation. They began to notice the same symptoms and quietly removed her from her role and replaced her with a younger director.

Lessons Learned:

- Reflect on the culture you find yourself in before you make any plans.
- Personal relations that are built upon trust are the foundation of planning.
- Teamwork can lead an organization to new heights by challenging the norm with a higher expectation for performance.
- When speaking of spending money, "You can lead a horse to water, but you can't make him drink." However, you can let him smell the water and want to take a drink.
- Be aware of internal threats—notice and wonder as you enter a new setting.

WHAT THIS TECHNIQUE IS ABOUT

This story shows several techniques discussed in this book: building alliances, communications and support. Part of the support is training to use the tools and terms, to adopt a renewed attitude and motivation to make the effort necessary to recover. Methods of *teaching* and *training* include job-aids, coaching, mentoring, online instruction and face-to-face instruction. Books and audio recordings can also be used. These methods are used and reinforced through the *ReNEW* meetings.

Creating Training

Before you begin to construct a lesson, you need to review the analyses you conducted earlier, including:

- Causes, desired outcomes and indicators (Chapter 11).
- Readiness and description of the community (Chapter 13).
- Objectives (Chapter 21).

When designing learning interventions, it is important to design for the way people learn. While it is true that there are preferences and variations in the way people learn, it is possible to say that generally, most people go through a similar sequence (see Figure 32.1). The learning sequence goes roughly like this: (1) information from the environment is perceived when it enters the senses as neural impulses, (2) we pay attention when we expect to learn from it and executive control directs our focus, (3) the information enters working (short-term) memory, where it is encoded in a form that we can connect it with information we already know and (4) remember it over the long-term; (5) when the information is needed at a later time, it is retrieved, and (6) we form a response such as speaking, writing or performing a skill. Like most models, this model is VERY simplified, but it provides a way to think about and remember the learning process.

Instruction that follows and supports the internal learning processes are more likely to be remembered. Gagné (1974) described the Events of Instruction (Figure 32.2) like this. A lesson starts by activating a learner's motivation to learn and informs the learner of the lesson objectives. Attention is directed to the key lesson features. Previously learned information is recalled so the learner can connect the new information with the old. Then information and learning guidance is provided allowing the learner to encode information for storage. Exercises that require the learner to retrieve what they just learned enhance the ability of the learner to recall the information. When appropriate, the instruction requires the learner to apply the information to a variety of situations, promoting the transfer of learning to other environments. Finally, the learner is required to demonstrate their new skill or knowledge, and feedback is provided to reinforce the learning.

There are several different types of learning to which this lesson structure can be applied, including cognitive skills such as problem-solving or creative thinking, learning concepts, rules, facts and names, motor skills and attitudes.

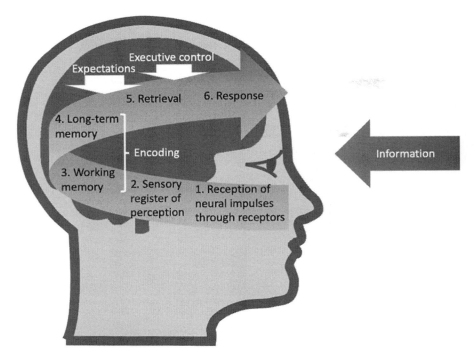

Figure 32.1 Events of Learning.
Source: Adapted from Gagné (1974).

HOW TO CARRY OUT THIS TECHNIQUE

About the Learners

You found some information about the learners when analyzing the readiness data. If you don't have enough information about the learners, you can do a survey to find out what they know about the topic, and their attitudes about it.

Analyzing the Content

Using this information, it is time to start to create the lesson plan. First, look at each objective and analyze what learners will need to know (knowledge) or be able to do (skills) in order to accomplish the objective. We don't want to forget to teach something important. This is like doing a cause analysis (Chapter 11) using the "5 Whys" questions, except we will ask five or more times "What do they need to know to accomplish this objective?" Ask until there is no more skill or knowledge needed, or until you are sure all learners will have the skill or knowledge needed.

Here is an illustration. The Hunger-free St. Michael initiative is planning to teach food preservation methods, and the first class will be on canning tomatoes. None of the learners have used a pressure

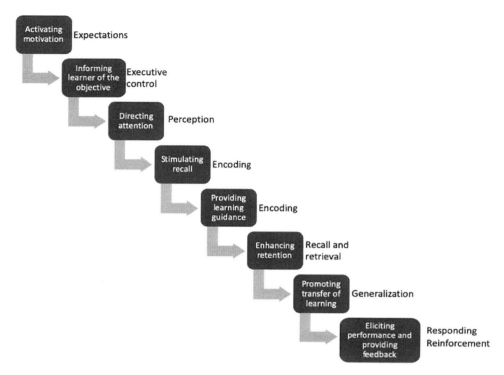

Figure 32.2 Events of Instruction.
Source: Adapted from Gagné (1974).

canner. The objective is canning whole tomatoes using a pressure canner. That is entered on a diagram (Figure 32.3) or list. The five things people need to know to can the tomatoes is how to:

1. Sterilize jars
2. Prepare tomatoes
3. Pack tomatoes in jars
4. Process the jars
5. Test the seal

Enter those items under the objective. For each of those you ask at least five times, "What do they need to know to accomplish this objective?" Focusing on processing the jars, the team found that learners need to operate the canner safely by following these steps:

1. Add 2" to 3" hot water in canner.
2. Place jars in canner on rack, not touching other jars.
3. Fasten pressure canner lid according to manufacturer's directions.
4. Turn on heat until steam escapes from canner vent.
   - Identify vent.
5. Put the gauge on canner.
   - Identify gauge.

6. Begin timer when gauge reaches 10 lbs.
   - Identify when gauge is at 10 lbs.
7. Adjust heat to keep gauge at 10 lbs. throughout.
8. Process for 10 minutes.
9. When 10 minutes has passed, remove canner from heat.
10. Let canner return to zero pressure on its own, about 30–45 minutes.
    - Do *not* run cold water over it.
11. Remove gauge and then lid according to manufacturer's directions.
12. Remove and place jars on rack to cool.

Notice that there are 12 main steps. There is also some information under four of the steps. This is because learners had no experience with pressure canners and did not know how to identify its parts. Also notice the dotted line in Figure 32.3. This is where the team decided the learners did not need to be taught how to place the jars on a rack to cool.

Each of the other skills (lid and jar sterilization, tomato preparation, packing jars and testing the seal) will be analyzed this same way. When the team is done with the analysis, the teaching methods can be planned, using the list or diagram of skills or knowledge to make sure nothing is missed.

THE LESSON PLAN FOR A FACE-TO-FACE TRAINING

Each of the steps in Figure 32.2 will be completed, but sometimes not in the exact order shown. There are nine steps or events of instruction that you will plan for.

Step 1. Usually the lesson begins with a "hook" or a way to draw learners in and motivate them. What will you do to make them curious and motivated to learn? Relevance of the lesson to learners is important to motivation. Challenge is useful to motivation, as long as learners feel they can accomplish the goal of the lesson.

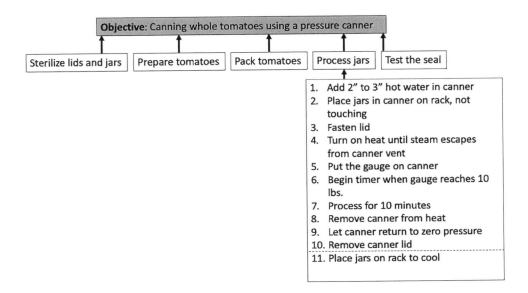

Figure 32.3 Analyzed content for processing jars in pressure canner.

Motivation is an attitude type of learning and may need to be reinforced throughout the lesson. Attitudes are hard to see except when they are demonstrated. Smith (2012) focuses on the behavioral aspect of *attitude* learning and emphasizes the importance of three key steps:

- Demonstration of the desired behavior by a respected role model.
- Practice of the desired behavior, often through role playing or exercises.
- Reinforcement of the desired behavior.

Step 2. Learners will need to know what they will be expected to learn, so you will need to share the objectives with them. This can help give them the big picture of what will happen during the lesson.

Step 3. Directing the learner's attention to key information usually happens at the beginning of the lesson, but also happens several times throughout the lesson. For instance, in order for the learners to know when to put the gauge on the pressure canner vent, the instructor will need to point out what the steam should look like.

Steps 4 and 5. Convey the lesson content to learners by demonstrating or explaining, using your choice of media. A small group can crowd around the stove and still see. A larger group may need to watch a projected image of the steps as they are demonstrated. At this time, the instructor will provide guidance on how to remember the steps, for instance by using memory aids. An example is when teaching learners to check the jars for a proper seal, you might teach this little jingle:

> A concave lid is safely sealed
>   When canning food for future meals.

At the same time the instructor demonstrates how to can tomatoes, learners can be doing the same thing, following the instructor's directions.

Step 6. Several times throughout the lesson an instructor can help the learners remember by asking them to recall something they learned. For instance, I might ask learners how they can tell that their tomatoes are safely sealed.

Step 7. To help learners generalize the concepts taught in the tomato canning lesson, you could tell them that a safe seal is important for everything they can, from beans to jams. Later, pass around jars of other home canned foods, such as apple pie filling, grape jelly or pickles and ask them how they can tell if the food is safe to eat.

Steps 8 and 9. Usually, the next step is to prompt performance of the new skill. In this case, learners may have been canning throughout the lesson. It is important to observe what is going on and provide feedback. If you were simply teaching concepts, the performance might be in the form of a quiz or game. Reinforcement might be in the form of a grade if the response is a quiz, or a good game score if the response is a game. In the canning lesson, reinforcement can come in the form of home canned tomatoes that learners can take home to their families.

At the end of the lesson, the instructor should bring closure by pulling together the most important points (synthesizing) and summarizing the lesson. This reinforces the key points.

Step 10. The last step is for the instructor, rather than the learners, so it is not part of the nine events of instruction. This step is *assessing the lesson*, so that it can be even better the next time it is taught. One thing the instructor can observe is if everyone accomplished the lesson goals and objectives: Did everyone learn canning safety? Did they learn to operate the pressure canner? Are all jars sealed properly? Another thing an instructor should do is reflect on the questions asked by the learners during the lesson. Was the instruction clear and easy to understand? Could the instruction be made even better?

Step 11. Describe the context for instruction. The description should include the following:

- *Resources required*: for instance, the canning lesson will need tomatoes, which the learners can bring from the community garden and jars with lids and rims. It will also require lemons, sinks, dishwashing supplies, stoves and pressure canners.

- *Timeframe*: for instance, the canning lesson can be accomplished in about two hours.
- Where learners will use the information (*performance context*) when instruction is done. The learners will do their own canning at home in their kitchens. The way you use this information is to decide what learners need to perform the skill on their own. Because canning is usually done only after harvest each year, and food safety is important, step-by-step instructions (a job-aid) should be provided for learners to take home to remind them what to do after a year has passed.
- *Learning context*: this face-to-face class can take place at a cooking school, a church kitchen, or similar place where multiple stoves and pressure canners are available.
  - If the planned learning will take place online or use technology equipment in a classroom, how will the instruction work? What equipment would be needed? How can demonstrations be simulated?

CREATING JOB-AIDS

If you have ever used a cookbook, or assembled furniture kits, you have used a job-aid. A job-aid is a quick reference resource providing support to complete a task. It is used just when you need it:

- When you were trained to do something but haven't done it for a long time.
- When you were trained to do something, but now there has been a change in how it is done.
- When you are trying to figure out something that has gone wrong.
- When you are trying to adapt a task to a unique situation.

A job-aid serves as a just-in-time reminder after training of how to do a task. When learners just need a reminder, a job-aid is more user-friendly than paging through copies of presentation slides from training. To create a job-aid, include only necessary information. The end result should be simple and concise, and it should provide information in small pieces using short words and short sentences in everyday language. Begin sentences with action words. Use simple drawings or graphics that clarify the directions.

A job-aid can be created in one of several forms, as seen in Figure 32.4. A few examples are:

- Step-by-step directions
- Checklist
- Form or worksheet
- Flow chart

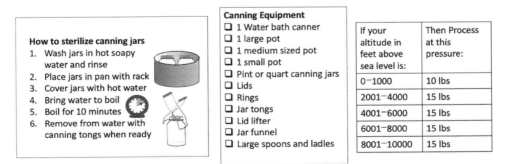

Figure 32.4 Types of job-aids.

MENTORING AND COACHING

Coaching and mentoring both involve learning, but not in the same formal way as teaching or training by a subject expert. **Coaching** is a one-to-one process that aims to improve performance of skills for use now. Mentoring is about developing knowledge and skills for the future. Coaching can be done by anyone with knowledge of the skills needed by the learner. In business, it is often done by someone's immediate supervisor. A key skill for a coach is asking the right questions to help the individual learn and work through their issue (Whitmore & Performance Consultants International, 2017). A coach also needs the skill to observe a student's performance and give effective feedback. Feedback becomes effective when it is provided in a timely manner and is relevant to the student's goals; the student can take action on it; it is friendly, specific and personalized. It should also be ongoing and consistent.

To help people learn, Whitmore and Performance Consultants International (2017) recommends that the coach work with those they will coach (the student) to:

- Set goals for each session, and for the short and long term.
- Define the current reality (what's happening now).
- Ask a student what options and strategy alternatives they have.
- Ask what, who and when will something be done (Whitmore & Performance Consultants International, 2017, p. 96).

Coaching could be done, for instance, by a community garden volunteer during a group gardening session to guide new gardeners to make their garden plans more productive.

Mentoring involves developing potential for the long term and is relationship-based. Usually mentoring takes place between more experienced people (mentors) and less experienced people (protégés). Those who are mentors need to be committed to learning and helping others learn and also need to be empathetic listeners. They can observe, reflect and help others see and reshape their thinking.

Many community, school and faith-based organizations use a mentoring approach with children or youth matched with a caring adult. There is evidence that mentored youth effectively develop improved attitudes towards school and better academic performance (Eby, Allen, Evans, Ng, & DuBois, 2008; Herrera, Grossman, Kauh, & McMaken, 2011). Mentoring can also be used within organizations to develop leadership skills (Allen, Finkelstein, & Poteet, 2009) for staff, volunteers and new board members. Whether the mentorship program is within a business setting or within the community, some of the same issues need to be addressed:

- Confidentiality.
- Relationship expectations and duration.
- Meeting frequency.
- Guidance provided to the protégé.
- The kinds of activities that will take place (Allen et al., 2009, p. 71).

There are some ways that coaching and mentoring overlap. So, when should an organization choose coaching, and when should they choose mentoring? Table 32.2 summarizes the main points:

Table 32.2 Choosing between coaching and mentoring.

When to choose coaching	When to choose mentoring
When specific task skills are needed now	When developing future new leaders
When staff or volunteers need a skill upgrade for specific tasks	When developing volunteers that balance work, volunteer work and personal life
When staff need new skills to take on new responsibilities	When an organization wants to retain expertise when long-term volunteers "retire"

TRY IT!

Imagine that you are on the Hunger-free St Michael Parish training team. Create a content list or diagram for how to prepare tomatoes for canning, including using lemon juice to acidify the tomatoes. If you have never canned tomatoes, look at the directions at Simply Canning (www.simplycanning.com/canning-tomatoes.html). Then, use the lesson plan form provided in Table 32.3 to describe the training you would create.

Table 32.3 Lesson plan template.

Plans needed	Your plans
1. Describe learners: ■ Describe the current attitudes, skills or knowledge levels of learners. ■ Describe the desired outcome goals including attitudes, skills and knowledge. ■ Describes the problem including symptoms, and possible causes for the deficit of including attitudes, skills and knowledge. 2. Describe selected solutions.	
Show content analysis shown using a list or diagram format. Show all necessary skills/knowledge/attitudes in the list or diagram.	
Indicate skills learners already have (prior or prerequisite S/K/A). These will not need to be taught.	
Describe teaching methods for the lesson and then for each objective. These include the following:	
Overall lesson strategies 1. How will learners get the big picture? 2. In what order will the content be learned? 3. How will the content be synthesized and summarized?	
Strategies for each objective (not all of these apply if they were done for the previous objective): 1. How will you motivate learners (in terms of relevance or challenge)?	
2. How will you inform learners of the objectives?	
3. What will help learners focus their attention on the important information?	
4. How will you help learners recall previously learned skills or knowledge applicable to this lesson?	
5. How will content be presented (including visual, verbal or media presentations)?	
6. How will you guide learners to remember (which supports encoding into memory)	

(Continued)

Table 32.3 (Continued)

Plans needed	Your plans
7. How will learners practice skills or knowledge (enhancing retention)?	
8. How will you help learners generalize what they have learned so they can apply learning to new situations?	
9. How will you prompt performance of new skills?	
10. How will you provide feedback?	
11. How will you assess the learning?	
Context for instruction. Description should include the following: 1. Resources required, including media. 2. Timeframe. 3. Where learners will use the information (performance context) when instruction is done. 4. Learning context If the planned learning will take place online or use technology in a classroom, how will the instruction work? (Describe anything known at this time about equipment required, target playback system.)	

SUMMARY

A program (a method planned in advance for achieving particular objectives) is often several interventions that work together. For instance, some self-help programs are intended to lead to new attitudes and behaviors, increase social support and create supportive environments, policies and resources. Policies will be covered in Chapter 33, environment in Chapter 34 and support in Chapter 35. This chapter focused on interventions leading to defined skills or knowledge, including training, job-aids, coaching and mentoring.

CITATIONS

Allen, T. D., Finkelstein, L. M., & Poteet, M. L. (2009). *Designing workplace mentoring programs: An evidence-based approach*. Hoboken, NJ: Wiley-Blackwell.

Eby, L. T., Allen, T. D., Evans, S. C., Ng, T., & DuBois, D. L. (2008, April). Does mentoring matter? A multidisciplinary meta-analysis comparing mentored and non-mentored individuals. *Journal of Vocational Behavior, 72*(2), 254–267. doi:10.1016/j.jvb.2007.04.005

Gagné, R. M. (1974). *The conditions of learning* (3rd ed.). New York, NY: Holt, Rinehart & Winston.

Herrera, C., Grossman, J. B., Kauh, T. J., & McMaken, J. (2011). Mentoring in schools: An impact study of Big Brothers Big Sisters school-based mentoring. *Child Development, 82*(1), 346–361. doi:10.1111/j.1467-8624.2010.01559.x

Smith, P. (2012). *Instructional design* (3rd ed.). New York: John Wiley & Sons.

Whitmore, J., & Performance Consultants International. (2017). *Coaching for performance: The principles and practice of coaching and leadership* (5th ed.). Boston, MA: Nicholas Brealey.

POLICY CHANGE

Figure 33.0

WHAT'S IN THIS CHAPTER?

Policies, regulations, procedures, rules and even laws may be modified when changing communities, organizations or government entities. Policies, by whatever name, may over time become outdated or unfair as conditions change over time; alternatively, they may have been illogical in the first place. They may be formal, written ways of doing things, or they may be assumptions shared by members of groups, communities or organizations. Changing formal or informal policies can change a community well into the future.

Objectives

By the end of this chapter, you will be able to:

- Determine if a policy change can solve community problems through policy analysis.
- Define the problem ("What's happening now?").
- Define the desired outcomes and indicators.
- Define the audience for the policy.
- Determine current and potential policy effects.
- Locate examples of effective policies.
- Plan strategies that should result in enactment of the policy, including:
  - Creating a persuasive story that emphasizes the positive benefits of the policy change.
  - Describing the timing for the campaign.
  - Describing how your team will network with the media, influential people and community members.
- Describe how the policy will be evaluated.

A STORY ABOUT THE 3RS PROJECT—READING REDUCES RECIDIVISM

On that Sunday morning when Tod, a local prison reform activist, walked into the Quaker meeting, he wore a worried look. All around the library in the Interfaith Center where they were meeting, he could view stacks and stacks of books on the floor and spilling across the library table. He had come to the Quakers to ask for help with a prison project he had been working on for several years to bring books to prisoners. Right before his eyes was the evidence that things were not going well. Too many books were coming into the Interfaith Center library, and too few of them were going out and into the hands of the prisoners. He already had one friend among the Quakers, Jill, who had also been involved in founding the project, so he felt less nervous about approaching a faith community for support. Normally, he placed little trust in religious people, but Tod was at the point of desperation. He had come to ask the Quakers, who have a long history of working for prison reform, to jumpstart the project. It was a long shot, but he was willing to take it.

Let's backtrack a bit to view the starting point for the founding of the statewide 3Rs Project. During the years of "law and order" edicts in America, prisons were being built at a rapid pace in rural areas to provide space for an ever-increasing prison population. Meanwhile, some prison activists began agitating for reform or reduction of state prisons. They settled on an initial strategy of delivering free books to prisoners. There had been no funds budgeted by the state government to supply books to prison libraries for many years; the legal education requirement was for providing only law books. It soon became apparent to the 3Rs organizers that without books on hand, there was no need for hiring prison librarians or staff. Barbara Kessell, the founder of the statewide 3Rs project, strategically moved higher up to make contact with lead administrators in the Department of Corrections, and eventually Barbara influenced a policy change, the hiring of more prison librarians once they learned that free books were available.

Barbara reached out to other activists to form new 3Rs chapters around the state. A new chapter was formed in a small midwestern college town by college professors and other prison activists. Tod was one of the prison activists who jumped on board. They initially began collecting donated books in a garage and at a campus ministry building for later delivery to prisons, but they soon found that the prison wardens did not trust them and would not allow many books to be delivered. They feared that the activists had a hidden agenda that might cause disruption, and that they might deliver contraband to prisoners in the book boxes. The way forward was blocked, so Tod looked for another way to achieve their goal.

The result of Tod's appeal to the Quakers was that Michael and Maurine offered to work with the 3Rs Project as volunteer coordinators. The first problem that had to be solved was the book storage. Maurine suggested to Tod that they approach a Christian pastor about storing books in the church annex. Tod was surprised and taken aback when he heard her message of hospitality. His negative stereotype of Christian ministers changed in response to Pastor Katherine's warm welcome. She even offered them a key to the building, so they could come and go with books. Why did she agree so readily? She viewed the project as fitting within the church's mission to the poor and disenfranchised. He then realized that he could safely relinquish his leadership of the project into the hands of others. Letting go is a really big step for a founder.

Next, Maurine invited Diana Brawley Sussman, the director of the public library, to join the project. She had been active for many years in social justice projects around town and was known to be sympathetic to social change action. She agreed to reach out directly to the prison librarians and made contact with three of them initially. Thanks to Barbara's influence with the Department of Corrections, the wardens gave the prison librarians permission to take vans to the local libraries to collect free books following quarterly book sales; another policy change! This also solved a problem for the Friends of the Library, who hated sending unsold books to the landfill. Everyone was happy.

Soon, another local public library joined the project. They also had a storage problem after their quarterly book sales, so having a place to send the overage was a boon to them. More librarians were being hired at the prisons, and eventually seven prison libraries and two public libraries connected to share free books with prisoners. Another local activist, Marilyn, collected and delivered books from used books stores and took them to the church book room which became a second location for librarians to make book choices. Now the prison librarians have amassed a significant collection of books to lend to the prisoners. The 3Rs regularly receives thank-you notes from the prisoners who are grateful for having books to read.

WHAT THIS TECHNIQUE IS ABOUT

Policies are the written or unwritten guidelines that organizations and individuals use to guide decisions. Policies guide decisions in organizations, schools, governmental agencies, foundations, funders and communities. When these guidelines become outdated or are found to be otherwise problematic, it may be time to change them.

Can a policy change solve community problems? Because policies guide decisions, they can change the way people do things in organizations and communities. This can lead to changes in attitudes and processes into the future. Policy change can be highly effective at solving community problems, but it can also take a long time, so patience is going to be required!

HOW TO CARRY OUT THIS TECHNIQUE

Who Should Be Involved?

Identify who should be involved in the formulation of a new policy. You will want to involve coalitions of organizations that work with the issue, agencies responsible for carrying out the policy, professional groups with concern about the issue and community groups representing all groups affected by or concerned with the issue. The coalition can be involved in participatory policy creation and strategic planning on how to get the new policy adopted and implemented. Those responsible for implementation need to be committed to the policy, or implementation will likely be ineffective. The involvement of a coalition ensures better decisions based on diverse perspectives and better chance of community acceptance of the new policy. These diverse perspectives should include those with opposing points of view. Open meetings inviting the public may also be a way to obtain a variety of perspectives.

What's Happening Now?

When examining a community concern for which your team has done a *cause analysis* and determined that one cause for the concern is a policy, you might look into a policy change by doing a policy evaluation. To make changes to policy that already exists, or to create new policy where none exists, we need to begin by:

- *Defining the problem* or issue the policy is meant to address (*goal*).
- If there is a current policy that needs to be updated, what is the *concern* with it?
- Who is the *audience* for the policy?
- What are the *effects*, both intended and unintended, of the current policy?

Hanberg (2001) adds that the following should also be considered:

- What is the context?
- How does the *implementing* organization work in practice?
- Are resources used effectively, and in the right way? (p. 49).

This is the "What's happening now?" phase. State what the issue is in evaluative terms (Bardach & Patashnik, 2019). For instance, in the complex problem of getting books to prisoners, research evidence indicates that education and reading is useful in reducing recidivism, but prison policies got in the way of getting books to prisoners. There was an unwritten policy held by prison wardens that they did not accept many books from activists. They did not trust prison activists, so they would not allow large numbers of books to be delivered. In addition, insufficient funding was going to the correctional system from the state budget for the prisons to purchase carefully selected books of their own for the prison libraries. Finally, there were too few prison librarians to process large numbers of books. Notice the evaluative terms "insufficient" and "too few" in the description of the issue? If possible, quantify "too few" and other evaluative terms. For instance, you might locate statistics showing that of two dozen state correctional facilities, only eight have full-time librarians.

The words used to define and evaluate the problem are important to the intervention of policy change. The rhetoric that is often used when discussing policy includes evaluative terms suggesting something is bad, wrong or a problem. Not everyone will agree that a particular policy is a problem, particularly in the public realm (governmental agencies, communities, schools). It is important to define the problem in a way that avoids a partisan (allegiance to a party or faction) or ideological view, because it may otherwise alienate possible supporters.

DESIRED OUTCOMES

The next step is envisioning desired outcomes. Policies exist for a reason, and they are formulated because they are thought to be necessary or to have benefits. The reasons or benefits should be stated by formulating *goals* and *objectives* for policies. For instance, a midwestern community with a diverse population was concerned about race relations and fair and impartial policing. Research had indicated a pattern of racial profiling. A number of community organizations met with the police department to create a policy that had as its goal "to lay the groundwork for positive community—police engagement." A few of the objectives formulated include:

- Police will take law enforcement actions based on behavior and not appearance.
- Police will provide equal protection regardless of racial and immigration status.
- The city will collect data on an ongoing basis on police actions including stops, searches and arrests to examine if there is evidence of bias or racial and immigrant status disparities.

Notice the implied measurable indicators. Data will be collected on stops, searches and arrests, to be examined for bias or racial and immigration status disparities.

Another thing that should be defined is the *audience* for the policy. In the example presented in this chapter, the policy audience consisted of the police department, the city government and the wider community, especially those potentially affected by racial profiling.

Finally, *policy effects*, both intended and unintended, of the proposed policy should be described. Intended effects are the benefits sought by the creation of the new policy or negative effects avoided by having a revised policy in place.

INFORMATION SEEKING

The search for evidence should begin with the current policy, if one exists. Your team will want to know how well it works, who supports it and who influences it.

In addition, you need to know about community readiness and resistance. Determine the readiness of the community to accept a policy change to understand what citizens will support, what they will resist and how they can be persuaded. Find out who the opponents are, how many there are, and what their arguments against a change might be. Concerns of opponents to the policy change need to be understood so your team can plan strategies to increase their readiness to accept a new policy. (See Chapter 13 for more on change resistance.)

PLANNING

With your new coalition in place, search for examples of best practices in policies dealing with your topic (see Chapter 14 or Appendix D for more on searching). You will also want to look for examples of alternative policies and how well they work. In addition, you can brainstorm alternatives. To choose from the best practices and alternatives, the planning coalition should determine criteria for evaluating the outcomes of the policy. Analyze the *policy effects*, both intended and unintended, of the policy alternatives and describe them. The intended policy effects for the Department of Corrections' policy allowing librarians to select books are that: (1) prison libraries would have a larger selection of reading materials for inmates, and (2) good books will keep inmates' minds engaged and entertained, thus promoting prison peace and safety.

An unintended effect might be the need for more space and shelves to store the books in the library.

A cost-benefit analysis for the top ranked alternatives might be a useful criterion for selecting among policy alternatives. A cost-benefit analysis allows your team to estimate the costs of a policy or project to gain the benefits you are seeking. You are looking for a policy in which the tangible and intangible benefits outweigh the costs. A simplified version can be conducted like this: your team will need to (1) brainstorm all costs and benefits of the policy, then (2) select measures for each of them and (3) translate as many of these as possible into currency (whatever form of money your community uses) if they aren't already, then (4) the outcome of costs and benefits will be predicted for a given period of time. Next, (5) add all costs and all benefits, then (6) subtract the total costs from the total for benefits. Examine trade-offs between alternatives. Then select attainable goals and objectives from among the brainstormed alternatives.

Plan strategies for getting the policy change *enacted* and implemented. Unless a policy is under your direct control, you will need a persuasive story to communicate that emphasizes the positive benefits of the policy change, good timing and networking with the media, influential people and community members. Depending on how large your opposition is, it might be more effective to work toward an intermediate goal of a policy that most of the community can accept, and then push for your final goal at a later time.

Tell Your Story

Begin to plan your communications by considering how you will tell your story. While it might be an easy story to tell those who are ready to adopt a change, but those who resist will need persuasion. Begin with the definitions and research your team did previously. If they did a cost-benefit analysis, show how the policy can benefit the community in tangible and intangible ways:

- Economically: savings in terms of reduced taxes or other costs.
- Greater health and safety: savings in terms of reduced pollution, safety (reduced injuries, for instance) and medical costs.
- Socially: a more satisfying community life as a result of reduced violence or drug availability, and a more attractive community as a result of reduced vandalism.
- Psychologically: a greater sense of individual safety and security.

In your message, your team will want to use the reasons you identified to communicate why change is necessary. It is important to give reasons when we ask for support. Cialdini notes that "when we ask someone to do us a favor, we will be more successful if we provide a reason" (2006, p. 4).

It is also important to mention both sides of the argument. People will be more likely to believe your message if you anticipate and bring up opposing viewpoints. Two-sided messages on non-advertising topics have greater credibility and persuasiveness (O'Keefe, 1999). After you bring up the opposing viewpoints, you can then show why they don't invalidate your argument. Always be ready to neutralize the opposition and counter the arguments of opponents, as they try to persuade others and attack your team's position.

Timing

Crisis often opens a window to policy change, but you do not need to wait for a crisis to work toward one. Other good times for advocating policy change can be:

- When there is a deadline for renewing a policy (such as an Act of Congress).
- An election year when a politician may be open for constituent input.
- When the public has become concerned because new information has become available or when a state or municipality is debating an issue.

Networking

Use networking to gather political support from community members and organizations. As your campaign for policy change progresses, keep your network informed through newsletters, emails and the media.

Reach out to those in power early in the process, including influencers and politicians. Power is as important as evidence in making policy changes. Make personal contact and use personal emissary work with local politicians, appointed officials, legislators and their aides, people at regulatory agencies and many others. Do what you can to make their life easier. For instance:

- Keep your questions polite and brief, but avoid simple yes-or-no questions.
- Bring business cards with your contact information to make it easier for the council person or representative to get back to you.
- Show up to meetings on time.
- Get to know the person and focus on the relationship first.
- Listen carefully.
- Provide written details of evidence you discuss for their reference.
- Always be pleasant and easy to work with.

Sometimes politicians have difficulty writing a policy that will be acceptable to everyone. If they are aware of your policy change efforts early, they may reach out to your team as one of the concerned organizations to help them work out an acceptable solution.

Just weeks before a vote in a city council, state or federal government, schedule an open meeting at which you deliver your message again, and ask the community to contact their city council, state or federal representative or senator, encouraging them to vote in favor of the policy.

Protect your credibility throughout your campaign by sticking to the facts, never shading them. A foundation of trust and cooperation is necessary to a successful campaign.

Finally, stick with it. Policy change can often take a long time and multiple attempts, so it takes patience and persistence.

POLICY ENACTMENT

Policy *enactment* is the official authorization to implement from organizations, school districts or governmental agencies. In organizations, this may require a simple vote of those involved. School districts may require a vote by the school board, municipalities may require a vote by the city council, and states or the federal government may require a legislative vote to pass a bill. This is where your networking with politicians and other people in power should pay off. If your message persuaded those voting, the bill may become law (Dove, 1997). Politicians also take note when a large community or constituent group indicates their concern by calling, sending emails or letters, attending open meetings or holding protests.

After a vote has been taken and the new or revised policy approved, it is time for implementation. This is largely the responsibility of the implementing agency, but others can sometimes help by providing resources or support. The steps for implementation include:

- Informing the people or organizations affected by the new or changed policy.
- Writing regulations or creating new procedures consistent with a new policy.
- Revising procedures, regulations, operations and systems to be consistent with a revised policy.
- Monitoring and/or enforcing the policy as needed.

POLICY EVALUATION

Evaluate results of the policy change after a time using your selected indictors to determine the impact of the policy. One thing you might want to determine is if there has been a change in impacts, and if the policy contributed to that change. Also, determine if there were unintended consequences. You might also want to know if there was any economic impact. Was your cost-benefit estimate accurate?

TRY IT!

Imagine that you are on a team working on a municipal task force (Community Energy Action Task Force) creating a clean energy policy for a city of about 60,000. The hope is to save citizens and consumers money, create local jobs, encourage local economic investment and protect the environment. Using the form provided in Table 33.1 and resources from the American Council for an Energy Efficient Economy (https://www.aceee.org/), make plans for creating a new policy.

1. Determine who should be involved in planning.
2. Define the problem ("What's happening now?").
3. Define the desired outcomes and indicators.
4. Define the audience for the policy.
5. Locate examples of effective municipal energy policies.
6. Plan a campaign that should result in enactment of the policy, including:
    a. Creating a persuasive story that emphasizes the positive benefits of the policy change.
    b. Describing the timing for the campaign.
    c. Describing how your team will network with the media, influential people and community members.
7. Describe how the policy will be evaluated.

Table 33.1 Policy planning template.

Who should be involved in planning?	
Define the problem ("What's happening now?").	
Define the desired outcomes and indicators.	
Define the audience for the policy.	
Locate and list Web addresses for examples of effective municipal energy policies.	
What is your persuasive message?	
Describe the timing for the campaign.	
Describe how your team will network.	Media
	Influential people
	Community members
Policy evaluation: ■ How will you collect data on your indicators? ■ What question should be answered?	

SUMMARY

Policies may be formal, written ways of doing things, or they may be assumptions shared by members of communities or organizations. Policies, regulations, procedures, rules and even laws can become outdated or unfair as conditions change over time, or they may have been illogical in the first place. This chapter discussed using cause analysis, cost-benefit analysis and policy evaluation to determine if a policy change can solve community problems. Changing formal or informal policies can result in positive change to a community upon implementation and into the future. Finally, we discussed how to plan for changing policy, including who should be involved in making the change, what research needs to be done and planning strategies for the policy change including creating the message, timing, networking and enactment.

CITATIONS

Bardach, E., & Patashnik, E. M. (2019). *A practical guide for policy analysis: The eightfold path to more effective problem solving*. Los Angeles, CA: CQ Press/Sage.

Cialdini, R. B. (2006). *Influence: The psychology of persuasion*. New York: Harper Business.

Dove, R. (1997). *Enactment of a law*. Washington, DC: U.S. Senate: Government Printing Office. Retrieved from www.congress.gov/resources/display/content/Enactment+of+a+Law+-+Learn+About+the+Legislative+Process

Hanberger, A. (2001). What is the policy problem? Methodological challenges in policy evaluation. *Evaluation*, 7(1), 45–62. doi:10.1177/13563890122209513

O'Keefe, D. J. (1999). How to handle opposing arguments in persuasive messages: A meta-analytic review of the effects of one-sided and two-sided messages. *Annals of the International Communication Association*, 22(1), 209–249. doi:10.1080/23808985.1999.11678963

PHYSICAL ENVIRONMENT

Figure 34.0

WHAT'S IN THIS CHAPTER?

Changing the environment can improve safety or access, encourage interaction and even enhance a sense of community. The physical environment can include the natural and built environments as well as infrastructure (basic facilities and systems required for the operation of a community). Changes can be either small scale, such as repairing playgrounds, improving transportation, parks and green spaces, and accessibility of public meeting spaces, or major developments such as toxic waste cleanup of a former industrial site to create a park or other recreational facility. This chapter covers how to approach small-scale environment change by creating concept plans that detail who should be involved in making the change and when.

Objectives

By the end of this chapter, you will be able to:

- Make plans for modifying the physical environment.
- Determine who should be involved in planning for a project.
- Describe what should be included in a concept plan for modifying the physical environment.
- Describe the timing and actions needed in planning small-scale changes to the physical environment.

A STORY ABOUT CREATING A MOUNTAIN BIKING TRAIL

Mountain biking trails seemed like a rather unusual idea when it was proposed in an area where there are no mountains. However, the rural region of southern Illinois has challenging terrain which has been adapted to create a mountain biking experience.

It happened that Southern Illinois University's (SIU) Touch of Nature Environmental Center outdoor education facility had a creative idea of making trails in unused areas. Since many bicyclists pass through the region on a trans-continental bike trail which crosses there, this provides an opportunity to expand the use of this area to the community of mountain bikers. The International Mountain Bicycling Association designed just under 30 miles of trails, and the Rotary Club of Carbondale–Breakfast volunteered to help cut trails and donated funds for the project.

The trail will soon be producing income for the rural region, which has few economic resources. Up to 55,000 riders per year are expected to use the trail, which means the money spent by visiting mountain bikers on food, lodging and biking equipment will go into the local economy. By using the beauty of the land, a new adventure experience will also produce new capital for the region. At the same time, Touch of Nature will be educating trail users about conservation.

WHAT THIS TECHNIQUE IS ABOUT

Making changes in the physical environment can mean many things, all of which can improve the well-being of community members, such as:

- Creating or improving open spaces in the community such as public parks and protected wild areas.
- Creating or improving open space for recreation.
- Creating or improving "third places" for socialization (Oldenburg, 1999).
- Creating or improving green infrastructure (such as right-of-way rain gardens, to filter runoff rainwater) and Bluebelt projects (to preserve and enhance natural drainage corridors, including streams, ponds and wetlands, to convey, store and filter runoff rainwater).
- Preserving historic buildings or monuments.
- Preserving or improving drinking water quality.
- Preserving or improving air quality.
- Local government efforts to reduce their own effect on the environment.
- Starting or improving recycling services for paper, plastic, metal and hazardous waste.
- Creating or improving environmental standards for business and industry.
- Providing support for public art.
- Improving accessibility of parks and buildings.

- Improving safety and cleanliness of streets and sidewalks.
- Developing affordable housing.
- Providing transportation choices.

The goals of physical environment changes can be widely varied. The change team might wish to:

- Attract visitors and new residents.
- Create a better quality of life.
- Protect the health of community members.
- Protect the natural resources of the community and maintain ecosystems.
- Preserve wildlife, particularly endangered species.
- Enhance the aesthetics of the community.
- Enhance the social life of the community.
- Sustain the local economy.

The purposes and ways that the physical environment can be modified to enhance a community are so broad as to be difficult to treat in a single chapter. In the case of the mountain bike trail, the project improved unused open space for recreation that became an asset for the SIU students, local community members, and mountain bikers from throughout the Midwest.

HOW TO CARRY OUT THIS TECHNIQUE

Who Should Be Involved?

Identify who should be involved in the formulation of a new environmental initiative. Just like policy initiatives, you will want to involve coalitions of organizations that work with the issue, agencies responsible for carrying out and maintaining the project and community groups representing all groups affected by or concerned with the issue. The coalition can be involved in strategic planning on how to get the new initiative adopted and implemented. The involvement of a coalition ensures better decisions and better chance of community acceptance of the project. Be sure to include those with opposing points of view. Open meetings inviting all members of the public that are concerned is also a way to obtain a variety of ideas and perspectives.

In the case of the mountain bike trail, the coalition included Southern Illinois University's Touch of Nature Environmental Center staff, who worked on planning, grant writing and building, and SIU graduate students studying recreation administration and outdoor recreation and resource management were involved in funding and development. The International Mountain Biking Association were involved in the design of the trails, and the Rotary Club of Carbondale–Breakfast were among the many community and student volunteers doing the hard work of building the trails.

WHAT'S HAPPENING NOW?

Often this type of project begins with an open meeting community-wide visioning process, in which community members express needs and aspirations for their community. Community organizations or officials consider frequently mentioned desires from the visioning session and examine "what's happening now." For physical environment initiatives, this includes the current uses and conditions of the building or land.

The director for the Touch of Nature environmental center knew that within the 3,100-acre property there were unused resources, which was an opportunity rather than a problem. He also knew that mountain biking is a popular sport, and that the southern Illinois region could use additional trails. It was also an opportunity to reach out to educate mountain bikers on conservation.

DESIRED OUTCOMES

The next step is to define your community's desired outcomes with indicators. Conduct a cause analysis (see Chapter 14) and focus on the causes, not symptoms. Finally, *prioritize* the causes you will address (Van Tiem, Moseley, & Dessinger, 2012). The gap between "what's happening now" and your desired goal may reveal many causes, including environmental, social and other factors. Priorities from a community-wide visioning session can inform the creation of a concept plan for high-priority items. Sometimes, in the case of environmental modifications, it is necessary to screen physical environment projects for possible environmental impacts.

> *Concept plan:* a short overview of a new project that describes the idea, existing conditions, opportunities and constraints, the audience (who will benefit) as well as key actions needed to create, implement and sustain the project. Timing for the project should be included and identify the team that will work on the project. For physical environments, a map or building elevation might be included. The concept plan should address the cost estimates, funding sources and uses of funds. When used for public meetings, the concept plan is very brief.

Touch of Nature's goal was to create a new environmental and recreational experience for the SIU community, southern Illinois, and the surrounding region. Indicators for a successful project of this kind might include:

- Sponsorships obtained and executed.
- Grants written and obtained.
- Trail builders trained.
- Volunteer hours for building and maintaining trails.
- Trails completed.
- Bikers served.
- Visitor ratings and comments.

INFORMATION SEEKING

Search for information about similar projects, how they were completed and what the results were. Searching can help you locate potential indicators for projects like yours. In addition, searching can reveal resources available, such as expert assistance, potential sponsors and grants and potential pitfalls of projects. Your team will also need to search for best practices. In terms of the mountain bike trail, best practices would include encouraging low impact riding and using methods of building and maintaining the trails that cause a minimum of damage to the ecology.

This research will help formulate a concept plan. Longer versions of a concept plan are often used for boards of organizations or city councils and public officials when they are making decisions. A brief version of the concept plan would be shared at a public meeting, and feedback would be gathered.

PLANNING

Using the concept plan, goals, objectives, indicators, organizational and public feedback, and information about similar projects and resources for guidance, the team can complete the planning process. Plans should be complete enough to result in the project completion and maintenance.

A key step at this point is to describe plans for funding and sponsorships. Next, describe the timing for the project once the funding is in place. As part of the plan, create a timeline for milestones and other activities, including who will do what. Key times to make environment modifications include when:

- New or renovated facilities are being planned.
- When old buildings are being removed or repurposed by community groups or government entities.

Any plans for state and local government facilities, public accommodations and commercial facilities should address accessibility (Department of Justice, 2010).

Create plans for communications media to be used to raise awareness of the project and generate interest and action on the part of potential volunteers. This should include creating a persuasive story that emphasizes the positive benefits of the built or natural environment change. Describe how your team will work with the media to keep the public informed of the project progress, and how your team will network with influential people and community members.

Plan training for volunteers, in the event that they will need specialized knowledge.

Describe how the project will be evaluated using the indicators identified earlier.

TRY IT!

Imagine that you are on a task force creating a concept plan for improving accessibility to an environmental education center in the Wisconsin north woods pine forest, including at least the nearest 30% (to the parking lot) of the total 12 miles of walking trails, so they can be used for those in wheelchairs or other mobility equipment. The purpose is to create better access to the forest and its wildlife, leading to a connection to nature and a sense of well-being through connections among nature, people and community. The center should be a neutral ground where anyone, regardless of social status, can come for

Table 34.1 Environment concept plan template.

Project abstract (short, stand-alone summary of the project)
Goals and objectives with indicators
Audience for the project (who will benefit)
Existing property conditions
Opportunities
Constraints
Timeline (What actions will take place to create, implement and sustain by what dates? Who is responsible? Gantt or PERT chart can be used)
Maps or illustrations needed
Cost estimates
Funding sources and uses of funds
Volunteer training needed
Project evaluation plans

recreation. They should not require visitors to spend money. Brainstorm how such accessibility can be created for the trails, parking and welcome and learning center. Create a concept plan that is accessible according to the 2010 ADA Standards for Accessible Design (https://www.ada.gov/regs2010/2010ADA-Standards/2010ADAstandards.htm) and the United States Access Board (https://www.access-board.gov/guidelines-and-standards/recreation-facilities/outdoor-developed-areas/background/committee-report/trails). A template for such a concept plan is found in Table 34.1.

SUMMARY

Changing the environment can be carried out to improve safety or access, encourage interaction, enhance a sense of community and many other purposes. The physical environment can include the natural and built environments as well as infrastructure such as stormwater filtration. Changes can be either large scale, such as cleanup of toxic waste, or small scale, such as repairing playgrounds, improving transportation by adding bike racks to public transportation or improving accessibility of public meeting spaces through entry ramps. This chapter focused on small-scale environment change by creating concept plans that detail who should be involved in making the change and when.

CITATIONS

Department of Justice. (2010). *2010 ADA standards for accessible design.* Retrieved from https://www.ada.gov/regs2010/2010ADAStandards/2010ADAstandards.htm

Oldenburg, R. (1999). *The great good place: Cafés, coffee shops, community centers, beauty parlors, general stores, bars, hangouts, and how they get you through the day* (3rd ed.). New York: Marlow & Co.

Van Tiem, D., Moseley, J., & Dessinger, J. (2012). *Fundamentals of performance technology: Optimizing results through people, process and organizations* (3rd ed.). San Francisco, CA: Pfeiffer.

SUPPORT

35

Figure 35.0

WHAT'S IN THIS CHAPTER?

Creating a healthy community sometimes involves changing conditions and providing support for community members to change behaviors and reduce risk. Types of support might include referrals for services, support events, self-help group meetings or alternative activities.

Objectives

By the end of this chapter, you will be able to:

- Assess conditions (incentives or disincentives) for desirable behaviors.
- Create an intervention to provide support for desirable behaviors, including who should be involved and when.

A STORY ABOUT COMMUNITY SUPPORT

Kara Dunkel, a community activist, related this story of how young people matter:

> Today and for many years "Young People Matter" has been the motto of the Jackson County Positive Youth Development Coalition (PYD). Our back history: We came together to collaborate efforts applying for a *Safe to Live* grant from the Illinois Violence Prevention Agency in 2003. This collaborative effort has become Jackson County Healthy Community Coalition (JCHCC), which is now under the broader umbrella of the Healthy Southern Illinois Delta Network (HSIDN).

The mission for JCHCC, straight from the HSIDN.org website is:

> "To serve as a catalyst for improving the health and overall quality of life of Jackson County residents by promoting healthy lifestyles, encouraging positive youth development, decreasing substance abuse, improving mental health, and increasing access to health care."
>
> Our Vision: We will be a catalyst for improving the health and overall quality of life within Jackson County, Illinois.
>
> Priority Work Areas and Action Teams include:
>
> - Behavioral Health
> - Cancer
> - Healthy Living
> - Joint Access to Care
> - Positive Youth Development (PYD)
> - Sexual Health
> - Built Environment
> - Preparedness
> - Diabetes Today Resource Team (DTRT)
>
> A coalition of Southern Illinois Healthcare, Jackson County Health Department, Southern Illinois Regional Social Services (which has since transitioned many times, now becoming Centerstone), Carbondale Park District, The Women's Center, Adolescent Health Center, Carbondale Police Department, Carbondale Public Library, SIU Touch of Nature, Carbondale administrators and The Church of Jesus Christ of Latter-day Saints Carbondale Ward came together regularly to address the grant requirements including specific organizations or agency sectors being represented. We coordinated a *needs assessment* survey and after evaluating the statistics, developed a strategic plan, measurable goals, and a timeline to complete tasks.
>
> One of the main goals was to *support* the launch of a Boys and Girls Club Carbondale (BGCC) which was accomplished. (BGCC has since flourished and has recently expanded to become Boys and Girls Clubs of Southern Illinois.) We also obtained cultural competency training for all involved in the collaboration and other trainings and developmental efforts to strengthen the agencies. We did a Study Circles discussion for eight weeks bringing the police and community members together

for a facilitated two hours of difficult and intense discussions. They also launched monthly PYD events called Family Vacation Nights (FVN), a free "vacation night" for all families to *support* the growth of youth developmental assets.

Focusing our efforts on strengthening families through best practices identified in *40 Developmental Assets* (Search Institute, 2006), we have just completed our sixteenth year of collaborative programming of FVN events. Assessments and grant requirements tend to motivate and direct much of the strategic planning for PYD and FVN events. Each agency chooses a month to be the lead or host coordinator for that month's FVN event, combining education with entertainment. For instance, a recent FVN featured family canoe experiences, water safety tips and ice cream at a nearby park. Another event provided child abuse prevention information with snacks and games for children. A third event had a presentation on "Current Teen Drug Trends," snacks and a session of yoga for kids and families. All events were designed to support the 40 positive supports and strengths that young people need to succeed, including external assets such as healthy relationships and opportunities and internal assets such as "social-emotional strengths, values, and commitments" (Search Institute, 2006).

Over the years we have collaborated, we have shared time, talents and resources. We have strengthened relationships between the agencies through: sharing trainings and contact information, networking being part of their meetings and recorded in shared meeting minutes, a shared Google Documents link so each agency in the PYD Coalition has equal access to the documents including by-laws and strategic plan, PYD listserv, Facebook page and website as well as consistent meeting dates, time and location.

(Dunkel, personal communication, July 27, 2019)

WHAT THIS TECHNIQUE IS ABOUT

This technique is about providing support such as help or advice regarding behavior changes and risk reduction. Support can help with a variety of situations, including:

- Diseases, injuries, or chronic medical conditions.
- Physical disabilities.
- Addictions.
- Eating disorders.
- Unhealthy or bad habits (smoking, or procrastination).
- Sexual identity questions.
- Emotional problems, mental illness or fears.
- Bereavement and grief.
- Parenting.
- Youth development.

While these issues vary widely, support groups for any of them have this in common: a peer support group is a regular gathering of people or their families with the lived experience of the issue. They might be face-to-face or online. The key factor in both approaches is emotional support. The groups come together once a month or more often to discuss challenges, struggles and successes, facilitated by a trained support specialist or peer. The people attending learn that they are not alone, and they are not judged in the same way they may be in other social settings. They are able to develop trust and hope in this setting. They can learn to show compassion and honesty. Most importantly, they work for a great number of people (Pistrang, Barker, & Humphreys, 2010) at a lower cost than more expensive interventions. Many people who come for comfort, leave with new confidence. Additionally, participation in self-help groups may have modest favorable effects on recovery outcomes (Markowitz, 2015).

Support to people with these concerns and their families might include one or more methods of providing:

- Information, resources and peer support provided during meetings or online.
- Referrals for services.
- Alternative activities as substitutes for risky activities.

HOW TO CARRY OUT THIS TECHNIQUE

Who Should Be Involved?

Identify who should be involved in the formulation of a new support initiative. You will want to involve coalitions of organizations that work with the issue, such as agencies and professionals responsible for health or mental health issues. In some cases, people working in the criminal justice system is warranted if your concerns are issues such as addiction. Community groups representing all groups affected by or concerned with the issue should also be identified and invited to participate. The coalition can be involved in strategic planning on how to get the new initiative started, planned and implemented. The involvement of a coalition encourages better community acceptance of the project. Don't forget to include those with opposing points of view. Open meetings at the inception of a project and after data gathering, inviting all members of the public that are concerned is also a way to obtain a variety of ideas and perspectives.

WHAT'S HAPPENING NOW?

With the help of the coalition, describe what's happening now. This will help determine the need for the project. One approach to this task is to *brainstorm* what's happening now and then describe the conditions and incentives supporting or disincentives blocking desirable behaviors. It is helpful during this phase to have members of the target audience at the meeting. Having a large number of knowledgeable people in your coalition can help with this difficult discussion, although it might be useful to begin the discussion in small groups first.

Another approach to assessing conditions is through *surveys* of the actual target group for your programs. There are many sources for locating reliable and valid assessments. An excellent searchable index for many tests with reviews is the *Mental Measurements Yearbook With Tests in Print*, available through academic libraries. Through this database, it is possible to locate surveys and inventories that can be used in your community. In the database, a link is also provided to the publisher's web page. It is important to visit the publisher's web page for up-to-date pricing information, because the information changes constantly. This approach is recommended when your project is comprehensive, like the Jackson County Healthy Community Coalition projects in this chapter's story. They located the Search Institute by doing a web search. The Search Institute (2006) has four surveys that can be used to assess the youth such as those in the communities served by the Jackson County Positive Youth Development Coalition.

The next step is to find out or estimate the size of the need. Ask your team this question: Are there significant numbers of people who could benefit from the project in your community? Answering this can be challenging for some types of issues, such as depression, because people living with depression may not wish to share that information. In this case, we may have to look to national statistics and use them to estimate the size of the local population. For instance, if we know that 7.2% of the U.S. population has a major depressive episode each year, we can estimate that 7.2% of your community may also have such an episode each year. This can be over 400 people each year for a city of 60,000.

DESIRED OUTCOMES

The desired outcome for a peer support group is generally for people to cope with their life situation or recover from their illnesses and develop skills to live more effectively in their communities. The specific desired outcomes depend on the needs being addressed. You will also want to select indicators that can be used when the initiative is evaluated. For instance, measures of resilience might be a useful indicator for a support group for those living with mental illness. In the story at the beginning of the chapter, the Jackson County Healthy Community Coalition selected the Developmental Assets Framework as desired outcome indicators for the young people and their families they served through their Family Vacation Nights.

INFORMATION SEEKING

Other questions that can be discussed with coalition members: Is there support in the community for your project? Is your concern a part of the mission of a group already within your community? If so, would that group be willing to help set up support programs or a self-help group? Are there national or regional groups that might be able to offer resources or assistance?

To locate answers to questions remaining after your meeting on "What's happening now," ask members of your coalition to search online or ask community influencers, doctors or other professionals in the field of your concern for their description of what's happening now and estimates of people who need support in the community. Survey potential attendees for their needs and preferences (Drebing, 2016). Members of your coalition may be able to help get the survey to potential attendees. Also look online and use networking for information on similar programs that have been found to be effective.

PLANNING THE SUPPORT GROUP

To begin a support program or self-help group, you will need to plan facilitation, meeting times and places, and plan communications to get the word out.

Facilitation of Support Groups

The team should identify someone comfortable with the expression of emotion, tension and conflict and willing to lead the group that can facilitate effectively. This is a job that takes energy, access to resources and the ability to facilitate. Depending on the issue focus of the support group (i.e. addiction, sexual identity, eating disorders), the facilitator should receive specialized training in facilitation of that type of group. Also, it is important that they receive training in cultural competency when the group includes people with a variety of cultures. Make sure the facilitator has the time to devote to the group. If not, you might investigate a co-facilitation arrangement. Look for national organizations that can help with this. Some offer how-to guides, or group starter kits.

Meetings

Determine where and when the group could meet. Also decide if the group will need to meet over the long term or if this is a short-term need.

Make decisions about who will be invited to attend. Will the group be open or closed? Will the group be only for people with the condition? Or will it be open to their families? Or would a separate support group meeting be better for the families?

Decide on the format for the meetings. Approaches could be:

- *Curriculum-based*—in which discussions center around issues from particular readings.
- *Topic-based*—in which topics are selected for each meeting's topic.
- *Open forum*—in which there is no topic determined before the meeting, and discussions depend on the topic that members bring up.

Before implementing the group, determine the guidelines for confidentiality and establish ground rules for group participation. Also decide what to do if an upset or angry person disrupts the meeting or dominates the group discussion. The facilitator could have an assistant help with these situations. Make plans *before* they arise. For instance, a co-facilitator can ask the upset person to move to a room next door to calm down before discussing the problem privately. It is important for the co-facilitator to show the upset person attention, empathy and respect.

Before starting the meetings, make sure you have a list of people to refer attendees to, when needed. These might include:

- Psychiatrists.
- Psychologists.
- Licensed clinical social workers.
- Clergy of all denominations and religions.
- Crisis hotlines.
- Medical doctors.

GETTING THE WORD OUT

Ask the coalition how you can get the word out to others who could benefit from attending the group meetings. They may have some excellent suggestions. Brochures or flyers can be printed and placed at:

- Local or state agencies serving people with the issues that concern you (disease, disability, mental health and so on).
- Churches, synagogues, mosques.
- Libraries.
- Colleges.
- Community centers.
- Supermarket community notice boards.
- Social service workers, clergy and physicians or therapists may also provide help or referrals to your support group.

ADDITIONAL SUPPORT MATERIALS

A web page can be created to share information about the support available. These might include information on face-to-face meetings, referrals for services, alternate events and activities to risky behaviors, job-aids (for instance, a tip sheet on how to share your experience in meetings) and online support. (See Chapter 31 for more information about brochures and other communications.)

IMPLEMENTING THE SUPPORT GROUP

After publicizing the support group, hold the first meeting. If the turnout is very large, it may be necessary to break the group into multiple groups.

- Do introductions and carry out any icebreakers you have planned.
- Share ground rules and confidentiality rules.
- Allow time for experience sharing if people are comfortable sharing at the first meeting.
- Pass a mailing/contact sheet for contacting members. Be sure to add a box to check if they want this information to be kept private.
- Discuss plans for the next meeting.
- Allow time for informal socializing after the meeting.

EVALUATING THE SUPPORT GROUP

There are three possible components to your evaluation:

- *Impact*: the effect on the target behaviors.
- *Outcomes*: the effect on health and quality of life.
- *Process*: how the program is run (including meeting activities) (Steckler & Linnan, 2002).

Many national organizations provide assistance with evaluation in the form of surveys and methods of administering them. Interviews, focus groups and observations are also data collection methods used for evaluating peer support groups. Before trying to create your own evaluation questionnaire, determine if validated evaluations are already available. (If you will need to create your own data collection tools, see Appendix E.)

TRY IT!

Imagine that you have just found out that your younger teenage sister has childhood cancer. You would like to find a support group for her and your family, but you have not found one.

1. What do you do to explore the need for such a group in your city of 100,000?
2. What do you do next?
3. Describe the steps you would take to begin a support group in your community.
4. Describe how you would evaluate the group.

SUMMARY

This chapter covered providing support for community members to change behaviors and receive emotional support. Types of support include support events, self-help groups, referrals for services, or alternative activities. The focus was particularly on creating support groups.

CITATIONS

Drebing, C. (2016). *Leading peer support and self-help groups: A pocket resource for peer specialists and support group facilitators*. Holliston, MA: Alderson Press.

Harris, M. J. (2016). *Evaluating public and community health programs*. Hoboken, NJ: John Wiley & Sons.

Healthy Southern Illinois Delta Network. (2019). Retrieved from www.hsidn.org/

Markowitz, F. E. (2015). Involvement in mental health self-help groups and recovery. *Health Sociology Review: The Journal of the Health Section of the Australian Sociological Association*, 24(2), 199–212. doi:10.1080/14461242.2015.1015149

Pistrang, N., Barker, C., & Humphreys, K. (2010). The contributions of mutual help groups for mental health problems to psychological well-being: A systematic review. In *Mental health self-help* (pp. 61–85). New York: Springer.

Search Institute. (2006). *The developmental assets® framework*. Retrieved from www.search-institute.org/our-research/development-assets/developmental-assets-framework/

Steckler, A., & Linnan, L. (2002). Process evaluation and public health interventions: An overview. In A. Steckler & L. Linnan (Eds.), *Process evaluation in public health interventions and research* (pp. 1–23). San Francisco, CA: Jossey-Bass Publishers.

MONITORING AND MANAGING CHANGE   36

Figure 36.0

WHAT'S IN THIS CHAPTER?

Whether the change is incremental or transformational, to manage it, the team needs to continually assess and adjust objectives, processes and outcomes. This chapter reviews the process of change and monitoring the outcomes to improve and make the changes stick. To manage change, it is necessary to examine potential risks and plan to respond, if risk-caused problems should occur. Quality should be defined so that all staff and volunteers are aware of the standards, and when exemplary work occurs, it should be reinforced. Finally, managing change requires evaluating and reporting results.

Objectives

By the end of this chapter, you will be able to:

- Monitor and manage change.
- Assess possible risk factors to create plans that will reduce risks.
- Create a plan to monitor and manage quality.
- Evaluate the project and report results.

A STORY ABOUT MANAGING CHANGE

Here is a story of social change which evolved from a small group of women who were meeting in a small city in the Midwest at the beginning of the feminist (US women's liberation) movement. This is a first-person account by Margaret Katranides, who is a seasoned feminist and a Quaker. As she approaches her 80th year of life, she has some valuable reflections about how change happens developmentally. In the late 1960s a small group of women, mostly highly educated wives of faculty members, gathered in a feminist collective to explore their identity as women. The city benefited significantly from the anti-nepotism policy at the university, which produced a pool of educated but unemployed wives who used their available time to make changes in the community. Margaret remembers:

> In the beginning, the Women's Center was meant to be a home away from home for women, a center for feminist organizing (we had art shows, poetry evenings, discussion groups, etc.); also, as a shelter for women living in abusive situations. In its early years the Center was very egalitarian and open in its organizational structure; an all-volunteer operation. The first building was heated by a stoker furnace, and one of the women gave classes in how to tend it. The volunteers kept a log so that the next woman coming on would know what problems might have been encountered; usually with a guest (i.e., a woman hiding) or occasionally with a man pursuing a guest.
>
> We had a board that functioned on a consensus basis. Board meetings were open, so if anyone had a problem or a suggestion they could come to the next meeting and state their case. If the suggestion was for a new project, the response often was "That sounds good, would you like to head it up?" I was a volunteer, and then a board member. After my husband died, when I was raising the kids and going to grad school, they let me out of regular work, but asked me to be ombudsperson, negotiating between people who were in conflict. There were only few times when people couldn't work out the conflicts themselves.
>
> After a few years, we appointed a director and counselor; these were volunteer positions, the counselor being on a traineeship from the Rehabilitation & Counseling Department at the university. Later, when the Center started getting grants to run the place, these were made paid positions. I felt a loss when it moved more toward being an institution, focusing on the shelter work; but it was obvious from the growing demand that we really needed that work to be done. And those early years had given a lot to those of us who ran the place—learning about our abilities and strengths for getting things done.

People and Their Roles in This Story:

- Feminists who initiated the Women's Center (informal group).
- Building managers (all volunteers).
- Director (appointed by the group).
- Ombudsman/conflict manager (appointed by the group).
- Counselor (interns/counselors in training at the university).
- Grant writers (volunteers).
- Guests: abused women seeking shelter from danger.
- Men who were hunting for their wives.

What is the dynamic (i.e. a force that stimulates change or progress within a system or process) driving this story of social change? There was a movement for social change among women in the 1960s that eventually led to providing safety for women who were living in abusive situations. This action was happening all over America in efforts to recognize the equal rights of women. In the university town where this story happened, there were educated women who had the time and the desire to engage in social change. As Margaret also indicated: "Of course, we weren't all helpless neophytes. Some of these women had organized to change city government and to pressure the school system to integrate, even before I arrived in town in 1967." Changes to the social power structure between women and men were occurring organically, from the bottom up.

Lessons Learned: how to sustain momentum from an organic movement until it becomes part of the infrastructure (using the story of the Women's Center as an example):

- **Coordination (the right hand needs to know what left is doing).** The board functioned on a consensus basis. Board meetings were open, so if anyone had a problem or a suggestion, they could come to the next meeting and state their case.
- **Monitoring progress and feeding the information back into the process.** The daily logbook became a significant way to report what was happening daily at the Women's Center even when there was changing leadership.
- **Assessing the process, partnerships, etc., and constantly seeking to improve outcomes.** An ombudsman was appointed to handle conflicts as they arose, as was a volunteer director and counselor; the counselor being on a traineeship from the Rehabilitation & Counseling Department at the university.
- **Communicating progress to stakeholders:** The center started getting grants to run the place; these were made paid positions.

WHAT THIS TECHNIQUE IS ABOUT

This technique is about managing and gauging progress of a change project as it unfolds. William Lofquist offers a structured way for consideration of how a community development project can be monitored (see Figure 36.1).

Community change begins with analysis of what's happening now, including indicators of the symptoms of a problem or opportunity. The change from the original description of "what's happening now" to the final achievement of desired conditions is closely monitored during implementation to make sure that progress is being made. However, much work happens between Conditions A and B. Expanding on

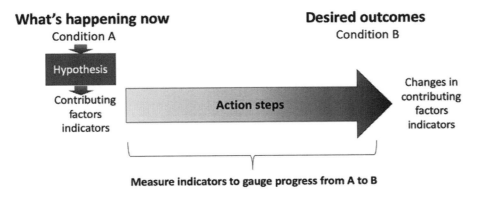

Figure 36.1 Gauging progress in community development.
Source: Adapted from Lynn and Lofquist (2007).

Figure 36.2 The change process.
Source: Adapted from Lynn and Lofquist (2007).

the arrow between Conditions A and B (see Figure 36.2), we find that a hypothesis is made, contributing factors are described during the cause analysis and action steps are planned and implemented, and changed conditions should lead to the desired outcome, if the hypothesis was accurate.

A *hypothesis* is made regarding the conditions, contributing factors and causes for the situation. *Planning* is then carried out to determine actions necessary to change conditions. When these steps are implemented, conditions should change, which should result in new conditions. When this change process is successful, those conditions produce the desired outcomes. While the change is in progress, indicators are monitored to make sure the project is on the right track to produce the desired outcome. Monitoring indicators when the project is in process is sometimes called a formative evaluation, because it can help form the project. If the project is not on track to successfully accomplish the desired outcome, a midcourse correction can be made. You won't want to get to the final evaluation to find out the project failed.

GET PEOPLE READY FOR CHANGE

In order to get people ready for change, you will want to *communicate* early and often with stakeholders the reasons and need for change and the form the change will take. *Engage* beneficiaries and stakeholders in the change process early, allowing them to participate in crafting the change.

In Chapter 13, we mentioned that resistance is natural, so you will need to anticipate and address resistance to change from the start. One way to do this is to engage people by asking them to help identify barriers to the proposed change and any anticipated problems so that they can be addressed. Listen, listen, listen! And pay attention to red flags sent up by the people on the front side of the process. They can see the roadblocks or the potholes and give warning signals that there is trouble up ahead. Using what you learn from those who resist, you can remove the barriers to change.

Implementing change often requires the beneficiaries, paid or unpaid staff to acquire new knowledge and skills, so your team will need to plan and implement methods to increase the capacity, knowledge or skill of volunteers by providing information, training and support. Also, make sure that change agents and beneficiaries feel safe to try out the change or new behavior.

MONITOR PROGRESS

Accountability can be created by using your indicators to *monitor changes continuously*. Someone will usually be assigned to *oversight* of the change implementation, sometimes a board of directors or the

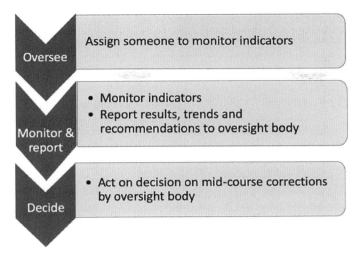

Figure 36.3 Monitor and manage implementation.

original change team (see Figure 36.3). The person charged with oversight will then assign someone to the task of monitoring progress. That person should periodically examine the selected indicators for the desired outcomes and objectives.

How often the indicators are examined depends on the nature of the goal or objectives. For instance, if the objective is to use social media to recruit volunteers, then the indicator (number of hits on a social media announcement) needs to be monitored every few days. On the other hand, if the goal is to *foster students' academic advancement and personal growth into self-motivated, resilient and responsible citizens* the indicators (the number of students remaining enrolled, graduating high school, completing a two- or four-year college degree) can be monitored only each semester or year.

Implementation and Maintenance

Implementation is defined by Moseley and Hastings (2005) as "the process of communicating, piloting, launching, and monitoring interventions" (p. 8). Implementation of change means not simply carrying out the planned actions, but also dealing with people and their frequent adverse reactions to change. As part of planning, your team assessed the community change readiness and planned strategies to cope with people's concerns, resistance behaviors and potential for relapse into old ways of doing things. To accomplish this, communication is a key strategy.

> *Change management*: the managing process of helping your community transition from the current state to the desired state. This process includes preparing, supporting and helping individuals, teams, organizations or communities make the transition.

Change Management

Implementing and maintaining a change involves several change strategies including change management. Remember that part of the plan to implement the solution is to monitor and manage the change process. Change management is a notion that is derived from business organizational or technology change but has found application in community change. It is the process taken to transition people (individuals or groups) efficiently from where they are now (often unaware of the need for change) to a desired outcome (adoption and internalization of the change) (Varkey & Antonio, 2010). Part of change management is assessing possible risk factors, planning to reduce risks as much as possible and creating a plan to monitor and manage quality.

Risks

Project *risks* can involve the potential for loss or even illness or injury. They include possible events, which, if they occur, can adversely impact one or more project objectives. The purpose for including a description of risks is to assess and manage them. To manage risks, you will need to anticipate and describe them and plan to reduce the potential of unpleasant incidents and barriers to your projects by these risks. For instance, if your nonprofit organization provides services such as an overnight homeless shelter, health problems among homeless people are common and can pose potential health risks for other shelter residents and staff or volunteers. Planning how to deal with health problems immediately when ill people enter the shelter can reduce the risk of spreading illness. In any change process, possible risks can be anticipated, contingency plans can be made, change implementation can be monitored and, if necessary, contingency plans can be activated.

Quality

When developing indicators, your team defined a level of quality desired for your organization's products and services. You may also need to develop policies and procedures needed to implement your quality definition. Many times, instruction for staff and volunteers is also needed to make sure your quality indicators will be met, so training, mentoring, coaching or job-aids will need to be developed and implemented. Finally, data collecting processes need to be carried out to monitor and evaluate (Chapter 38) whether or not work is being done according to definition, policies and procedures.

Report Results

The person monitoring the implementation will need to report to the group charged with oversight of the project, as well as key stakeholders such as a board of directors, collaborators and major donors. They should provide answers to questions, about trends regarding the progress (or lack of progress) toward goals and objectives.

Old structures, policies and systems sometimes create barriers to progress. If any such barriers have been identified through examining the indicators, make recommendations about the status and any actions needed by the management or change team. In addition, stakeholders and volunteers need to be able to communicate openly about issues. Support the organization's ability to make these changes by listening and acting to remove the barriers.

Reinforce appropriate actions and successes. If culturally appropriate, publicly recognize actions of exceptional volunteers, staff, members of your change team and collaborators, so the rest of the volunteers and staff remember their contributions. People from some cultures prefer private recognition. Finally, talk about success on visible short-term milestones and progress on long-term goals every chance you get. Tell success stories about the change process to the team and the community.

Even when the indicators of change are showing significant progress, don't declare victory prematurely. Transformational change runs deep, and quick wins are only the beginning of what needs to be done to achieve long-term change. Launching one step of a long-range change is great, but don't let your task force disband after the first success. If you can sustain that progress, it means the change is working. Keep looking for improvements. Each ongoing success provides an occasion to build on what went right and identify what you can do differently. Make a mid-course correction when things aren't working properly. Maintain quality performance through reinforcement.

HOW TO CARRY OUT THIS TECHNIQUE

Monitor Progress

Assign someone to the task of monitoring progress. Periodically examine your selected indicators for your desired outcomes and objectives and ask this question: Are desired outcomes (goals) and objectives being achieved? If they are, then recognize, reward and communicate the progress. If not, then consider the following questions:

- Will the goals be achieved according to the timelines specified in the plan? If not, then why not?
- Should the goals or target dates for completion be changed? Are the desired outcomes and objectives realistic? (Warning: be cautious about making changes to your plan—determine why efforts are behind schedule before goals or times are revised.)
- What are the barriers to accomplishing the tasks? Do staff and volunteers have adequate resources (money, equipment, facilities, training, etc.) to achieve the goals?
- Should priorities be changed to put greater focus on achieving the goals?
- What can be learned from monitoring progress so we can improve future planning and implementation? Can we improve future monitoring and evaluation efforts?

REMOVE OBSTACLES

Make changes to remove barriers to change. Anticipate resistance to change from the beginning. Communicate and engage people, inviting them to participate in creating the change. Provide information, training and support so people can learn about the change. Maintain a sense of safety for people to try out the change or new behavior.

BUILD ON THE CHANGE

Don't declare victory too soon. Keep looking for improvements. Build on what went right and identify what you can change and do differently. Make a mid-course correction based on evaluation data when things aren't working. When things are going well, reinforce quality performances by staff and volunteers.

MANAGE RISKS

Identify and describe with your team the risks that might affect your project or its outcomes. Analyze the risks: Determine the likelihood and consequence of each risk, and then evaluate or rank the risks by likelihood and consequence (Pinto, 2015). The steps for dealing with risk are:

- Analyze the risk to determine the likelihood and consequence of each risk.
- Evaluate and rank the risk by determining the likelihood and consequence of the risk actually happening.
- As a team, determine whether the risk is acceptable or if it is serious enough to justify doing something to mitigate the risk.
- Select the highest-ranked risks and make a prevention or contingency plan to treat or modify these risks to achieve acceptable risk levels.

- Monitor and review the project as it is implemented, including the potential risks identified.
- If any anticipated risks occur, implement the contingency plan to treat the risk.

MANAGE QUALITY

Develop and document definitions of quality products and services for your organization. Develop policies and procedures to implement your quality definitions. Next, develop and implement instruction for staff and volunteers. Finally, develop and implement evaluation data collection processes to monitor if work is being done according to the definitions, policies and procedures.

REPORT RESULTS

Report the answers to the questions about progress to the oversight group. Describe trends regarding the progress toward goals and objectives. Make recommendations about the status and any actions needed and recognize exceptional people (staff and volunteers). Talk with staff and volunteers, stakeholders and the wider community about progress every chance you get.

TRY IT!

Imagine that you are on the staff of a nonprofit organization supporting at-risk youth and their families. These teens include those who are (select one):

- Involved in drugs or alcohol.
- Abused sexually, physically or emotionally.
- Living with mental illness.
- Neglected at home or living in stressful family environments.
- Lacking social or emotional support.
- Involved with delinquent peers.

Your program includes support groups, alternative activities for youth and individual counseling. The support group project is new this year, and it is your team's job to monitor and manage the project. Describe how your team will:

1. Assess and plan for risk factors to reduce them as much as possible.
2. Define and support quality.
3. Monitor and manage the project.
4. Evaluate the project and report the results.

Feel free to do some research on this particular type of support group to support your recommendations.

SUMMARY

This chapter reviewed the change process and then examined monitoring and managing change. To manage change, your team needs to continually assess and adjust processes to obtain your desired outcomes. To manage change, we saw that it is necessary to examine potential risks and plan to respond if known risk-caused problems should occur. Quality should be defined so that all staff and volunteers are aware of the standards, and when exemplary work occurs, it should be reinforced. This chapter also covered monitoring the processes and outcomes to improve project performance and make the changes stick, as well as evaluating and reporting results. More on evaluation will be covered in Chapter 38.

CITATIONS

Lynn, D. D., & Lofquist, W. A. (2007). *BreakAway*. Tucson, AZ: Development Publications.

Moseley, J. L., & Hastings, N. B. (2005, April). Implementation: The forgotten link on the intervention chain. *Performance Improvement*, 44(4), 8–14. doi:10.1002/pfi.4140440405

Pinto, J. K. (2015). *Project management: Achieving competitive advantage* (global ed., 4th ed.). New York: Pearson.

Varkey, P., & Antonio, K. (2010). Change management for effective quality improvement: A primer. *American Journal of Medical Quality*, 25(4), 268–273. doi:10.1177/1062860610361625

STAGE 6
Evaluation and Conclusion

Monitoring and improving implementation require evaluation of the process, partnerships and outcomes of the change initiative. This stage provides information on sustaining the change, developing leaders and developing plans for evaluation, evaluation methods and using evaluation to improve the initiative. We then address issues of how facilitators gracefully disengage from a project.

Figure S6.0 Facilitation of Change Model Stage 6: Evaluation and conclusion.

LEADERSHIP, SUSTAINABILITY AND RENEWAL

37

Figure 37.0

WHAT'S IN THIS CHAPTER?

An initiative is sustainable when it can continue without depleting the resources, including human energy, upon which it depends. To achieve sustainable change, the practices that the change initiatives introduced need to continue to be used and not regress to an earlier stage. They must become the new way of life, including being integrated into mind-sets, practices and behaviors rather than something added on top of people's already overloaded lives.

Paradoxically, sustainable change must also continue to be consistent with shifting values of the community, or it won't continue. This suggests that values embodied in an initiative sometimes need to change as community conditions change. The change team needs to provide feedback to the community on progress toward successful outcomes. An organization, community or business group that plans to continue into the future will also need to prepare a succession plan and to develop new leaders. This chapter covers creating a plan to develop future leaders and teams that can envision goals, motivate, manage, represent the team, build bridges, networks and connections with potential partners and communicate clearly and persuasively. This chapter addresses strategies for enhancing the sustainability of the change initiative and the organization.

Objectives

By the end of this chapter, you will be able to:

- Describe strategies for sustaining an initiative.
- Describe the strategies used by leaders who can lead a change process as conditions change.
- List strategies to renew an organization in the face of changed conditions.
- Create an action plan for leadership development for yourself.

A STORY ABOUT MENTORSHIP FOR LEADERSHIP DEVELOPMENT

In the early 1990s, a facilitator encountered several powerful guides who guided her work in the field of community development and prevention. One powerful influence on her as an emerging leader was a well-known consultant in this field named William Lofquist. Bill is well known in community development both nationally and internationally. He is a slow-talking Southerner with the heart of a diehard radical. That Southern drawl of his provides great cover for his social change agenda. Here is an example. In 1954, after the *Brown v. the Board of Education* decree of the U.S. Supreme Court, Bill along with several other college students, created and led the strategy that nonviolently integrated the University of North Carolina in 1954. He had learned this technique from Quakers and became a master of this framework of community development over time.

When the facilitator was teaching a prevention course at a small college, she took the bold step of introducing herself to Bill by telephone and asking him to come to speak to her college students the next time he was in Illinois. He generously offered to do so without charge, which is very characteristic of Bill. Not long after that she received a call from him inviting her to join his national training team. What a surprise! He was choosing her, an unknown quantity, as his traveling partner. Like any good mentor, he had recognized her hidden gifts and knew that they would make great team partners. She leans on Bill for courage because he always hones tightly to the truth, although experience indicates there can be painful consequences. He is a role model for showing fierce courage in a world that fears change. With him in the world, she doesn't feel totally crazy for being who she is. With Bill as her mentor and role model, she can always count on someone being just a little bit farther out on the limb than she is.

WHAT THIS TECHNIQUE IS ABOUT

Preventing Rollback

To sustain and make a change stick, strategies should be planned for enhancing commitment and minimizing resistance. People involved in planning may be more likely to find the change *acceptable*.

Your team will need to plan strategies to *raise awareness* of community members about the need for change, so they will *recognize* and accept it, make a *commitment* to adopt the change, *explore* and

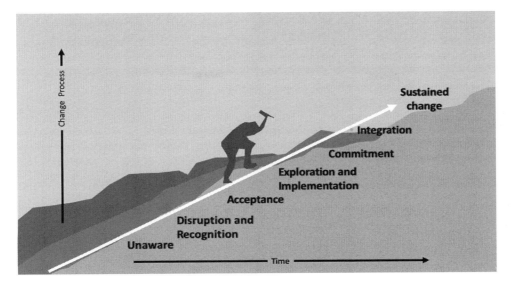

Figure 37.1 Change commitment timeline.

implement it, and ultimately *integrate* it into their lives. Ultimately, you want the change to be part of the organization and the community's way of doing things, integrated into the infrastructure (see Figure 37.1). The last thing you want is for people to feel that a change is simply added on top of already complicated lives with no infrastructure to maintain integration such as policies, procedures, rewards and so on. This is when the behaviors roll back to the old way of doing things.

When leading a change initiative, the leader should convey a vision of the change, the "what" and "why" of it, and should demonstrate support for it by showing their own commitment. It must be clear that their own beliefs and behaviors support the change. They should also provide feedback and communicate the outcomes to stakeholders. If the change is a new or revised program of an organization, the leader should communicate the vision, and later the outcomes to the community, and especially those directly affected outside the organization.

LEADERSHIP FOR ORGANIZATIONAL RENEWAL

For an initiative to be sustainable, the organization also needs to continue to renew itself, rather than continue to use paradigms, frames of reference and even technologies that are no longer appropriate for the contemporary environment. Organizations and their leaders need to create plans to develop (as in this chapter's story) or hire new leaders as replacements as old leaders move on. Leaders who can lead in the renewal of a change process as conditions change have different characteristics from those necessary to begin an organization and get the ball rolling. Founders usually begin with a powerful idea and the self-confidence to create their own path. They don't just talk about it, they do it. They create an organization to carry out their vision, as they work hard and persistently to make it successful. But founders are not always the best leaders to continue to renew the organization once it reaches a mature level. For example: one organization was successfully founded, and then it became stuck. When it came time to replace the founder, the board of directors wisely hired a new leader with a profound understanding of the value of working together in shared leadership. Each had a distinctive role to play at the proper time.

How can we tell what kind of leadership an organization needs at a given point in time? We need to ask these questions:

- At what phase of development is the organization? (See Figure 37.2.)
- What should the leader focus on, as the organization develops? Growth? Renewal?
- What should the leader's style be for the phase of development?

When an organization moves past the start-up phase through growth, their growth may begin to level off as conditions in the community change. At this point the leaders need to begin thinking of renewal before stability leads to stagnation and decline.

What are the characteristics of leaders who can lead in the *renewal* of the change process as conditions change? In many of the stories in this book we have reviewed different styles of founders that lay the foundation for a change process. Pastor Christine (Chapter 1) was an inspirational leader who had a fresh viewpoint on the issue of homelessness in her town, which led to a team effort by many community influencers to start the Homeless Coalition. Fern, with a collaborative style, worked alone at first, knocking on doors and inviting pastors to come to a new understanding of racism in her town (Chapter 19). When that initial effort failed, she partnered with the library director, the Human Relations Commission and others to eventually establish the Race Unity group. On the other hand, in the story of the two corporate adventure trainers, it was mainly through innovative and dynamic leadership of a single person who founded an international organization for teaching peace through cooperative play (Chapter 29). Everyone has their own leadership style. All of these styles of leadership were employed at the right time and the right stage of the change process.

As William Lofquist frequently said, "conditions are always changing" (personal communication, March 18, 2016). As a result of changing conditions, it is necessary to continue to plan and implement changes that move our communities toward well-being (Figure 37.3).

At some point, a shift in the leadership paradigm can either renew the organization or stall it under a single leader's command. What happens when the founding leadership style must change because of new

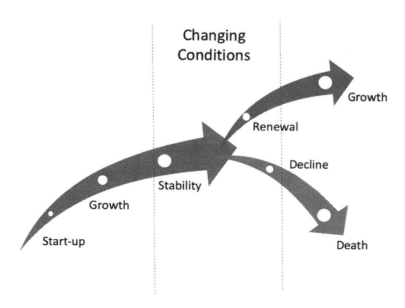

Figure 37.2 Organization change phases.

Figure 37.3 Continuing planning.
Source: Adapted from Lofquist (1989).

conditions? In the "Trouble on the Team" story (Chapter 29), we saw how the founder was confronted by unit leaders for standing in the way of growth of the organization. His style was a driven, top-down autocratic leadership style, which was necessary in the beginning. One self-driven person with an inspiring vision making strategic decisions for the organization made sense when the organization was in the start-up phase. Later, however, an autocratic style became a block to further growth as the organization spread from the U.S. to other countries and cultures. Leadership needed to be shared with the leaders in each country because only they knew how the organization's branch could be sustained in their cultural context. He needed to give his teams the tools they needed and the space to get the job done. When the board of directors eventually requested that he "step down," he was replaced by a leader with a collectivist and collaborative style of leadership, which renewed and grew the organization from six nations to 40. The new international manager was selected to create a new model of shared leadership while maintaining the balance from the center. Like a hub in a wheel; she kept the organization together while sharing the power. She brought a new vision and a strategy for transformation to the organization. She kept what worked while reinventing the relationships between the hub and the branches.

Founder's syndrome can become a real problem for the renewal of organizations and must be addressed as the organization grows and changes. Eventually the founders must disengage in order to allow for new leaders who can promote growth by responding to the changing conditions. (Disengagement will be discussed in Chapter 39.) In Chapter 32 we told the story of the *ReNEW* organization. After analyzing conditions using a SWOT analysis, the board decided to pursue the opportunities offered by the Internet and collaboration with other groups. This led to a renewal of the organizational vision.

Leadership and management are linked but are not the same thing. *Leadership* is the act of inspiring others to work toward achieving a goal. *Management* is coordination of activities and exercising the responsibility to make decisions and oversee an organization. What facilitators and leaders need to do are a combination of management and leadership skills (Bolea & Atwater, 2015). When any of these are missing, the team and the whole organization can flounder. Further, a leader needs to know when to lead and when to manage in order to achieve renewed organizational excellence.

While every nonprofit organization is different, a few attributes of excellent organizations and their programs can be identified. According to social analyst Lisbeth Schorr (1997), successful programs have these characteristics: They are comprehensive, flexible, responsive and persistent. They see clients in the context of their families and communities. They have a clear mission, take a long-term preventive orientation and evolve over time as communities change.

Flexibility, responsiveness to changing conditions and persistence are the keys to sustaining the organization. The practices and interventions of these organizations must all be consistent with and support their missions and programs. Schorr (1997) says that *practices* of successful programs include hiring competent and committed people to manage them, and training and supporting staff (and volunteers) to provide excellent and flexible service; staff and volunteers build relationships with clients based on trust and respect.

Finally, excellent organizations plan for the sustainability of the organization itself through developing leadership skills in others in advance of a change in leadership. Before disengaging, leaders need to plan for the future of the organization by developing future leaders that have the ability to create and maintain team chemistry, effective and efficient communication and a compelling vision for the team, including multiple constituencies, clear expectations and low turnover. They need to be able to delegate without micromanaging (such as controlling and directing the smallest actions taken by team members), bullying or playing favorites.

LEADERSHIP DEVELOPMENT

Although each organization is different and requires some specialized skills, some skills typically used by a nonprofit leader include:

- Working and inspiring others to work toward achieving a vision/mission.
- Managing change.
- Managing, influencing and delegating tasks to board, staff and volunteers.
- Working with people that have considerably different backgrounds from your own.
- Collaborating with stakeholders.
- Managing operations in resource-constrained environments.
- Developing next generation leadership skills in others.
- Analysis and creative problem-solving.
- Communicating internally and externally.
- Managing effective and efficient meetings to handle formal business.
- Managing conflict while respecting differences and maintaining trust.
- Assuring that the organization complies with all federal, state, and local requirements.

Looking at the list of management and leadership skills listed here, ask yourself where your strengths and weaknesses lie. If you see many weaknesses, don't despair; leaders are made, not born. You can grow your skill set by creating a personal action plan. How do you get started? Do a self-assessment to determine what areas need development. You will discover valuable insights by examining your skills, traits, competencies, abilities and experience. There are many leadership skills assessments available online and in book form that can be useful. There is also a "Change Leadership Skills Self-Assessment" online in eResources that can be used.

Learn how other people perceive you. It is often the case that when we assess ourselves, we are inaccurate, so determining what others think can be a reality check. Find out what your team values in a leader. Use this information to create a personal development plan. You can find a mentor, read books and blogs on leadership, and take leadership training or use a combination of these methods of learning.

Study your organization, community and the field of endeavor your organization's mission is focused on. Study how to run effective meetings, and then apply your new ideas. Revise them based on feedback from your team. Study effective communication and apply what you have learned. Innovate, take risks, evaluate how your innovation worked and *learn from your mistakes* (Dyer, Gregersen, & Clayton Christensen, 2011).

HOW TO CARRY OUT THIS TECHNIQUE

Sustaining the Change

The goal of a change is to get the change started and then sustain momentum as necessary at least until the change becomes the new normal and part of the organization's and the community's infrastructure. Coordinate the change so the right hand knows what the left hand is doing.

- When planning strategies to *raise awareness*, plan to communicate a vision of change that people affected by the initiative will *recognize* and value (see Figure 37.1). Highlight the advantages of changing.
- Involve affected people in the planning early and often within a climate of trust, increasing the likelihood that they will find the change *acceptable*.
- Ask well-respected people in the community (especially those well respected by people directly affected by the change) to model the new behavior and show how they find it rewarding.
- Make the changes as simple and easy to do as possible. Point out compatibility with their values and the ways things are already done. Avoid burnout caused by too much change all at once.
- Provide support for the change such as job-aids, training, coaching incentives or recognition as people *implement* the change.
- As people explore and implement the change, recognize success (early successes need to be planned—plan to do something achievable in a short time that makes individuals and groups feel good—and celebrated, as well as the long-term successes). Provide incentives if necessary. Knowledge of results and recognition is often sufficient.
- To enhance *commitment* to the affected people and the wider community to the change, be patient and flexible while people learn ways to *integrate* the change into their lives.
- Monitoring progress and feeding the information back into the process. Assess the process, partnerships, etc., and constantly tweak to improve. Evaluate the outcomes and plan further strategies as necessary. Provide feedback to stakeholders and the community on successful outcomes.

RENEWING THE ORGANIZATION

A sustainable organization is one that can renew itself when growth has stalled. To renew or transform an organization is an internal change initiative. Leading change takes courage because leaders need to be able to question policies, practices, values and ways of thinking. And they need to be able to recruit followers who disrupt business as usual. Change, moving from an existing state to a new and different one, is challenging, and there is no guarantee of success. Like all change initiatives, it begins with the leader and board of directors (your change team) asking, "What's happening now?" and then their desired outcomes and indicators (see Figure 37.4). They should then gather data on the organization's readiness, and effective organizations and programs that can be used as a model for renewal. Then, following data collection and review of research for model organizations, they can describe the situation much as the *ReNEW* team did (Chapter 32), using a SWOT analysis (Harrison, 2010). (See Chapter 19 for more on SWOT analysis.) Using these models, they can plan strategies to make the changes, implement and evaluate processes and outcomes. All the while, they need to be on the lookout for things that derail change, such as disengagement and negativity of team members or beneficiaries of the change. Instead, working with the team, the leader needs to model the change for the organization, demonstrating his or her commitment.

Figure 37.4 Organizational renewal cycle.

LEADERSHIP DEVELOPMENT

When leaders, whether volunteer or staff, are nearing the end of their term, their time as a committee chair is up, or they wish to move on, they need to plan ahead to develop skills of someone who can replace them. To begin to plan leadership development for promising members of staff, a leader might begin with their own job description if one exists. If one doesn't exist, it may be a good time to create one. Knowledge and skills needed for their job should be listed there. This list can be reviewed with the committee or board of directors and updated as necessary. Another thing the director can do to create a comprehensive list of skills is to research lists of skills required for nonprofit directors by examining posted job openings.

Next, they can seek someone that can develop the skills to lead, and mentor them by asking them to serve on the board with them. It is helpful to debrief the developing leader after meetings. Finally, the former leader can serve a year as past chair or past president. As the current leader, you might also recommend books or other leadership development opportunities for the developing leader. Many organizations "institutionalize" this leadership development method by creating elected positions of president-elect and past president.

Using a skill list the leader feels is complete, they can meet with the potential leader to go over the list and compare skills already demonstrated by that staff member, crossing off the list those items that the staff member has obtained. The remaining skills are used to create a leadership development plan. While many organizations offer leadership development for nonprofit organizations, any skills unique to the organization will need to be taught through mentoring, coaching or college programs. For instance, the director of Touch of Nature Environmental Center, discussed in Chapter 34, has a master's degree in recreation administration, and program leaders have degrees or certifications in their program specialties such as recreation, therapeutic recreation and environmental education. After completion of these kinds of programs, there will still be some skills unique to that particular workplace.

Let's say you are the potential next leader. You might actively pursue learning the needed knowledge and skills by seeking a mentor. A mentor is a person with whom a future leader (protégé) has a long-term relationship focused on growth and development. A mentor will challenge and encourage you to think through issues and practices by asking stimulating questions and guiding thinking. They also provide feedback, but they do not give day-to-day advice or micromanage your work.

Occasionally you might find a senior leader looking for someone to mentor, as Maurine did in the story in this chapter, but generally you will have to make the move yourself. To find a mentor, begin by spending some time looking for someone with whom you feel a natural fit. Make a list of people who might make good mentors. These people do not necessarily need to be in your organization, but they should be in a position similar to the position you aspire to. Think about what to say when approaching a potential mentor. Speak to them and plan a short meeting. Focus on building a relationship first. If it looks like it will work out, agree to a schedule and stick to it. Show your appreciation for their assistance. Follow up after the meeting with an email thanking them for their time.

At a future meeting, you should discuss the tentative number of times the you will meet with the mentor, confidentiality, boundaries, expectations and termination. At your meetings, speak honestly about your goals. When he or she asks a challenging question, rise to the occasion, and don't back off. If you need time to think about it, be honest. Follow through with an answer at the next meeting. The U.S. Office of Personnel Management (2008) suggests other good topics to discuss:

- Managing conflict within the office or unit.
- Career progression.
- Networking.
- Influencing others.
- Managing politics in the office and organization.
- Newest trends in technology.
- Time management.
- Work/life balance.
- Leadership development (p. 12).

Maintain a healthy, professional relationship between you and your mentor, but make the relationship mutually beneficial—it's not just about you. Think about what you might offer them in return. I (Jeanne) once had a wonderful mentor who felt that performance appraisals were punitive, so he was uncomfortable and sometimes procrastinated on scheduling those meetings. While discussing it, I offered an alternative perspective that put a positive, developmental spin on appraisals. I could see him relax and smile, so I knew I had offered something valuable to him.

The first person on your list of potential mentors is not always the best possibility. It is acceptable to speak to more than one person until you find that potential mentor that is a good fit. Also, it may be necessary to find more than one mentor because some possible mentors can offer one type of knowledge and others are best at other types of knowledge. I have had several mentors over the years as my career evolved.

Beyond discussions, other methods of career development include shadowing the mentor on the job, then discussing the experience as part of a mentoring experience. A next step in developing skills and knowledge would have the mentor and his or her protégé (or mentee) work together doing leadership-level tasks such as writing grant applications, doing presentations, working with large donors, designing processes or organizational structure.

Some larger organizations have formal mentoring programs, but if not, you may need to take the initiative. Many potential leaders know in advance of being selected for mentorship that they are interested in leadership positions. It is up to them to determine what knowledge and skills they want to develop and to create a development action plan for themselves. This might include completing degree programs, taking training courses, attending conferences, reading books and seeking a mentor relationship.

TRY IT!

1. Take the change leadership skills self-assessment located online in eResources to assess your skills. Summarize strongest skills and weakest skills.
2. Imagine that you are a staff member working for an organization like Action Against Hunger USA or a similar organization. Select a larger nonprofit that interests you. They often list job opportunities with a job description. Research the organization. Locate information on a position that interests you, including their required qualifications and experience. Compare your skills (as assessed with the inventory) with those listed to see what skills you would need to develop for a job you find listed.
3. Create a leadership development action plan for yourself. State your goal and objectives, and create a list of action steps consistent with your goal. Later, you can reflect on how you are doing and revise the action plan if it isn't working. Your action plan should be no more than one page and no more than 10 actions.

SUMMARY

An initiative or an organization is sustainable when it can continue to work toward their vision and mission without depleting the resources that support it. To achieve change without regressing back to earlier behaviors, the practices of change initiatives must become integrated into mind-sets and behaviors rather than something added on top of all the other things people need to do. People involved need to believe in the benefits of the change to make a commitment to the new way of doing things. Because conditions are continually changing, the change initiative needs to be flexible enough to accommodate the new conditions. An organization or community group that plans to continue into the future will also need good leaders to renew the organization to meet changed conditions. This chapter covered creating a plan to develop future leaders that can manage as well as lead.

CITATIONS

Bolea, A., & Atwater, L. (2015). *Applied leadership development*. New York: Routledge.

Dyer, J., Gregersen, H., & Clayton Christensen, C. (2011). *The innovator's DNA: Mastering the five skills of disruptive innovators*. Brighton, MA: Harvard Business Review Press.

Harrison, J. P. (2010). Strategic planning and SWOT analysis. In J. P. Harrison (Ed.), *Essentials of strategic planning in healthcare* (2nd ed., pp. 91–97). Chicago, IL: Health Administration Press.

Lofquist, W. A. (1989). *The technology of prevention workbook*. Tucson, AZ: AYD Publications.

Schorr, L. (1997). *Common purpose: Strengthening families and neighborhoods to rebuild America* (1st Anchor Books ed.). New York: Anchor Books, Doubleday.

U.S. Office of Personnel Management. (2008). *Best practices: Mentoring*. Retrieved from www.opm.gov/policy-data-oversight/training-and-development/career-development/bestpractices-mentoring.pdf

EVALUATION

38

Figure 38.0

WHAT'S IN THIS CHAPTER?

Evaluation of any community development project begins when the team describes the project's framework for (1) what the endeavor is trying to accomplish (goals or desired outcomes for the short, intermediate or long term) and (2) how the project is going to accomplish the goals. A clear description of intention is necessary to keep the team on track and give them the satisfaction of seeing results. This description is also useful when a team applies for grant funding or seeks in-kind donations. When the team first describes "where we are now," they should have identified indicators and sources where they can obtain or collect valid baseline information (using methods such as interviews, observations or surveys). This data can be used as a starting point for their project, describing in detail "where are we now."

After project implementation, data can be obtained or collected again and compared to the original data to determine progress from the starting point toward their desired outcomes.

Objectives

By the end of this chapter, you will be able to:

- Create a list of steps to carry out your evaluation.
- Plan and implement an evaluation of the process or outcomes of your project.
- Locate existing data that will provide information for your desired outcomes.
- Describe observation checklists, surveys and interviews.

A STORY ABOUT EVALUATION

As a result of wars and turmoil on parts of the African continent, a large influx of new immigrants came to a midwestern community. As a way to ease the transition for the adults, a school district adult basic literacy program applied to a local community foundation for a grant to teach a customized adult English literacy program and help them integrate into the community. The main employers for many of the men were supportive of the program: they publicized it to employees and provided space for the after-work program. As usual, the granting agency required an evaluation plan for the grant application.

The plan was to use surveys or interviews after the program was delivered, and an advocate (a member of the immigrant community that had been in the midwestern community for a few years) was enlisted to help develop the program in a clear and culturally appropriate way. Mainly, the survey objectives were to ascertain the following:

- How satisfied were the project participants?
- Did participants' behaviors on the job change because of improved understanding and use of English?
- Did community-level indicators change for interactions with community support agencies (such as the local Social Security office or the local office of the state Division of Motor Vehicles)?

The first objective was appropriate for a survey or interview of the program participants, but the second and third objectives required personal travel to the workplaces and community support agencies that served the immigrants.

The school district was given the grant, and the project was developed with assistance of the immigrant community advocate and delivered to the immigrant men in an after-work program. A short survey in English was developed for program and tested by the community advocate with a few volunteers from the program. Generally, the survey directions and questions were clear, but one question was confusing to the advocate—a question asking about a critical incident. The question was revised using different words, but it was still confusing to the volunteers. That question was finally taken out of the survey and revised to ask the men during an *interview* in their first language to tell a story about a time they used English in an important situation. After several revisions, this question finally gave the program planners useful and trustworthy information that helped them revise the program for the next offering, and it satisfied the granting agency's evaluation requirement.

Lessons Learned:

- Language and culture have an impact on the choice of evaluation methods.
- Testing a survey for clarity to the actual respondents is an important step to make sure your data is trustworthy.

- Data collection tools such as interviews or surveys implemented in a language other than English should be translated accurately and in a culturally appropriate way. If it will be translated to another language, translate and back-translate (translate from the new language into English) to ensure accuracy.

WHAT THIS TECHNIQUE IS ABOUT

Planning and starting up a new initiative can be exciting and fun for the participants when things are going well. Later on, when the real work of executing the carefully laid plans begins, volunteers may begin heading for the exits, especially when difficulties arise. The obvious next step is to evaluate the progress on the plan and make course corrections. This step is sometimes ignored because of a "failure to communicate."

There are key times when data should be collected: at the beginning of a project, when assessing needs, opportunities or readiness and when you need to gauge progress. This does not necessarily mean when the project ends, but it might be when a funder or sponsor requires evaluation data on the effectiveness of a project. There are two kinds of evaluation:

- **Formative** evaluation is evaluation conducted at a formative stage before implementation for the purpose of improving the project, including: (1) learning what processes work, and (2) improving how things get done.
- **Summative** or confirmative evaluation is evaluation conducted following the project to make judgments about the effectiveness, sustainability and impact of outcomes, including: (1) discerning the effects of the project with individuals who participate, and (2) discerning the effects of the project on the community.

Ideally, the project should use both types of evaluation using the indicators selected early in the process. It is also useful to examine and evaluate the processes of planning and implementation as well.

HOW TO CARRY OUT THIS TECHNIQUE

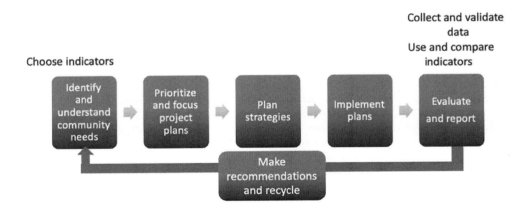

Figure 38.1 Evaluation process.

WHO SHOULD BE INVOLVED?

To collect and analyze evaluation data, you should involve stakeholders, including those directly impacted by the project. In the case of the story in this chapter, language was clearly a barrier to involving the adult language learners before they completed the program, so the community advocate was asked to help plan and write the evaluation questions and assist with testing the survey and interview until they were clear to all the people who would respond.

WRITE THE QUESTIONS

The next step is to determine what questions you need answered. To evaluate outcomes, you want to write questions for your survey or interview that address the indicators selected when envisioning your desired outcomes early in the project (Kim, 2016). For instance:

- How many people were aware of the project?
- How satisfied are project participants?
- How many people were served?
- Did behaviors of participants change?
- Did community-level indicators change? (Examples of community-level indicators include crime rates, homelessness, number of people living in group quarters, age of the population, enrollment in public schools, primary home language, family income levels, poverty levels or unemployment levels.)

SELECT THE DATA COLLECTION METHOD

After you know what information you need, select data collection methods. For instance:

- Surveys about satisfaction and importance of the project.
- Interviews with key participants.
- Observations of behavior and environmental conditions.

More information on each of these methods is found in this section, and in Appendix E in eResources.

The next step is to do some research to identify instruments (surveys, interview guides or observation checklists) similar to what you want to create. These can be used as guides to write your survey. Many surveys are available online for adult literacy programs, so the project designed in the story had several good guides that were used to develop and customize their evaluation survey and interview questions. (See Appendix E for more guidelines for writing survey questions.)

Data collected for any part of your project must have four qualities. (1) It must be **useful** to the decisions your project team must make. (2) Considering the availability of resources and time, the data collection needs to be **feasible**. (3) The data collection and analysis need to be conducted ethically, lawfully and with sensitivity that it is acceptable by the individuals and organizations involved, so it must be done with **propriety**. (4) Finally, the information needs to be **accurate**, so that you collect the data you need, and the instrument would produce consistently accurate information (Anderson, 2010). One of the most challenging part of data collection is to create accurate instruments. An instrument is accurate when all users understand the questions in the same way, so clarity is extremely important. The information in the following paragraphs will help you write an accurate survey, interview guide or observation checklist.

Surveys

A **survey** is a data-gathering instrument in which survey takers answer questions by selecting a choice or answering in writing. Surveys can be used in a change evaluation to find out about satisfaction and importance of the project and process. Survey items begin with the questions you want to have answered. They may gather facts as perceived by the people taking the survey, or they may ask for opinions, beliefs or attitudes. While surveys are frequently used, they are sometimes poorly written, making survey results untrustworthy.

Whether you hand surveys to people, mail them or use web surveys, there are things that need to be explained verbally or in a cover letter or directions. (1) Explain survey purpose and importance, and help the respondent feel that the study is significant. (2) Mention the value of the information that the survey taker can provide. (3) Offer to send results. (4) State the length of time the survey will take to complete. You will know this because you tested the survey. (5) Assure the survey taker that their individual answers will be kept private. The information will be shared only as compiled information. (6) If the survey is mailed, request a return date (mailing time plus one week). If the survey taker is invited by email with a link to an online survey, tell the survey taker when the survey will close. (7) Thank the respondent.

Interviews

Interviews with key participants are another possible option for collecting evaluation data. Many people would rather talk than write, and a good interviewer can establish a relationship and gather information that the person being interviewed may not want to put in writing. This is especially true for sensitive topics. Keep in mind that some topics are sensitive in some cultures, but not others. When asking about sensitive topics, interviewers must be chosen carefully. In some cases, a woman may be a better choice for interviewer when interviewing women, and men more appropriate to interview men. Race, culture, nationality or ethnicity, or class identity may also be considered when selecting interviewers. In the story in this chapter, the immigrant community advocate carried out the interviews in the first language of the interviewees.

Sometimes interviews may work better than surveys because both the interviewer and the person interviewed can probe or ask questions to clarify the question or answer. If your project benefits young children, those who do not read and write well, or people with visual impairments, an interview may be the only way to collect the information. If you collect data from children, you *must* get parents' permission.

Interview question development and testing follows many of the same procedures as developing a survey. Instead of creating survey questions, however, you will create an *interview guide* which includes notes or a script for explaining the interview purpose and directions and the questions. If a team will be involved with collecting interview data, each of the interviewers should interview in the same way. More information on creating and administering interviews is available in Appendix E.

Data can also be collected from small groups in interviews. Questions are asked in a group setting where participants interact with other group members. This method can generate many ideas through interaction of group members and may allow the synthesis of many ideas.

With the permission of the people being interviewed, audio or video recordings may be made of the interviews to make sure the data was recorded by the interviewer accurately.

Observations

Data about behaviors or environmental conditions can be collected using an observation checklist (Harvey, 2013). A checklist is a list of things that an observer is going to look for when observing behaviors or environments. It is useful to help the observer remember what to look for. All observers will need to evaluate in the same way, using the same definitions. A training session or discussion of examples done before collecting the data will help all observers to evaluate consistently.

A community group was concerned about safe play areas for children. They created a checklist (shown in Table 38.1) with definitions which all volunteer observers agreed to use. This checklist was designed to be used at the outset of the project to help inform "what's happening now," and for an evaluation

Table 38.1 Playground observation checklist.

Playground checklist	Yes	No	Comments
Does playground equipment appear to be in good repair? (Free from broken parts, corrosion or rust)			
Is equipment free of vandalism? (Graffiti or damage)			
Are there protective surfaces under play equipment? (Acceptable: rubber mats or poured rubber, wood chips or rubber mulch at least 9 inches deep, pea gravel/play sand. Not acceptable: concrete, blacktop, packed earth, grass)			
Are all sharp corners, edges or points covered to protect children?			
Are all moving parts covered to avoid hazards to children? (including pinch points)			
Is playground free from litter?			
Are there fences along busy streets? Proper openings in playground equipment are small enough to avoid body or head entrapment.			
Guard rails are located and in good repair on all elevated surfaces (Avoids gaps or similar hazards).			
Avoids entanglement hazards (such as gaps or protrusions that could catch children's clothing)			

of outcomes at the conclusion of the project. Each volunteer went to a designated community park to observe and record the conditions of the playground. In the initial assessment, they were also encouraged to take snapshots to document serious problems.

When observing behaviors, you can record what people actually do or say, rather than what they say they do. You thereby avoid people's desire to look good (or bad) to others and also their tendency to forget what actually happened. In Appendix E (found in eResources online) you will find details on making observations.

Archival Records

Archival records with data on community concerns are often available. Records might be in the form of paper or electronic documents, or other media, and may be in the form of numbers (quantitative information about how many, how much or how often) or non-numerical or qualitative information. Qualitative data is about attributes, characteristics, properties of things. They are not limited to verbal or textual records; images or video records can also be informative. Information from archival records can be analyzed to identify patterns or trends over time and used to *verify findings* from other data sources and methods such as surveys or interviews.

Look for archival data sources for information that can address your assessment and evaluation questions. There are many forms of archival data, often collected and compiled yearly. This data can be used initially as part of an assessment of needs, and later, subsequent data can be used for evaluation by comparing to the earlier data. Archival can be found at governmental, commercial and nonprofit websites, such as:

- U.S. government data.
- State data.
- Larger city websites.
- Hospital, universities and nonprofit organizations.

U.S. government data available on websites include information from the U.S. Census Bureau such as the American Community Survey, general population and housing characteristics (population, age, sex, race, households and housing, etc.); population by race and Hispanic or Latino origin; Hispanic or Latino by type (Mexican, Puerto Rican, etc.); households and families (relationships, children, household size, etc.).

From the Bureau of Labor Statistics, information can be found such as state and local employment and unemployment; state and county wages; worker health and safety statistics; and wages by area and occupation. The U.S. Department of Justice has information such as asylum statistics, juvenile crime statistics, gang statistics, violence against women and environmental crimes.

Examples of data that can be located at the state level include Department of Education educational attainment by district, Demographic Center population counts and projections by county and Department of Health statistics on diseases and conditions.

Larger city websites often include data on population, housing, income, age, education, race and ethnicity. Statistics may also be found at www.city-data.com.

Hospitals, universities and nonprofit organizations may also provide reports appropriate to their mission that can be useful to your evaluation. Validate archival data by comparing it with community data such as the information collected with your survey.

TEST THE SURVEY, INTERVIEW OR OBSERVATION FORM

After a draft of the survey or interview questions is complete, ask a couple of members of the population you will be serving to review the questions and make sure they are clear. If the target population is not readily available, like homeless people who change locations frequently, ask for their help in formulating survey questions when they come for the services you are offering. This is a key step when the survey will go to people who speak English as a second language. Using the resulting information, revise your survey or interview questions and directions for clarity.

If you will be using an observation form, test that with the users to make sure it is clear to everyone, and they interpret the firm items in the same way.

PREPARE TO ANALYZE THE DATA

After the data is collected, you will need to make sense of it. It is best to prepare for analysis as soon as you create the questions, long before collecting the data. If you use a survey creation web page, the data might be placed into a spreadsheet, or it may be tabulated for you and placed in graphs. For reporting purposes, community members are generally familiar with reading graphs such as:

- Pie charts.
- Horizontal or vertical bar graphs.
- Line graphs.

If you will have survey or interview comments to analyze, plan to read interviews multiple times to become familiar with your data. Then you will use thematic content analysis to find common patterns across a data set (collection of data). Code or label the text, classifying the information. These choices are directed by your original questions, by your indicators, by input from stakeholders and by the data available. Search for themes with broader patterns of meaning, then review themes to make sure they fit the data. Name the themes and write up a coherent narrative that includes quotes from the survey respondents or interviewees.

COLLECT AND ANALYZE YOUR DATA

After you have decided how your data will be analyzed, your survey or interview is ready. Collect and analyze the data according to your plans.

If you used more than one method of data collection, such as a survey and interviews, compare the results. If results from both methods say the same thing, you can trust the results. If they contradict each other, you may need to look for reasons why. As your project progresses, keep your eyes open for indicators you hadn't thought of. For instance, a project focused on neighborhood safety may have identified a reduction in police calls to the neighborhood, but a consequence of increased safety that the project planners later noticed was that pizza places now delivered to the neighborhood.

REPORT RESULTS

Organize your data to create a picture of the project results. The final step to evaluating a project is to report results and make recommendations. There are multiple ways to report results. One method is a *formal written report*. This may be needed if your project has used grant money or has sponsors. Many community-wide projects *present a report* to a city council or they may call a *community meeting* (Fawcett et al., 1995). If it will be shared with community members, it should be easy to display, explain and defend. If your results are quite positive, creation of a *press release* and sharing it with local media is also a possibility.

If this evaluation is done formatively (conducted at an early or formative stage during implementation), then the next step is to use the information you have learned to revise the project implementation as needed and continue the implementation process.

TRY IT!

Imagine that you are on the project team for the safe play areas project. What kind of data collection method would you use besides observation? Why? List steps that would you take to develop your evaluation, collect data, analyze it and report it.

SUMMARY

This chapter covered methods and steps to carry out your evaluation, and introduced observation checklists, surveys and interviews. It also provided suggestions for locating archival data related to your desired outcome indicators.

CITATIONS

Anderson, J. L. H. (2010). Collecting analysis data. In K. H. Silber & R. Foshay (Eds.), *Handbook of training and improving workplace performance* (Vol. 1, pp. 95–143). San Francisco, CA: John Wiley & Sons.

Fawcett, S., Francisco, V., Paine-Andrews, A., Lewis, R., Richter, K., Harris, K., Williams, E. L., Berkley, J. Y., Schultz, J. A., Fisher, J. L., Lopez, C. M. (1995). *Work group evaluation handbook: Evaluating and supporting community initiatives for health and development*. Work Group on Health Promotion and Community Development. Kansas: University of Kansas. Retrieved from https://ctb.ku.edu/sites/default/files/chapter_files/work_group_evaluation_handbook_2.pdf

Harvey, L. K., DiLuca, K. L., Hefner, K., Frabutt, J. M., & Shelton, T. L. (2013). Systematic observations of neighborhood order: Assessing the methodology in evaluating community-based initiative. *Journal of Applied Social Science*, 7(1), 42–60.

Kim, Y. (2016). *Community wellbeing indicators and the history of beyond GDP* (Research & Policy Brief, 73). Cornell University's Community & Regional Development Institute. Retrieved from https://cardi.cals.cornell.edu/sites/cardi.cals.cornell.edu/files/shared/PolicyBriefJune-16_draft5.pdf

39 DISENGAGEMENT
It's Been Nice, but I Really Must Be Going

Figure 39.0

WHAT'S IN THIS CHAPTER?

Facilitators and leaders can be most effective at facilitation when they stand apart and objectively observe the action. Staying neutral or disengaged is necessary for facilitators because they have the responsibility to guide their community or team to make wise decisions to create changes that they accept, commit to and implement. Effective facilitators don't take participants' behaviors personally or try to achieve their own ends. They simply try to help the team or community successfully make the changes necessary.

Secondly, a facilitator needs to know when to walk out and close the door. The ego of a leader or facilitator can get easily engaged, and then it may be hard to let go, but it is essential to the health of an organization. A formal disengagement reduces the risks of ongoing *scope creep* (continuous or uncontrolled growth or changes in a project's scope) and reduces the ongoing labor of the person facilitating. A formal exit meeting is useful to learn effectively from the process and to create closure so that the next leader or facilitator can begin with a clean slate.

Objectives

By the end of this chapter, you will be able to:

- Describe how and when to step aside as a facilitator.
- What plans to make for the exit of a facilitator.
- What needs to take place at the exit meeting.

A STORY ABOUT DISENGAGING FROM THE ACTION

One example of this behavior of over-engagement is found in the story of the *Elephant in the Living Room* where the leader had brilliantly established a global peace organization but nearly destroyed it with his egocentricity. By declaring himself to be the sole founder, he insulted many other volunteers who were equally important in the founding story. They eventually left the group, quietly and angrily, because their gifts of time and talent were never fully acknowledged. The absence of team member involvement in planning, discussion of concerns and appreciation underlaid the difficulties.

Some people are good at starting new ventures but not at managing them: The founder's ego attachment nearly crashed the organization when he could not recognize that he was the wrong person for the management job. He had not learned this important lesson: there comes a time to stop participating in gatherings or activities and move on. Another way to say it, is "*Well, it's been fun, folks, but it's time for me to cash in my chips.*"

WHAT THIS TECHNIQUE IS ABOUT

As mentioned earlier in this book, a facilitator sets the stage for disengagement early in the project. At the beginning of your engagement with any group, the facilitator needs to pose some questions:

- What is your relationship to the group? Leader or facilitator, or group member?
- Are you being paid or just volunteering as a facilitator?
- What is your timeline for leaving the group, and under what conditions?
- Will your departure harm the progress of the project, or give an opening for new leadership?
- Do you have a plan for passing the baton? How are you preparing new leaders?
- Is there a post-project role for you?

Sometimes you will need to be in the role of a leader "for the long haul" until the bumps are all worked out. Training and transferring skills do take some time in order to build confidence and competence within the organization. However, there is always a terminus to engagement, and eventually the role of leader/facilitator will be passed on to the next leader. Going back to our original metaphor of riding on a train, the conductor eventually trades places with a new one coming on duty. How are you preparing yourself and the organization for the moment when your role will be ending?

There are several ways to view your role as a facilitator. You can pick which one fits your personality. There really is no one-size-fits-all for this pattern.

Mentor—a person who is a model for leadership and serves primarily in the role of developer of new leaders or guides to the active leadership.

Midwife—a person who assists with the "laboring" of a new idea or assisting when a group is in deep conflict. This role is short term and deals mainly with conflict situations that need a cool-headed person to intervene with subtlety and then leave when the work has been accomplished.

Guide from the side—a wise counsel whose advice is sought by the current leadership without being actively engaged in a leadership role. This person can also serve as a mentor if requested.

Expert—an outside person who has knowledge and experience that is useful from a technical standpoint.

Institutional memory—someone who has "been there and done that" in an organization and carries a timeline in his mind of what has happened before but is no longer an active leader. This person can be very helpful to advise the newcomer who arrives in the third act of the play and thinks they know about acts one and two.

Servant leader—set of practices that enriches the lives of individuals, builds better organizations and ultimately creates a more just and caring world (Greenleaf & Spears, 2002).

One role to avoid is:

Meddler—someone who has officially left the leadership role but lurks in the background, advising or controlling the action. This person has not fully disengaged and can cause trouble for the new leaders.

A facilitator's role includes encouraging action, providing ideas and support, and enabling participants to succeed. How and why does a facilitator gracefully exit from the facilitation role? The answer to this question depends on the goals and objectives for facilitation *established at the beginning of the facilitator's participation* in the project. Planning prior to facilitator participation is important to an exit that leaves a project with new leadership and the organization healthy and sustainable (Hormozi, McMinn, & Nzeogwu, 2000). This planning should involve team members in the decision-making process for ending the facilitator's role at the appropriate time and preparing new leadership (Ford, Krahn, Wise, & Oliver, 2011; Harrigan, Fauri, & Netting, 1998; Keyton, 1993). This team participation increases team member loyalty and commitment, which leads to sustainability of the change (Ford et al., 2011; Harrigan et al., 1998; Keyton, 1993; Looney, Shaw, & Crabtree, 2011).

WHEN TO STEP ASIDE

A facilitator needs to recognize when it is time to step aside. There are three points in which stepping aside is necessary:

- Temporarily, when *expressing a personal opinion*—Let team members know that you will take off your facilitator (neutral) hat for a moment to express a personal opinion. This should happen infrequently and be very brief.

- When the facilitator finds it *impossible to remain neutral*, open and objective during meetings. There is a big difference between facilitating and excessive psychological reliance on someone by others. At this point, you must leave to allow someone who can remain neutral to step in.
- When the objectives agreed upon at the beginning of the *project have been accomplished*. Be prepared to demonstrate success—you have improved your client's situation. The agreement to serve as a facilitator should include measures of progress and success (Janich, 2016).

HOW TO CARRY OUT THIS TECHNIQUE

How to Step Aside

Long before the exit of a facilitator, plans need to be laid for sustaining of the project efforts. People should be selected who are open to coaching and will continue their efforts after the facilitator is gone. The facilitator can coach these apprentice facilitators on how to conduct effective meetings and how to support collective efforts at continuing the change efforts so that the positive results are maintained.

All team members should be aware of the facilitator's approaching exit, and they may even be included in that decision. There should be a formal exit meeting planned, including a discussion of concerns, the process, challenges, difficulties, recommendations for the future and appreciation for the work done and accomplishments of facilitator and team. Consider some sort of celebration.

WHEN OBJECTIVES ARE COMPLETE

Agree to the goals and measures of success for facilitation at the *beginning* of the facilitator's participation in the project.

As part of the planning early in the process, make plans for sustainability of the organization or the project. New facilitation or leadership is one piece of the sustainability. The team should plan for guidance, support and teaching of the new facilitator/leader when needed. This may include interpersonal skills, process improvement, problem-solving, team building, data analysis, advocacy for the organization and its mission, fundraising and financial management.

FORMAL EXIT MEETING

At the concluding meeting(s) when the facilitator will be stepping down, a formal meeting with team members allows for closure and learning. Concerns and appreciation should be expressed, and accomplishments and outcomes of the project should be communicated during a review (Keyton, 1993; Hormozi et al., 2000; Looney et al., 2011). It is particularly important for leadership to express appreciation and reward accomplishments of the team, enhancing motivation (Looney et al., 2011). Team discussion and review of the process, accomplishments and challenges allows teams to learn from their experiences, enhancing learning that can apply to future efforts.

Decide who needs to be at the meeting that has a high stake in the results. Before planning the agenda, think about what you as a facilitator need from the meeting. Also, ask the team what they want from the meeting and be sure to include those important items. Allow sufficient time for discussion.

Plan your feedback to the team, making it non-evaluative and descriptive. Identify elements of feedback that could possibly trigger defensiveness and consider what form it would take to avoid difficulty. Determine how can you ask for feedback on how the facilitation went. If there is resistance to speak on the part of any attendees, consider how can you get it *expressed*.

THE AGENDA

There are some topics that *must* be covered in the final meeting. Create an agenda including the following:

- Discuss the outcomes, using evaluation data. What were the accomplishments and challenges?
- What was the final understanding of the problem cause or solution? Was this different from the team's initial recommendations?
- What were the final costs and/or cost per beneficiary?
- Was there resistance from the community? What form? How was it addressed?
- What would you do differently next time? What recommendations should be made for the future.
- Give feedback to the team on the process and how they managed the project. Tell them what they did to make it a good project
- Ask for feedback on the process. Ask the team what you did to make it a good project.
- Celebrate your successes.

FINAL WRITTEN REPORT

Lastly, facilitators that are completing their tenure should be encouraged to provide written documentation summarizing successes, difficulties and recommendations for the team, following the exit meeting (Looney et al., 2011). This report can help support the team efforts at implementation because members often forget verbal comments (Thor et al., 2004). Feedback can also be welcome to an organization's leadership where they are not members of the change team, such as overseeing entities.

REFLECTION FOR CONTINUED PROFESSIONAL DEVELOPMENT

At the exit point, the facilitator can also review, reflect and learn from the process as an individual (Block, 2000). Neil Thompson, in his book *People Skills* (2015), suggests that there are six steps to using reflection to improve your work: reading, asking, watching others, paying attention to your feelings, talking to others about your experiences and thinking about your work. While Thompson was not writing specifically about facilitation, his steps apply:

1. *Read*—about methods of facilitation, change and related topics you want to learn more about and skills you want to develop.
2. *Ask*—other facilitators about the way they do things and why those things work.
3. *Watch*—what other facilitators do to learn from them.
4. *Feel*—pay attention to your emotions, what elicits them, and how you deal with them. What works, and what doesn't?
5. *Talk*—share your experiences with others doing the same work and learn from one another.
6. *Think*—take time to think about your facilitation and how to improve it.

This process allows you to look at your ideas in new ways in order to learn from the experience and revise what you do to become more effective.

TRY IT!

Imagine that you have served as facilitator of the Hunger-free St. Michael team. Your service will be complete within the next three months.

1. Make a plan for the mentoring of the next leader. Include the list of topics.
2. Create an agenda for the exit meeting.
3. Write an outline for the final report.

SUMMARY

This chapter covered the process of disengagement from a project by the facilitator. It described how and when to step aside as a facilitator, what plans to make for the time when the facilitator disengages and what needs to take place at the exit meeting.

CITATIONS

Block, P. (2000). *Flawless consulting: A guide to getting your expertise used*. San Francisco, CA: John Wiley & Sons.

Ford, J. H., II, Krahn, D., Wise, M., & Oliver, K. A. (2011). Measuring sustainability within the Veterans' Administration mental health system redesign initiative. *Quality Management in Health Care, 20*(4), 263–279. doi:10.1097/QMH.0b013e3182314b20

Greenleaf, R. K., & Spears, L. C. (2002). *Servant leadership: A journey into the nature of legitimate power and greatness*. New York: Paulist Press.

Harrigan, M. P., Fauri, D. P., & Netting, F. E. (1998). Termination: Extending the concept for macro social work practice. *Journal of Sociology and Social Welfare, 25*(4), 61–80.

Hormozi, A. M., McMinn, R. D., & Nzeogwu, O. (2000). The project life cycle: The termination phase. *S.A.M. Advanced Management Journal, 65*(1), 45–51.

Janich, N. (2016). Facilitator withdrawal from organizational change initiatives. *Group Facilitation, 13*, 43–55.

Keyton, J. (1993). Group termination: Completing the study of group development. *Small Group Research, 24*(1), 84–100.

Looney, J. A., Shaw, E. K., & Crabtree, B. F. (2011). Passing the baton: Sustaining organizational change after the facilitator leaves. *Group Facilitation: A Research and Applications Journal, 11*, 15–23.

Thompson, N. (2015). *People skills* (4th ed.). New York: Red Globe Press.

Thor, J., Wittlöv, K., Herrlin, B., Brommels, M., Svensson, O., Skar, J., & Ovretveit, J. (2004). Learning helpers: How they facilitated improvement and improved facilitation—Lessons from a hospital-wide quality improvement initiative. *Quality Management in Health Care, 13*(1), 60–74.

INDEX

Note: Page numbers in *italic* indicate a figure and page numbers in **bold** indicate a table on the corresponding page.

3Rs project (Reading Reduces Recidivism) 106, 296–297
5 whys approach to cause analysis 74

abstract, grant 187–188
Academy for Co-Teaching & Collaboration 145
acceptance of change 100
accessibility, improving 307–308
accountability 183–184, *184*, 189–190; communications 273; creating by monitoring changes continuously 168
accurate, quality of data collected 342
acting quickly, perceived need for 65
action planning 5
actions, meeting 218–219
action steps 114; in change process 320, *320*; in gauging process *112*
activity traps 16–17, 64, *64*, 118
ADA Standards for Accessible Design 308
advertising, relative impact of word of mouth *versus* 274, *274*
African American Museum 155
agenda: city council meetings 136; creating for meetings 32, 34; final exit meeting 352; meeting planning 217; opening meeting 218; for visioning meeting 86
agreements: alliance/collaboration 199–200; meeting 218–219
alliances 194–202; agreement or compact 199–200; bridging cultural, social and community values 198–199, 201; building community 199–200; due diligence 197; formative evaluation 200; fundraising as an alliance 198; how to carry out technique 200–201; integration, level of 197, *197*; maintaining 199; with outside organizations *196*, 196–198; resources 201–202; strategic 194, 198
allies for awareness-building and information-sharing 155
ambiguity 83, 223
American Community Survey 145, 345
Amiable communication style 208–209, *209*, **209**, 211
Analytical communication style 209, *209*, **209**, 211

anchoring **25**
Angel in the Night (play) 37
answers, responding to 242
appeasement 248
archival records 345
Arenas of Action framework 119, 120, *120*; example of use 122; quadrants of *120*, 121–122
asking good questions 235–245
assessment of the situation 82
attitude learning 290
attitudes: spectrum of 67–71, *69*; story about attitudes toward beneficiaries of change 68
autonomy, volunteering and 42, *42*
Avenue of the Righteous 37, 185, 198
awareness: change readiness and 100; dialogue that raises 279; raising in fundraising campaign 185

balance, changing 125–126
barriers to change, removing 323
beginning a change 3–9
behaviors: communications for public behaviors that others will emulate 277; facilitator responses to participant **233**; of others, predicting 206
beneficiaries of change: as resources 157; spectrum of attitudes toward 68–71, *69*; steps in change adoption 134, *134*; story about attitudes toward 68
benefits, analysis of 264–265
Berger, Jonah 274
bias: common and strategy for reducing **25**; confirmation 64; definition 24; explicit **25**; implicit 25–26; journaling buttons and biases 24–27; as listening barrier 224; observer 64; social biases 25–26
Blake, Robert 119–120
blame, avoiding 17–18
blind spot 52
blind-spotting 248
board members: accountability 189; donations by 186; fundraising 180–181, 185–187
body language 143, 226, 231–232, 234

boundaries 86, 87
brain switching 83
brainstorming: alliances/collaborations 200–201; card storm process 52; community support 312; contributing factors and causes 109, 114; fundraising and 180, 185; gathering the wisdom of the group 86–88, *87*; identifying play and players in community 135; methods 87–88; policy change 299; prison library example 108, *109*; reverse 88; strategies 167, 169–170; team culture discussion 217; visioning 85, 86–88, *87*; what's happening now? *73*, 73–74, *76*
brainwriting 88
brochures 278–279, *278*, 314
Brown v. Board of Education 330
budget 266–268
Bureau of Labor Statistics 345
buttons 24
by-product 113

capacity building 140, 143
card storm process 52
cause analysis: 5 whys approach to 74; root cause analysis 109
causes: brainstorming what's happening now *73*, 74, *109*; in gauging process *112*; matching solutions to 265, **266–267**; in prison library brainstorming example 108, *109*; reducing multiple 119; root 74–75, *75*, 109, 240; symptoms differentiated from 240
CBPR (Community-Based Participatory Research) 138, 142
change: getting people ready for 320; incremental 93–94; individuals and 95–96, *95–96*; opposition 98; resistance 95, *96*, 96–97, 100; timeline *99*, 99–100; transformative 93–95, *94*; types of 93–95
change adoption: steps in 134, *134*; timeline 97, *97*
change commitment timeline *99*, 99–100, *331*
change cycle: ideal individual 95, *95*; individual with resistance 95, *96*
"Change Leadership Skills Self-Assessment" 334
change management 321–324; *see also* managing change
change process 320; data collection points in *147*; drawings of 60–62; questions through 239–241, *240*, 243; what's happening now? 320
change process model, Lewin's 60
change readiness 91–103; analyzing qualitative data from interviews or surveys 101; assessing 98–99, 101–102; elements of 98–99; interviews 101–102; levels of 100; making plans 100–101; opposition 98; story about 92–93; SWOT analysis 158, 161
change team 26, 30–32, 73–74, 78, 87–89, 101, 120, 132–136, 146–148, 160, 174–175, 203, 220, 230, 321–322, 330, 335, 352; attitudes 68, 70; change readiness 95–96, 100–101, 103; creating

belonging 227; definition 31; recharging stuck 88; volunteers 36
changing conditions: community development principle 7, 31, *31*; in gauging process *112*
choreography: of conversation 203–213; definition of 204
clarifying questions 226–227
clarifying the issue/problem 105–106; action steps 114; contributing factors 109; fishbone diagram 109–111, *110–111*, 114–115; gauging process 111–112, *112*; hypothesis 107–108; hypothesis testing 113–115; indicators 110–113; searching for data on indicators 112; story about reading in prison 106; technique description 106–107
clearing mental space for facilitation 26, 46–49; mindfulness 48–49; story about 47–48; technique 48
clear the space 21–22, 86
close-ended questions 239
coaching 292, **293**
coalitions 297, 299, 305, 312–314
coding data 102
cognitive biases 24–25, **25**
collaboration 194–202; agreement or compact 199–200; alliances with outside organizations *196*, 196–198; bridging cultural, social and community values 198–199, 201; building community 199–200; due diligence 197; factors leading to effective 141–142, *142*; formative evaluation 200; goals 196; how to carry out technique 200–201; methods of 199–200; reasons for 141–142; resources 201–202; structure creation in arrangement 197; sustaining partnerships 144–145; *see also* partnerships
Columbo (TV series) 131
commitment, change readiness and 100–101
common ground, finding 207–208
common purpose, creating sense of 54
communication planning template 281, **281**
communications 271–282; about support group 314; across cultures 231; breaking up tensions in a group 209–210; change readiness and 101; choreography of conversation 203–213; demonstrating accountability and stewardship 189–191, **190**; with donors 189–191, **190**; evaluating 280; meta-message 206–207, 206–208; in partnerships 144; personal emissary work 272–274; physical environment change 307; plan to raise awareness and encourage participation 273; policy change 299–300; poor 254; in print and visuals 278–279; for public behaviors that others will emulate 277; reporting results 279–280; sharing ideas and stories 277; in social and other media 279; stewardship **190**; stories in local news media 277–278; story about 204–205; story about communications as a strategy 272–273; technique description 273; word-of-mouth *274*, 274–276
communication styles 208–209, *209*, **209**, 211

community: general description of 133–134; identifying culture and values 132–134; identifying the play and the players in a community 130–137; overlapping 132, *133*
community change: beginning of initiatives 3–9; reflection, observation, and wonder 10–14
community description 136
community development 257, 257–325; choosing and developing a solution 259–270; communications 271–282; conflict role in 249; definition of 5–6, 11; framework 5–6; gauging progress in *319*; monitoring and managing change 317–325; physical environment 303–308; policy change 295–302; programs 283–294; as radical method 6; strategies, examples of 167; support 309–316
community development principles: changing conditions 7, 31, *31*; participation 6, 31; responsibility 7, 31
community identity 142
Community Police Officer 68
community problem-solving 122
community readiness 98–99; analyzing qualitative data from interviews or surveys 101; assessing 98–99, 101–102; components of 98–99; definition 94; interviews 101–102; levels of 100; making plans 100–101; for policy change 299
community strengths 142
community support *see* support
Community-Based Participatory Research (CBPR) 138, 142
concept plan 306
conditions, focus on 7, 120
confirmation bias **25**, 64
confirmative evaluation 341
conflict 246–255; addressing in healthy way 249–250; avoidance behaviors 248; how to carry out techniques 251; issues that can cause 250–251; poor communication 254; resolutions 251–252, *252*; role in community development 249; situational blindness 252–254; story about 247–248; team 250–251; technique description 249; what's happening now? 248
connection, sense of *225*, 227
consensus: building with I-to-We thinking 53, 54, *55*; root cause analysis 74; used as methodology for team building 51; on vision 89
conservatism bias **25**
constraints **268**, 306, **307**
context: for instruction 290–291; partnerships and 145
continuous improvement model of development 60, *61*
contributing factors 109, *112*
conversation facilitation 203–213; breaking up tensions in a group 209–210; communication styles 208–209, *209*, **209**, **211**; cues 207; cutting in 205; dance metaphor 204–207; facilitation observation practice 212–213; finding common ground 207–208; how to carry out the technique 210–211;

observation and reflection 206–207; technique description 205
Conversation for Race Unity *see* Race Unity
conversations, for identifying play and players in community 136
cooperative overlapping 208, 210
core group 29–31
cost-benefit analysis 264–265, 299
creativity, visioning and 83, *84*
credibility 262, 300–301
cues: nonverbal 206; taking from facilitator 207; verbal 207; visual 207
cultural issues: accommodating meeting attendees 216; communications across 231; eye contact *225*, 225–226, 231; gestures 226, 231; private recognition 322
cultural liaison 200
curriculum-based meeting format 314
Customer Relations Management (CRM) software 191
cutting in 205

Dalio, Ray 12
dance metaphor 204–207
data: demographics, local 145; graphs 346; key times for collection 341; local 18, 111, 113–114, 138–141, 145, 148; preparing to analyze 346; qualities of collected 342; searching for data on indicators 112
data analysis 146–148, *148*
data collection 138–149; acquiring research partners 143–144; in change process *147*; collaboration, reasons for 141–142; community-based participatory 141; conducting participatory data gathering and evaluation 145; how to carry out the technique 148; local 140–141; sharing findings and decisions with the team 146–148; sharing findings with the community 148; story about 139–140
data collection methods: archival records 345; interviews 343; observations 343–345, **344**; selecting 342–345; surveys 342–343
daydream 88, 148
debriefing 27
decision-making: accountability and use of financial data for *184*; in alliance/collaboration 199–200; team decision process 263; top-down 247
decisions, at meetings 218–219
deep listening 22–23, 195, 222–228, *225*; barriers to 224; components of 224–227, *227*; how to carry out the technique 227; interpersonal level *225*; intrapersonal level *225*; overview 222–223; story about 223; technique description 224
deep thinking 23
defining problems 106, 108, 114–115, 296, 298, 301, **302**
demographics 145, 345
denial 96, 100

design: of change strategies 159, *159–160*; solution creation 265
design charrette 88
desired outcomes 73, 74, *75*; analyzing qualitative data from interviews or surveys 101; change management 322; in change process 320, *320*; creating a vision of 83, 86; envisioning 298; in gauging process *112*; indicators of 240–241; for monitoring change 319, *319*; physical environment change 306; policy change 298–299; support group 313
detours 15–18
development: definition of 5; process characteristics 6; solution creation 265
disabled participant meeting accommodation 216
disengagement 348–353; final written report 352; formal exit meeting 351–352; how to carry out the technique 351; how to step aside 351; reflection for continued professional development 352; story about 349; technique description 349; when to step aside 350–351
disruption, change readiness and 100
distractions 206, 219, 224
doing for others 69, 70
doing it with others 69, 70
doing to others 69, 70
donations 178–179; by board members 186; conducting meetings seeking 185–186; individual giving *180*, 180–181; in-kind 182, 187; *see also* fundraising
donor pyramid *185*
donor stewardship 181, 183–184, 190, **191**
donors: accountability to 184; communications with 189–191, **190**; cultivating relationships with 181; objections of, managing 186; recurring 184, *185*
dreaming 22, 85, 88
dream team, creating your own 51–53
Driver communication style 208, *209*, **209, 211**
drivers 126, 274–275
due diligence 197
Dunkel, Kara 310–311

elders, accommodating meeting attendees 32, **33**, 216
Elements of Change (Lofquist) 72, *75*
elephant in the living room 247–249
emotional distractions 219
emotions, word-of-mouth promotion and 275
energy: draining of 17; re-energizing a stalled project 17–18
engagement, participant 230, 232, **233**
environmental concept plan template **307**
episodic volunteering 39, 41
equilibrium, upsetting 125
escalated resolution process 252, *252*
ethics 199
evaluation 339–347; collecting and analyzing your data 346; of communications 280; formative 341; how to carry out the technique 341; involved parties in 342; of policy change 301; preparing to analyze data 346; reporting results 346; selecting data collection method 342–345; story about 340–341; summative or confirmative 341; support group 315; technique description 341; testing survey, interview and observation form 345; writing questions for 342
evaluation process *341*
events: fundraising 182, 186–187; promoting 278
exit meeting 351–352
expectations, as listening barriers 224
expert (facilitator role) 350
experts 140
explicit bias 25
exploration, change readiness and 100–101
Expressive communication style 208, *209*, **209, 211**
eye contact 143; breaking 226; listening and 224, *225*, 225–226; observing 231; rapport building 239

face-to-face training, lesson plan for 289–291
facial expressions 226
facilitated resolution process 251, *252*
facilitation: clearing mental space for 26, 46–49; story about preparing to facilitate 47–48
facilitation observation practice 212–213
Facilitation of Change Model 8, *8–9*; Stage 1: issue awareness *1*, 1–8; Stage 2: getting to know you *19*, 19–25; Stage 3: information seeking *57*, 57–150; Stage 4: facilitation of planning *151*, 151–255; Stage 5: community development *257*, 257–325; Stage 6: evaluation and conclusion *327*, 327–353
facilitation of planning 151–255; alliances and collaboration 194–202; asking good questions 235–245; choreography of conversation 203–213; effective learning objectives 172–176; fundraising and stewardship 177–193; listening deeply 222–228; observing the action 229–234; planning for change 153–163; setting the stage for productive meetings 214–221; strategies and tactics 164–171; what to do when things fall apart 246–255
facilitator: disengagement and 348–353; views on roles of 350
feasible, quality of data collected 342
feedback: nonverbal *225*, 226; for volunteers 41–42, 44
fee-for-service 183, 187
feelings heuristic 25
fidget toys 219
first meeting, calling 30–35; agenda creation 32, 34; carrying out technique 32–34; first steps for facilitator 32–34; story about 30–31; technique consideration 31–32, **33**
fishbone diagram 109–111, *110–111*, 114–115, 240, 253
flexibility, as process facilitator quality 83
FOA (Funding Opportunity Announcement) 188

focus: on listening 224–225; on outcomes and conditions 120, *121*; planning perspectives 120, *121*; on relevant local issues 142
focus continuum 120, *121*
focused attention 23
focus groups 146
focusing on conditions 7
focus question 207
food insecurity 65, 86, **168**, 170, 174–175, **175**
Force Field Analysis 124–129, 253; diagram 127, *127*; how to carry out the technique 126; retreat center example 128, *128*; skateboard park example 126–128, *127*; story about skateboarders 125; strategies and tactics and 167, 169; SWOT analysis 158, 161; technique description 125–126
formal written report 346
formative evaluation 200, 341
Foundation Directory Online 188
founders 331–333
founder's syndrome 250, 333
framework: definitions 61–63; mental model and 61–63, *63*; team culture discussion 216–217; tent structure analogy 62, *63*
fun, volunteering and 41–42, 44
Funding Opportunity Announcement (FOA) 188
fundraising 177–193; as act of love 178; as an alliance 198; goals 177–178, 185; how to carry out techniques 184–185; methods of 179–188; partnerships 144; resources 192–193; software to assist with 191; story about funding homes for veterans 178–179; strategies 185–189; timeline 185; viral model 181, *182*
fundraising methods 179–188; building fundraising network 181–182, *182*, 186; events 182, 186–187; fee-for-service 183, 187; grants 183, *183*, 187–189; individual giving *180*, 180–181; in-kind donations 182, 187; sponsorships 179–180
fundraising network, building 181–182, *182*, 186
fundraising plan 179–180, 180, 184–185

Gantt chart 169, *169*
gardening metaphor 20–22, 86
gatekeepers 31–32
gauging process 111–112, *112*
generativity 40
gestures 226, 231–232, 234
getting on board 4–5
getting to know you *19*, 19–55; building rapport and unity 50–55; clearing mental space for facilitation 46–49; meetings 29–35; recruiting and retaining volunteers 36–45; reflective facilitation 20–27
Ghais, Suzanne 46
Gilbert, Thomas 109
goals: alignment of tactic, strategy and goal 166, **168**; breaking into smaller achievable 17; of collaboration 196; fundraising 177–178, 185; identifying common 207; of meeting 218; monitoring indicators and 321; of physical environment change 305; for policies 298
Goldboss, Ruth 37
Good Samaritan Shelter 11, 16, 140–141
Google Scholar 262
governance 51, 81, 183, 189
grants 183, *183*, 187–189; abstract 187–188; contents of application 188–189; funding agencies 188
graphs 346
grassroots organizations 32, 180, 182, 196, 199, 201, 211, 215
grids 119–120, *120*
group brainwriting 88
groupthink 249, 253
guidance, for volunteers 41–42, 44
guide on the side (facilitator role) 350
gun violence 215

habits of the heart 23, 69
halo effect **25**
headline news 88
high-priority, high-yield issues 75, 76
Holocaust 37, 195
Homan, Mark 97
Homeless Coalition: activity traps 16; beginning of 4–8; calling a first meeting 30–31; Community Police Officer 68; data collection 139–141; observations that started 12; planning perspectives 118–119
homes for veterans 178–179
Honor of Humanity Project 37
hot button 24
human needs, Rock's SCARF model 42, *42*
Human Relations Commission (HRC) 154–155, 332
Hunger-free St. Michael scenario 170, **170**, 174–175, *175*, **175**, 287, 292
hypothesis: in change process 320, *320*; clarifying the issue/problem 107–108; definition 74, 108, 173; in gauging process *112*
hypothesis testing 113–115

icebreakers 53, **54**, 65
identifying the play and the players in a community 130–137; community description 136; how to carry out the technique 137; identifying community culture and values 132–134; influencers 135; information collection 135–136; key members 135; plan identification 136; story about 131–132; technique description 132; who is outside the community 135; who needs awareness of plan 134
If . . . Then form 108, 114
images, brochure 278
implementation: change readiness and 100–101; communications 280; definition 321; maintenance 321; monitor and manage 320–321, *321*; policy 301; support group 314–315
implicit bias 25–26

incremental change 93–94
indicators 75; characteristics to select for 111; clarifying the issue/problem 110–113; definition 73; in gauging process *112*; identifying 110, 240–241; locating and establishing 77–78; for monitoring change *319*, 319–321; physical environment change 306; for policy change 298; in prison library example **112**; searching for data on 112; visioning and 86
individual giving *180*, 180–181
influence 135
influencers 31–32, 135
information: bias 25; too much with too little meaning 64
information seeking 57–150; change resistance and readiness 91–104; force field analysis 124–129; getting grounded (collecting data together) 138–149; identifying the play and the players in a community 130–137; mental models and frameworks 59–66; physical environment change 306; planning perspectives 117–123; policy change 299; Spectrum of Attitudes 67–71, *69*; support group 313; visioning 80–90; what's happening now? 72–79; wondering and hypothesis testing 105–115
in-kind donations 182, 187
institutional memory (facilitator role) 350
instruction: events of 286, 288; *see also* training
integration, change readiness and 100–101
intellectual distractions 219
interactive activities, meeting 217
intercultural participants at meetings 32, **33**
Interfaith Council 11, 16
interrogation, suggestive 239
interruption: as listening barrier 224; skill of 205
intervention: attributes of 262; budget and 266–268; choosing and developing solutions 259–270; consensus for group commitment 264; cost-benefit analysis 264–265; design and development 265–268, *267*; designing learning 286; how to carry out the technique 261–262; matching solutions to causes 265, **266–267**; searching for 261–262; story about 260–261; team decision process 263; technique description 261
intervention design template **268–269**
interview guide 343
interviews 340; for change evaluation 343; data collection 146; selecting interviewers 343; testing 345; writing questions for 342
intrinsic motivation 37
introductions 53, **54**
Ishikawa, Kaoru 109
issue awareness *1*, 1–8; beginning a change 3–9; detours (stalled projects) 15–18; reflecting, observing, and wonder 10–14
"I" statements 252
I-to-We thinking 53, 54, 55

Jackson County Healthy Community Coalition (JCHCC) 310, 313
job description, volunteer service 38
job performance 109
job-aids 291, *291*
Jones, Bernie 157
journaling buttons and biases 24–27, **25**

Kanter, Rosabeth Moss 95, 97
Katranides, Margaret 318–319
Kessell, Barbara 296
key logs 15, 17–18
key members of the community, identifying 135
knowledge sharing 140
Kübler-Ross, Elisabeth 96

language, accommodating meeting attendees 216
Lazarus, Emma 51
leadership: alliance/collaboration 199; "Change Leadership Skills Self-Assessment" 334; definition 333; mentoring 330, 336–338; for organizational renewal 331–334; shared 331, 333; skills used by a nonprofit leader 334; story about 330
leadership development 334, 336–338
leading questions 239, 242
learning: attitude 290; context 291; events of 286, 287; instruction events 286, 288; *see also* training
learning objectives: definition 174; effective 172–176; how to carry out technique 175–176; Hunger-free St. Michael Parish example 174–175, *175*, **175**; SMART 176; story about 173–174; tactics different from 174; technique description 174
lesson plan for face-to-face training 289–291
lesson plan template **293–294**
Lewin, Kurt 125–126
liaisons 200
library, prison 106–107, *109*, **112**, 113–114, 138, 296–299
life stages of volunteers *39*, 39–40
liminality 250
listening: barriers to 224; change readiness and 101; components of 224–227, *225*; deep 22–23, 195, 222–228, *225*, 238; instead of defending or rebutting 207; public listening sessions 136; story about 223
listening barriers: biases 224; distractions and interruptions 224; expectations 224; talking and not listening 224
listening components 224–227, *225*; asking questions *225*, 226–227; connection *225*, 227; eye contact 224, *225*, 225–226; nonverbal feedback *225*, 226; presence 224–225, *225*
local data 18, 111, 113–114, 138–141, 145, 148
local news media: for community information 136; getting stories in 277–278

Lofquist, William 11, 23, 73, 330, 332; change readiness story 92; community development definition 5; community development principles 6–7; *Elements of Change* 72, 75; on framework 61; on monitoring community development 319, *319*; relationship building process 51; Spectrum of Attitudes 7–8, *8*, 69, *69*; *The Technology of Development* 5
log jam 17–18
lost opportunity cost 267–268

maintenance, implementation and 321
Malcolm X 106
management, definition of 333
managing change 317–324; building on the change 323; getting people ready for change 320; removing obstacles 323; reporting results 322–323, 324; risk 322, 323–324; story about 318–319; technique description 319–320
managing quality 324
managing risk 323–324
mandatory fee 183, 187
maze, finding way through 16–17
meddler (facilitator role) 350
meeting facilitation *see* meetings
meeting planning 214–221; accommodating attendees 216; agenda 217; how to carry out technique 219–220; interactive activities 217; language and cultural differences 216; older or disabled participants 216; preparing yourself 217–218; recording key information 217; for reporting results 279–280; room set-up 217, *218*; socializing 216; team culture discussion 216–217; technique description 216
meetings 29–35; acquiring research partners 143–144; calling first 30–35; calling subsequent 30–34; choreography of conversation 203–213; concluding 219–220; context 205, 210; distractions 219; face-to-face 143; finding common ground 207–208; formal exit meeting 351–352; to gather community information 136; icebreakers 53, **54**; observing during 218; open 136; openers 53–54, **55**; opening 218, 220; planning for productive 214–221; practicing observing 212–213; reporting results to community 279–280, 346; to seek donations 185–186; setting the stage for productive meetings 214–221; sharing findings with the community 148; special considerations for intellectual, older or disabled participants 32, **33**; staying on task 218–219; support group 313–314; visioning 86
membership fees 187
memory: limits of 65; working 65
Mental Measurements Yearbook With Tests in Print 312
mental model 12, 59–66; defined 59; framework and 61–63, *63*; habits of thought that sabotage efforts 64–65; how to carry out technique 65; identifying your group's 63–65; power and limits of 63; story about 60
mentor (facilitator role) 350
mentoring 292, **293**, 330, 336–338
messages, two-sided 300
meta-message 206–208
micro-volunteering 39, 41
midwife (facilitator role) 350
mindfulness 26, 48–49
minutes, meeting 217
mirroring 226
mission 82–83, 94, 178–179, 183–187, 189–192, 236, 241, 251, 275, 279–280, 334, 338; alliance/ collaboration 199; definition of 178; failure 81; fundraising and 178, 181
mission statement 83, 139, 201
monitoring change 317–324; how to carry out the technique 323; quality 322, 324; reporting results 322–323, 324; what's happening now? 319, *319*
monitoring progress 320–321, *321*, 323
motivation: intrinsic 37; learning and 290; of volunteers 40
mountain biking trails 304
Mouton, Jane 119–120
multi-voting 75
mutual revelation 208

NAACP 272–273
networking: locating promising practices or interventions 262; for organizational and community resources 155; policy change 300–301; snowball 136
neutral guidance, providing 26–27
neutrality, of retreat location 52
newsletters 280
nonprofit organization (NPO) 17, 41, 45, 94, 134–135, 143, 149, 183, 185, 194, 201–202, 336, 345
nonverbal behaviors, observing 230–234
nonverbal feedback *225*, 226
"notice, wonder and ask" method 238, 243
noticing 236; conflict 250; in group communication 207; techniques, how to carry out 13–14
NPO *see* nonprofit organization (NPO)
nurturing, as process facilitator quality 83

objectives: effective learning 172–176; monitoring indicators and 321; for policies 298; SMART 176; surveys 340; *see also* learning objectives
objectives, meeting 33
objectivity 206
observation 11, 229–234; for change evaluation 343–345, **344**; conversation facilitation 206–207; facilitation observation practice 212–213; how to carry out observations of participants 231–232; how to carry out observing and noticing techniques

13–14; making observations 12–13, **13**; during meetings 218; nonverbal behaviors 230–234; playground observation checklist **344**; practicing 232–233; reflecting on 12; story about 230; as subjective 12–13; technique description 230–231; what to look for 13, **13**
observation form, testing 345
observer bias 64
obstacles, removing 323
older participants, accommodating as meeting attendees 216
On Death and Dying (Kübler-Ross) 96
one-on-one resolution process 251, *252*
open-ended questions 180, 186, 195–196, 199, 226–227, 238–239, 243
openers 53–54, *55*
open forum meeting format 314
opening dialogue, story about 195
openness, as process facilitator quality 83
opportunities, in SWOT analysis 76, *77*
opportunity cost, lost 267–268
opposition 98
organization change process 332, *332*
organizations: leadership 331–334; renewal 331–334, 335, *336*
otherness 68
outcomes: focus on 120; *see also* desired outcomes
outreach programs 280
overlapping speech 208, 210
oversight 320–321, *321*
oversimplified thinking 119

Palmer, Parker 23
parking lot 208, 218–219
participation 279; community development principle 6, 31; encouraging 242
partnerships: acquiring research partners 143–144; capacity building 143; with community groups 140; promoting equitable 143; sustaining 144–145
People Skills (Thompson) 352
performance assessment and evaluation 190
personal emissary work 155, 198, 272–274, 300
personal invitation, recruiting volunteers by 41, 43
Personal Resilience Inventory 96, 97
PERT (Program Evaluation and Review Technique) chart 169, *169*
photovoice 146
physical distractions 219
physical environment change 303–308; desired outcomes 306; goals 305; how to carry out technique 305; information seeking 306; involved parties 305; planning 306–307; story about 304; technique description 304–305; what's happening now? 305
planning: in change process 320; continuing *333*; disengagement 350; meetings 214–221; physical environment change 306–307; policy change 299–301; for raising funds 179; support group 313–314
planning for change 153–163; allies for awareness-building and information-sharing 155; cooperative creation of new resources 155–156; design of change strategies 159, *159–160*; how to carry out the techniques 160–161; networking for organizational and community resources 155; perspectives, paradigms and sources of design 159–160; race conversations story 154–156; reviewing your research 157; strategies and tactics 160; SWOT analysis *157–158*, 157–159, 160; technique description 156, *156*
planning perspectives 117–123, *118*; Arenas of Action framework 119–122, *120*; example 122; focus continuum 120, *121*; focus on outcomes and conditions 120, *121*; grids and units of change 119–120, *120*; how to carry out the technique 122; purpose 121, *121*; story about 118–119; technique description 119
players, identifying in the community 130–137
playground observation checklist **344**
play identification 132, 136
policy: audience for 299; desired outcomes 298–299; implementation 301; for volunteers 38–39
policy change 295–302; communications 299–300; desired outcomes 298–299; evaluation 301; how to carry out the technique 297–298; information seeking 299; involved parties in 297; networking 300–301; planning 299–301; story about 296–297; technique description 297; timing 300; what's happening now? 297–298
policy effects 299
policy enactment 301
policy evaluation 301
Post Traumatic Stress Disorder (PTSD) 178
power, speaking truth to 173
practices: attributes of promising 262; searching for promising 261–262; of successful programs 334
presence 224–225, *225*
press release 346
prison library 106—107, *109*, **112**, 113–114, 138, 296–299
prison reform 37, 236–237, 296–297
problems: defining 106, 108, 114–115, 296, 298, 301, **302**; joint ownership of 140
problem-solving, community 122
problem statements, checklist for clear 108, 114
procedures, for volunteers 38–39
process: partnerships and 144; team culture discussion 216–217
process facilitator 82–83
processing, conflict and 250
process knowledge, building 140
process questions 239

programs 283–294; definition 283; story 284–286; training 286–294
progressive muscle relaxation 26
project management software 169
project timeline 168–169, *169*
prompt questions 242
propriety, quality of data collected 342
protocol, definition of 68
PTSD (Post Traumatic Stress Disorder) 178
public listening sessions for identifying play and players in community 136
purpose: alliance/collaboration 199; of collaboration 144; of meeting 218
purpose continuum 121, *121*
push and pull forces 125–126, *126*

Quakers 23, 37, 51–52, 165, 296, 318, 330
qualitative data 345
quality: definition 322; managing 324
quantitative data 345
questions: asking good 235–245; asking simple 207; asking while listening *225*, 226–227; change process and 239–241, *240*, 243; cheat sheet to use through planning cycle 243, **244**; clarifying 226–227; closed-ended 239; delivering 242; effect of powerful 239; favorite 241; focus question 207; how to carry out technique 243; leading 239, 242; open-ended 180, 186, 195–196, 199, 226–227, 238–239, 243; process 239; prompt 242; recall 239; redirecting 242; responding to answers 242; rhetorical 239; story about 236–237; team decision process 263; teamwork and *238*, 238–239, *243*; technique description 237–239; types of 239; why people ask 237; writing for evaluating outcomes 342

Race Unity 22–23, 154–156, *158*, 204–205, 223, 272–273, 332
Racial Taboo (film) 154–155
rapport, building 50–55, 238
readiness *see* change readiness; community readiness
reading in prison, story about 106
recall questions 239
recharging a group that is stuck 88
recidivism 106–108, **112**, 113, 296–298
recognition: change readiness and 100; private 322; of volunteers 42
recording key information 217
recruiting volunteers 36–45; first steps in 38–39; story about 37–38; strategies 40–41
redirecting question 242
reflection 11; conversation facilitation 206–207; on disengagement 352; importance of 12; story about 22–23
reflective facilitation 20–27; clearing a mental space 26; how to carry out the technique 24; intentional gardening metaphor 20; journaling buttons and biases 24–27, *25*; neutral guidance, providing 26–27; technique description 23
relatedness, volunteering and 42, *42*
relationships: building rapport and unity 50–55; using questions to establish *238*, 238
renewing the organization 331–334, *335*, *336*
reporting results 279–280; evaluation 346; monitoring change 322–323, 324
Request for Proposal (RFP) 188–189
requested fees 183
research: acquiring partners 143–144; Community-Based Participatory Research (CBPR) 138, 142; reviewing yours 157; *see also* data collection
researchers, external 141
resilience 96, 97
resistance to change 95, *96*, 96–97, 100; causes of 96; change cycle with 95, *96*; increase with negative focus 120; managing 320; to policy change 299; *see also* change readiness
resolution, conflict 251–252, *252*
resources: beneficiaries of 157; cooperative creation of new resources 155–156
response rate 101
responsibility, as community development principle 7, 31
restraints 126
results, reporting *see* reporting results
retreat center example: Force Field Analysis 128, *128*; situational blindness 81–82; visioning and 52
reverse brainstorming 88
RFP (Request for Proposal) 188–189
rhetorical questions 239
risks: managing 322, 323–324; steps for dealing with 323–324
Rock, David 42, *42*
room set-up 217, *218*
root causes 74–75, *75*; analysis 109; fishbone diagram 109–111, *110–111*, 114–115

scapegoating 248
SCARF model of human needs 42, *42*
Schorr, Lisbeth 333
scope creep 349
searching for data on indicators 112
seed money 183, 188
self-awareness, social biases and 25–26
self-motivation action 37
Senge, Peter 63
servant leader (facilitator role) 350
sharing ideas and stories 277
shunning 248
silence, using 242
situational awareness 252, *253*
situational blindness 81–83, 239, 252–254
skateboarders 125–127

SMART (Specific, Measurable, Achievable, Realistic, Time-bound) acronym 176
Smith, Huston 20
snowball networking 136
social biases 25–26
social currency 274–275
socializing: at meetings 216, 219; planning for 216
social media: creating communications in 279; evaluating communications 280; recruiting volunteers 41, 43
software to assist with fundraising 191
solutions: choosing and developing 259–270; consensus for group commitment 264; cost-benefit analysis 264–265; design and development 265–268, 267; how to carry out the technique 261–262; intervention design template **268–269**; matching cause to 265, **266–267**; selecting 263, *263*; story about 260–261; technique description 261
Southern Illinois University's Touch of Nature Environmental Center 304–306
speaking: eye contact during 225; knowing when and when not to speak 206; overlapping 208, 210; talking and not listening 224; truth to power 173, 250
spectrum of attitudes 7–8, *8*, 67–71, *69*; examining for your group 70; reviewing your team's 157; technique 69–70
sponsorships 179–180
stakeholders 167–168
stalled projects 15–18
statistical methods of data analysis 146–147
status quo bias **25**, 42
stewardship 181, 183–184, 189–191
story: in local news media 277–278; sharing 277
strategic alliance: definition 198; functions of 194
strategy 164–171, 241; alignment of tactic, strategy and goal *166*, **168**; community development strategies, examples of 167; definitions of 166; differences between 166, **167**; how to carry out the technique 169–170; how to develop 167; Hunger-free St. Michael scenario 170, **170**; planning change 160; for policy change implementation 299; project timeline 168–169, *169*; revising 241; story about 165; story about communications as 272–273; technique description 166–167
strengths, in SWOT analysis 76, 77
structure, partnerships and 144
success, measuring 240
successful programs, characteristics of 333–334
summative evaluation 341
Supplemental Nutrition Assistance Program (SNAP) 175
support 309–316; desired outcomes 313; how to carry out the technique 312; information seeking 313; involved parties 312; story about 310–311; technique description 311–312; what is happening now? 312–313
support group: attendees 314; desired outcomes 313; evaluation 315; facilitation 313; getting the word out 314; implementation 314–315; information seeking 313; meetings 313–314; planning 313–314
surveys 312, 340; for change evaluation 342–343; of change readiness 101–102; data collection 146; explanation provided with 343; identifying play and players in community 136; testing 345; windshield or walking 136; writing questions for 342
Sussman, Diana Brawley 297
sustainability 329–338; how to carry out the technique 335; leadership development 334, 336–338; leadership for organizational renewal 331–334; long-term 142; preventing rollback 330–331; technique description 330–331
sweeping conflict under the rug 248
SWOT analysis 76, 77, 253; for Conversation for Race Unity *158*; external factors 158, 161; internal factors 157–158, 161; planning for change *157–158, 157–162, 162*; ReNEW example 284, **285**, 333, 335; in sample scenario 162, *162*; strategies and tactics and 167, 169
symptoms: brainstorming what's happening now 73, 74, *109*; causes differentiated from 240; contributing factors and 109; definition 74, 173; in gauging process *112*; of success 77

tactics: alignment of tactic, strategy and goal *166*, **168**; definitions of 166; different from learning objectives 174; explicit 167; how to develop 167; how to write **168**; planning change 160, 241
taking sides 248
talking stick 22, 30, 50, 52–53
Tannen, Deborah 200
target populations 134
tax-exempt status 180, 185, 196–197, 202
team building: icebreakers 53, **54**; I-to-We thinking 53, 54, **55**; story about creating your dream team 51–53; technique 53–55
team conflict 250–251
team culture discussion, planning 216–217
Technology of Development, The (Lofquist) 5
tension, breaking up 209–210
tent structure analogy 62, *63*
Thompson, Neil
thought-habits 12
threats: conflict and 251; in SWOT analysis 76, 77
"Three Strikes You're Out" laws 236–237
time frame 86, 87
top-down decision-making 247
topic-based meeting format 314
training 286–294; analyzing the content 287–289, *289*; coaching 292, **293**; context for instruction 290–291; creating 286; disengagement 350; instruction events 286, **288**; job-aids, creating 291, *291*; lesson plan for face-to-face 289–291; mentoring 292, **293**

train ride metaphor 4–5
transformative change 93–95, *94*
transparency 101, 189, 273
Transtheoretical Model of Behavior Change, Prochaska's 95
Tri-Ethnic Center for Prevention Research 98
triggers 274–275
trust: change readiness and 101; eye contact and 225; restoring 83; volunteering and 41–42, 44
truth, speaking to power 173, 250
turnaround strategy 82–83
two-sided thinking 119

United Way's 211 Information and Referral System 143
units of change 119–120
unity, building 50–55
urgency 17
U.S. Census Bureau 145, 345
U.S. Department of Justice 345
useful, quality of data collected 342

values: alliance/collaboration 199; bridging cultural, social and community 198–199, 201; conflict and 251; shifting community 330
verbal cues 207
veterans, homes for 178–179
vision: of collaboration 144; definition 81; focused 83; keeping team focused on 89; reviewing yours 157
visioning 4–6, 30, 52, 80–90, 285; brainstorming 85, 86–88, *87*; carrying out the technique 86; creativity and 83, *84*; data collection 139; focus questions 85; initial event 85; large-scale 85; recharging a group that is stuck 88; situational blindness 81–83; small-scale 84–85; technique described 83
vision statement 86
visual cues 207
voluntary donations 183, 187
volunteer management tools 44
volunteers: characteristics of 39–40; data collection 139, 142, 148–149; gender, marital, parental and educational status 40; job description 38; life stages *39*, 39–40; making doers out of supporters 43; motivations 40; policies and procedures for 38–39; recruiting 36–45; recruiting strategies 40–41; retaining *41*, 41–42, 44; service 38–39; strategies and tactics and 167–168; what potential want to know 41
vulnerable populations 38

walking survey: data collection 146; identifying play and players in community 136
weaknesses, in SWOT analysis 76, *77*
What do you see? 22
What's happening now? 6–7, 11, 64, 72–79, 119, 207, 236–239, 343; brainstorming 73, 73–74, 76, *109*, 114–115; in change process *320*; conflict 248; high-priority, high-yield issues 75, 76; intervention 263; locating and establishing indicators 77–78; method 2 for large groups 78; method 1 for small groups 78; monitoring change 319, *319*; physical environment change 305; policy change 297–298; renewing the organization and 335; reviewing your analysis 157; story about what's happening now and desired outcomes 73; support 312–313; SWOT analysis 76, *77*; visioning and 81, 85, 86
What's really going on here? 250–251
what to do when things fall apart 246–255
white space 279
who will benefit? 86, *87*
Wilkinson, Michael 6
windshield survey: data collection 146; identifying play and players in community 136
wisdom of one 146
wisdom of the group 86–87
Wise, Will 238
Women for Change 272–273
wondering 11, 13, 207, 236, 238, 250
word-of-mouth communications *274*, 274–276
working memory 65